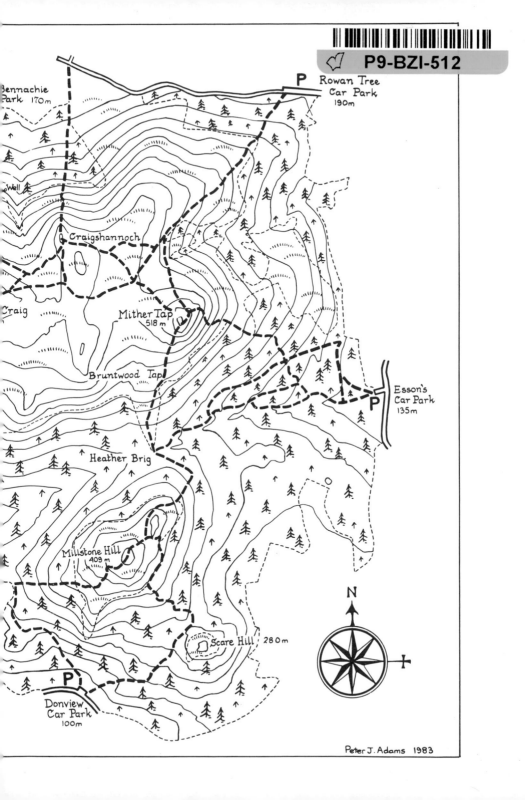

Bennachie
Park 170m

Rowan Tree
Car Park
190m

well

Craigshannoch

Craig

Mither Tap
518 m

Bruntwood Tap

Esson's
Car Park
135m

Heather Brig

Millstone Hill
409 m

N

Scare Hill 280 m

P
Donview
Car Park
100m

Peter J. Adams 1983

BENNACHIE AGAIN

Bennachie Again

Edited by
ARCHIE W. M. WHITELEY
M.B.E., M.A., J.P., F.S.A.Scot.

Published by the Bailies of Bennachie
Clerk: Mrs Helen P. Fraser
1983

ISBN   0   900323   59   0

Printed by
William Culross & Son Limited
Coupar Angus, Perthshire, Scotland

John Mearns entertains the Bailies at the Summer Rally, 1982

Photo – R. Henderson

Foreword

SIR MAITLAND MACKIE, C.B.E., J.P., B.SC., LL.D., F.E.I.S.
Lord-Lieutenant of Aberdeenshire and Second Guardian of Bennachie

Flora Garry in her poem asks 'Foo Aul' 's Bennachie?' It doesn't seem to me to matter. What is important is that it is there, it's aye been there and it will aye be there. In a changing world that is comforting. As a boy, in less affluent and sophisticated days, it was part of an annual holiday to climb and enjoy Bennachie. I believe I passed on that enjoyment to my family and I think in turn they to the next generation.

However old the Hill is, it's there and it's easier to climb and tidier because of the Bailies – Bless them. I'm proud to be associated.

Preface

To reprint the 'Book of Bennachie' or to edit a new one, that was the question which occupied the minds of the Council of the Bailies of Bennachie for quite some time. The first book had been an outstanding success. It went into five impressions – all sold out. It was still being asked for. On the other hand, in answer to a request in the first book for new material relating to Bennachie, we were inundated with replies. In addition we received a most welcome gift of One Thousand Pounds towards the publication of a new book from Miss Elizabeth G. Whitelaw, Edinburgh, and her brother, James H. Whitelaw, Canada, in memory of their mother, on condition that the new book should contain an illustrated article on the Bennachie Distillery at Jericho, which had been leased to their grandfather in 1884. This magnificent gift tipped the balance, and so 'Bennachie Again' was born. We hope you enjoy reading 'There's Nae Sair Heids in Bennachie' and the rest of the book.

We are very grateful to all our contributors and especially to the following for allowing us to reproduce articles, poems and photographs: –

The Aberdeen Journals Ltd.; The Aberdeen Art Gallery and Museums; The Deeside Field Club; The Forestry Commission; Ordnance Survey; Flora Garry; H. J. L. Mantell, A.R.I.B.A.; The Library, King's College, Aberdeen; The University of Cambridge; Professor J. K. S. St. Joseph, C.B.E., M.A., LITT.D., F.B.A.

Our thanks are also due to all those who helped to type articles and to proof-read, with a very special thanks to our hard-working and very efficient honorary secretary, Mrs Helen P. Fraser.

Once again the Council of the Bailies of Bennachie warmly appreciate the valuable assistance received from our Printers, Messrs. William Culross & Son Ltd., Coupar Angus.

The Editor.

Opposite: The Editor *by* Sandra Mutch

Contents

CONTENTS – *continued* *Page*

Standing l. to r. L. Mackay, M. White, T. Michie, T. Hutchison, I. Grant, M. Davidson
H. Cadenhead, J. Kelman, A. Watson
Seated l. to r. G. Ingram, D. Stewart, J. Mackay, H. Fraser, D. Gordon, M. Simpson

THE COUNCIL OF THE BAILIES OF BENNACHIE

Senior Bailie: ALGY WATSON, Springbank, Oyne.
Deputy Senior Bailie: JAMES T. KELMAN, 6 Westholme Terrace, Aberdeen.
Clerk: MRS HELEN P. FRASER, Templar Croft, Aquhythie, Inverurie.
Treasurer: GORDON R. INGRAM, 10 Cuninghill Road, Inverurie.

MASTER OF FORBES, Castle Forbes; SIR ARCHIBALD GRANT, BT., Monymusk
House; G. R. T. SMITH, Pittodrie House; ROBERT G. AITKEN; DR DANIEL
G. GORDON; IAN GRANT, Conservator, East of Scotland Conservancy;
C. E. I. HARDING; MISS DOROTHY DUGUID; TOM M. HUTCHISON;
TOM MICHIE; MISS MARY SIMPSON; DR MARION WHITE;
A. W. M. WHITELEY.

Warden of the East Marches: JOHN OGSTON.
Warden of the West Marches: GORDON R. INGRAM.
Warden of the North Marches: MRS. SHEELAGH MARTIN.
Warden of the South Marches: JAMES R. MACKAY.
Wardens of the High Tops: HERBERT CADENHEAD, MICHAEL
DAVIDSON, LESLIE G. MCKAY.

EDITORIAL COMMITTEE

The Master of Forbes, Mrs Helen P. Fraser, Dr Daniel G. Gordon,
Tom M. Hutchison, James R. Mackay, Miss Mary Simpson, Dr Douglas
L. Stewart, A. H. Watson, A. W. M. Whiteley (Convener).

Dr Danny Gordon, Founder Senior Bailie

TO MY LITTER ALLIES

By Tom Michie

This mak's me conceited
   Fin I tak' a look doon there,
An' see aroon a table
   Folks, as if in prayer!
Solemn words being bandied
   A' aboot Bennachie,
Its walks, its fields, its bushes,
   An' even its lavatorie!

A' ken a'body likes me,
   They widna climb if they didn't,
The folks that come are a mixture –
   The young, the aul', and the wisn't.
The view is worth the effort,
   O'er bonnie Garioch side,
They a' reach the same conclusion
   'Fit a bonnie place tae bide.'

A' eence heard a Roman sodjer
   Sweerin' at the sleet,
His ablatives were absolute –
   An' him wi' soakin' feet!
His thochts were o' sweet Italy
   An' maybe o' his dame –
It's a' this Empire buildin' –
   He should hae bade at hame!

Fin I look back o'er a' the years
   An' see the web that's spun –
Bottles, sweetie papers
   Littered o'er ma grun'!
A'm gled o' your existence
   An' the love ye bear tae me!
Let's hope yer indicator
   His a lang pedigree!

For those less classically-minded in verse 3, lines 3 and 4, could be thus –
   Shiverin' in his shortened kilt
   An' soakin' sandelled feet.

The above effusion prompted by attendance at a Council Meeting of the Bailies of Bennachie at Thainstone House Hotel on 25th March 1980.

The Guardian of Bennachie, Sir Maitland Mackie (*second from left*)
with the three successive Senior Baillies – *Left to Right* –
Danny Gordon (1973-78), James MacKay (1978-82) and Algy Watson (1982 onwards)
Photo – W. Rankin

Rally below Esson's Croft

Photo – J. R. MacKay

THE BAILIES OF BENNACHIE – TEN YEARS ON

By James R. Mackay

In *The Book of Bennachie* published in 1976 our Founder Senior Bailie, Dr Daniel Gordon, gave a resumé of the activities of the Bailies from their inception in 1973 to that time. (Incidentally the fifth and last impression sold out at the end of 1979 – 4,500 copies in all and we thought originally that we would have difficulty in selling 500!). This article takes up the story from where Dr Gordon left off.

The pattern begun in these early days has been maintained. The Rallies at the Back o' Bennachie picnic area attended by over 500 continued to be dogged by parking problems so in 1979 we looked to the other side of the Hill and found a delightful spot beside Esson's Car Park – a grass park (kindly made available to us by Mr George McWilliam of Tullos) sheltered from the north and west with a very fine view of the Mither Tap soaring above. There was enough space to park the 150+ cars in the same field. The Clachie burn flowing through the middle presented a bit of a problem but our friends in the Forestry Commission provided a bridge and helped us to position it. By this time the toilets at Esson's Car Park were completed and the knocking down of part of the drystane dyke gave access from the field. This pattern continued for three years and very enjoyable Rallies they were. The field was cultivated in 1982. We were reluctant to return to the parking problems of the Back o' Bennachie until the Forestry Commission offered us the use of the park adjacent to the picnic field for cars. This proved to be absolutely ideal in 1982.

At these Rallies the Guardian of Bennachie, Sir Maitland Mackie (we congratulate him on his knighthood), welcomes the company and the Forestry Conservator, latterly Mr Ian Grant, brings greetings and information from the Commission. While we are waiting for the superb hot sausage rolls from Insch, May Thomson, John Mearns or Jim Glennie delight us with monologues.

For many people the Rally has become a most enjoyable reunion. Bailies come from far and near to enjoy the company, the scenery and the fine weather. For ten years now the sun has shone and there hasn't been a spot of rain during the Rally – although it has been raining before and after. We must be looked after well from on high.

The pattern of the Annual General Meeting in the autumn remains also largely unchanged. Inverurie Academy Assembly Hall has always been the venue. After the business part there is normally tea, entertainment and an illustrated talk. Speakers have included Ian Strachan (the Cairngorms), George Dey (Forestry in Focus), Charles Gimingham (Heaths and Moors of Scotland – we congratulate him on his elevation to the Reguis Chair of Botany at Aberdeen), the Senior Bailie (Bennachie) and Mark Young (a Naturalist in the Hills). We have been entertained by John and Alice Mearns, Tom Reid of Bothy Ballad fame, James Kelman, Brian

Cruickshank (violin), Tom Michie (piano), Jacqueline Norrie (violin), May Thomson and James Glennie who has been writing some excellent doric verse.

In 1981 we departed from this format to have a concert of some of the poems and songs from the Bennachie Ballad Competition. There were 146 entries from 96 contributors. The main sponsors were Grampian Television Ltd. whose director, Mr A. Mair, presented the prizes. The award for the best work in the doric was donated and presented by Dr George Philp of Scotsoun. It was a most worthwhile exercise and our printers already have in hand the production of a booklet entitled *Poems of Bennachie* featuring about 50 selected examples. We are also investigating the possibility of producing a Bennachie cassette.

In 1979 we organised a Bennachie Art Competition with 135 entries from local primary schools. The standard was high and six prizes were awarded. In the previous year the competition was based on an essay 'Why I like Bennachie.' Fifteen prizes were presented by Councillor John Sorrie (we congratulate him on taking office as Convener of Grampian Regional Council).

Also at that meeting in 1978 Dr Gordon resigned as Senior Bailie. Anticipating this we had changed the constitution so that he became a Council member for life and we still benefit from his ideas and enthusiasm. Little did he think in 1973 that in ten years time membership of the Bailies would rise to 2,400.

Another important change in the constitution drawn up by our legal expert, Robert Chalmers, was designed to give us charity status and this has been accepted by the Commissioners of Inland Revenue so that we do not have to pay tax on our assets.

A further change in 1978 was the promotion of our old friend, Conservator Morrison, and his replacement by Ian Grant who has taken a great interest in the Bailies and has supported us in so many ways. Only recently he assured us that there were no plans to sell off any part of Bennachie. The thought of a private developer getting his hands on this priceless asset does not bear thinking. He also accepted our arguments for not charging for car parking at any of the Bennachie car parks (contrary to Commission policy).

Bennachie Forest used to be administered from Banchory under District Officer A. A. Cuthbert who left us a permanent reminder of his influence in the chapter he wrote on 'Bennachie Forest' in the *Book of Bennachie*. When the control switched to Fochabers we found ourselves with a new District Officer – Ron Marnie. The relationship has been a very happy and fruitful one. Ron has a soft spot for Bennachie. He was instrumental in persuading Mr Morrison that a path from Esson's Car Park to the Mither Tap would be a worthwhile venture. Algy Watson and I marked out a possible route and Ron approved. The opening of the re-designed Esson's Car Park and the new path in 1978 was attended by Conservator Morrison, Assistant Conservator David Paterson, District Officer Ron Marnie, Dr Jean Balfour, Chairman of the Countryside Commission for Scotland, Lady Grant of Monymusk and many others including Bailies.

David Paterson has given us valuable service both at Bailies Council Meetings and on the Hill. He too has moved south. Lady Grant of Monymusk attended her last Council Meeting in November 1979. We greatly appreciate her active interest in Bennachie. She is of course now Lady Tweedsmuir. She it was who suggested that it would be appropriate to celebrate the Queen's Silver Jubilee by planting 25 trees in Paradise Woods. We decided in fact to plant more than 75 specimen trees and a pleasant evening was spent in April 1977 filling the gaps created by the loss by windblow of some of the magnificent trees planted by Sir Archibald Grant over 200 years ago.

In the context of tree planting it is worth mentioning that in spring 1976 we planted a considerable number of native trees provided by the Forestry Commission for amenity purposes in the Monymusk triangle in order to attempt to break up the hard fence line of the division between heather and the Forestry Commission plantations. Incidentally, after the planting there was a prolonged drought and not all the trees have taken.

Ron Marnie was also involved in the production of the *Guide to Bennachie*. We are grateful to him for many suggestions. We printed 5000 Guides initially of which the Commission took half so enabling us to produce them at a very economic rate. Due to demand we have had to print another 3,000. The comments on the *Guide* have been very encouraging and we feel that it is fulfilling a need in answering many of the questions that people have about Bennachie, its routes and its history. Ron and his

1982 Rally – Handing out the sausage rolls
Left to Right – Leslie McKay, Jas. Kelman, Charles King, Cuthbert Graham
Photo – R. Henderson

colleagues have done a great job in re-designing and changing the emphasis of the Donview Centre. It is now an interpretive facility of the highest order.

Before we leave the Forestry Commission personnel one other member of their staff must be mentioned, viz. Bob Aitken who has been Chief Forester on Bennachie since the inception of the Bailies. He too is a regular attender at Council Meetings and not only gives us advice but practical help on the Hill as well as in many different ways.

Coupled with the Forestry Commission we must also thank Gordon District Council on the erection of the much needed toilets at the Rowan Tree Car Park. Being of timber to a Forestry Commission design they blend in well with the environment but surpass those of the Forestry Commission in that they even have HOT water!

Working parties of the Bailies have been active in various ways. The erosion on the Rowan Tree-Mither Tap path has been tackled by draining as well as by removal of all the cairns and using their stones to fill the erosion channels. This work was initiated by one of our younger Council members — Mike Davidson. We purchased a scrub saw and have used it to cut the whins and heather on certain of the paths. More and larger stepping stones have been laid. The Esson's Car Park-Heather Brig paths have been re-surfaced in all the boggy areas. The turf table at Shannoch Well has been completely reconstructed. A new indicator has been made of stainless steel which needs no protection and has survived two winters and the attempts of summer vandals. Once again we are grateful to Jim Jamieson and Ron Doughty of Inverurie Academy Technical Department for masterminding the reconstruction.

We have located the Gouk (Cuckoo) Stone which was a very old marker of the Commonty or Free or King's Forest of Bennachie. It has been signposted by the Forestry Commission and a path made to it. Not so easy to find was the Cup and Saucer Stone. Armed only with the information provided by James Milne in *Twixt Ury and Don* and in *Bennachie* by A. I. McConnochie, Mike Davidson and I had many fruitless searches before Mike found it completely overgrown with moss and shrubs. According to Milne it was 'laid into the west side of the boundary dyke between the parishes of Chapel of Garioch and Oyne west of the farm and ruined house of Tullos.' The stone is according to McConnochie 'about two and a half feet square and ten inches thick. The 'Cup' is circular of 5 inches diameter and 2 inches deep but slightly raised in its centre.' We will be delighted to take anybody to see the stone especially if they can give us a clue as to its origin! Esson mentions it in his letter to Robert Cormack (see chapter on p.98 so it must have been well known at one time.

The enigma of the Maiden Causeway continues to exercise our minds (and our backs!). Old maps of Bennachie show what is called the Maiden Causeway going from the fort on the Mither Tap in roughly the same direction as the present Rowan Tree path and petering out in Pittodrie Woods. McConnochie (1890) describes it as being only visible in places, roughly paved and about fourteen feet wide. We were unsuccessful in locating it until a study of aerial photographs showed a double line in more

The new stainless Indicator about to be positioned
Left to right – Ron Doughty, Dave Brown, Bert Cadenhead, James Kelman, Leslie Mackay
Algy Watson, Jim Jamieson and Kenneth Mackay

Photo – J. R. Mackay

or less the correct position. Nothing was visible on the ground but excavating down two feet we found the stones just as McConnochie described. It is amazing that such a massive structure had almost completely disappeared from human ken. It must be of great antiquity. It is mentioned by Alexander Keith in 1732 and was at that time considered to be at least 300 years old. When it was built, by whom and for what purpose are mysteries which we hope to unravel although the associated legends make interesting reading. Gordon District Council and the oil industry in the form of BP are actively supporting us in various projects including attempting to date the Causeway by radio-carbon means. We see this as a long term project but very exciting.

The probable site of Hosie's Well has been located. With the help of Kemnay Scouts we dug it out and lined it with stones. Again the Forestry Commission did the needful as far as signposting is concerned. We feel that there should not be a proliferation of signposts over the Hill and the Commission have wherever possible used discreet colour coded arrows to be read in conjunction with the map boards at the car parks or with the map attached to the 'Guide.'

The other archaeological discovery that has excited us is the discovery, by Emeritus Prof. J. K. St. Joseph of Cambridge University (pioneer of aerial photography) of the largest Roman fort north of the Antonine Wall at Logie Durno. This makes it almost certain that Bennachie is *the* Mons Graupius of Tacitus. Much remains to be done in tracing the past history of the Hill, for example in *Scottish Notes and Queries* 1888 J. Esson refers to 'hundreds of tumuli on a moor to the south of Bennachie near the farm of Auquhorsk' suggesting that 'the spot at some remote age was the scene of a battle.' He asks for information. We are still trying to find them.

Many bailies when they climb the Hill take with them a plastic bag into which they deposit the occasional crisp bag or can which continues to be dropped by the thoughtless. Pitcaple Scouts and Cubs have also been active in litter collection. The litter problem is not too bad but it is a constant battle. Perhaps it is because of our efforts in this respect that we won national recognition in being awarded a Special Mention Certificate by the Keep Britain Tidy Campaign. It is however perhaps not widely realised that the Forestry Commission organise litter collection in their car parks and it is only right that they should be associated with this Award. It must be rather galling for them when they so often read of the Bailies being given credit for something in which they too have been involved. It seems that the Bailies have captured the imagination of the media more so than a group of civil servants! Credit must go where it is due. If it was not for the pioneer work of the Forestry Commission it is possible that the Bailies would never have been formed.

In recent years we have led parties from various schools and adult societies as well as Bailies to places of interest on Bennachie. If there is a demand we shall continue to do this. Algy Watson and I and James Kelman have been giving many illustrated talks on Bennachie to WRI's, Rotaries, Guilds, Round Tablers and so on. Everywhere we go the reaction is the same – 'I never knew there was so much to see on Bennachie!'

We have become affiliated to the Scottish Rights of Way Society and the North-East Mountain Trust. In 1980 we co-operated with the Grampian Federation of Conservation Societies in hosting a Countryside Conservation Conference with speakers from the Institute of Terrestrial Ecology, Nature Conservancy Council, Countryside Commission for Scotland, Forestry Commission, Scottish Wildlife Trust, North-East Scotland Mountain Trust and Conservation Society. Delegates were present from Aberdeen Civic Society, Banff Coast Conservation Society, Moray Society, National Trust for Scotland, Scottish Ornithologists Club and Grampian Regional Council. Never before have so many conservation interests met together. It is only a pity that because of lack of time we could not have formulated a plan of action to educate the public with regard to the urgent need to think in terms of conservation and to press the Government to realise that conservation must be taken from the bottom of its list of priorities (receiving only a matter of pence for each man, woman and child per annum) and given urgent attention and finance otherwise the future for mankind is bleak.

On the publishing side in addition to *The Guide* we produced 1,200 copies of a Bennachie calendar for 1981 with colour photographs of the Hill at different seasons. They were all sold. For 1982 we selected 13 black and white sketches relevant to Bennachie, increased the number printed to 1,500 and sold them all. We have just taken delivery of 2,000 copies of the 1983 calendar – colour reproductions of water colours of Bennachie and hope to sell all of them. Next year we are having a photographic competition from which the pictures for the 1984 calendar will come. We have postcards with three different views; lettercards have also had two different pictures. Membership scrolls are an attractive and permanent record of belonging to the organisation. Peter Adams in co-operation with Grampian Orienteers produced for us the only accurate and up-to-date map of Bennachie in existence. Many have been bought unfolded and framed. Enrolment forms are available to simplify the process of Membership.

The Council has continued to meet approximately four times per year either in the Rowan Tree restaurant or in one of the local hotels. We would dearly like to have a place of our own which could be manned for so many hours per week. Bailies and others could drop in and study our superb collections of old books and photographs (donated by Miss Cormack and others), old maps and artifacts from the Hill. This could be a great boon for the local people many of whom are incomers and are just as fascinated and delighted with Bennachie as the rest of us.

The popularity of Bennachie is not difficult to understand. It has a distinctive profile with the shapely peak of the Mither Tap rearing up Fujyama-like at its eastern end. It has all the features of a true mountain – precipitous rocks, ravines, well defined tops, tundra type vegetation and a great feeling of wilderness in spite of its accessibility. Within a quarter of an hour of leaving Inverurie or three quarters of an hour from Aberdeen one can be tramping on its vast windswept heather-covered flanks or breathing in the pine scented air in the lythe of one of the recently constructed forest walks. To all, native or incomer it is a 'friendly' hill. It is this universal affection for it which enables me to predict with certainty that the Bailies of Bennachie will be in an equally healthy state ten years from now.

THE FOUR SEASONS OF BENNACHIE

By Dr R. J. House

When Winter lays her icy hand
On Bennachie all clothed in white,
And all is still on frost-bound land,
And Wintry sunshine shafts its light
On Bennachie, on Bennachie,
Then that's the sight I long to see.

When vernal sunshine melts the snow
From topmost crags of Bennachie,
And babbling burns in frolic flow
Chuckling their way towards the sea;
Then that's the place I long to be,
On Bennachie, on Bennachie.

When Summer in her glory glows,
And verdant beauty clothes the land,
Then to the North my fancy flows
Longing that I could once more stand
Upon the slopes of Bennachie,
For that's the place I long to be.

When fruitful Autumn paints the scene,
And heather decorates the bens,
And early frosts make senses keen,
And berries ripen on the glens;
Then that's the place I long to be,
On Bennachie, on Bennachie.

BENNACHIE RULES O.K.

By Joanne Gordon

Countless times I've heard, and hope often to hear again, that from such-and-such a place 'You can see Bennachie.' There is a unique contentment for some of us in being at, or summoning up recollections of those places, and this need lose nothing even when age or exile preclude ascent of the tops.

It is an open question why some mountains are particularly significant visible symbols of happiness, as Bennachie has been to so many, through the generations and around the world.

'High ridged mountains are the mountains of Bashan!
Why look ye with envy, ye high ridged mountains
At the mountain where God has chosen to dwell?'

The psalmist here refers to Mount Sion and its election as successor to the hill of Sinai, where the Lord conversed with Moses. The Samaritans revered a different eminence, Gerizim, and the 'people of the land' had their own mountain shrines at which the Israelites were strongly tempted to join in their rites. All the peoples of the Old Testament appear to have heard some version of the same call: 'Lift thine eyes to the mountains, from whence cometh thy help,' though they might point each to a different summit as the mountain 'where God has chosen to dwell.'

A mountain to which the eyes of many turn with delight, and awe, and hopefulness (and all those blessings looked for from the unsleeping 'keeper of Israel'), is almost always, like Bennachie, visible from a long way off. It is not necessarily very high; I have met no-one with this particular feeling for Ben Nevis. Outliers and tip ends of mountain chains have special advantages. Mount Carmel, for instance, is a bluff crowning a promontory into the Mediterranean (and Carmelite spirituality is misunderstood if thought of as a way of hiding from the world). Bennachie, though hardly high enough to be a mountain at all, is visible from far and wide because it projects from the Eastern extremity of the Grampians into the lower ground between the hills and the sea, while the Garioch at its feet flattens out still more to the North-East and the Buchan peneplain. The change from the rounded outlines of such foothills of Bennachie as Old Flinder, Christ's Kirk, Rothney, and Dunnideer to the heavily glaciated, longer and lower, elliptical outlines of the Buchan horizon is extraordinarily subtle, and, short of living half a lifetime, or, better, two lifetimes, one in each, there is no better way to observe the gradation than to look down into it and out over it from the Mither Tap, on a clear day.

To reach that point, one has climbed well above the highest cultivated fields, and passed through plantations of conifers, which give way to rocky heathery ground at the highest levels. Here too, people once lived, but if there was tillage, its traces are lost unless to the eye of a specialist. I remember once trying to distinguish, in what I could see from that viewpoint, what was man's handiwork from that which was not. In the whole expanse below me, only some of the absolute bones of the landscape, the watercourses and their governing framework of slopes and levels appeared unaltered by the hand of man. Some of the trees and wild plants might be self-sown, but in all the low ground are certainly there on sufferance. Only the heights of Bennachie preserve, in contrast, some ecological autonomy.

Sudden changes of character at and near the tops of mountains are commonly delightful and dramatic, as at Monte Alvernia, where St. Francis received the stigmata, and the natural wooded hill-top, preserved at his request, waves spectacularly above the monastery and the overworked slopes where tiny fields and terraces alternate with eroded scree. Bennachie's own dramatic high point is, of course, man-made, the Mither Tap having been crowned with fortification; but being prehistoric, this strange architectural feature hardly disturbs the sense one has of being above and beyond the consuming tide human occupation of the landscape. Active persons may seek to perfect the impression by walking along the ridge to the actual summit at Oxen Craig.

Such contrasts, and the feeling of liberation to be found by climbing above the levels of present-day cultivation, are much to the modern taste. Infinitely more world-weary than the Romantics, at the end of the 18th century, who invented that particular game, we still have to acknowledge that the symbolic significance of Bennachie has accumulated, and fed on itself, to a great extent because this has been an inhabited mountain. The inhabitants of the Common of Bennachie, the Wildgooses, are a legend in themselves. I met one once in a formal context which prevented me from adverting to the family history, and still do not know if he noticed that I watched with fascination the way he walked. It was a pace which would have carried him effortlessly over the stony, tangly, peat-pitted expanses of the heights of Bennachie. It remains, I believe, uncertain just how high up the hill the Wildgooses actually lived. But there is no uncertainty as to the advantages, well understood from very early times, of living half-way up a mountain. And Bennachie possesses, in Chapel o'Garioch and its near neighbourhood, a 'mezzanine floor' of unrivalled amenity. The Maiden Stone is an outstanding piece of material evidence that Pictish inhabitants, who preserved also their own pre-Christian art-forms, favoured that area. On those slopes they could grow some cereal crops in good soil with natural drainage. Game must have abounded in the wild country higher up the mountain, while their own farm animals would find more grazing at those intermediate levels than would have been safely accessible in the wet woodlands choking the bottom of the valley.

I was grown-up, unfortunately, before I ever saw Bennachie, but as I picked up the threads of its magic, it dawned on me how much of the history and legend of the place seemed ready-made for being 'told to the children.' No doubt every generation of Aberdeenshire children has received echoes of it: strange distorted echoes some of them, such as the legend of the Maiden Stone, which features a very mediaeval Devil. I have heard also that the mirror among the Pictish symbols on the stone was taken as a representation of a girdle, and that the Maiden was making oatcakes when she was turned to stone. The oatmeal, on which the Picts indeed depended as a staple food, is the sole link between that legend and the reality of the Maiden Stone – and how tenuous! The Forbes and Leslie heroes (and villains) of feudal and Jacobitish tales might recognise themselves more readily in stories now being told about their exploits. Their surviving castles also materially fix the legends – though the uses of a castle may soon be as remote from our experience as were the real uses of the Maiden Stone from that of the mediaeval people to whom the Devil was real enough to have made it out of a petrified girl. All of this wealth of stories, through the spectrum from scholarly research to pure fantasy, and especially those told to children, have fed and still feed the widespread awareness that it is always good when one can be within sight of Bennachie.

And when one cannot? Such is the power of words that a single line of verse,
'I would I waur far Gadie rins'
may bring back awareness of the look of that landscape more effectively than any picture. Perhaps because each picture of Bennachie conveys only one impression of one facet of a view, whereas a nostalgic poem 'brings up Samuel' whole and entire, pictures may be less disquieting – a better solace daily for the exile in his home. One wants, of course, both the picture and the thing itself. A world-map of the distribution of pictures of Bennachie would undoubtedly show the highest concentration of all clustered round the foot of the mountain – many of these as highly prized as the souvenirs which have been carried to the ends of the earth. My own favourite, which now has pride of place in my home in Cambridge, is an etching made by my grandfather, Arthur John Lewis Gordon of Ellon. From Ellon, it requires good eyesight, a fine day, and a measure of faith to see Bennachie at all. The etching process has produced a reverse impression of an Ellon scene dominated by Bennachie on the far horizon, with the Mither Tap showing up at the right hand side. If one is sufficiently familiar with the outline, seeing it inside out is rather refreshing!

Besides his pictures, poems and ballads, the fixated exile may resort to another form of expression for his feelings that 'Bennachie Rules O.K.'

This is to select an accessible local surrogate, perhaps calling his house 'Craig Shannoch,' or merely feeling reminded of Bennachie by some local scene which may be supposed to have common or comparable features. Trans-Volta Togoland in West Africa is the furthest I have ever been removed from Bennachie and obliged to reside for long enough to feel the full effects of separation. There I lived for many months looking out over a baking red laterite plain, poorly covered in grass and low scrub, out of which rose an isolated pyramidal chunk of mountain, called Adaklu. Unlike Bennachie, Adaklu is precipitous – one side a cliff from summit to base, the menacing appearance of which is enhanced by tales of people being thrown over the edge, supernaturally and otherwise. It is altogether more spooky than any thing in Scotland. The summit area, in marked contrast to the gentler slopes, has never been exploited for food-gathering or planting of cassava or banana trees. It is preserved for use as a fetish grove, where the rain-forest canopy still keeps out the light and one moves with comparative ease over the dead leaves on the dark, dry, floor. Strange as it may seem, Adaklu became my local substitute for Bennachie, perhaps because it is an outlier hill, dominating a coastal plain, and it took the eye every time one looked Southwards from the town of Ho, as insistently as Bennachie fills the South view from my home at Insch. I retain a conviction that Bennachie had something to do with my desire to get to the top of Adaklu, and with my satisfaction when I did so – though I was rapidly washed off it again by a tropical rainstorm, and had to have sixteen thorns removed from my feet, some poisonous.

When I came back to live within sight of the real Bennachie, I brought some Adaklu folk-lore and adapted it for home use. All mountains are looked to for weather signs, and in Africa, of course, the important thing is to know IF it is going to rain. (In Scotland, we only need to know WHEN). Adaklu is a rain-bearer, anxiously watched for signs. A little wreath of mist floating free above the summit does not give much hope. Adaklu is 'smoking his fetish pipe,' and may or may not be intending rain. But if the mist becomes a cloud, and settles on the peak, Adaklu has 'put on his fetish hat' and rain may be expected. Bennachie, too, possesses a fetish hat and a fetish pipe, and, as my father pointed out, can also wrap himself completely in a fetish blanket, which means that the rain is NOT GOING TO STOP.

When it eventually does so, one is well advised to wait awhile before setting out for yet another walk on Bennachie – unless, that is, one is content to keep strictly to the excellent paths maintained by the Bailies. For Bennachie is a mountain of deep heather and other lush greenery, walking among which one may very quickly be soaked to the skin for several hours after rain ceases, or on a morning of heavy dew. But there is the special delight at such times of the rivulets carrying the water off the slopes and forever finding new courses down the changing face of the hill. Sandy stretches of any small path receiving a convergence of these rivulets are rapidly channelled and cut back round the bases of big stones, which shift and again divert the flow. The human foot-passenger must literally watch each step, or trip and stumble and splash. I was enjoying a leisurely descent by the path to the ford above Hillfoot Cottage in such conditions, making frequent halts as the only safe way of looking around me more widely, when I had the luck to see a beautiful young roe-buck feeding just below me, and to see him before he happened to notice me. I kept still and saw the huge differences in the aspect of the creature undisturbed, and, when he saw me but was not sure that I had seen him, of the alerted animal, head raised and suddenly still, and then of the fugitive. He decided, though I remained frozen, that I must have seen him, and fled in great floating bounds high over the deep fern and heather, delicate feet touching down, it seemed, only occasionally, to rebound from some hidden rock.

Common sights of the mountain, the rain running off it, the animals and birds which are to be seen by anyone who can stand still, live long in the memories of all Bennachie people, besides a lesser number of impressions of stranger, once-in-a-lifetime incidents, captured more carefully and consciously as memories. After the greatest heather fire of my experience, which blackened the North face of Bennachie from end to end, my father and I walked a little way up from Oyne, above Hillfoot. The dark expanse of the slopes above us was flecked with white. I thought at first that white quartz boulders had been exposed by the destruction of undergrowth. But stones do not hop! Each white fleck was a hare, still in its winter coat, suddenly deprived by a cruel fate of both camouflage and cover.

Just as the situation of Bennachie is so exposed and its outline so clear and memorable as to make it visible and recognizable over a much wider range than are most mountains, so its legends and history, its common and uncommon sights and sounds, the whole feel of the mountain, are, in the old senses, both highly agreeable and distinctly peculiar. In modern parlance, 'Bennachie Rules O.K.,' and it remains a great recommendation if one can say of any place, 'from there, you can see Bennachie,' or of some association of ideas and memories that by them Bennachie is brought into focus before the mind's eye.

MY MITHER, MY MAGIC MOUNTAIN

By Prasong Sananikone

'There's braver mountains ower the sea
An' fairer haughs I've kent, but still
The Vale o' Alford – Bennachie
Yon is the Howe, an' this the Hill.'

Charles Murray.

Motoring home from Aberdeen, at the top of Tyrebagger, I always see her. There she is, pavilioned in splendour, on the distant horizon beyond Blackburn and the rich and rolling farm lands of Kinellar. Like a Heraldic Lion on a sometime azure, sometimes vert, or sometime even on a sable ground, welcoming she lies. Along the bonnet of the car, and through the windscreen she looks and says 'Hello!' When this happens I know that I am home. Beyond all possible shadow of doubt I know that I am Home.

Not having being born in the North-East, I find it difficult to explain why I am so attached to Gordon District's very own and very special mini-mountain. The high ranges and cloud-piercing peaks of my native Laos, in distant Indo-China, dwarf Craigshannoch and Oxencraig any day. But it is Bennachie above all that holds a permanent and very special place in my heart and affections.

Maybe Bennachie means so much to me because during my happiest years I was fortunate enough to be brought up on a farm in the pleasant little parish of Daviot, under the shadow of what was to become and what shall for ever remain my own, my very own Magic Mountain.

During my impressionable teens, as I trudged to the Gunhill Junction to join the Inverurie school bus, a mere glance at the colours and contours of the Hill never failed to chase away any Monday morning gloom I may have had. During my University days, a return from Aberdeen to Gadie and Garioch was sheer refreshment of spirit.

With rod and line, constant and pervasive, the backdrop scene was always friendly Bennachie. Fishing on Don and Ury, so all-seeing was my Hill that when I kept an undersized trout or fished in an unsporting manner I couldn't see Mither eye to eye. Later when I overcame my fish-hungry phase and became a true angler, I used to look up to Mither who, I am quite convinced shared my pride whenever I was lucky enough to grass a salmon!

With gun in hand, and before sneaking across a neighbour's field in an attempt to bag a wild duck, pheasant or partridge, invariably did I give Mither a conspiratorial little nod. And such was our amazing rapport, through a cloudy eyelash, she always, I swear, returned a slyly jovial and encouraging wink! Mither always knew that my shooting skill was far from perfect; and a blank day would greatly disappoint an enthusiastic young sportsman.

Nor did Mither ever mind my using her as a sign-post. Minus map or compass, unfailingly and by very simple bearings, could I find my way around the vast Meal Girnal of the Garioch. To head for home was straight forward in the extreme. I just had to cut across to the East of Mrs Tap, look for the TV mast beyond Westertown and the Cross of Jackston, and that was it. It was as easy as that.

Came a dowie day when I could no longer see or be near my Magic Mountain. In my mind's eye only could I picture the forest at her foot, the heather-clad purple of her waist and the boulder-strewn bulges of her breast. I am in hot and steamy tropical terrain.

Full of zest, I went back to my native country, the little land-locked Royal Kingdom of Laos, hoping by precept and example to help my fellow-countrymen to achieve a measure of the prosperity of the Scottish good life I had known and left. All went well for a time. But alas!

A Western education was suspiciously regarded once the infiltrating Communist finally came to power. The political and cultural background from whence I had returned was anathema to them. Under the cold eyes of malevolent guards, it was forced labour for me. The encroaching jungle had somehow to be turned into what it was hoped would one day be happy and productive farm communes. At pistol point those who were regarded as enemies of the usurping regime were, in tense and back-breaking conditions, made to do the job.

The stench and steamy heat, the hunger and exhaustion, the cramped bamboo sleeping quarters, the unspeakable primitive prison conditions, none of these deterred me from thinking longingly – in the delerium of despair – had all my Scottish past been but a beautiful dream? – of my beloved Bennachie. Not once, however, and for fear of being locked in solitary confinement, did I dare tell my fellow prisoners, let alone my unsympathetic guards, that my own poor old Aberdeenshire Mither had far more charismatic charm than all the tropically-rich ranges put together. (By this silence I did my Magic Mountain less than justice. I can honestly affirm, however, that this was the only time I let my own, and very dear Bennachie down).

Now I see her again! I wasn't dreaming after all. There, she smiles her immemorial smile as the car tops the brae of Tyrebagger. I have made amends for my shameful prison-camp silence and I have been forgiven; therefore I am at peace.

Fate couldn't have chosen a more auspicious – or maybe should I say symbolic? – hour for my re-union with my own, my very own beloved Bennachie. It was an April Fool's Day, nineteen hundred and eighty-one, that in quietness together, and after a long twelve year absence, we celebrated our oh! so happy re-union. The torrrid horrors of tropical Laos under its invaders were erased and, I hope, laid to rest forever by the caller North-East breezes as in solitude – it just had to be in solitude – I climbed from Pittodrie to the Tap.

'Weel, Mither,' I thought as I looked down on a train snaking slowly through the fertile Oyne valley at my feet. 'Weel, Mither, I've come hame. After experiences that are best forgotten I've come hame to bide wi' ye for gweed. An' if y're daft eneuch to visit ye'r cousins in South-East Asia, I'm nae, I'm definitely nae, gyan wi' ye.'

Foot-note by Mr James R. Mackay.

Prasong Sananikone arrived at the home of Mr & Mrs Jack Philip, Lumphart, Oldmeldrum, in 1962 as a teenager from S.E. Asia. Unable to speak English, he attended Inverurie Academy where his delightful personality endeared him to staff and pupils. Under Dr Norman Dixon, he did extremely well during his three happy years there. Four years later he graduated B.Sc. in Agriculture.

Determined to improve the standard of living of his fellow countrymen, he became an Agricultural Adviser in Laos. When the communists took over he was arrested, imprisoned and brutally treated, including being foot shackled. He was even made to dig his own grave.

He escaped across the Mekong River on the night of 8th December, 1979 in a sinking canoe with ten escapees aboard, including his wife and children. Other parties tried the Mekong crossing that night were all slaughtered by bullets and rocket-propelled grenades.

Prasong and his wife and family are now living in Aberdeen and are very thankful to be alive.

PARADISE

By Thomas L. F. Burnett of Kemnay

As ye gang doon the Lord's Throat
On Paradise ye come,
The bonny Don a'round it
Reflects the setting sun.

The purple heather carpets
The slope o' Bennachie;
The firs stand out like sentinels
For all who come to see.

The beauties of the country
God made for tired man
Who each his road must travel
Since ere the warl' began.

The peat reek rises frae the burn
Of cottar house and mill;
The shacking briggie stands alone,
And a' the earth is still.

If I canna gain the Paradise
We read of in the Book
When my weary work is over
Then find for me some nook

Between the Don and Paradise
And northwards to the hill:
And I shall be contented,
And my tired spirit still.

'THERE'S NAE SAIR HEIDS IN BENNACHIE'

By Michael G. Kidd

In the summer of 1976 I came across in the possession of Mr McIntosh of Wembly an old advertisement, exhorting me to 'ask for Benachie Pure Highland Malt Whisky' and assuring me that 'there's nae sair heids in Benachie.' The advertisement further informed me that this was the product of Callander and Graham at Benachie Distillery which had been founded in 1824. That I knew was the year after the famous Excise Act of 1823 which laid the foundations of the modern distilling industry. An early licensed distillery then, quite near my one-time home at Pitmachie, and I knew nothing about it. I was intrigued.

Preliminary enquiries confirmed that there had indeed been a Benachie Distillery and that it had been situated at Nether Jericho in the parish of Culsalmond. A visit to the farm provided me with the unusual sight of a large cattle byre with barred windows down the length of its sides and with the further clear evidence of a distillery in the form of a dilapidated and roofless kiln in a line of otherwise unruined buildings giving some indication of their former use.

The first pieces of a lost jigsaw had been found. Local enquiries revealed that a lot of people were unaware of the distillery having existed but that some of the older folk did have recollections of an enterprise that had closed just before the First World War. I wanted to know more and a search for the rest of the jigsaw began. This article is not a chronological history of the distillery but tells of that search and shows the jigsaw picture so far as I have been able to reconstruct it. It is as yet incomplete: one or two tantalisingly intriguing pieces are still missing, despite extensive search. Perhaps some reader of this article will be able to help towards finding them. I and the other Bailies of Bennachie will be delighted and grateful if further information is forthcoming.

Mr William Gordon, late of the shop at Pitmachie, a fertile source of ideas and snippets of information throughout my search, suggested to me the first person I interviewed, the late Mr James Beattie of Mill of Bonnyton, who was to provide me with information, confirmed by others, as well as with his personal recollections. He recalled as a lad, in the first decade of this century, driving barley to the distillery from Mill of Bonnyton. As he was rather young he had to look after the horses and not lift the two-hundredweight bags. He also remembered seeing carts, drawn by two horses, carrying three huge barrels at a time from Jericho to the station at Insch. He further recalled an outlet for the product in Insch, stating that William Callander rented a shop nearly opposite J. & A. Forsyth's in the High Street in Insch where two-gallon pigs and bottles could be bought.

The late Mrs P. Chapman of Auchingoul told me of carts in the Glens of Foudland, nose to tail, going and coming from Jericho, and often scarce a sober carter amongst them. She told me of dances held in the loft over the Malt Barn to a band from Inverurie in the days after the distillery had ceased production. Mr Harry Fraser of Insch confirmed that his grandfather, Mr Robert Ingram, who died in 1935, had at one time driven the barrels of whisky from Jericho to Insch station.

Mrs J. Mennie of Auchencrieve Croft, Methlick, contacted me to say that she has in her possession a two-gallon Benachie whisky pig. This she kindly allowed me to photograph. Mr Norman Robertson of Netherton of Largie is another who is lucky enough to own such a pig and he still keeps whisky in his one! He also allowed me to photograph his pig and gave me a photocopy of the bill, still in his possession, dating from 1906, when his father purchased the two gallons of whisky for £1.15.0 from Messrs. Callander and Graham.

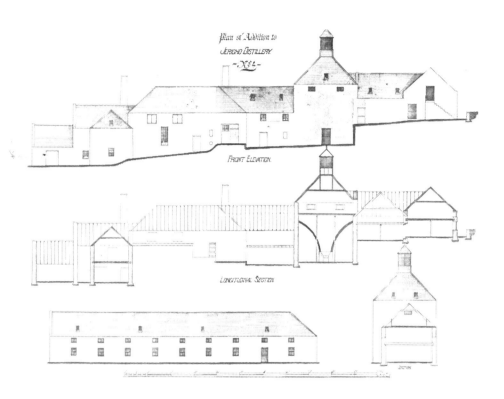

Reproduced by courtesy of the late Mr Frank Duncan, Nether Jericho

Mr Thomas Milne of Rothes, who was aged 85 when I visited him in 1977, was particularly informative. His father, William Milne, came from Westhall in 1870 to be grieve at Nether Jericho farm and distillery when John Maitland was the distiller. He was an expert in the breeding of Clydesdales and was in charge of the distillery carting. There were apparently six horses to do all the work of the farm and the distillery. Loads were carted to Insch station twice daily.

The workmen were, as was usual, housed in a bothy and were looked after by Mrs Milne, and it was while there that Mrs Milne gave birth to my informant's eldest sister. William Milne left Jericho for Thomastown of Auchterless, where Thomas was born, and around 1900 moved to Rothes.

He became friendly with the publican at the Victoria Bar, one Andrew McKenzie Grant, and persuaded him, according to my informant, to stock Benachie Whisky, which he doubtless enjoyed until his death in 1913, the year in which production ceased at Jericho. Thomas Milne remembered well the slogan on the bottle labels, 'There's nae sair heids in Benachie,' and vouchsafed that it had indeed been a very mild whisky. He also thought that there must have been whisky in the warehouse at Jericho for a while after 1913, because he could clearly recall the product still being on sale at the Victoria Bar when he went off to the war in 1915. There was, however, none left when he came back!

Mr Steve Sillett of Aberdeen, author of *Illicit Scotch*, whom I contacted, told me an anecdote recounted by his late father-in-law. Mr Adam Gordon. At a wedding in Insch, not long before the outbreak of the Second World War, a long-hoarded cask of Benachie, in all probability the last, was emptied and enjoyed. It was reported to be extremely mellow if a trifle woody.

I enquired of the late Mr Frank Duncan, a prominent Blackface breeder and owner of Nether Jericho until his recent death in 1981, whether he possessed any old documents relating to the distillery. To my delight he was able to produce the architect's building specifications and plans, dated 1884, for the additions and alterations to Jericho Distillery when William Callander and John Graham had taken over the lease of the distillery and farm from the representatives of the late John Maitland. There was also a plan of the distillery dated 1919. These he very kindly allowed me to photocopy.

Reproduced by courtesy of Mr N. Robertson, Netherton of Largie

It is, however, to the late Mrs Grierson of Cairnhill, near Huntly, that I am greatly indebted for putting in touch with me her friend, Miss Elizabeth Whitelaw, who lives in Edinburgh. Miss Whitelaw's late mother, whom I had the privilege to meet in 1977, was the last surviving child of the William Callander, who had operated the distillery with his brother-in-law, John Graham.

Mrs Whitelaw, née Leila Graham Callander, who died in 1981, was able to confirm that on economic grounds whisky production had ceased in 1913, and that her brother, also William Callander, had carried on after her father's retiral the farming side until his death during the Second World War. She had in her possession two photographs of Nether Jericho as a distillery, taken probably around the turn of the century. As far as she could remember the office wing in the later of the two photographs was added to the family dwelling house about ten years before the distillery ceased operations. John Graham, the brother-in-law and financial partner of William Callander, ran a grocery business in Banff. This was doubtless another outlet for the product.

Mrs Whitelaw further recalled that there had been employed a brewer, two maltmen, two ploughmen, two orra men, and a carter. She said there were occasionally dances to fiddles in the barn and she spoke of the men sweating freely as they jigged and birled in their heavy boots. She remembered the names of three of the gaugers: Messrs. Apedaile, Woodcock and Laing, as well as the name of the carter, one Tom Adam, and that of the housekeeper, Kate Catto.

Gradually the pieces of the jigsaw were fitting together to portray a lively industrious and very human enterprise. However, the widening but incomplete picture posed many interesting questions, some of a more dry and statistical nature, and some of which, alas, remain still unanswered. How much whisky was produced per annum? Where did the whisky go from Insch station? Were there ever any irregularities discovered? Who had taken out the first licence to distil in 1824? Had there been a still there prior to the Act of 1823? After all Mr Robertson's pig did claim the distillery had been established in 1822.

To find answers to as many of these questions as possible I should have to have recourse to official records of one sort or another. I began a systematic search.

My first move was to get in touch with the Grampian Regional Archivist, Mrs Brenda Cluer, whom I had recently met. After search, she informed me that there was nothing relevant in the Regional archives, but she suggested I approach the Business Archives Council of Scotland, the Scottish Record Office for their Customs and Excise records, and the Aberdeen City Library where I could consult Valuation Rolls and such books as might be available.

The Business Archives Council of Scotland was interested in and sympathetic to my enquiry, but unable to help. The Scottish Whisky Association, to whom I also wrote, could provide no information other than to refer me to Alfred Barnard's book, *The Whisky Distilleries of the United Kingdom*, published in 1887, which contains an entry on Benachie

Reproduced by courtesy of Mr McIntosh of Wembly

Distillery. The Librarian and Curator of H.M. Customs and Excise Library, Museum and Records in London carried out, at my request, a search of material there, but without success, stating that 'all the surviving records of both the Customs and Excise in Scotland are housed at the Scottish Records Office.'

To the Scottish Record Office in Edinburgh I went. There I found that two registers are closed to public gaze until the year 2000, but that I was able to consult the Register of Periods from Distilleries, 1811, the Fine Register, 1827-60, and the Fraud Register, 1827-50. The last two were particularly intriguing as shedding a fascinating light on the life of the times, but in none of them could I find any material attributable to Jericho Distillery. The folk there must all have been honest or undetected! What was particularly disappointing was to discover that there is no surviving register of the granting of licences to distil and that the letters of district excise supervisors to the Board of Excise anent each new application for a licence have not been kept. These have either been destroyed long ago as no longer important or have been lost in the various removals of the records from one place to another. This shattered my hopes of learning there who had taken out the first licence to distil at Jericho.

I contacted *The Press and Journal* in Aberdeen and through their columns made one or two personal contacts, but the first real breakthrough in information, a considerable assemblage of pieces of the jigsaw, came from the Aberdeen City Library, where I was able to consult the Valuation

Rolls, delve into issues of *The Aberdeen Journal* for 1823 and 1824, and read the entry in Alfred Barnard's book.

The Valuation Rolls date back to the middle of the last century and the first entry I found for Nether Jericho on the Estate of Sheelagreen, the proprietor of which was Andrew Gammell, Esq., was that for 1855-6. The tenant and occupier of Nether Jericho was one William Smith and the annual rent or value was £70.0.0. Six years later a Mr Livermore sublet a house from Mr William Smith, and it is tempting to wonder if he was an Excise Officer.

In 1864 William Smith retired and the tenancy of the farm and distillery was taken over by Mr John Maitland. In 1867 the resident Excise Officer is named as Mr F. W. Heighton, and by 1869 Major Andrew Gammell of Countesswells had succeeded as proprietor of the estate. Ten years later the tenancy appeared in the hands of the representatives of John Maitland, distiller, and the Excise Officer was now Mr William Morgan. The yearly rent or value of Nether Jericho farm is given as £116.6.0 and that of the distillery machinery and buildings as £60.0.0.

In 1884 Messrs. William Callander and John Graham took over the tenancy of the farm and distillery from the representatives of the late John Maitland, the proprietor of the estate now being The Right Honourable Lord Forbes. The distillery was now to become known as Benachie Distillery.

1884, as we know from the extant architects' plans and building specifications, was the year of additions and improvements to the distillery. The General Conditions laid down in the Specifications are fairly standard. The particular instuctions were as follows: 'The Employers will take off the wood-work of old roofs. Clear out the foundations. Supply the Rubble stones and sand to the Mason, and perform the Cartage of all Materials from a distance no exeeeding the Insch Railway Station.' Further, the Mason 'must have the walls ready for the roof before the 6 Sept. 1884,' the Carpenter is 'to have the roof ready for the slater within ten days after the walls are ready for him,' and the Slater likewise has ten days 'to execute his department.' The whole work is to be completely finished 'on or before 6 Oct. 1884.' The Specification is dated 18 June, 1884, and is signed by Messrs. George Matthews, Alexander Tocher, James Pirie and Charles Duthie.

The Valuation Rolls go on to show a fluctuating yearly rent or value of the farm and distillery and a succession of Excise Officers: Mr Joseph T. Apedaile, 1892; Mr Walter D. Evans, 1897; Mr George Woodcock, 1904; Mr Clement E. Ablitt, 1911. And so, sadly, I came to the last entry for Benachie Distillery, that of the years 1912-3. The next year shows that the proprietor is still Lord Forbes, that Mr William Callander, Jnr. is now tenant of the farm and house of Nether Jericho, but that nonetheless there is still an Excise Officer in residence, Mr Patrick Laing. After 1915 he departed. Great Britain had embarked upon the social upheaval of the First World War; Mr William Callander, Snr. had retired; the distillery had ceased production; an era had come to an end.

By 1919 the Estate of Sheelagreen itself was no more. It was split up and sold and in the Valuation Roll for 1920-1 William Callander is given as proprietor of Upper and Nether Jericho as well as of Colpy and St. Sairs; Lord Forbes's other former tenants were now tenants of Mr Callander and one William Kidd was the grieve. On Mr Callander's death in 1942 the properties were purchased by Mr James M'Intosh, Wembley, who in turn sold them in 1947 to Mr Francis Duncan.

The weekly editions of *The Aberdeen Journal* for 1823 and 1824 were, of course, enthralling. In that year for Wednesday, May 21, 1823, I was excited to find a Notice of Farms to Let in the Garioch, which listed all the farms on the Estate of Sheelagreen, to be let for nineteen years from Whitsunday, 1824, but was disappointed to find Nether Jericho omitted. Clearly its tenancy was on a different basis.

I read with interest many Notices of Sale of seized Highland Whisky by order of the Commissioners of Customs, and accounts of clashes between Excise officers and smugglers from the Cabrach and Glenbucket, but these are outwith the scope of this story. However, I was thrilled to come across the following advertisement in *The Aberdeen Journal* for Wednesday, Nov. 17, 1824, repeated in the editions for Nov. 24 and Dec. 1:

JERICHO WHISKY

Whisky, from Jericho Distillery, is to be had in Aberdeen,
only at the shop of Will. Milne, 39 Broad Street.

These premises have disappeared but they stood near where St. Nicholas House now stands.

Jericho Distillery is not mentioned in Samuel Moreword's list of distilleries of 1821, published in 1824, and reproduced in J. A. Nettleton's *The Manufacture of Whisky and Plain Spirit* in 1913. However, on p.243 of Alfred Barnard's *The Whisky Distillers of the United Kingdom* (1887), the reader will find the heading, 'Benachie Distillery, by Insch, Aberdeenshire.'

The entry describes the distillery buildings as being in a line sloping down towards the stream. First, at the top of the hill, were two Malt Barns, each 140 feet long and 25 feet broad, with two floors, the top used for the storage of barley, the lower for malting, and with Steeps of concrete and iron placed at each end of the barns. A doorway from the Barley Loft led into the Kiln, 'an apartment floored with perforated iron plates, and measuring about 24 feet square, where peat only is used for drying.'

At the lower elevation was the Malt Store, consisting of two lofts, into which the malt was conveyed by chutes from the Kiln floor. Underneath was the Mill Room, containing a pair of iron malt-rollers, driven by water power. From the Mill the ground malt was conveyed to the Mashing Hopper, 'situated in the Mashing House further down the hill, and placed above the Mash-tun.' The Mash-tun was an iron vessel, 12 feet in diameter and 4 feet deep, with 'revolving stirring gear, driven also by waterpower.' Below the Mash-tun was the iron Underback, from whence the Worts were pumped up into the Coolers at the top of the building. The Worts, when cooled, were run into four Washbacks, each containing about 3,000 gallons. The Tun Room was contiguous to the Still House, which was situated at the foot of the hill and contained, 'besides the Wash, and Low-wines, and Feints Chargers, two old Pot Stills and their respective Receivers.' The Stills, we are told, held 1,400 gallons and 706 gallons respectively.

The Spirit Store adjoined the Still House and contained a Spirit Vat holding 1,100 gallons, 'and all the necessary appliances for filling and weighing the casks of Whisky.' There were four Warehouses, but a new Warehouse was under construction which would be larger than all the four combined. There were, in addition, a small Cooperage, a Smith's shop, cartsheds and stables.

The annual output is given as 25,000 gallons but with the enlargement of the premises the firm of Callander and Graham expected to be able to turn out 40,000 to 50,000 gallons.

This whisky pig is the property of
Mrs J. Mennie, Methlick
Photo – Michael Kidd

The bulk of the jigsaw was now complete and I became even more keen to find those pieces still missing. A further visit to the Scottish Record Office revealed in the register of defunct companies a few unexpected pieces in the form of an apparent intention to restart the enterprise.

I came across a Memorandum of Agreement by Benachie Distillery Syndicate, Limited, having its registered office at 46a, Union Street, Aberdeen, to purchase from Lawrence McDonald Chalmers of Aberdeen 'rights, interests and claims' acquired by him 'under Contract or Agreement entered into between him and William Callander, Farmer, Jericho, in the County of Aberdeen, by missives dated in March and April 1919.' The Memorandum, dated 1920, was subscribed by the said Lawrence McDonald Chalmers; by John Rattray Flockhart, Chartered Accountant, as Director of the Syndicate; and by James Bisset Davidson, Solicitor, the Syndicate's Secretary.

The Memorandum of Association of the Syndicate, dating from March, 1920, sets out the objects for which the Company was established: inter alia 'to acquire and hold, manage, develop, improve or otherwise turn to account the buildings connected with the farm of Jericho . . . including the buildings adjacent, formerly occupied as a distillery, and the water and other rights connected therewith, and any moveable property and rights pertaining thereto, all of which have been agreed to be purchased from William Callander, Farmer, Jericho.' The Statement of Nominal Capital was £2,000, divided into 2,000 shares of £1 each.

The Company was formally dissolved by notice in the *Edinburgh Gazette*, dated 1st July, 1960. The last director was Mr L. E. F. Chalmers of Lethenty House, near Inverurie.

I contacted Mr Chalmers, who now lives in Aberdeen, and who is the son of the man who entered into the Agreement with William Callander. He explained that his father, who died in 1959, had been very friendly with Mr Callander and had formed the Company with a view to starting distilling again, but that it had never got off the ground. The necessary return was made every year under the Companies Act just to keep it alive and in case it could be used in some way.

This discovery filled in the picture up to the present time. But what of the early years? The first tenant of Nether Jericho of which I knew was William Smith in 1855. Nowhere had I seen him referred to as a distiller, but it seemed a reasonable assumption that he was. Had he been there since the start? Had he, with an eye to business, taken advantage of the 1823 Act and taken out a licence to distil the next year? Had he, like his famous namesake, George Smith of Glenlivet, had to go around with pistols for his own protection against the illicit traders, rivals whom he was likely to put out of business? Had the folk of Jericho been previously engaged in the illicit trade themselves? In getting their wares to Aberdeen had they to run the gauntlet of the celebrated and indefatigable Excise Officer, Malcolm Gillespie? All these questions clamoured for answers.

William Smith had been the tenant of the Gammell family: it might, therefore, be helpful to have access to Gammell family records if available. I was very fortunate to be put in touch with Mr Edward Gammell, who lives in Hampshire, through whom I was able to trace relevant Gammell papers to the Archives Department of Aberdeen University. These proved interesting and frustrating. In rent collection lists William Smith was mentioned as being in Nether Jericho in 1839, 1838, 1837, 1834 and in 1833, the earliest reference. No mention is made of the distillery. The most tantalising document of all is a description of the farms on the Estate of Sheelagreen with conditions of lease, dated September 1823. It mentions Mains of Sheelagreen, Boghead, Old Wrangham, Little Wrangham, Croft of Little Wrangham, St. Sairs, Upper Jericho, Scares, Fordmouth, Waulkmill, and Garden's Mill. The omission of Nether Jericho is significant and would suggest that even prior to 1824 the property was a separate entity. Does this go some way towards explaining the discrepancy between the date 1822 on Mr Norman Robertson's whisky pig and the founding date of 1824 declared elsewhere?

So near and yet so far!

It was at this point that Mrs Helen Fraser, Clerk to the Bailies of Bennachie, and a source of encouragement to me in my research, came up with a vital piece of information contained in Henderson's *Aberdeenshire Epitaphs and Inscriptions*. It was the very brief inscription on a stone to be seen in Oyne Churchyard which reads thus: 'The Burial Place of Wm. Smith, Distiller, Jericho, who was born at Mill of Ardoyne, January 4, 1793, and died 22nd February, 1873.' The same book quotes a headstone in Tullynessle : 'In Memoriam James Smith, A.M., Preacher of the Gospel, for xxxvi years Schoolmaster of this Parish. Died 27th December, 1861, aged 63 years.' The book goes on to say that this James Smith was the son of Alexander Smith, Mill of Ardoyne, and a direct descendant of Patrick Smith, tenant of that mill in 1674, who was a brother of William Smith of Mill of Tiftie, the father of Mill of Tiftie's Annie. The book does not state whether William and James Smith were brothers.

Clearly, however, William Smith would have been of an age to establish a distillery around 1823, and if the two men could be shown to be brothers, it would seem that he was descended from a background that would have fitted him for that kind of occupation.

A visit to New Register House in Edinburgh provided some answers. The Register of Births and Baptisms for the Parish of Oyne showed that 'on Jany. 6, 1793 Alexr. Smith in Mill of Ardeen had a son baptised William.'

The Distillery, circa 1900. The late Mrs Whitelaw's photograph

His death certificate showed that he had died at Westhall Cottage, Parish of Oyne, that his father had been Alexander Smith and his mother had been born Elizabeth Rough. He left a widow, Jane, née Bisset. The death certificate of James Smith showed the same parents and was witnessed by Wm. Smith, his brother, resident in Jericho. A search in the records of the Parish of Culsalmond revealed that on 20th June, 1847, William Smith and Jane Bisset from the Parish of Old Machar were 'contracted in order to marriage' and had their banns published before the congregation.

The jigsaw now seems very nearly complete, but not quite. We do know for certain that Jericho Distillery did not merit mention in the list of 1821; we do know that as a property it was separate from the other farms on the estate in 1823; we do know that the distillery's product was on sale in Aberdeen in 1824. We do not know just when distilling started, or much about the distribution and marketing of the product down the years. We do not know for certain if William Smith founded the distillery and took out the first licence to distil, though it does seem likely. We are not sure if the distillery began operating in 1822 and was licensed two years later.

Perhaps one day the uncertainties will be resolved. In the meantime I am happy in the knowledge that at least one Benachie whisky pig is still being appropriately used, even though the original brand is no longer available.

TAM STEPHEN
or The Cairter o' Benachie

By Michael G. Kidd

Tam Stephen tyaaved at Jericho,
A buirdly cairter he,
He cairtit tae the trains at Insch
The casks o' Benachie.
He tyaaved tae William Callander
'Twixt Skares and Sheelagreen,
Fa was it made the Highland Malt
Brocht twinkles tae the e'en.

Sing airie additie airie an,
Fill up your stoup; be ree!
There's nae sair heids,
There's nae sair heids in Benachie!

Young Tam was yet a single chiel
Fa ettled tae be wed,
He set his he'rt upon fair Kate
Fa was the kitchen maid.
But Kate sae sonsie an' sae braw
Was thirl'd tae anither,
A plooman lad fae Gadieside,
Jock, the maltman's brither.

Sing airie, etc...

Tam wasna blate an' coorted Kate
He tint nae chance ava,
But bonnie Kate rejeckit him
An' caa'd him gyte an' aa'.
Tam was sae sair distress'd at this
He kicket owre the theats,
He got blin' drunk an' raced his cairt
Through Insch's windin' streets.

Sing airie, etc...

It was a mercy nane was killed
As oot the toun he fared,
An' syne again fan couped the cairt
At Mill o' Knockenbaird.
Fan Callander he heard o' this,
Tae Tam he said, 'Ye'll see,
Ye'll flit your kist an' cairt nae mair
My casks o' Benachie.'

Sing airie, etc...

Noo Tam tyaaved neist at Bonnyton,
An' dyod, it's nae a lee,
But he 'gan cairtin' barley tae
The still made Benachie.
At Bonnyton there bade a deem
Caa'd Muckle Anne by aa';
She fairly socht tae please the loon
But fleggit him awa'.

Sing airie, etc...

Tam swore he'd hae nae mair tae dae
Wi' kittly kitchie deems,
But fan he took a fee again,
He'd ither thochts it seems.
For syne he married weel-faured Jean
Fa cookit at Pitbee,
An' noo they bide wi' bairnies twa
At Back o' Benachie.

Song airie, etc...

Author's Note.

I have carried out research into Benachie Distillery which, between 1824 and 1913, at Nether Jericho, near Colpy, produced a Highland Malt called at first 'Jericho Whisky,' then later 'Benachie Whisky.' I have adopted the distiller's spelling of Benachie. The research suggested the material for the ballad. From 1884 the distillery was operated by Messrs. Callander & Graham, and one of their advertising slogans was 'There's nae sair heids in Benachie.' The places mentioned in the ballad are all real and William Callander was the distiller: all other persons are entirely fictitious. The tune I have selected for the ballad is 'John Drumlie,' though I have no doubt others would be suitable.

Michael G. Kidd.

JOHNNY GIBB AND BENNACHIE

By Cuthbert Graham

The Mither Tap of Bennachie must have dominated the western horizon of William Alexander, the creator of *Johnny Gibb of Gushetneuk* for the first quarter of his life, for he was born in 1827 at Resthivet, about a mile and a half north-east of Pitcaple in the parish of Chapel of Garioch, the eldest son of James Alexander and his wife Anne Wilson. At Resthivet his father carried on the trade of blacksmith, but when young William was still at Daviot School (which he attended as being nearer his home than the school at Chapel) his father gave up his blacksmith business and removed his family to the farm of Damhead, Pitcaple, of which he had become tenant.

As eldest son, William Alexander might well have anticipated eventually succeeding to the tenancy of Damhead and he flung himself into the work of the farm until the accident in which his leg was crushed and had to be amputated. During the long illness which followed this calamity he read extensively, came under the influence of the Mutual Improvement Association, then at the peak of its influence in Aberdeenshire, acquired a useful knowledge of Latin and taught himself to draw so that he could illustrate his own humorous stories and verses. A prize essay about farm servants, jointly written by William and his brother for the *North of Scotland Gazette*, brought him into contact with William McCombie, Cairnballoch, part-proprietor and editor of the paper. McCombie gave Alexander a job on the *Gazette* in 1852, and he transferred to the new paper when the *Gazette* was transformed into the *Aberdeen Free Press*, which was to become the great Liberal organ of the North of Scotland for the next seventy years. On McCombie's death in 1870 Alexander succeeded him as editor of the *Free Press*.

It was in the previous year that the *Free Press* commenced publishing in instalments Alexander's most famous fiction 'Johnny Gibb of Gushetneuk in the Parish of Pyketillim, With Glimpses of the Parish Politics about A.D. 1843.' There was never any secret of the fact that 'Pyketillim' is largely modelled on Chapel of Garioch – though the actual name Pyketillim appears to derive from an actual farm name, that of Pictillum just to the north of Kemnay on the Kemnay-Port Elphinstone road. In his *Place Names of Aberdeenshire* William Alexander's namesake, W. M. Alexander, notes that Pictillim is quite a common farm name in Aberdeenshire with examples at Ellon, Meldrum, New Deer and Tarves. Curiously enough he does not mention the Pictillim at Kemnay. The name also occurs in England where it is usually applied to a modest land-holding entirely surrounded by hedges.

'Johnny Gibb' was first published in book form in 1871 and by 1912 it was accepted as a Scottish classic and had run through seventeen editions, including the *edition de luxe* produced by David Douglas of Edinburgh in 1880 with illustrations by Sir George Reid, President of the Royal Scottish Academy, engraved by M. Durand of Paris. Latterly out of print for some years, it was last re-issued by the Heritage Press, Turriff, three years ago.

The structure of 'Johnny Gibb' suffers a little from its having been initially written as newspaper instalments. All the chapters are uniformly short and some of them are very deliberate side-issues. But in the main it is a very thorough and satisfying picture of the ways in which the Disruption affected rural life in Aberdeenshire, with Johnny Gibb, a small farmer, occupying the centre of the stage.

The Rev. N. L. A. Campbell, minister of Chapel of Garioch, remarks in the *Third Statistical Account* of the parish (1960): 'If a picture of the social life of the parish 100 years ago is desired it will be found in *Johnny Gibb of Gushetneuk*.' Yet Mr Campbell himself points out that in at least one respect the Disruption took a different course in Chapel of Garioch than it does in 'Johnny Gibb' for the established minister of the parish, the Rev. Henry Simson or Simpson, who wrote the *New Statistical Account*, 'went out' in 1843 and carried many of the parishioners with him. The opposite happens in 'Johnny Gibb' where Mr Sleekaboot stays put and is depicted as 'the very incarnation of Moderatism.' It is thus left to Johnny Gibb himself to take the lead in the great kirk controversy in the parish, for during the visit to the wells at Tarlair, which opens the novel, he had heard from Maister Saunders the sad story of the Marnoch intrusions case and returned to Pyketillim an ecclesiastical radical, just as he had already been a political radical since voting Liberal in defiance of his Laird after the

Reform Bill of 1832. Johnny ranges himself with the non-intrusionists, breaks with the parish minister and becomes the leading promoter of dissent in the district. A public meeting is held in the Gushetneuk barn at which Hairry Muggart gives a graphic account of his experiences at the futile settlement of an unacceptable presentee at Culsalmond. A site is found for a free Church and after the Disruption of 1843 a regular minister is called, and eventually a manse is provided for him.

This is the Disruption side of the story, but it is not obtruded unduly. Of much greater importance to modern social science students is the clash of classes within the farming community. Dr Ian Carter sums this up in his book *Farm Life in North-East Scotland* when he says apropos of 'Johnny Gibb':

'The heart of the novel is a systematic contrast between the socially and morally admirable relations between farmer and servants on Gushetneuk, a middle peasant farm with an incomplete farm family, and the immoral atmosphere on the neighbouring capitalist farm of Clinkstyle – an atmosphere that corrupts both the farm family and the farm servants.

'Alexander also attacks lairds' land policies: when, Tam Meerison inseminates the kitchen maid, the newly married couple can find no farm cottage in which to set up house, for all the neighbouring lairds have pulled down croft houses and cottar houses to avoid a heavy Poor Law assessment. They are compelled to move to the Bennachie squatter colony, and Tam, a skilled horseman, is forced to take to day-labouring. 'Johnny Gibb' is not the couthy tale of country folk – the MacArchers – that later bourgeois commentators made of it . . . Alexander makes conflict over church government – the novel's ostensible concern is the course of the Disruption in the Garioch – a stick with which to beat landlords and capitalist farmers. In this magnificent novel we see the defence of peasant interests moving from the religious to the political sphere.'

Now the Marxist Communism of Lewis Grassic Gibbon in *A Scots Quair* was naked and unashamed. Here we have Dr (now Professor) Carter revealing William Alexander, Gibbon's great predecessor, as a Radical whose attack on capitalism on the land was Marxist in all but name. I wonder what Alexander himself would have said about that.

The reader of 'Johnny Gibb' will certainly be largely unaware of this deep political undercurrent. He will see the nastiness of Clinkstyle as due, not to its being a capitalist enterprise, but to its subservience to the greed and ambition of Mrs Birse, a woman of masterful machinations which, unfortunately for her and her husband and children, gang aft agley. It was the appalling character of Mrs Birse which struck the Victorian readers of 'Johnny Gibb' as William Alexander's greatest *tour de force*.

Today our reading of 'Johnny Gibb' can be enhanced, certainly, by some thought on the social issues which Dr Ian Carter has raised. But if we belong to Aberdeenshire or even more closely to the farming country around Bennachie, our keenest pleasure will surely be in the *language*, the rich Doric dialogue which is the distinguishing stamp of the book. We are introduced to it and to Tam Meerison as well as to Johnny himself in the

opening words of the book, said to have been uttered at 4.30 a.m. on a June day in 1839:

'Heely, heely, Tam, ye glaiket stirk – ye hinna on the hin shelvin' o' the cairt. Fat hae ye been haiverin at min? That cauff saick'll be tint ower the back door afore we win a mile fae hame. See't yer belly-ban be ticht aneuch noo. Woe, lassie! Man, ye been makin' a hantle mair adee about blaikin that graith o' yours, an' kaimin the mear's tail, nor balancin' yer cairt, an' gettin' the things packit in till't.'

Some of the best dialect in the book occurs in scenes connected with Tam Meerison and Jinse Deans, the good-looking kitchie deem at Gushetneuk. Chapter Three, called 'Rustic Courtship' describes what happens at Gushetneuk while Johhny and Mrs Gibb are temporarily absent on holiday at Tarlair in 1839. Once he gets the 'loon' Willie McAul safely tucked up in bed in the chaumer Tam 'under pretence of going to the stable slipped down the trap and out by the door, which he quietly locked to make sure that Willie McAul would not follow him. In somewhat less than two minutes thereafter, Tam Meerison and Jinse Deans were seated side by side on the 'deece' in Johnny Gibb's kitchen.'

As the hilarious scene which follows has been extracted from 'Johnny Gibb' and reprinted in *Grampian Hairst* (1981) the schools anthology of North-east prose, I will not repeat it here. Comedy has turned to something like tragedy by the time we get to Chapter 26, called 'A Start in Life.' By this time 'about a week before the Whitsunday term of 1842,' Tam Meerison has flitted from Gushetneuk to Clinkstyle, where he is not at all happy, but he is constrained to 'bide on' for another term for a very special reason – and that reason is Jinse Deans whom – not at all unwillingly – he is obliged to marry. Johnny Gibb is startled and annoyed when he learns that Jinse is 'needin awa.'

When Jinse unexpectedly bursts into the kitchen, where Mrs Gibb is attempting to explain to her husband why Jinse must leave, Johnny gives vent to his bewilderment.

'Fat haiver's this't ye've taen i' yer heid noo?' demanded Johnny, addressing Jinse. 'Are ye gyan clean gyte to speak o' leavin' yer place; and it only an ouk fae the term tee? Faur wud ye gae till?'

'Hame to my mither's,' answered Jinse, exhibiting somewhat of discomposure at Johnny's vehemence.

'Jinse's mother lived not far off Bennachie in a very unpretentious residence.' This is in fact all that we are told about Jinse's mother's but-and-ben save it was three miles from Gushetneuk and Clinkstyle and 'very barely afforded room for two beds in its dark and diminutive extent.' The Bennachie squatter's colony is not explicitly mentioned, so perhaps Dr Carter is assuming too much when he identifies it with a squatter's clay bigging.

A few hours later we are again shown Tam and Jinse seated side by side on the deece at Gushetneuk and this time Jinse is in tears.

'Tam put his arm about her and there was genuine feeling in the poor chap's words . . . as he said in his tenderest tones 'Dinna noo, Jinse – Ye'se never want a peck o' meal nor a pun' o' butter as lang's I'm able to work for't'.'

They were married as soon as the banns could be cried, and we next meet Tam when that malevolent underling Dawvid Hadden, Sir Simon Frissal's officious ground-officer, orders him to stop carting sand from a march burn (probably at Burnhervie) to help build the Free Kirk of Pyketillim. Tam is unmoved.

'Na, sang aw, Dawvid. As lang's I've Gushetneuk's orders to full san', it's nae you 't 'll stop me, nor a' the grun-offishers i' the kingdom.'

Hadden vapoured about an interdict, but 'Tam said he might get a 'dizzen o' enterdicks' if his taste lay that way, but he would take his loads of sand in the meantime.'

Several years now pass and when Willie McAul leaves Gushetneuk to obtain enlarged experience in big farming he suggests to Johnny Gibb that Tam Meerison might take his place.

'Faur is he?' asked Johnny.

'Dargin, an livin' in a bit hoosie near the fit o' the hill. I'll speak aboot it till 'im gin ye like.' Tam jumps at the opportunity. He was now the father of a family of three. 'It seemed to him to be in a measure Paradise regained, when he had the kind of work day by day which he liked and was fully competent to do, and when Johnny Gibb, not merely did not grudge his going once a week to see his family, but made Jinse Deans and her offspring heartily welcome to spend a day at Gushetneuk at all times when they chose to do so.'

Two further points can be made about topographical issues in 'Johnny Gibb.' In April 1843 a historic meeting of the Synod was held in Aberdeen and Mains of Yawal, as the Pyketillim ruling elder was bullied into going so that his vote could be cast in the cause of the Moderates.

'As the newspapers had just announced, the Aberdeen Canal was 'again open for navigation,' after some temporary stoppage, and Mains was decidedly favourable to going by the 'swift gig boat' as the cheapest means of conveyance. So next day he had his old-fashioned gig a-yoke to convey himself and the minister to the Canal Head (at Port Elphinstone) . . . Rev. Andrew Sleeaboot, as became his dignity took his passage in the cabin of the fly-boat, but this course his ruling elder resolutely declined to follow. He could save a shilling by going in the steerage, and why should he not do so?'

The second point is that whenever it is mentioned in the book 'the Broch' refers not to Fraserburgh but to Inverurie – it being equally with Fraserburgh a 'burgh.' That Inverurie is meant is clear when on one occasion Johnny Gibb and his cronies are so keen to attend a meeting in 'the Broch' that they walk there on foot, which of course could easily be done from Chapel of Garioch.

At the end of the day Johnny Gibb, having disposed of the operation of Gushetneuk to a younger generation recovers briskly from a spell of illness and the book ends, as it began, with an outing to the seaside. As Mrs Hairry Muggart tells Meg Raffan the hen-wife:

'Na, na, Gushets is courin up fine; and him an' the goodwife is makin' ready to gae doon to the Walls for an aucht days or sic like; an' that's a hantle better for the constiteetion nor a' the doctor's drogs that ye can pit in'o yer inside.'

Reproductions of Sir George Reid's drawings is by courtesy of
Aberdeen Art Gallery and Museums.

BIRDS OF BENNACHIE

By David Merrie
with ornithological data provided by Steve Buckland

As I write this it is winter. Ten inches of snow have lain for a week and are now melting away. In that spell of beautiful, crisp, clear days with the temperature well below zero, you could have travelled, if you had wished, on skis from the pastures of Oyne across the tops and down to the Don, even in some places over the Don itself. These days so full of beauty and the pleasure of living for humans in warm houses stocked with food, were hard on our wildlife, and on birds in particlar. The small animals, mice, voles, moles burrowed below the snow and in their well established runs through the earth and surface vegetation. I saw a tired Tawny Owl sitting on a gatepost in bright sunlight leaning against the cap of snow atop it. He would have had a hard job finding his customary prey.

Other birds of prey I have seen in this weather, hunting over the low ground, are Sparrowhawks and Kestrels. The Kestrel normally seeks small mammal prey but when this is hard to find, will go for small birds, hoping to surprise them and catch them on the ground as they feed round byres and cornyards. The Sparrowhawk also hunts around these places, but catches its prey on the wing. That is to say, the Sparrowhawk is on the wing. It can, and very frequently does, pursue and catch flying prey, but it can just as easily drop a leg as it makes a pass over a small bird and snatch it up with scarcely a hesitation in its flight.

One of the birds on which the Sparrowhawk preys is the Wood Pigeon, 'though normally only the larger female bird can successfully kill them. I don't need to tell folk of the Garioch how common Wood Pigeons are at any time of the year. To pass a wood where they have just come into roost about dusk of a winter's evening is like being subjected to a volley of .22 rifle shots as they fly out in panic.

The Rook is also present in large numbers in the farmland around Bennachie. At Oyne we have a large roost of 500 or more birds in the Petmathen woods. At dawn each day they spread out in groups, some large, some small, to forage for grubs in the fields. Life is difficult when the ground is frozen and the Rooks have to try other things to eat, like turnips, 'though those must be frozen too. A few come to our bird table, and can make short work of all the scraps we have put out for smaller birds.

It is at the bird table or the cornyard that one can see the greatest variety of birds in our area in the winter. At the bird table concentrate all the species that remain in the garden environment throughout the year. The harder the weather, the more they come, the more they fight for room, for priority; sometimes holding on for longer than they need to feed adequately; sometimes being driven away. The Great Tits and Blue Tits are the most successful. They will eat anything and can solve any problem of access. We can identify some of our regulars. There was a female Great Tit we called Curly-tail. She obviously roosted in a small hole that gave her tail a permanent leftways bent. She died a year ago by flying into a window. This year a male Great Tit has occupied her roost for his tail has become bent in exactly the same fashion. We feed our tits with good Scots oats, and last summer our local pair of Blue Tits fed their young on small green caterpillars and frequently brought these to the bird table and coated them with oatmeal before taking them to their chicks.

Many other birds watch the tits and learn, but do not have the strength of claw to hang in impossible positions. Robins and Dunnocks hover and make snatches at hanging food or jump into coconuts, sitting sideways so that they can feed and keep a lookout at the same time. The Coal Tit is a regular but less frequent visitor. Blackbirds are a numerous and noisy clientèle. Squabbling Starlings and plebeian House Sparrows split their time between the bird table and the farmyard next door.

Around the cornyards, and also in the turnip fields, especially when the ground is not frozen, one will find the wintering flocks of Finches and Buntings and occasionally Skylarks. Commonest amongst these are the Chaffinch and Greenfinch, and with them, in varying proportions every year, will be Bramblings, Yellowhammers, Reed and Corn Buntings; sometimes a few Tree Sparrows or Goldfinches. All of these species, except for the Bramblings, breed in the area, but many of our winter birds will have come, like the Bramblings, from Scandinavia in the hope of a milder climate and better food supply.

In the woods, apart from the Wood Pigeon, the main winter inhabitants are the tits, Coal Tits the most numerous, followed by Blue, Great and Long-tailed Tits. They rove around in flocks, sometimes as many as fifty or more, of mixed species, and frequently accompanied by Goldcrests and a Treecreeper or two. A wood may seem deserted until you come across such a party. You may hear the chirrup of Long-tailed Tits, delightful little birds looking like pink, white and black lollipops, with their round bodies and long tails, or the chitter of Blue Tits; and then, if you stand still and watch, you will see them. At first you may have difficulty seeing even one or two. But they move all the time, and you will see, first here, then there, small birds flitting from tree to tree and losing themselves almost immediately in the foliage. They will seem oblivious of your presence if you keep quiet, and soon they will be all around you. You will see some very well; even to see the lovely red and gold crown of the male Goldcrest; or to have a Treecreeper announce itself with a thin 'pseep' and to alight on a tree trunk nearby, zigzagging upwards, sharp tail spread out pressed against the bark as it probes with its curved bill in the crevices for grubs.

The other places to look for birds in the winter are the rivers and watermeadows. As long as there is some clear water, and it must be a very exceptional winter if there is not, one will see the Dipper, in dinner jacket, white front and dark red cummerbund. He sings much at this time of year, for Dippers select territory along the riverbanks and guard this jealously. They nest from April onwards, having up to three broods. Other winter water birds are the dabbling ducks, Mallard and Teal, and diving ducks, Goldeneye and Goosander, which may all be seen in small numbers on the Don. An all year round regular is, of course, the Heron which not only feeds on suitably sized fish, but frogs, beetles and even small mammals and birds if it can catch them. We do not have any large heronries in the district, and mostly see Herons in just ones and twos.

In the riverside fields, Greylag Geese and Whooper Swans, visitors from Iceland, feed during the day. At dusk the geese fly to roost at the Loch of Skene, and the swans might go with them, but more usually roost on a river pool. The Loch of Skene is also the roosting site for thousands of Common Gulls. Every winter, morning and dusk, these may be seen drifting to and from their feeding places. Over Oyne the morning procession takes an hour or more from first light as parties move leisurely across the valleys of the Gadie and Urie in a general north-westerly direction.

The first signs of spring come on a fresh February day when the Song Thrush returns to the garden and tries a few notes, or when the first Oystercatchers come up the river valleys and fly, piping loudly, over the lower fields. As often as not a spell of cooler weather silences this first overture, but by mid-March, whatever the weather may bring, the Oystercatcher will be there. By day they will prospect the fields for nesting sites. Most will have found a mate on the seashore where they have spent the winter; some may have retained the same mate for many years, as Oystercatchers can live for up to twenty years. At night they assemble in roosts in sheltered places along the river banks, or sand quarries and the like.

With the early Oystercatchers often come Golden Plovers who may stay in our fields for a week or so before passing on to the higher moors inland. Although the Bennachie moorland looks similar to many a Golden Plover moor, very few stop there to breed. The top country is almost the sole province of the resident Red Grouse and there is a limited number of them as the feeding is not very rich. Of the other game birds, the Blackcock is found sparsely on the lower south-western slopes of Bennachie; the naturalised Pheasant is common and ubiquitous; and the Partridge is found well-distributed but in small numbers throughout the farmland.

In the often forbidding weather of March and early April, spring can creep up on you almost unnoticed, the migrant birds marshalling themselves in sheltered places, the young plants and tree buds swelling and brightening to a yellow-green. Then, on what we like to call a real spring day, we awake to the voices of Larks, Blackbirds, and Thrushes singing to a cloudless dawn. The haggling of the Oystercatchers resound over the fields; Curlews and Lapwings spell us with their wistful cries, always evoking day dreams of wild and distant places. The Tits have temporarily abandoned the bird table and aggressively claim their territories around the garden. Robins, Wrens and Dunnocks will be singing from their particular vantage points on or in the garden shrubs. The Tawny Owl, whose hootings filled the early winter night, is quiet now for it will have found its nest hole, and is already by mid-April expecting the emergence of its fluffy brood.

New forms, new voices, now arrive. Sand Martins flit along the river courses. Grey and Pied Wagtails bob in the ditches and build their grassy nests in corners of bridges or buildings or crannies in wall or bank. Swallows chitter from telephone wire and dash around byre and barn in nuptual flight.

Now is the time to go to the woods, when even the Commission's seried ranks have evidence of life. One day you will hear the first Willow Warblers and in the next day or two the woods will be full of them. From some tall tree a Mistle Thrush will be warbling his terse but melodious song. In the evenings you will see the Woodcock roding. This is a peculiar display flight in which this heavy snipe-like bird flies slowly just above the tree tops, making repeated circuits over its chosen territory. As it goes it utters two sounds, so dissimilar that it is difficult to believe they come from the same bird. One is a low frog-like croaking, and the other a high call, best described as 'tsiwick.'

Jays also become especially noticeable with their loud raucous cries. The call belies the appearance of the bird, for it is a beautifully dressed creature in pinkish grey with a black tail, black and white wings with a patch of bright blue barred with black. The Bullfinch is another handsome woodland bird. In the winter they roam far, and our resident population may even be joined by some of their brighter continental cousins. They feed on buds and seeds and are often found right out on the moor eating heather seeds. In the spring they return to the woods, or to gardens with trees, especially fruit trees, where they can do considerable damage. Fortunately, they are not so numerous round here as to be a general nuisance.

Resident with us all year round are the two woodpeckers, Great Spotted and Green. The Great Spotted is black and white and in the spring proclaims its territory with loud drumming. The Green Woodpecker is larger, of a yellowy-green colour with a red head. It did not formerly exist round here, but a northward expansion of the species range has occurred in the last twenty years or so. It has a loud laughing cry.

As May becomes established the last of our summer visitors arrive, at the time when the early resident breeders already have flying young. About the first or second week of May, the Swifts arrive, very suddenly. They are a very well regulated species whose annual rhythm is almost totally unaffected by climatic conditions. You could almost set you calendar by the time of their arrival. At first they congregate in hundreds over areas rich in insect food, such as rivers and ponds. For some days they will dash ceaselessly to and fro hunting small flies and recharging themselves after their long flight.

They will then move onto their traditional nesting places under the eaves of old houses, barns and churches. On still summer evenings they will chase each other, shrilly shrieking in the way which has earned them the name 'devil birds.' Apart from the time they are at the nest, hidden in some dark place, they are continually on the wing, even roosting aloft many thousands of feet up.

Another late arrival, perhaps the latest, is the Spotted Flycatcher, which occurs in small numbers around Bennachie. It is a garden or woodland bird which lives up to its name. Its technique is quite different from the Swift, as it makes short fluttering sorties from a perch to snap flies or even small moths.

As the leaves start to grow in the hedgerows, so birds such as the Whitethroat, Greenfinch and Chaffinch start to build. On whin or broom you'll find the Yellowhammer and in the wetter places among rush and willow the Reed Bunting and Sedge Warbler.

How can one keep pace with everything that happens in the three months of early summer? By the time the conscientious gardener has tilled the soil and nursed the first seedlings till they are ready to plant out, half of the breeding season is over. Throughout May the wader ducks will be hatching. Lapwings who nest in grassy fields will be frantically protecting their youngsters from the clumsy hooves of cattle. Oystercatchers who prefer drier places, often ploughed fields, may have an easier time of it for the most part, but run the risk of total loss, when the fields are rolled or sprayed. Both species may also lay in hay fields and are at risk during silage cutting. Many a sympathetic farmer has moved eggs or rescued young if he has seen them before his machine has caught up with them, but they cannot save them all.

Around the marshy edges of the woods and moors the Curlews will be showing the same anxious concern over their precocious young. And quite right too. For crows and gulls and birds of prey are breeding too, and require tasty tit-bits for their broods. Few gulls breed on Bennachie, but many on the nearby Correen Hills and they cover a wide area in search of food. In some old Crow's nest or on a quarry ledge, the Kestrel will be bringing up its brood of four to six young; and the Sparrowhawk will have its nest next to the trunk of larch or pine. The Buzzard only occurs on the south-west side of Bennachie, and then sparingly. It usually has a brood of up to three and builds its large nest high in a mature tree, preferably deciduous, but not always. Those colourful relations of the Crow, the Jay and Magpie are also a danger to smaller birds, and will take both young and eggs. Most people will be familiar with the domed nest of the Magpie, often built in hedgerow or garden trees; but many will not have found the untidy nest of the Jay hidden deep in the forest.

The Rook is commoner in Aberdeenshire than in any other part of the country. This is probably due to three circumstances: first the good arable land in which it can find the grubs it needs; second the distribution of trees of the right size and type for building nests; and third the climate, which being not too hot in summer permits the better survival of the young. For this is their critical period. If the ground dries out and becomes too hard, the grubs will burrow deeper, and the Rooks, especially young and inexperienced ones, cannot penetrate the soil and get food. Jackdaws frequently share the nesting colonies with Rooks, but equally, they may nest in unused chimneys or old ruins.

There are two relations of the Wood Pigeon that I have not yet mentioned. One is the Stock Dove, a quiet, grey bird of woodland edges. It nests in holes in trees and occurs sparsely all round the district. The other is the Collared Dove, a recent coloniser from eastern Europe, now to be found almost throughout Scotland wherever there is cultivation. It is a very successful species, but not always popular with farmer or gardener. Always hanging around the barns or feeding amongst the vegetables, it advertises its presence with a most penetrating and monotonous 'cu-coo-coo.' Last year our resident pair of Collared Doves produced three broods of two young from a pair of nests in spruce trees, that they used alternately.

Many other resident birds produce three broods. For them the building season is a very strenuous period lasting from March to August, or April to September. Blackbirds and Song Thrushes may produce up to twelve young. The reason that the Blackbird population does not increase out of hand is that mortality is very high, especially in the first month or two after fledging.

Among the summer migrants perhaps only the Swallow is capable of producing three broods. They make full use of the available season and it is always touch and go with the last brood as to whether it can survive the early autumn storms and cold spells in September that may make its food supply unavailable for several days on end.

In years past, the Cuckoo was common almost everywhere and its far-carrying call heralded the start of summer. To Bennachie only a few come now. They are most vocal in May and rarely heard in June. Their most common foster species is the Meadow Pipit, which in summer returns to join the Red Grouse in the heather on the high moors.

Almost before one realises it, summer for the birds begins to end. By late June the wader chicks are beginning to fly and by July flocks will be forming and moving gradually to the coast, where they will gather into congregations of thousands in preparation for the autumn migrations. In August many of the young of our summer visitors – the Willow Warblers, Martins and Swallows for instance – will be travelling south to warmer countries, whilst their parents are still toiling with their last brood.

The countryside is quiet now. No song is broadcast to claim a territory. Birds are either busy with their growing youngsters, or undergoing moult in preparation for winter. No bird wishes to draw attention to itself when moulting. It is weak from the exertions of the season, and because of the energy requirements of feather growth. Also it cannot fly well. During or following the moult comes a period of 'body building.' Those migrants with far to travel need to build up a fuel supply of fat, often as much as half their normal weight again, in order to sustain them on their journey.

During the migration time we may see or hear birds passing through our area which do not normally live here. I have heard Whimbrel over my house in an August evening, en route from Iceland to Spain or Africa. On top of Bennachie I have seen Peregrine, visiting for a brief space the land over which an ancestral pair used to hunt perhaps, when they nested on Mither Tap many years ago. Along the rivers one might see Osprey fishing, a grand sight this, and one that we can witness almost anywhere in Scotland, with luck, during the autumn migration, now that so many pairs have become established.

September comes, the end of summer, departure of the last of the avian visitors, harvest-time. Will the barley be in before the geese arrive from Iceland? Perhaps this question does not mean so much to farmers of the Garioch as to those of Buchan, where many thousands of grey geese, Pink-footed and Greylag, settle for a while before dispersing south and west to spend the winter. However, we see them overhead, their long skeins weaving and interweaving like smoke in the wind.

In October come the finches and thrushes. A clear night and a light breeze in Norway will see the departure of hundreds of thousands of Redwings, Fieldfares and Blackbirds. With them will be Chaffinches, Bramblings and many other species, even to fluttering Robins and diminutive Goldcrests. If the good weather holds most may reach our shores. If not many will perish over the sea, as witnessed some autumns from the oil platforms. On favourable migrations many of the stronger birds will overfly the coastal region and alight in the centre of Scotland. In such a year we may only see a few Redwings and Fieldfares. At other times they hit the coast in ravenous condition. At this time the Rowan crop is mature. The great flocks make short work of the berries and in just two or three days have stripped those on Bennachie and have passed inland in search of more. Fieldfares are very likely to come to the garden at this time, for they love to feed on fallen apples.

Other migrants from northern Europe that we may see are birds of prey such as Hen Harrier and short-eared Owl, though the Short-eared Owl may also breed on the south side of Bennachie.

Whether these autumn migrants stay with us for long or not depends on the availability of food. They do not stick to a chosen area like the breeding birds must. Winter is the time for survival, and if the food is used up or unobtainable due to weather conditions, then the birds must go. With every cold wave from the north, the birds tend to go further south and west, to southern Ireland or even to France; but adverse conditions further south may initiate a reverse migration.

When the snows come then one may be lucky to see the Snow Buntings. Striking white patches on their wings and a liquid call, a flock of them in the sun can look like snowflakes and their massed calling sound like the tinkling of snowbells. Further west they are often found feeding on the edge of snowfields, or on snow patches high in the hills. Although food is not plentiful here, it is obvious; and the close observer can see them picking up seeds or insects blown by the wind on to the top of the snow. In hard weather I have seen them locally with the other finches and buntings around the cornyards.

So now the year has come full circle. The Tawny Owl with whom we started our narrative, for a month or two, has filled the nights with its hooting as it establishes its territory. The heathery summit range of Bennachie is left to the Red Grouse. The woods are quiet except for the cry of Jay or fright of Wood Pigeon, and the roving bands of tits. More and more, birds come to congregate around the artifices of man, gleaning from his harvest, or crowding his bird table, seeking the means of survival over the lean months.

A SEUCHIN' WIN' AFF BENNACHIE

By James D. Glennie

A seuchin' win' aff Bennachie
Gid quaetly ower th' Ury,
An' A sweir it fusper't in ma lug
This wird for Inverurie.

'Think ye weel o' th' Muckle Bass
That stan's aside th' Ury,
For sene ye'll a' be trystin' there
Wi th' lave o' Inverurie.
A've seen them a' pit by their trock
An' chainge their silk for linnen,
Then lanely lanely wan'er doon
Far waters deep are rinnen.
Ye've mairket oot wi' muckle steens
Th' rank that pairts th' livin',
Bit ken ye nae yir een an' a'
Fin wi' life's sair dirl ye've striven?
If big ye growe, ae lesson mair
Gang doon bye Bass an' Ury,
An' a little filey ponder there
Wi' th' lave o' Inverurie.'

Th' seuchin' win' aff Bennachie
Gid quaetly ower th' Ury
Syne furl't roon th' Muckle Bass
An' up throwe Inverurie.

MEMOIR WRITTEN BY ALEXANDER BISSET, ARTANNIES, INVERURIE, 1855

I, Alexander Bisset, in Artannies, this 10th day of May 1855, being in good health for a man of fourscore and seven years completed, one day took a thinking about what I had witnessed during a longer life than many of those who were my school-mates but are now gone to their long home. The changes in life coming thick into my memory, I formed the resolution of committing some of them to writing, with beginning among my own Ancestors.

In process of time, my grandfather removed to Mill of Inveramsay, and at the flitting, carts, it seems, were not then in use, for my father was carried in a creel upon a horse's back, being balanced with a calfie.

I come to speak of things relating to home, of what I have been told, and what I have seen – and first of what I was told. There lived at Artannies a man in my younger days. His name was Alexander Murray (he was the Miller), and from him I had part of the following relation. His father once lived at Upper Boat (then only a boat croft), and, so scarce were tenants to be had, that as an inducement to farm the half of Artannies, along with a Baillie Keith, his father received Marts (as he called them) out of my Lord's Byres, to yoke his plough with. He lived at what is called Old-Hall. In process of time Baillie Keith flitted to Boynds, and, if I mistake not, the Miller's father flitted to Ratch-hill. They were succeeded by Mr Alexander Innes, from Mill of Auchleven – who, it appeared, had obtained a nineteen years' lease. He had two sons, but none of them inclining to farming, he removed to his property now called New Inn, and gave up two of the years of his lease to my father to begin with.

My father is now under the hands of a housekeeper (as I have already said). My mother, daughter of George Jackson, Farmer in Mill of Carden, was living with her mother, life renter in Inverury, was now set upon both by father and friends. Suffice to say they, after a while, were married in August, 1768. I, the eldest son was born the following year, the 10th of May, named Alexander.

There were three other sons, William, James and John. William died in the prime of life, of fever he contracted when at his studies in Aberdeen. James was married at Artannies to Janet Lawson, daughter of Archibald Lawson, Farmer, Milton of Kemnay. They had sons and daughters. John became a minister of the Church of Scotland, at Moneyfith, and married Isabella Dick, a farmer's daughter in the parish. They had sons and daughters. But to resume the narration.

My father lived scarcely eleven years with his family. The cause of his death was a white swelling in one of his knees. After his death, the two uncles took charge of the widow and children for the space of about four and a half years. I was begun to the charge under the eye of my mother. Her old servants were not my friends. My father on his deathbed had given the old Millart an advice to look after things, and he, being of the old school (but with no bad intention), stirred up my mother to oppose me, until at last her eyes were opened, so that what at first was the watch-word with my mother's superiors 'NO change of plans,' I, in part, was allowed to get my own way. I was grieved to see the oxen get so much half-threshed straw – I was for raising turnips to improve the land, and give to the cattle. About this time, we had not above half an acre of turnips. The best help I got, was to change my mother's old servants, and engage some of those who had been where turnips were raised. I got one from Cluny – a good hand – to be our ploughman (a learned hand). He began us to raise turnips on lime, as I said, but in part, that I was allowed to take my own way with the dung.

Our laighland formerly was in three divisions. It was dunged always the third year (for Bere). Being of a light soil and never cleaned with green crop, the Bere that grew upon it was half wild oats – and this is the reason that, whilst other farms in the Earl of Kintore's interest paid farm bere, the farm of Artannies paid malt. I have paid some of it under the old lease, but in general was paid with money.

Let me resume the narration of things at home, by saying that 1782 brought a bad crop – commonly was called the snowy harvest. The crop, in many places, never came to maturity, and in the end to be frosted. Artannies is an early soil, and that year we only took in the last part of the crop upon Martinmas Day. In many late places in the country, the crop was entirely lost. As rents then were paid in meal and grain, more than with money, farmers paying largely grain were ruined. We had forty bolls of farm meal for the mill to pay, and only gathered fifteen for crop, 1782. Money and work was then scarce, and many would have died of want. But Man's extremity is of God's time the opportunity. The American War ceased, the Prayers of God's people are heard, the threatened famine is averted by the King's stores finding their way home to us, and many a Boll of Bere and white pease is ground at our Mills to save a starving people: suffice it to say, the winter passed through until seedtime, and then the consternation begins about what was feared – frosted seed. A mystery was now discovered to many a man's cost. The best looking and bonniest corn was the frosted, and did not spring in the ground, while the green coloured, that appeared never to ripen came to be the best crop. The crop of 1783 was early, but then good seed the next year of 1784 made all the meal kists to run over.

Tenants that fell behind with their rents had sad haggling with their landlords – some finishing them altogether, whilst others allowed them time to recover, as did the Earl of Kintore. That Nobleman coming to the North at this time to live at Keith-Hall was a great blessing to his tenantry by his indulgence. Baillie Bruce the factor that lived at Brigellows being dead, His Lordship made choice of Dr William Thom of Craibstone as his factor, whose lot it was to have to begin with these ill years, and leave them in the hands of his nephew, Dr Alexander Dauncy – unfinished.

His Lordship letting his eye upon me, at this time, I was liming and making some appearance. Having got a settlement of arrears of farm meal, and his Lordship wishing to settle business with all his tenants, and having called a valuator from the Border in order to give them all leases, I was put upon to go with him – which I did. His name was Mr Low. Travelling with him about 14 or 15 days over the farms, I had a hand in doing good to many, which I do not repent of. Mr Low, seeing what I was doing in putting the Braes above the road into cultivation, was for Lord Kintore to give me assistance, but his death put a stop to it, and in place of help, I had a rent put upon the Braes in the new Lease.

Again I cannot help repetition. I am now to speak of her that left me. I was married at Aberdeen the 23rd Sept. 1799. I remember to come home by the old road – the turnpike was about to be opened. My brother James was married a month before me. Our mother, James and me some years back had signed a 22 years' lease, James then being averse to farming. Only the Meal Mill and two cows' meat, with the then accommodation of having a wright's shop to make machinery, and keep apprentices, was his reason for signing the lease, but long before the end of the lease, he saw reason to change his mind, and turn to the farming, when he took New Mill of Crimond, three years before the Lease of Ardtannies was out. James at last leaving me, I had his Inventory of the Meal Mill and Farm Steading to settle.

Alexander Jackson and James having a new settlement three years before the Lease was run, out-cropped the land they were leaving – Alexander Jackson taking twelve white crops, one after another, of some of the land. It was ascertained that he did not carry away more than two seeds with his flitting crop. The old Mill House was about done, I had to rebuild one – being told by the proprietor I would get no help. My brother took away his kiln with him, I got a new kiln, and succeeded wonderously for a time, and was well employed until the kilns and Mills at Port Elphinstone appeared – I now find I am in the background.

I am again under the necessity of repeating. As I said before, my brother James was averse to farming, and joining his mother against me (not without cause) a rough concern of a farm to take out of the natural stake – but as I said already, I had the countenance of Lord Kintore, and as an inducement, the farm meal of 68 Bolls and 2 Pecks, converted into money with the exception of 20 not converted – at the value of 18/- per Boll. The 12 Bolls of Malt to be the price of farm bere – the two Mill swine he asked to be paid for – but they were never required. The three dozen of fowls – one of them capons – only one dozen to be required, of hens.

I must repeat again, before all this is accomplished. The Mill Multures originally paid by the Proprietors or Portioners in Inverury, being taken into consideration as too high, by Dr William Thom, present Provost of Inverury, and Factor to the Earl of Kintore, with his Lordship's consent, agreed to reduce the Multures, which was done by a new Act of Stipulation – and since that time, Lord Kintore's tenants are set free from paying Multures, and the other Portioners as Heritors, may be set free also, soon.

I come now to speak about Inverury, when I was put to school. There were no slated houses then in the Borough – with the exception of the Kirk, and the present Old Tolbooth, now the dwelling house of Mr Donald the Saddler – the Parish Church being flitted up in 1775 from the burial ground beside the Bass – besides getting old (a storm that came about Martinmas, if I mistake not, was the principal cause, the ice giving way by a partial thaw, and settling at the Damdyke of Thainston, turned Don about by Urybank for 8 or 10 weeks, that there was no getting to the Kirk or Yard). The Parish Church was lifted to the site where the Manse once was, and has since undergone some repairs, and last of all, been rebuilt and enlarged. The landward part of the Parish is not so well peopled as once it was – but it is better cultivated, and many an acre which was once barren is now brought under cultivation – so that the upper part of the Parish is growing grain, turnips, grass or planting, in the place of Bent, broom, whin and heather – which it did in my younger days. I cannot omit taking particular notice of the improvement in houses and to farm steadings in the Parish. Beside the steading that our forefathers occupied in their days, the walls in general built of dry stone and loose earth put in to keep out the cold and to fill up the heart of the wall. This was the state of our farm steadings in general before 1782 – commonly called the snowy harvest.

But as I have said before, the appearance of the Earl of Kintore in the north at this time, was a great blessing to his tenants in the way of improvements. In general, owing to bad years, we were dispirited, as tenants. Being in arrears, what could we do? His Lordship soon saw the state, and with Dr Thom, the Factor, entered into a remedy with the tenantry by giving them new leases, and time to pay up bye runs, and coming under new regulations of improvement, promising to assist in building new houses with stone and lime and stob-thatched, all with straw and heather.

The raising green crop in greater breadth took place, by dividing the arable land into seven portions, so as to give a 7th part for cleaning clean crop or fallowing only; feeding of cattle and growing of bere, for the breweries and the distilleries. 'Now' was the order of the day among the tenants, and as to raising young cattle, let it not surprise that where four calves were reared upon some of our farms, there are now generally ten yearly – as our forefathers required ten or twelve oxen to yoke the plough. I remember three old ones being sold to a dealer, that had carried the yoke thirteen years upon the farm, in the long team. So you'll easily perceive that the training many young oxen was not needful (until they failed on the feet, they were not to be laid aside). They were denominated good old servants. It is generally known, I understand, that John, Earl of Kintore went out at Sherrifmuir with the rebel side that lost the battle. When he returned home to Keith-Hall, what offended him most was – they had shortened his long plow, and must immediately everything as it was – which was done – until his Lordship was satisfied.

I am now to speak of the state of farms, and manner of farming which in a great measure did depend on natural causes. Some were easier dealt with than others. Some were more rugged than others, yet of a kindly soil. Others were most easily tilled, but less productive. From experience, for my part, I would prefer the rugged because, once overcome, I have always the best soil. A tenant should not take advantage by cropping what may be called good, with a view to indemnify himself, for in the end, he will be a loser. As I said, I shall now speak of the state of some of the best of our farms, and how few turnips were to be found at Keith-Hall. When Mr Walker came with his Lordship in 1782, to farm the Mains, as then farmed by Baillie Bruce, the Factor, then living at Kintore.

About this time of reformation, almost every long plough of cattle was made shorter, and in place of ten or twelve to one plough, four to six did the work. The first drilled turnips upon our farm was done with eight oxen in the plough, and our potatoes after the same way. Want of tools was a great impediment to us in getting forward; being often under the necessity of making things to answer the end, from our own imagination – having no pattern to direct us. Just to mention the threshing mill – there was not another in Lord Kintore's interest, and so much did his Lordship interest himself, that he came to Artannies, accompanied with a neighbouring gentleman, to see the work. There was no Foundry at Aberdeen at this time, none nearer than Carron. We had all the machinery to make of wood. His Lordship, seeing this, gave us to be wheels from the old wood at Keith

Hall, what was sufficient for the water wheels and axle also. At first we attempted flails, and threshed a rick of bere, and did it well, but with little speed. Afterwards we attempted something like the present plan now adopted – all the machinery being made of wood, with the exception of Journals, that were iron. We had no shaker, but a brander behind the Mill that the corn fell through about 2 ft. high. This did for some time until we were more experienced, and not a turning shaker, when all this in time wore out and needed to be renewed, metal took the place of timber, but had I my time to begin over again, and the experimental knowledge I now have, I would have the barn beside the byres, as they now stand, and thrash mill driven from the present mill-lead with a chain or rope. Had this been the way at present, one man would have done the work that requires two, having all the straw, etc. to carry up the Brae to the byres, as at the present time. I say one man wanted two or three seasons, would pay the cost of removing, and the remover to be a gainer in several respects in time to come. When we began to think of any alteration to the Mill Water, we had to consult the Baillies of Inverury – they being bound for payment of Multures and Services about the mill-water and damdyke, and keeping the mill-house in repair – particularly in thack and rapes. Before that we could not interfere with the lead, to cast any foundation for the Thrash Mill, and at the first, were not allowed water, but when the meal mill was not going. The Wauk Mill was upon the same footing. The Tacksman of the Mill – if need required – sent a call to the Baillies of Inverury, and they, through their Town's Officer, sent what was wanted of services for the meal mill. I have seen at a time in the winter, in the middle of a storm, perhaps an hundred men working in the mill lead, in casting out the snow and ice – and in the time of summer, in bigging the damdyke. I have seen in a bonny day, a far greater number of Burgh Heritors – some of them with their help-mates – as wives and daughters – for they all knew their place in the dyke – where to work. Suffice it to say, there is an original copy of the division of the work – I have an extract of it in my possession – for the mill-master's use.

I am to tell something about the origin of the Waukmill – this happened in Mr Innes's time. David Walker, a Bleacher and Waulker in the Parish of Glenbervie, seeing an advertisement for one of his calling, at Monymusk, took it into his head to come north and enquire after it – but it would not suit, it wanted a main article – a stream of water to drive his Waukmill. Being disappointed, he turned himself east, to come by the Kemnay road, and when opposite the back rush of Mill of Artannies, he formed the resolution of applying to Mr Innes – then tenant of Artannies – for liberty to erect a Waulk Mill, with consent of the Majestrates of Inverury, upon condition of being allowed the use of the Mill-water when the sucken did not require it – the Mill, with a Croft was agreed to, and David Walker, being a wright, soon had all in order. He was living after I was running about as a boy, for I remember upon his burial. Himself and wife and part of the family are interred at Inverury. Jean, their eldest daughter, lived long after the last of the rest of the family were gone, and in part carried on the business, until one night she had her house rifled and burned. (This was in a singular way found out).

There were cruives in the damdyke in John, Earl of Kintore's time, and were kept in regular repair for the use of the family. I cannot help mentioning that, during the old millart's time, there was no change allowed by the Mill-water course, that could be prevented by him or the sucken (until the Multures were reduced). The idea of a threshing mill must not be mentioned, but in the event of more mills appearing, a wider mill-lead was wanted, with a big sluice to keep out floods from the bleaching. I have seen at a time 28 or 30 long webs upon the side of the Mill-lead, and the green opposite the meal mill-wheel almost covered with yarn. I had almost forgotten to mention that the Earl of Kintore's tenants had also their appointed Ells of the Damdyke to keep in repair (living in the burgh or vicinity) also their Ells of the Mill-lead to keep clean.

Lastly upon this subject of thirlage, let me note that the want of a Fanners was a great hindrance to the work at the Mill. I have seen the Milling put a stop to for four or five days, there being no wind. At last a fanners was procured by the Tacksman of the Mill and to all appearance, like to do well, but the sucken being divided and the Heritor part of the Burgh being against her – claiming the right of receiving or of rejecting whatever might be brought into the Mill house in virtue of being bound to uphold the same. One day, a number of the disaffected, headed by a deputation of the Magistracy, took it into their heads – one of them bringing an axe to destroy the fanners should the Mill-Master object to turn her out. After a long conference, instead of turning out the fanners, but obliged by ocular demonstration to own her usefulness, the matter was referred to two Arbiters chosen, namely George Cruickshank, Farmer in Balhaggarty upon the sucken's side, and John Glennie, Farmer in Mill of Lethenty upon the Mill-Master's side. The value of the winnowing to be paid in money and not in part of the stuff, as usually. As soon as the original cost was made up, we made a present of the winnowing to the sucken.

I am now to speak of the state of roads in my younger days, and I shall begin with the road from Huntly to Aberdeen. The order in planning to keep it straight – it is up brae and down hill, so that a horse and cart fully loaded in the out going, must be overpowered upon one of these braes (how absurd) – when I look back to former days in journeying with what I accounted a loaded cart in the winter road to Aberdeen, with generally six bolls of meal – travelling in a dubby road all the way – and at the journey's end, upon Thursday night had to stand in the meal market and sell the whole out in retail – we had no grain market to go to.

As I have said already, the Infield was divided into three parts, and dunged every three years, and sown in Bere. This was turned into Malt – partly, if possible, smuggled and sold to the Whisky Brewers – perhaps turned into meal for family use, and the offals (as there was very little green crop raised) given to the beasts.

The oat crop, managed as follows – for much did depend upon it. First, the money rent, second, the farm meal, and as for cattle, they were much in the background – as a milk cow was the readiest market. Fat cattle were scarce to be found, as green crop was not much in use – ten or sometimes twelve oxen were used in the Plow — some of them carrying the yoke ten or more years until their feet began to fail them — then laid aside. Originally when young valued at from £6 to £8 and now sold to the dealers at £3 or £4. It will be easily seen that want of turnip was an unspeakable loss — oats had the greatest thing to do to the farmer, it was his only support. The farm was generally divided (as I have said already) into Infield, Outfield, Haugh. Our Intown, as it was called, being dunged once in three years carried a grain crop always — every third year being Bere or Barley, the two next, oats. Our Outfield was divided generally into ten folds, as they were called. They underwent a revolution of five grain crops, one after another. The sixth year was allowed to lye untilled, and go to natural grass, and allowed to lie five years. Then the old dykes that remained always about the fold were built up to confine the cattle and sheep during the night and mid-day, for dunging the fold that was to be cropped next year.

Haugh, for the sake of pasture to the cattle, was not kept much in crop — but when the grass needed renewing. Faughs, as they were named originally, made out of the roughest of land when carts were not in use, to drive the stones away to build dykes (after this manner) — when the land was to be put into cultivation, what was intended to be plowed was first cleared of stones by throwing them aside where they were allowed to lie; after plowing another stoning took place after the same manner, and plowing until all intended was finished. So much for Faughs.

I now come to speak of servants' fees for the half-year. Leaving the school, and giving up the learning during the harvest, as usual, (being the eldest son), I then formed the resolution of engaging with the farming, and laid hold of the plow — being then in my fifteenth year. Engaging with my father's farm — a rugged subject — my father being taken away from his family early, scarcely living with them as to have time for much improvement (as I have already said), the first thing I did after coming home from school, was to fee a man to stand the side of the threshing and the plow — his fee £1/5/- to drive, the plowman's fee £2 — to thresh the other side. A horseman about £2, a little boy to make straw to the two plowmen £1, a shepherd to gather in the sheep, and harrow 10/-. One of the boys to act as little horseman, two women £1, the other 12/-. The horseman was allowed something additional for going to Aberdeen with the meal etc., and making market, and the plowman for sowing the corn, two day's wages. A common labourer 6d, a wright 10d, a mason 1/1, a tailor 4d, a blacksmith by the half-year, a man to the moss 6d. All the above with their meat.

The Editor is grateful to Dr James Gill, Inverurie, for this Memoir.

AGRICULTURE IN ABERDEENSHIRE IN THE EIGHTEEN-SIXTIES

By James Allan

Commencing in 1862 at the age of eleven, I experienced on end eleven years of farm-servant life, and served upon eleven different farms. My fee for the first six months was thirty shillings, and my last fee as grieve to Mr Alsop, Butcher, Inverurie, was £18.10s. Wages were high in the Seventies after the Civil War in America and the Franco-Prussian War, and before the great depression in Agriculture in the Eighties. When I started work the Ordnance Survey of Scotland was being prepared by Soldier Engineers. They had a camp on Bennachie.

My father before me was a woodman and crofter, earning his living like other crofters from a double source. In the Twenties of last century he took a lease of a patch of moorland on Bennachie for nineteen years at a rent of £7. This croft of Blindburn still appears in the Valuation Roll of Chapel of Garioch in my name, but at a rent of £24. It was twenty-four acres of moorland, and my father proceeded to build for himself a dwelling house with barn, byre and stable. The walls were built of stone and clay, faced with lime mortar inside and out.

The mason, one Esson, a squatter on Bennachie, did his part of the work for twenty pounds. My father, a woodman, with the aid of a neighbouring joiner did the woodwork. The house had no upstairs; just a but and ben with a middle closet for the meal girnal, with a bole window. The two rooms had each a window 3½ feet by 2½ feet, with four 'lozens.' The fireplace was wide open with no 'sway,' and we children could stand or sit within it. The couples were of rough wood with only one squared edge. Circle saws were not yet in use. Trees were sawn by water power, by means of several frame saws working upright. The rough boards so produced were squared and trued by hand ripping saws. The sarking of the croft consisted of split young trees, called 'divot lath,' cut with a frame saw by two men, one above, and one in a pit below. On this sarking, sods were placed grass downwards, cut thin at the ends and thicker at the centre by means of a 'flauchter' spade for the purpose. The thin ends of the divots overlapped each other on the wooden lath, and the sods were cut of a size to suit the intervals in the divot lath. Divots would not lie on a flat sarking. This roof was then thatched with heather and clay from the eaves to the ridge. A runner of wood, nailed through the heather and divots to the couples along the eaves, kept the heather from being lifted by the wind; and the ridge was heavily clayed. Sometimes the thatch was of broom stobbed into the divots, or straw tied down with 'reps.' Kirk Session Records frequently mention that a common punishment inflicted on wayward young parishioners was to make them fetch heather to re-cover the kirk, manse, or school. The floor of the croft was of earth and became muddy in wet weather. We said 'ben' to the kitchen and 'but' to the room. The chimney of the kitchen-end was of wood, called a 'hingin lum,' and was four feet wide over the fireplace, tapering to eighteen inches at the top. This chimney was tied round with straw ropes over clay. The room or 'horn' end of the house had a stone chimney of the same shape, In the spate of 1829, a lonely woman had her house surrounded with water at Orton in Morayshire. She climbed up the chimney and stood on the 'rantle-tree,' or crossbar of iron which supported the crook for the kettle. A man in a boat saw her head protruding from the chimney, and rowed to rescue her. Quoth she, 'Ye're the blithest sicht I've seen!' Quoth he, 'Ye're the blackest bezom I've ever seen!' The triangle end of the gable was built of divots, and clay divots lasted well. In the fireplace, the deep 'well' fire was cleared of its ashes once in three weeks. The fuel was wood or peat from Bennachie. On a rainy Sunday, the church had a strong smell of peat from the heavy damp clothing of the hearers.

My father then commenced in his odd moments of leisure the reclamation of the waste land, which he added to year by year, until at the end of the first lease he had about half of the land reclaimed. His next lease cost him £14 per annum, the double of his first rent, for there was a land famine before the hungry Forties. He continued to reclaim during his second lease, and then his rent moved up to £18. The present lease, still held in my name, James Allan, No. 2, is for £24, and is overshot by a few years, and will be given up at Whitsunday, 1927. But the laird built a new house and steading. Of the 24 acres now arable, twenty-one were reclaimed by my father or myself, and three by the proprietor. I would have you note that it was the peasantry in these parts after the Forty-five, that brought into cultivation and enclosed with dykes most of our arable land. And the strange thing today is, that although the proprietors got all this labour of generations as a gift, yet they are unable to live on the estates handed over to them by their forefathers. Can we conclude then that this reclaimed, enclosed land, is in itself, in modern conditions, valueless and not worth holding? Certainly today it would not pay to reclaim waste land, and build farm houses and steadings thereon.

Now a word about reclaiming or trenching moorland. In the winter of 1873-1874, in my early manhood, leaving farm service, I helped at home to reclaim the last part of our croft. Agriculture was thriving then and this was the last great phase of enclosing land in Scotland. Smith, in his *New History of Aberdeenshire*, 1875, speaking of Dyce, page 316, Vol. 1, says: – 'During the past forty years the extent of arable land has been about doubled, and whole has been more or less improved by thorough drainage, which has been effected in many cases by the tenants.' We were not yet in the barren Eighties.

I had for a mate at trenching, one of the strongest men I have ever seen, physically, but not mentally. When at work, he worked with all his great might, and when resting for a little, he told some of the most ridiculous lies you ever heard. But his stories did no harm to any living soul; on the contrary, they were amusing and concerned himself and his exploits. One day, he told me, he was digging a pump well at the edge of a wood, some distance from a steading. About 25 to 30 feet down he struck rock, in which he drilled a hole and put a charge of powder with a fuse. He lit the fuse and began to climb the ladder. Half-way up, the ladder gave way, and own he fell. Effecting a hurried repair, he was scrambling up again, when again the ladder gave way. As he fell the second time, the charge went off, and blew him right to the topmost branches of a high tree, where he hung helpless all the three days of Auld Yule, before he was discovered and taken down! I am convinced that by dint of repeating his stories, he firmly believed they were true. Poor old man, he took his own life in the end, and your humble servant was one of the five who bore him to his last resting place in the churchyard of Blairdaff.

Well, Geordie Lamb and I agreed to trench moorland for my father for £8.10s per acre. This gave us a wage of about 15s per week each. First we opened a trench three feet wide and ten inches deep, and barrowed the stuff out of our way. This gave us room to work. Then we peeled the sod off the next strip of three feet, and buried it face down in the empty trench. Next, one of us, and we took turn about, with a tramp pick, alias a Lumphanan auger, slacked the stones from the earth to a depth of ten inches, while the other, with a shovel, lifted the earth on to the sods in the empty trench. The stones and roots of whins, etc., were put on the top of the new field to be gathered off before seed-time. This new field got a dressing of old guano from Peru, and oats were sown for two or three years on end. A deep ploughing brought up the rotting sod from below for a crop of potatoes or turnips. The whins and broom were difficult to eradicate, and often persisted for many years. The stones carted off were used to make the field drains and dykes. If you have seen the consumption dykes near Kingswells or Glassel, or Port Lethen, or Blackhall, you will have a faint idea of the hardness of the labour of trenching. The Peruvian guano was powdery as flour, and so was contained in sacks of fine cotton, out of which my mother made all my 'slips' or pinafores for school.

Before the railway was opened in 1854, this manure was transported to us as far as Port Elphinstone by canal, upon which I travelled once to Aberdeen in the fly boat, an infant in my mother's arms.

After the trenching, we had to put in drains. In this we followed a herring-bone pattern, making the side drains about three feet deep, and the leader drain a little more. In the bottom of each drain we put two rows of stones, two long parallels, about a foot apart, and big cross stones bridging these. Then we filled in small stones to a depth of a foot for filtration down into the drain. An iron brander at the mouth of the leader drain kept out the rabbits. In clay land these old stone drains were superior to modern clay-pipe drains. The Government gave loans in those days for drainage, and for these, interest had to be paid. The rough ground around a newly reclaimed field, upon which we dumped stones, roots etc., was called the 'baulks.'

And now for the farm worker proper in my day, and first of all ploughing. I can remember assisting at a championship ploughing match in 1872 at Balhaggarty near Inverurie, at which nineteen thousand spectators paid for admission – all farmers and farm servants keen on speeding the plough. At this national match, only those ploughmen competed who had been champions at their own district ploughing matches. Why has all this enthusiasm for work well-done almost disappeared? Men are losing their truest source of happiness – namely skilled work well done. Nineteen thousand men will now gather to watch professional footballers, but is the pleasure the same, and does the satisfaction last? The chief ploughmakers of the day were Buchan of Balquhain, Newlands of Inverurie, and Sellar of Huntly, and the common plough was the long board. The makers encouraged the champions to use their particular ploughs. I can remember ploughing for a squatter on what was called the Free Forest of Bennachie; the squatter repaid my employer with service at busy seasons. There we made the rigs narrow, high in the feering and low and shallow in the mids – an antiquated easy method of drainage on the brae-face practised by our forefathers, who shared rigs time about in the open field, and pooled their diminutive oxen to the number of eight to twelve to draw the clumsy wooden plough owned in common. The crown of the rig did well, being piled up with mould, but nothing grew in the mids, or open drain. No reaping-machine could have been used on this uneven surface. I have just seen photographs of rigs of this sort in the year of grace 1926 in Brittany, where the reaping is still done by hook on rigs of three feet, on which a scythe could not be used, and where the knife and teeth of a reaping-machine would be destroyed upon the humps and howes. In 1870, I ploughed the Pleyfold or Battlefield of Harlaw in narrow sixteen-foot rigs. Sometimes I had to plough with a pair of strong oxen instead of horses; 'owsen' we called them. The yoke or wooden pole over their necks made them hang their heads; the yoke was fixed to the horns, and round the neck, and was attached in the centre to the soam or plough rope. But many oxen wore collars and 'hames' like horses, with a common swingle-tree fitted to the plough.

All sowing of grain was done by hand and the harrows, of wood with iron teeth or tines, were made at home.

We worked ten hours a day in two 'yokins' of five hours each; from six to eleven and from one to six with no half-day on Saturday. In addition, we got up at five or earlier to feed and clean our horses before breakfast at five-thirty: and the horses required attention in the evening. In harvest we worked an eleven hours' day from six to ten, from eleven to two, and from three to seven. All our food was brought to us in the field. Harvest was a big job, for all the grain was cut by scythe. Many extra hands were engaged, mostly Highland men. At Balquhain in 1871, four of us scythed 140 acres of crop. For one day of eleven hours, our record for the four of us was twelve acres cut. Shearers often used to compete with each other, and in their haste went on beyond the grain to cut whins in the baulks! A good scythesman cut from two to two and a half acres per day of eleven hours. We four shearers had four women to gather, and four men to bind, and one man to pull the shoulder rake behind the others. At the end of a 'bout' we sharpened our scythes, while the others finished the gathering, binding and raking. For two weeks before harvest two women baked oatcakes, continuously, in order to be free to gather on the hairst rig.

Although the Rev. Patrick Bell of Carmylie, Forfarshire, was experimenting with his first reaping machine in 1826, such machines began to appear in Aberdeenshire only about 1872-73. The first type was the common tilter, which needed one man to drive and one man to tilt off a pile of grain at intervals. Then came the 'back delivery.' Then there came the 'side delivery,' which had this advantage that it could go on cutting in the field for any length of time without gatherers in attendance; and finally the binder appeared in the middle eighties. Harvests varied much with the weather. The year 1867 gave the heaviest grain crop in my experience, with the latest harvest. It rained all summer, and in November, one week before the term, we were binding oats. The crop was still green and frozen, and the bands broke clean over. As a rule with a standing crop, scythesmen followed each other, but that year each man was set to cut a rig of this bad crop, lying in all directions, and level with the ground. One hundred acres of crop made one hundred good stacks, but all of straw, with very little and very inferior grain. The following year, 1868, was the year of the short crop. There was not a shower from seedtime till harvest. Straw was very short, and ear of oats never shot properly, and was never fully disclosed. Most farmers threshed the sheaves twice, to try to extract the grain. That year I was at West Harlaw, and there we managed to bind the crop in short sheaves, and had it all in on 23rd August. I went to see the Highland Show in Aberdeen that year, at the end of July, and the farmers near Inverurie were then making their grain crops into 'coles.' The crops measured only from 15 to 18 inches. Rain fell in late August and only then did the grass seed, sown in April, germinate.

The threshing on big farms was done mostly by portable steam engines. The mill and engine were moved from farm to farm by horses. There were no traction engines. Small lots were threshed by water mills and horse mills. My father, like all small crofters, threshed with a flail from five o'clock every morning and as a boy I had to assist.

The price of dead meat in 1865 was about 68s per cwt., whereas in 1874, it rose to 105s, thanks to the world disturbances of the Civil War in America and the Franco-Prussian War. The high price of meat encouraged farmers and crofters to trench more land, and this was the last period of real land famine in Scotland. With the dismal Eighties, trenching and draining ceased, and rents fell as leases expired. Certain banks were said to be in financial difficulties then.

Regarding our food in farm service, I had no complaint to make; it was clean and wholesome. At five-thirty we had water brose and milk, and oatcakes ad libitum. At noon we had perhaps vegetable broth, or milk broth, potatoes stoved or chappit, or milk brose, whey brose, ale brose, cabbage brose, kale brose or turnip brose. Seldom or never did we have meat, until I entered service with Mr Alsop, the Butcher at Brand's Butts. For our third and last meal, we had a plate of porridge or some kind of brose, with oatcakes and skimmed milk to fill any void. For sauce we had the very best – namely a keen appetite engendered by hard work. On this diet, I weighed 14 stones 4 lbs at eighteen years of age, and I am still able for my turn at the turning lathe or sawbench at 75. I spent two half years in farm bothies, where we had to make our own food. We had time only to make brose. On Sundays we pooled our resources, and bought something extra, and the kitchen 'deem' came and helped to cook. Bothies should be made illegal; I did not like them. On some farms on Sunday morning we got each one cup of tea, small pat of butter and sometimes as a great treat, a red herring. There was no bread or flour.

My first 'chaumer' (French chambre, a bedroom) at Tullos was a hut resembling a pig-house, the floor of which was eighteen inches below the ground level. In rainy weather the water came in at the door, and ran out under the wall at the other side of the hovel. There was no fireplace. I had planks to walk on to get to bed with dry feet. Any modern pighouse is infinitely superior. And I was a boy and alone. My next home was on the west side of Monymusk, and there with another fee-ed man, I slept in a loft above the stable, in the atmosphere which the horses had first used below. The roof was of the common type, rafter divot lath, divots, and thatch of broom. The stable rats burrowed regularly in this roof. We had to acquire the habit, in the morning, of refraining from opening our eyes until we first shook our heads downwards over the bedside to clear the dust which fell overnight from the rats upon eyelids! At other farms I found the 'chaumer' reasonably good, in some cases very good.

On the subject of feeing markets and six-monthly engagements, I am convinced that, if these were done away with, then that restlessness and shifting among farm servants would disappear also. Wages should be paid monthly with a month's notice on either side. Masters and men would get to understand each other better. Feeing markets always remind me of the old days when slaves were bought and sold by their general physical appearance, as one would buy a horse in St. Sair's Fair. I myself have had my wrists examined by farmers, to see what appearance of strength there was about them. After fifty years of experience in the wood trade of employing men at a weekly wage, I can say I have had no bother at all about changes every few months. Men have been with me for fifteen and twenty years; they take as much interest in the business as I do, for we all know that we sink or swim together.

I consider that farmers in Aberdeenshire have little to learn from those of any other part of Scotland. In the Annandale district of Dumfriesshire, I found the farmers many years behind in method. They were still using the old cart with wooden axle. In 1885, the reaping-machine of the back delivery type was the rule in Aberdeenshire, whereas in Annandale one found everywhere the old tilter. Instead of the modern broadcast sowing-machine, a bedsheet round the neck was the rule. The oat, straw and boghay for feeding in Annandale did not produce quality meat. The skilled cattleman in Aberdeenshire found his counterpart in the byre-woman, who earned as much as a ploughman. Women were still on heavy outdoor work in Dumfries, driving turnips and filling dung. Life was a less serious affair for the Annandale farmer, who would pay a horseman 10s or 15s more, if he were an expert curler, and a strength to the farmer's rink. As milk production and bacon curing were more important in Dumfries than beef production, male calves were sold in Lockerbie at from 1s to 4s each to be railed off to Glasgow to make veal pies, whilst calves in Aberdeenshire were selling at that time at £4 each, to be fed. Young pigs were much dearer in Lockerbie. Aberdeenshire produced Shorthorn and Black beef, whilst Dumfries bred Ayrshires for milk. Each breed has its particular value.

I have vivid memories of the awful thunderstorm of July 1873. It commenced about midnight and continued until five in the morning, and later in some parts of Aberdeenshire. The lightning was incessant and the thunder almost one continuous roar. It began again, equally severe, about ten in the forenoon and lasted until half past three in the afternoon. Much damage was done all over Aberdeenshire to houses and to animals. After the storm the farmer at Tillywater, Monymusk, went to see if his animals were all safe. He saw them from a distance all lying on a knoll, and assumed they were all right. He went back in a few days and thought it strange that again they were all lying on the same knoll, but on closer inspection he found that all his eight animals were dead. I have never seen such a storm since. On the eve of the storm there was a great blasting of rock in Kemnay Quarry. A Welshman had worked for three years, tunnelling below a large face of rock, and cut out one chamber to hold about three tons of explosives. The country folks firmly believed that these explosions were the cause of the thunderstorm.

A winter storm in 1881 made a strange change upon agricultural land on the river Dee near the Inn of Coila-creich, above Ballater. The river was jammed with ice, and the trees along the banks were skinned by ice-floes. The river overflowed, cut a new course, and formed an island. The island part was in turnips, and has never since been cultivated, but the heather can be seen on it now, in wavelets upon the old turnip drills.

All animals in the Sixties were sold in fairs to butchers, and I can remember the founding of the first cattle Auction Mart in Aberdeen, namely John Duncan's in King Street in 1867. John Duncan was a dealer, importing large numbers of cattle from Orkney. He took an open stance in King Street, where he sold by private bargain. Soon the stance was divided up by means of 'flakes' or portable wooden fences. Then the rostrum was erected, and permanent buildings later, and that was the evolution of the modern Auction Mart. My mother always went to Lawrence Fair in Old Rayne, a three days' fair for cattle, horses and timber chiefly. There she bought wool and spun it on a big wheel. I carried it to the only surviving hand-loom weaver in the district, Birnie at the Glinton, near the Lord's Throat, and he made for us wincey, blankets, suiting as required. Burnhervie Wool Mills killed out the individual hand-loom weavers of our district and at the mill we could get wool carded. But alas! the small rural industry at Burnhervie, with its water power, has in turn disappeared, with the rise of the big industrial factories in large towns. Lawrence Fair had its beauty competition, and the bonniest lass got a bouquet. Brawls were frequent among the gallants who were keen to escort her home. For holidays, we held the Fast Days, much like Sundays.

In my childhood in the middle of last century, before our Poor Laws were the finished article they are today, and before the dole was even dreamed of, a lot of 'gangrel bodies' travelled the country, peddling their wares from farm to farm, and they had their centres where they lived for possibly a week at a time. An old woman of this type used to put up at my home. In her younger days she had followed the fife and drum with her husband, who was a soldier, and whom she lost along with her three sons in the Continental Wars. After that she took to the road, to peddling and to drinking whisky. I can see her yet making through our land to our house, with her old coal-scuttle bonnet, and a roomy black cloak covering innumerable bundles tied about her shoulders. She looked like a balloon. In her cups she used to fall down, and roll about until she found her feet again, when, like a drill instructor, she barked out the order 'As you were!' which was the name we ever knew her by, or for short, 'Ashie.' At times she took fits of weeping for her lost ones, and annoyed the whole house. My father, who knew her little ways in drink, used on such occasions to break into song, 'Wha wadna be in love with bonnie Maggie Lauder?' whereat an instant change came over 'Ashie.' Jumping to her feet, she would dance round the house, with a fold of her skirt between her finger and thumb, and then sit down and laugh in the best of good humour. 'Ashie' must have departed this life nearly seventy years ago.

For a newspaper, we took in the *Aberdeen Journal,* which was then a weekly. It cost threepence, including twopence of a tax stamp. The stamp was abolished on 9th June, 1855, and on 25th August, 1876, the *Journal* became a daily. Six families joined to buy one copy weekly, and this copy went round, one day on each croft. The man who got the first day of it paid the biggest share, and was the official subscriber. My uncle, Alexander Allan, who succeeded the famous botanist John Duncan as tenant of Longfold, got the paper last. He carefully preserved all the numbers, and brought them to the half-yearly cash settling, at the house of the official subscriber, where the copies were divided among the six subscribers. Uncle Sandy of course paid the smallest share, because he got the paper on the sixth day. I can remember as a child holding a fir candle, while my mother read to my father of the Sepoy atrocities to children during the Indian Mutiny. The tales made my hair stand on end. War Passion seems always to exaggerate and even to breed such tales concerning the enemy. The fir candle was a strip of fir log from a moss bog, which burned like a candle, being full of resin. These logs are quite common in mosses many feet below thr surface, and stand there where they once had grown as trees. Some crofters had a standard for holding the fir candle, called a 'peer man,' because it performed the duty often assigned to poor travellers seeking a haven. The fir candle gave a better light than the cruisie, for which however, I had to gather 'rashes' for wicks, always at full moon, when the 'rashes' were said to be in best condition. We commonly had two 'rashes' in each cruisie, peeled of course, and sometimes more for additional light. Then came the naphtha lamp, a dangerous contrivance, and then the paraffin lamp.

Events, which today would make no impression upon the public, were in the middle of last century, matters of great interest. For example, the performance of the 'Messiah' in Aberdeen was talked of in our districts for weeks before the event. James Macdonald, a crofter, heard his friends discuss it, and resolved to go. On his return he had a strange story to tell.

'We were a' sittin' fine an' quate,' he said, 'when a brazen-faced hizzie jumped up and shouted that she was the King o' Glory. Weel, the wirds were hardly oot o' her mou, when a bit mannie up and roart 'at he wis the

King o' Glory; an' then afore we cud say Jake Robinson a hale crood o'
folk a' yell't oot o' them that they were the King o' Glory. Nae only that,
bit stanin' i' the middle o' them wis a mannie wagerin' a stick. I didna bide
to hear ony mair, for Ah thocht they wad settle their quarrels better amon'
theirsel's, so I took ma bonnet, an' crawlt awa oot. Yon wis nae place for
me.' Such was the untutored mind of the small crofter.

And now a word about a peculiar form of land tenure that I experienced.
I mentioned that I had once been sent by a farmer to plough the small field
of a squatter on Bennachie. There had been squatters on the south slope of
Bennachie before living memory. Bennachie up to 1859 was a Free Forest or
Commonty. These commons were used as resting places by drovers, driving
the cattle south in the autumn to the great markets of Falkirk and Perth.
The first squatter is said to have settled on Bennachie in 1801, and many
settled in the Twenties. The squatters in my time were very respectable
people with nothing of the tramp or gipsy about them. Each had built his
own little homestead, and reclaimed his garden and arable land. The largest
holding or pendicle was of 12 acres. The houses were like my father's,
which I have described to you, walls of stone and clay, and divot roof
thatched with broom or heather. There was no trouble about the title deeds.
As families grew, extra rooms were added. One house had an excellent
museum in my time, namely, 'Esson's Collection,' now dispersed. That
squatter's son was a detective, and died as Sergeant of Police at Alford. Let
me think now. In the Sixties there were seven or eight families; George
Esson, third of his line, is the only one left on the hillside today, still
cultivating his croft. His grandfather settled in the Twenties, and married a
daughter of the earliest settler of 1801. The Essons were masons and
champion dykers, and their works in the estates around, and on their own
croft will live long after them. Macdonald, a retired contractor, with the
biggest patch, had two cows, two or three yearlings, but no horses. The
ploughing was done by neighbouring farmers in return for help in busy
seasons. Each squatter had pigs and a few ewes and lambs. The Littlejohns
had housing for two or three families. They were thatchers by profession.
Farthest west were the Gardens. Then there was Sandy Lindsay, the cadger,
who drove fish from Peterhead and Aberdeen, specialising in herring, fresh
and salt, and in dried dogfish. Susie Findlater, a sister of Mrs Esson, was
unmarried. She knitted stockings, doing what was called 'Factory' work,
working wool handed to her by the travelling grocer. All women knitted
'eidently' to add to the sombre income. Then the Mitchells engaged in
draining, woodcutting, thatching, dyking or farm work. A surviving
daughter, now in the household of Professor John Morrison, D.D.,
Edinburgh, never fails to visit the old settlement annually. The squatters
jointly constructed a road east and west from the main road near Tullos
Castle. Below the commonty on this road, Sandy Porter built for himself a
house, on the estate of Fetternear. His house had two wooden 'hingin'
lums, and around it Sandy trenched and dyked a considerable area. He paid
a nominal rent of five shillings, receiving on rent day half yearly, like the
other tenants, a fine dinner when he went to pay his half-crown. All these
crofts I have mentioned were in full cultivation from 1860 to 1870. No

parish recognised the squatters officially, as the neighbouring parishes dreaded doubtless considerable claims for poor relief; and then no official proprietor of Bennachie was entered in the Valuation Roll. Proclamation of marriage was a problem; Oyne proclaimed a squatter as resident in Chapel of Garioch, and Chapel of Garioch proclaimed him as resident in Oyne! In 1845 the whole hill of Bennachie was surveyed by Alexander Smith (who later wrote the *New History of Aberdeenshire*) with a view to its appropriation by the neighbouring lairds.

The case dragged on in the Court of Session until 1859, when the hill was divided among nine neighbouring lairds, with moss privileges to other estates. The squatters made no opposition at the time, and a protest from them later was of no avail. A small rent was imposed on each. All paid until the Littlejohns, Hugh and James, taking further thought, declined to continue to pay. They were both forcibly evicted in 1878 by Robertson, Sheriff's officer in Inverurie, two policemen, and workmen from the owning estate. Even in face of such odds, the Littlejohns declined to move their furniture. This was done for them, and immediately a course of masonry was torn from the front of each house, and the two houses were laid low. When the rent was imposed, the tenants had legal protection for their crops, which they did not have as settlers on a commonty, where the herds of others might break in upon their crops. With the lean agricultural Eighties, the others departed, with the exception of the Essons, who are still there. They were far from rail and school, and there was less work for them in the countryside. Dyking ceased when reclamation of land ceased, thatching ceased, knitting did not pay, and with the modern agricultural machinery there was not much casual labour on the farms. Some went to America, and did wisely. Their little fields were at once planted with trees, and these trees were cut down during the Great War. It was near the old 'colony' of the squatters that the remains of the lost child from Dorlethen were found by woodmen, engaged cutting these same trees. Now the area is a waste of broom and heather and rotting brushwood. It has not been replanted. But one can follow the old road still from near Tullos Castle westward, and find beyond Esson's, the little fields where the broom is most luxurious. Look for the old holly tree, the wild cherry, the laurel, and the honeysuckle, and in their midst you will always find the pile of stones and clay, which once were a homestead. Listen and you will hear the trickle of water from the spring of clear pure water, now overgrown. And as you look around, picture the writer at break of day, with well-groomed pair, shining harness, new 'theats,' and a 'Buchan' plough, lilting up the old road to do a 'yokin' for a poor squatter.

Finally, as I look around me, at the vast amount of reclaimed land in Aberdeenshire, I take off my hat and salute our forebears, who from the '45 rebellion onwards, turned moor and bog into these smiling fields, trenching, draining and enclosing, working early and late in all weathers, waging a hard warfare with nature, but winning for themselves and their descendants that grit and that indomitable perseverance, that characterise the natives of the North East. God grant that generations to come remain true.

Reproduced by courtesy of the Deeside Field Club.

A NEW LIFE FOR NORTH EAST TOWERS

By Marc Ellington of Towie Barclay

'I will build me a house
As thieves will need to knock at, ere they enter.'
William Forbes, after the sacking of Corse Castle.

The North East of Scotland possesses the greatest concentration of castles and fortified houses anywhere in Britain, arguably anywhere in the world, reversing the well-known quip of that arch-Englishman Dr Samuel Johnson – for, when it comes to castles, the noblest prospect is most certainly the high road that leads to Scotland, particularly its North East.

Valuable agricultural land in constant need of protection, a lack of effective strong central government, religious, political and social turmoil, and, less easily understood, a long persisting fashion favouring rather aggressive-looking buildings – all led to the castle and the tower house as the chosen dwelling of the North East laird as late as the middle of the seventeenth century. Quite often these buildings were commissioned by merchants, magnates and entrepreneurs with little aristocratic pretension. The great master-mason, Bel, was still chiselling splays on the gun-loops and shot-holes of Craigevar Castle long after such buildings as Hardwick Hall ('more glass than wall') were an accepted part of the English countryside.

Many of our finest castles and tower houses remain in excellent repair in many cases still lived in by the descendants of the original owners. Some have been greatly altered, but many are in a surprisingly genuine state of preservation. As fashion changed and the need for defensive dwellings disappeared, many fine early buildings were abandoned in favour of the more fashionable and socially more suitable mansion house. By 1677 the Earl of Strathmore was able to remark: 'Such houses are truly quite out of fashion, as feuds are, the country being generally more civilised than it was of ancient times.'

Derelict, ruined and crumbling castles became very much part of the rural landscape; nearly every parish had one. It is interesting to note that in the past hardly an example exists of a small North East castle or tower house being taken up as a dwelling for folk outside the landed class upon abandonment by the laird and his family, perhaps not surprisingly as the castle has always been recognised as the outward and visible sign of feudal power. The presumption of living in a laird's house would have for many violated a system strongly observed and adhered to:

'The rich man in his castle,
The poor man at his gate;
God made them high or lowly,
And order'd their estate.'

though, in times of acute housing shortage, the temptation must have been great. There is still a strong social stigma attached to castles and those who choose to live in them, which can show itself in subtle ways even today, though fortunately this is fast disappearing.

We are now witnessing the greatest change in the fortunes of the fortified architecture of the North East to take place since the tower house building boom of the late sixteenth and early seventeenth centuries. A reappraisal of the value of the fortified house as a modern family dwelling and a rebirth of interest in the merits of historic architecture, tempered by a healthy dose of romanticism, has brought about the reconstruction and restoration of some of our best hitherto neglected and ruined castles and tower houses.

Though the restoration of castles is nothing new – many outstanding reconstructions have taken place in the past – a few marked differences in style and approach make this current phase of restorations worth noting. In nearly every restoration of a North East castle or tower house to take place recently, there has been an extremely high degree of commitment to the original architecture and historic merits and values of the buildings which has been based on thorough research and solid historic investigation. As a direct outcome, historic and architectural compromise has been kept to the minimum, leading to a careful blending of the needs of this age with the well restored fabric of the past. Perhaps the most dramatic and least expected aspect of this current restoration activity has been the direct personal involvement by the owner/restorer in nearly every aspect of the actual reconstruction and restoration work. It is this high level of involvement and commitment by the owner which, more than anything else has assured such a high degree of success.

The Victorians, while feeling a strong affinity with the values of Scottish baronial architecture could rarely resist the opportunity to 'improve' upon history. This most often resulted in restorations which lost the very essence of what the building was all about. The vast wings and additions needed to house the family, guests, and the legions of servants required in a Victorian household usually smothered the original house, often overwhelming a basically simple, honest building with a grandiosity never originally intended. The Victorian lifestyle by its very nature was at odds with the original requirements needed to keep the small castle or tower house ticking over.

The small North East castle or tower house was originally intended as an easily defended family home with perhaps a small group of retainers all living closely together in what can only be described as a communal lifestyle. The successful running of the tower house household depended very much on the closest integration of family and retainers, a situation quite different from the later 'Upstairs, Downstairs' type of master/servant relationship reflected in Georgian and Victorian architecture and lifestyle. One only has to look at the rapport that exists between the master and servant in any of Shakespeare's plays to get a clearer idea of how this earlier social structure differed. If good architecture reflects the social conditions of the age of which it was born, the small castles or tower houses in their very form can tell us a great deal about the lives of their earlier inhabitants.

The tower houses of the North East, while possessing many individual design and detail differences, share a certain uniformity of style and form which allows generalisation: typically smallish (by castle standards), more vertical than horizontal, with crow-stepped gables, dormer windows, a vaulted ground floor, great hall on the first floor, a turnpike stair interconnecting and leading to accommodation above, pepperpot turrets, small windows usually heavily barred, perhaps an open parapet, shot-holes and gun-loops, and often an iron gate (or yett) to give protection to the one door for access. These are not the great military fortresses such as Edinburgh Castle or Stirling and are rarely even large enough to be called stately homes, but these buildings present a delicate grace and style combined with the Scot's love of economy and effectiveness (in all things save government) which confidently allows the tower house of the North East to assume its place in the forefront of outstanding European domestic architecture. These buildings nearly always possess what can be described as 'couthiness,' or a slightly homely atmosphere, tempered with an honesty of purpose and just the right touch of drama. There is nothing quite like the presence of a North East tower house standing, a stalagmite of harled stone, rising into the sky unashamedly, even a little fairy-tale-like.

Udny, Abergeldie, Balfluig, Tillycairn, Carnousie, Aswanley, Davidston, Harthill, Aboyne, Allardyce, Midmar, and my own home Towie Barclay have all recently undergone complete reconstruction and restoration from ruin, all to a very high standard, some winning major architectural awards. Each of these restorations has been carried out with a total involvement and commitment from the owner, sustained by a high degree of enthusiasm. Most of these owner/restorers have been young or youngish, often with small children, and without exception no past experience of the building trade. More than once, a visitor to a restoration site has been surprised to find the laird or even his lady, carrying sacks of plaster or mixing cement, a state of affairs in no way out of context with the historically traditional role of the North East laird who was in the past nearly always a working man. It's worth remembering that when the sons of the seventeenth century Gordon Laird of Knock were murdered by the Forbeses, they were not playing backgammon, listening to music or in flippant conversation with the ladies, but were digging peats. So it is fitting that when John and Gillian Gordon of Abergeldie and Knock were restoring their castle they became totally involved in every aspect of the restoration work, a pattern to be seen throughout all these current tower house restorations.

The information shared between the restorers and the craftsmen involved in these different restoration projects has greatly added to their individual successes. The exchange of ideas and theories with regard to tower house restoration, where so far very little serious academic work has been carried on, has been of immense value and of great benefit to those involved. Though much very useful advice and information is freely given by the various government bodies concerned directly with the preservation and restoration of the heritage, it is extemely helpful to be able to call on others who have been through it all before. Such diverse questions as 'Where can I get the best Caithness flagstones?' 'Who's good at doing complex roof leadwork?' or 'What's the best way to repair fractured vaults?' are all the sorts of topics that arise when two restorers meet. This vast accumulating pool of knowledge and resources which has grown out of this sharing of common experience easily leads one to view these present North East restorations as a group or school. Perhaps we are looking at a group of restorers not unlike the old schools of master masons and builders who originally erected these buildings.

Through this shared information one is beginning to see a pattern of improving excellence emerge with each new restoration. As skills increase the pool of knowledge becomes greater and one is able to learn from the mistakes of a previous restoration. New standards of excellence seem to be set with the final coat of harling on each newly-restored building. As one involved in one of the earlier tower house restorations, this is a hard confession to make and, as one is forced to live with the odd minor mistake inadvertently made during the restoration, it is at least comfortng to know that by sharing information the chances for error in future restorations are less likely.

As a direct outcome of these restorations, we in the North East have gained perhaps the finest group of tradesmen in the country, able to work with confidence on historic architecture. Two such men deserving special mention are Alistair Urquhart of Aboyne and Slessor Troup of Premnay, undoubtedly two of the finest stonemasons at present working in Scotland. Both have of late been solely involved with the restoration of tower houses and castles. A valuable function of these restorations has been the assured preservation of the skills, crafts and trades, no longer required in the building trade at large, which otherwise may have been lost forever. Fortunately their survival seems assured for the near future at least, as they are daily being passed on to the assistants and apprentices at work on these restoration sites. This, for me, is perhaps the most heartening outcome of the current phase of restoration work.

The restorers and owners of these buildings have come from backgrounds as varied as the buildings themselves. Ranging from the direct descendants of the original owners to oil-related businessmen, farmers, architects, an antique dealer – even a folk singer (will surprises never cease!) has chosen to restore and make his home in one of these splendid buildings.

As to the future, we can look forward to the completion of restoration work to a very high standad on Pitfichie and Leslie castles and I am certain a few more reconstructions will take place, though it must be said that ruins are becoming few and far between. Someone recently remarked to me in a moment of cynicism: 'The trouble with all these restorations is that there won't be any beautiful old ruins left.' Though I can scarcely think of anything more enjoyable than an afternoon spent clambering over a crumbling mass of ivy-covered stone and lime, there is for me no greater thrill than seeing a family living in a beautifully restored tower house which had shortly before been a hopeless ruin with no apparent future other than a steady return to the earth from whence it came.

These buildings were erected for habitation by people living in a world which at first glance seems very different from our own – or was it? I feel a great many similarities exist between the present and that age when most of these buildings were erected. Intense religious questioning, an obsessive quest towards the unknown and extreme social and political uncertainty, were all the common experience of the majority of the country in the late sixteenth and early seventeenth centuries. Most of Scotland was then, as now, very much in the economic doldrums, with one marked exception – Aberdeen and the area around. While a principal branch of the Douglases, one of the most powerful families in Scotland was living in a cramped and what must have been a highly uncomfortable (even by sixteenth century standards) tower on a small island in Loch Leven, magnificent buildings were being erected all over the North East. Even a minor branch of the Ogilvie family was capable of building a house as beautiful, innovative and complex as Carnousie castle near Turriff, while in the rest of the country there was a marked decline in such building activities, despite the newly-acquired church lands which had recently come into secular hands.

Then, as now, the North Sea provided the principal economic cushioning given to the North East, formerly as the great trading route to the Baltic and the Low Countries, presently as the source of Britain's vast petroleum wealth, with Aberdeen as its capital. It cannot be denied that the oil industry has brought a wealth and confidence to our area from which a wide section of the community has greatly benefited, but so also has our vast wealth of heritage been greatly increased by these present restorations which have given rebirth to one of our most valuable continuing assets, the North East tower house, an asset which will still be with us long after the last drop of North Sea oil has been extracted.

My wife and I have been privileged to restore and make our home one of these very special buildings and can both feel a strong sympathy with the satisfaction of the sixteenth century builder who wrote:

'This undertaken and begoun at Whitsonday in an. 1590 but would never have been perfyted giff the bountiful hand of my God had nocht maid me to tak the work in hand myselff, and furnished strangelie to my consideration all things neidfull, sa that never week passed but all sort of workmen was well peyit, never a dayes intermission fra the beginning to the compleitting of it, and never a soar finger during the haill labour. In Junie begoun and in the monethe of March eftir I was resident therein . . . thair for justlie I may call it a speckyakle of God's liberalite.'

Marc Ellington of Towie Barclay is on the National Executive of the Historic Houses Association and also sits as a member of the Historic Buildings Council for Scotland, without whose grant aid many of the restorations discussed in the preceding article could not have taken place.

PITFICHIE CASTLE

By Colin Wood

Referring to castles of the modified 'L' Plan in his book *The Earldom of Mar*, Dr Douglas Simpson writes: 'Perhaps the most interesting example of this earliest form of firearm defended house in our Province is Pitfichie Castle.' During the reign of Mary, Queen of Scots, around 1564, when it was thought the Castle was built (for the Hurry family), a laird's insurance policy was very much his castle-home. Pitfichie, situated on rising ground, with walls five feet thick in places and shot holes at various points round the building, was a truly fortified house, ensuring a high degree of security to its inmates against any ill-intentioned intruders.

Habited at different times by Hurrys, Cheynes and Forbeses until into the 18th century, the castle is recorded as a ruin on a map of c.1770. In 1936 the north wall and the south gable fell, leaving only a weakened shell with no floors, no roof and only a truncated staircase leading nowhere. The ruin had become the haunt of the owl and the raven. (Pitfichie, I am told, means the Place of the Raven). With this major structural collapse, Dr Simpson stated emphatically that Pitfichie was beyond all hope of restoration. However his words 'Irremediable ruin' came to me as a challenge. I have always been saddened by the sight of what was once a proud castle, a fortified house or a stately home, fallen into ruins, and for some time it had been my ambition to restore such a place. I wanted above all to have the satisfaction of seeing restored some crumbling part of Scotland's architectural heritage. So here was my opportunity, Dr Simpson notwithstanding. So, hopefully, I acquired what remained of Pitfichie.

Embarking on such an enterprise, the first requisite is to find a first-class mason, and such a one was ready to hand in the person of Slessor Troup of Auchleven. He it was who had so splendidly restored Harthill Castle. Despite a prolonged search for original plans, only a Victorian architect's drawings and measurements of the first two levels of the five-storey building could be found. So my own architect, Mr W. Cowie, had to be guided largely by what remained of the castle and by existing plans of other similar fortified houses.

I resolved from the start that authenticity should be the keynote of the restoration. This, amongst other things, entailed searching for local granite of the right shade and texture. Over a thousand of the 'right' granite stones were carved and dressed on site. Old, durable pitch pine was selected for the beams, the floors and the window frames. Hundreds of beams had to be gradually acquired from old warehouses, and countless nails removed before the wood could be re-used. Old, well-seasoned Scottish oak (which had to be searched out) was chosen for the doors and some wall linings, and all were adzed as the originals would have been. Door fittings, hinges, special nails, handles and latches, were made by the skilled local blacksmith, Bill Cobban, all in the pattern of the period. The roof of the castle was carefully slated by John Rhind and Sons of Inverurie, under the supervision of Andrew Rhind, using Ballachulish slates, acquired for the most part from a jute mill in Dundee. The Great Hall and basement floors and the near approaches to the castle were laid with flag-stones, painstakingly cut over a period of two

years in a small Caithness quarry. Water was divined in the woods high above
the castle and piped into the building. The 'Toy Cottage' nearby has been virtually
rebuilt by Slessor Troup and will house the heating system. The original courtyard
has been reclaimed, as has the former garden ground, partly framed by old sycamore
and ash.

At the time of writing, the castle itself is structurally complete but much remains
to be done, such as the laying out of the grounds, the planting of trees and shrubs,
and the making of a new entrance. This will all take time, but with the co-operation
of mother nature and the weather clerk, the castle will eventually take on a lived-in
aspect.

I cannot be too generous in my praise of Slessor Troup and his loyal team, Lea
Henderson, Robbie Keith, George Cook and Mike Bates. The building, whether
viewed as a whole or examined stone by stone, reveals pride in craftsmanship. Without the dedication of those named and the help of others, the restoration could
not have been completed. I may add that the Historic Buildings Council, who
gave a generous grant towards the project, have highly praised the standard of
all the work carried out.

If ever the ghosts of the former inhabitants should visit their old haunts, I would
like to think they would be happily surprised and gratified to see Pitfichie so restored,
standing strong and dignified against the fitting background of Bennachie.

LADY JEAN FORBES OF PITFICHIE CASTLE

Near the close of the 17th century, William Forbes, the young laird of
Monymusk, brought his young bride, Lady Jean, the eldest daughter of the
first Earl of Kintore, to Pitfichie Castle.

> 'Hoo dee ye like Pitfichie,
>   Hoo like ye there to dwall;
> Hoo dee ye like Pitfichie,
>   Gentle Jean o' Keith-hall?'

> 'Oh, weel I like Pitfichie,
>   An' I like there to dwall;
> Oh, weel I like Pitfichie,
>   But nae half sae weel's Keith-hall.'

> 'Oh, ye'll get wine an' wa'nuts,
>   An' servants aye at yer call,
> And young Monymusk to dawt ye;
>   Ye had na that at Keith-hall.'

> 'Oh, I had wine an' wa'nuts,
>   An' servants aye at my call,
> An' the bonny Laird o' Fyvie
>   To see me at Keith-hall.'

Pitfichie Castle – 1983

Photo – Colin Wood

Pitfichie Castle circa 1900

Photo – Sarah Cormack

HARTHILL CASTLE

By Mrs M. Erica Smith of Pittodrie

The Castle of Harthill, situated in the Garioch close to the small hamlet of Kirkton of Oyne, is now a magnificently restored building, having been a ruin for three hundred years. The earliest date recorded is 1638 but one is doubtful, as if true, it would make it one of the latest fortified houses, and it was always believed to be a good deal older than Leslie Castle.

Of course there must have been a much earlier castle on the site as it was the residence of the Abercrombie family of Birkenbog granted to them by Robert the Bruce in 1315. One of the family fell at Flodden in 1535, leaving a son who had a son and grandson, both Alexander, successive owners of Harthill. It is not clear when or why the Abercrombies left the Castle but it passed to the Keiths and then to the Leiths of Barns and Leith Hall, possibly and very probably through the marriage of daughters, as in those warlike and unruly times the young men of any family had but a short expectation of life.

Patrick Leith was granted a charter by James V which must have been between the dates of 1513 and 1542 as he reigned only 29 years, being an infant at the time of Flodden where James IV was killed. There followed a succession of Leith lairds, a second Patrick, John, William, and then three Patricks. The whole family were ardent royalists and fought bravely for Charles I. One of the Patricks was executed in Edinburgh by the Covenanters together with a young Gordon ancestor of my own.

The last Patrick laird of Harthill seems to have been a violent and quarrelsome man and it is said that he burnt down the Castle, living for a time in a cave on Bennachie. Another story runs that his tenants burnt it in revenge for his ill deeds. It is impossible now to know the truth. There was evidence of the fire in the blackened stumps of the rafters protruding from the masonry. The ruin and the lands fell into the hands of the Erskines of Pittodrie.

It was never repaired until the year 1974, when the ruin was bought by a young American couple, Steven and Ann Remp, who with great courage and determination set to work to repair this huge building, a truly herculean task. All they had to work on were the massive walls, still standing, no roof, major parts of the staircase fallen, gatehouse almost destroyed. The ground floor had been used by a local farmer to house cattle, poultry, etc. and it was in a filthy and deplorable condition. Flocks of pigeons had made it their home with results you may imagine.

The Remps did an enormous amount of work with their own hands. I myself saw Mrs Remp sitting astride one of the great beams which were to carry the roof, with a sheer drop below her of six storeys. They obtained the services of a master mason, Slessor Troup of Premnay, who, with an assistant, brought forth a miracle of reconstruction. He is a perfectionist; every detail had to be correct and indeed is so.

Mr and Mrs Remp collected 40,000 slates from various barns and farms in the neighbourhood. They were assisted at times by some young people from round about, Eric and Brian Dalgarno, Audrey Hay and Garry Simpson, who worked at week-ends and in the school holidays. Many of the slates collected with such hard labour had to be re-cut to fit the turrets; much of this work was done by the brothers Rhind of Inverurie.

The marathon work, completed in 1977 unbelievably quickly, is an outstanding success and I hope and believe will be a thing of beauty and a joy for ever. The owners have perfect taste. The beautiful furniture, mostly oak, refectory tables, four-poster beds etc. are exactly right as are the decorations. They have won the Saltire Award 1979, Civic Trust Award 1978, the Good Workmanship Award among others, richly deserved.

Troup has left his mason's mark on many of the stones. He will always be remembered for his work on Harthill which is scheduled as Category A listed architecture building. It is a superb example of Scottish baronial architecture.

BALFLUIG CASTLE

By Joe Sutherland

In the Book of Bennachie, Mr Jim Buchan described the castles of Bennachie so eruditely and so well that anyone attempting to write on a similar subject would be wise to emulate the Lord of the Isles, advance discreetly to the rear and leave the Rector in command of the field. Then, from a safe distance, one might be bold enough to write, not on a castle of Bennachie, but on a castle from which Bennachie might be seen.

By this criterion no better subject could be found than Balfluig. No wonder James Giles chose the view of the Mither Tap from the Howe of Alford as the background of his 1840 watercolour of the castle.

On the 14th of February 1921 the Society of Antiquaries of Scotland held a meeting with Lord Lyon Balfour Paul in the chair. It was addressed by a youthful W. Douglas Simpson on the subject of five Donside castles – Pitfichie, Tillycairn, Asloun, Colquhonny and Balfluig. The speaker described the state of Balfluig at that time. 'Now uninhabited, the structure is falling into rapid decay. The roof is leaking and the walls stand in urgent need of repairs. There is a huge vertical rent in the east face of the wing, evidently caused by a settlement, which will soon bring all to the ground.' He then drew a graphic picture of Balfluig – 'the bare, unadorned, loopholed walls, the high pitched roof, the strange bulky chimneys, the three tortuous stairs, and the gloomy vaulted cellars with their shot holes and rusty iron cleeks, complete the toute ensemble of an old world fortress.

Little is known of its history although it is believed that the tower was fired and damaged by the revengeful Gordons after the Battle of Alford. However this little Aberdeenshire castle was the scene of a strange and melodramatic incident, more reminiscent of hot-blooded medieval Florence than of the homely Howe of Alford.

It involved the two proud families of Forbes of Balfluig and Skene of that Ilk, armigerous and autochthonous, and both of such ancient origin that, by comparison, the Gordons, the Irvines and the Burnetts seemed newcomers to the North East.

In the early years of the 18th century George Forbes, the Laird of Balfluig, had married Jean, daughter of the sixteenth Laird of Skene. They had two children, John, the heir, and a daughter Mary who was very beautiful but had the misfortune to be dumb. According to Skene of Rubislaw Mary Forbes was seduced by her cousin, George Skene of Skene who then seriously wounded her brother in the brawl that followed. 'Upon which occasion the aged father of the lady is said to have imprecated the judgement of Heaven upon the family, that they might be cursed in their generation and come to a speedy termination.' The next scene in the melodrama was the marriage of George Skene and Mary Forbes – but the last act was one of tragic retribution. Among the seven children of the marriage was Alexander who succeded in 1825 as the last Laird of Skene. Born deaf, dumb, simple and almost blind, he shuffled through the darkened rooms of Skene House until his death in 1827.

In 1921, when the ruinous condition of Balfluig was being described, there seemed little hope that it would ever be saved. In that year Sir Robert Lorimer was at the height of his powers and was completing the restoration of Balmanno in Perthshire. With its white harled walls, its panelled rooms, its fine plaster ceilings and its vigorous ironwork, it was a worthy successor to his previous work at Earlshall in Fife and the transformation of Dunderave from a gaunt ruined tower on the shore of Loch Fyne to one of the most delightful houses in the Western Highlands.

In the North East, however, apart from the work of Dr Kelly at Dunnottar, Birse and Castle Fraser, under the patronage of Lady Cowdray and the Hon. Clive Pearson and the later restoration of the House of Schivas by Lord Catto and Mr Fenton Wyness, little was being done. In 1921 it would have seemed incredible that, sixty years later, three of the five castles described would have been magnificently restored.

Balfluig was the first and probably one of the most successful of all the post-war restorations in the North East. Today the white tower gleams in the sunlight, its turret miraculously replaced.

Inside, its cheerful vaulted kitchen is again in use and, on the first floor, its Great Hall, with its handsome fireplace from Longford Castle in Wiltshire, has become a splendid drawing-room. From its flagpole flies the quartered banner of the Tennants, proclaiming that the Baron of Balfluig is at home.

LESLIE CASTLE

By David C. Leslie.

Leslie Castle, Leslie, Near Insch (Ordnance Survey Map No. 37; grid ref. NJ 599249) is located at the west end of the Bennachie range in the fertile valley of the Gadie Burn. The castle is situated on a moat approximately 100 metres from the burn and has existed in its present form since 1661 when William Forbes, on marrying the widow of the last Leslie of Leslie, reconstructed the dilapidated Castle of Leslie. The site itself as the original seat of all the Leslies, dates back to the 1070's when Bartoff, a Hungarian Noble in the service of Queen Margaret (Margaret Atheling) was granted land charters in various parts of Scotland but specifically in this area. Due to a misunderstanding by Malcolm Canmore of the old words 'less' and 'lyn' the name Lesslyn (now Leslie and other various spellings) evolved and the title Lord Lesslyn created. The title remained with descendants of Bartoff at Leslie until circa 1349, when it was transferred to the Rothes branch of the family leaving Leslie to become a Barony and this title has endured to the present day.

On the death of William Forbes, the Barony and Castle passed to his son John who sold the lands of Leslie shortly after to the Leiths of Leith Hall in whose hands the castle remained until acquired by the present owner in 1979. The castle was in constant occupation until circa 1800 when the main roof, slates, all timbers and stone flags were removed for use on other estate buildings. The north-east corner and kitchen vaulting collapsed during the storms of 1958, but despite this unfortunate incident, the remaining structure has withstood the ravages of time remarkably well.

The architectural designation of the Castle is 'L-plan' with a square stair-tower located in the re-entrant angle. The building is a Scheduled Ancient Monument and is probably the last of its type to be built in Scotland. Consequently, when the Renaissance Movement was spreading throughout the civilised world and fine mansion houses rather than fortified buildings were being constructed, Leslie Castle was rather an anomaly. However, an almost unwilling acknowledgment of sophistication is apparent, as the designer/builder has conceded a few touches of refinement by incorporating larger windows, cornices, diamond-plan chimney stacks and a pediment over the entrance door bearing the inscription 'Hoec. Corp. Sydera Menterm' translation (This (house) is the Body, Heaven is the Soul). The Corbells at the bartizans have an 'egg and dart' motif incised on the stone and the tower was capped with a stone balustraded parapet.

Internally the main stair is wide and divided into four short flights with quarter landings between each floor including the cap-house level and is built round an unusual hollow square stone newel with slits on each face, so placed as to be above the pitch line and on the vertical centre line of each flight. Many theories have been put forward to explain this feaure; but it is now generally accepted that the shaft may have housed oil lamps which were lowered from the top by means of a chain, and the light from the lamps illuminated each quarter flight through the slit. At a time when female apparel was becoming bulkier and 'flounced to the ground,' to light the stairs more efficiently was highly desirable for personal safety.

An arrangement of corbelling, similar to that used on the bartizans, is to be found at the head of the main stairs, and the egg and the dart relief on the stone here has been well preserved, due to its protected location. The function of this feature is to support the top of a small flight of stairs, housed in the wall thickness leading from the top of the main stair to the lower tower room. In plan this stair resembles the letter 'J.'

The re-construction of the kitchen vaulting in the north-east corner has been remarkably rewarding; the large span fire opening arch and associated vaulting intersecting the main barrel vault has, once again, produced a very pleasing form. The fireplace is lit by a slit window on the east, located above a 'bink.' These features, including the small vaulting leading to the main flue gathering, emphasises the importance of the kitchen fire in the day-to-day running of the castle, far exceeding in quality the design of the fire opening in the Great Hall.

The environs of the Castle were protected by a barmkin wall, tower and gate-house which were probably erected in association with Castle Leslie. These structures have sadly disappeared, although their foundations and under building have been exposed as work proceeds. A 'hanging stone' has also been discovered which has been set aside for incorporation in the external layout.

Reconstruction of Leslie Castle began on 21st October, 1982 under the personal direction of David C. Leslie, Baron of Leslie, Dip.Arch.Abdn., A.R.I.B.A., A.R.I.A.S., F.S.A.Scot., after overcoming many hurdles and obstacles encountered by the owner of a ruinous building of architectural and historic interest. Slesser Troup, the well known master mason and expert in the complexities of castle construction, is leading the team of artisans in the practical and physical aspects of the project.

At the time of going to press, the restoration is progressing very favourably, with one section of the building roofed and the other portion approaching second floor level. By the end of the summer the fabric will be well protected from the elements and thoughts will be turning to internal fittings which will finally transform the building into a splendid family home.

THE HILL FORT

By Flora Garry

The Romans marched by Don
Herriet the laich countrie;
But heich in their fort on the Mither Tap
The Picts fan sanctuary.

BENNACHIE AND THE SEARCH FOR A BATTLEFIELD

By J. K. St. Joseph

The granite mountain of Bennachie stands in an isolated position a little forward, that is to the NE, of the high ground forming the edge of the Highlands, 32km W of the coast near Newburgh and 42km S of a point between Banff and Whitehills on the N coast of Buchan. Not only does Bennachie command wide views, but the mountain is easily distinguished from afar because of its distinctive profile with a number of separate peaks standing out against the skyline (see p.89). There is no high ground between Bennachie and the E coast, and the summit at 1,733 ft. (528m) above Ordnance Datum is high enough for mariners at sea to recognise the mountain even when the coast and hinterland are fog-bound. 12km from Bennachie, the E to W ridge extending between the Hill of Corskie and Tillymorgan hides the mountain from the N save from some high vantage point like Knock Hill. The most distinctive, though not the highest of several peaks of Bennachie is the easternmost, Mither Tap, a granite tor, site of a small hill fort, where massive dry stone walling on the accessible sides makes a fortification of unusual strength.

Bennachie has long been recognised as one of Aberdeenshire's most notable mountains, celebrated in folk-lore and legend: a recent discovery suggests that it may have appeared on the stage of history earlier than had been thought. The evidence for this is largely circumstantial: to appreciate its significance, reference is necessary to Roman military operations north of the Forth-Clyde isthmus. That Roman forts and camps extended for a considerable distance beyond the Antonine Wall has long been known. The first detailed plans of these works were made in the mideighteenth century under the direction of General Roy, and published posthumously in 1793 in his *Roman Military Antiquities of North Britain.*

Excavations sponsored by the Society of Antiquaries of Scotland at Ardoch in 1896-97 and at Inchcuthil in 1901, added considerably to knowledge of both places, while similar work along the Gask Ridge established the existence there of a series of watch-towers. By 1939, four more forts had been recognised, at Carpow on the S shore of the Firth of Tay, where a bath-house had been partially excavated in 1793[1], at Fendoch[2] in Glenlomond, and at Bochastle[3] near Callander, both as a result of fieldwork, and at Cardean,[4] near Meigle, by observation from the air. The last three sites had been recorded in the eighteenth century, but since then had been so levelled by ploughing as to have been temporarily lost to knowledge. The tally of Roman military sites north of the Forth-Clyde isthmus now stood at nine forts, large and small, eleven watch-towers and thirteen temporary camps.

Crawford's brief aerial excursion to Scotland in 1939 provided a foretaste of what was to come. Increased opportunities for flying, and experience in observation gained during the war of 1939-45, heralded a new era. Ft. Lt. Bradley, an instructor at the E.F.T.S. at Scone airfield, in the course of his flying duties, discovered a small Roman camp at Gourdie and a small fort at Cargill, both within his training area of his base at Scone. After the war, a series of reconnaissance programmes over Scotland, planned as an aid to research in many fields, began in 1945, and have continued ever since. From 1948, these were undertaken for the Committee for Aerial Photography of the University of Cambridge, while for the last seven years the staff of the Royal Commission on the Ancient and Historical Monuments of Scotland have also been engaged in aerial photography in support of the Commission's work. Since 1939, yet four more forts, four watch-towers and no less than forty temporary camps have been added to the map.

Historical records of Roman military operations in Scotland are meagre. For Agricola's operations in the eighties of the first century, virtually the only source is the famous biography of Tacitus, and it was not the author's intention to give particulars of places or of troop movements, so necessary to reconstruct the sequence of campaigns. History provides even less information about the Antonine occupation in the mid-second century, and the Severan campaigns of 207-8, both of which extended north of the Forth-Clyde isthmus. There are tantalisingly brief references to further campaigns or punitive expeditions, but precisely where these took place or whether any of them penetrated beyond the isthmus is not known. Archaeology has very notably supplemented the historical record, but care is needed in attempting to assign camps to a given campaign, particularly as temporary camps are notably difficult to date.

Bennachie lies far to the N of any area permanently garrisoned by the Roman army, and it is with the temporary camps marking the movements of troops on campaign or on the march that we are concerned. Three main results have come from the recent great increase in the number of known camps: firstly, the recognition that Roman troop movements extended much more widely over Scotland than had previously been supposed; secondly, that at some sites camps of different size or type occupy in part the same ground, so that careful excavation at points of intersection of their defences may reveal the order of succession, and thirdly, that some of the camps fall into groups distinguished by size, or shape, or plan of gates. As this matter has been considered in detail elsewhere,[5] the discussion need not be repeated here, but three of the groups are of concern in the present context. One, comprising twelve examples, ranging in size from 3·5 acres to about 60 acres, has gates of distinctive plan, including an external *clavicula* and oblique ditch. At Dalginross, which alone was planned while the defences still existed in relief, the rampart was also turned inwards to form an internal *clavicula*. Four of the camps[6] lie each beside a fort seemingly planned or established by Agricola, so that all in this group are in all most certainly to be linked with his operations. The two northernmost, 23·7km apart, at Ythan Wells and at Auchenhove, appear to agree in size (*c.* 33 acres) and proportions and would seem to be successive members of a series, others of which clearly await discovery. If their ditches are consistently as small as those of the two known camps, they may have been so reduced by ploughing that little trace remains.

Next to be mentioned are two camps in Strathearn, at Dunning (115 acres)[7] and near Abernethy (111 acres), a reasonable day's march of 15km apart. Although the shape of each camp is irregular in detail, there is close approximation to a square. Both camps seem to have been provided with six gates, each with a traverse: this fact, and the correspondence in size and proportions link them together. A small piece of samian recovered from the bottom of the ditch-filling in a section across the S side of Abernethy, points to a Flavian date. It has been suggested that these two camps mark the advance to the Tay, mentioned by Tacitus,[8] at the end of Agricola's third campaign, *vastatis usque ad tuum (aestuario nomen est) mutionibus.*

A third group comprises seven '130-acre' camps, which extend in unbroken series from Ardoch to Kair House, overlooking The Howe of the Mearns. In shape, these camps are designed to be rectangular, but with such a large area, inevitable irregularities arise owing to uneven ground: that the departure from the average size hardly exceeds 1% is remarkable. The average ratio of the axial dimensions is 1:1.36, though one member of the series (Grassy Walls) is closer to a square (ratio of 1:1.13). There are six gates each with a traverse. At Ardoch, where a number of camps are clustered round the fort, observation has shown that there the '130-acre' camp is the latest Roman work on the site: later than a 63-acre camp (one of a series closely resembling the '130-acre' camps, but of half the area), later than a 30-acre camp, a 10-acre camp, a watch-tower, and an annexe to the permanent forts occupied in both Flavian and Antonine periods.

Up to 1975, five large camps were known in NE Scotland (Fig. 1), namely Raedykes (93 acres), Normandykes (minimum area 106½ acres), Kintore (110 acres), Ythan Wells (111 acres) and Muiryfold (109 acres). The last four do not differ greatly from the average size of 109 acres, appreciably smaller than the '130-acre' camps further S, with which they have often been considered. Raedykes is the most irregular of any mentioned so far, owing to the awkward ground that it occupies. It is smaller than the '130-acre' camps by 28%, and than the 109-acre camps by 15%. It thus conforms most closely to the second of these two series. Raedykes is the closest to the sea of all the large camps. It has been conjectured[9] that its size may be explained by a need temporarily to detach a contingent of troops for special duties in connexion with a trans-shipment point in Stonehaven Bay, 5km away. Normandykes, which is set along a ridge, is a rather elongated rectangle in shape, Kintore and Muiryfold are more regular in outline, but the first of these, to judge from the ratio of the axial dimensions (1:1.30), is nearer a square than are most members of the '130-acre' series. Ythan Wells is a parallelogram in shape.

On 26 July 1975 a large Roman camp was observed from the air at Durno, 9km NW of Inverurie. Further observations in 1976-77, together with fieldwork, established the greater part of its perimeter, and this was confirmed by digging a number of ditch-sections. The outline of the camp (Fig. 2) may be described as a rectangle having its long axis aligned NW-SE, but with the northernmost sector of each long side inclined northwards through about 30°, perhaps to take advantage of the uneven ground which ranges in height between 100 and 135m above Ordnance Datum. Five gates

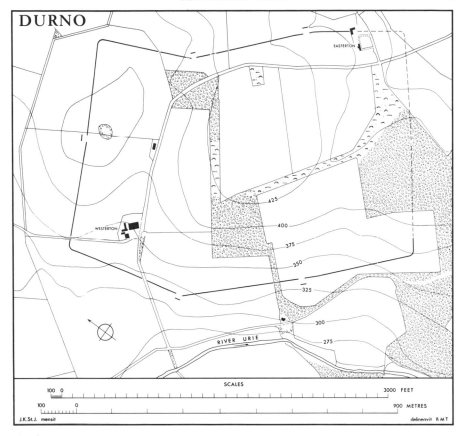

Fig. 2

were identified, each with a traverse: two lay in each of the long sides, and one at the centre of the short NW side, and there will no doubt have been a matching gate in the SE side. As drawn in Figure 2, the area is about 144 acres (58.25 ha). For most of the perimeter the ditch had been cut in brown brashy subsoil, occasionally penetrating the thinly bedded shales from which this was derived. However, igneous rock outcrops towards the NE corner, near the steading of Easterton. Where such rock was encountered, the ditch profile conformed to the irregular rock face, no doubt after any loose blocks had been prised off. South of the steading, the rock presents an unbroken face, so that the position of the SE angle and of the adjoining lengths of side could not be determined. The defences there may have consisted only of a rampart of earth and stone gathered from the surface. Durno lies in the 25.75km interval between Kintore and Ythan Wells, 14.1km from the former and 11.7km from the latter. It is the largest camp known N of the Antonine Wall, exceeding those of the '130-acre' series by some 14 acres or about 11%.

What is the signifance of this exceptionally large camp, and how did the forces quartered there reach Durno?

The uniformity of size shown by the large camps that can be grouped into series suggests a close relationship between the composition of a Roman expeditionary force and the area of its camps. Durno will thus have held a force appropriate to a camp of 144 acres. Undoubtedly many more camps await discovery in Scotland, but is it likely that in the country extending back to the Forth a whole series of 144-acre camps (hardly less than eleven in all) have escaped observation both from the air and on the ground? The possible lines of march for such a large force are quite limited in number. Moreover, if the size of the ditch at Durno is any guide, crop marks would be expected at some members of such a series. As to the other five northernmost large camps (Raedykes to Muiryfold), there is a reduction in size of about 17% compared with the camps of the '130-acre' series. That an imperial expedition – for such was the nature of Severus' campaign in Scotland – should have required camps uniformly 130-acres in size for the first 120km of its advance beyond the Forth, and for the next 80km when the army was increasingly remote from its base, and therefore most vulnerable, camps no more than 109 acres in size on average, calls for explanation. There are several possibilities: a component of the main force might be detached for independent operation, or a large baggage train be left behind. However, no small camps are known that might throw light on the matter, even assuming that such action was likely.

The suggestion has been made that the northernmost large camps should be attributed to Agricola[10]. This was prompted by the fact that there are no longer other camps known thereabouts large enough to have held his field army. In contrast to Tacitus' statement, relating to the sixth campaign, that Agricola 'divided his army into three parts and so advanced,' in the following year 'with his army in light marching order, and strengthened by the best of the British soldiers . . . . . he advanced to Mount Graupius.'[11] The attribution mentioned above raises the question of the whereabouts of Agricola's large camps further S. Lengths of ditch which seem to belong to a camp beneath the Severan works at Carpow, may provide a hint,[12] but six marching-intervals (that is five camps) would be required between Caprow and Raedykes.

If Durno held an exceptionally strong force appropriate to the size of the camp, that force was assembled, so far as known, at this one locality. Is it chance that the average areas (109 + 33 acres) of the only two types of camp that have come to light within 55km of Durno, when added together correspond so closely to that of the large camp there (144 acres)? The 33-acre camps are indubitably Agricolan, and if this equation is correct, the 109-acre camps, and Durno itself must also be Agricolan. Durno represents a concentration of exceptional military strength called for by some special situation. History tells of one such occasion, namely the battle that formed the climax of Agricola's seventh campaign.

The camp at Durno occupies uneven ground sloping in large part towards Bennachie, so that the mountain is visible from much of the camp. Proximity to the small river Urie, the only adequate water supply, may have determined the choice of site: a slight change of position to the NE would have afforded much better ground. A strong impression is gained that the view of Bennachie was an important factor in laying out the camp. The careful choice of position here, as at the other large camps, and of the very route taken by the army, implies adequate reconnaissance. If the 33-acre camps represent a force moving ahead,[13] reconnaissance may have been its principal rôle. This smaller force could well have returned to link up at Durno with the main concentration of Agricola's troops.

If Agricola's aim was to subjugate the whole country, it may be wondered how this was to be achieved. His seventh campaigning season saw his troops approaching the Moray Firth, but reconnaissance would have shown all too clearly the difficulties ahead. That his army could over-run the whole of northern Scotland within the span of his governship must have seemed increasingly unlikely. The more extended his lines of communication, the more difficult would it be to maintain his accustomed speed of operations.

In his very first campaign, Agricola had brought resistance to an end in Wales when, after a hazardous crossing of the Menai Strait, he inflicted a decisive defeat on the Ordovices in their island fastness of Anglesey. Similarly, a pitched battle with the assembled Caledonian tribesmen may have seemed an easier way of ending effective resistance in the north of Britain, than an attempt to over-run the whole country. Already in the preceding campaigning season the Caledonians had resorted to force to the extent that in one particular attack upon a legion, only immediate action seems to have prevented a dangerous situation from becoming a defeat.

How closely military operations were concerted on the Caledonian side is unknown. The progressive advance of Roman forces along the front of the Highlands would have been easy to watch, allowing time for sending out a general call summoning warriors to fight. Once the ineffectiveness of surprise attacks on individual units came to be realised, what choice remained save the concentration of a large force for a pitched battle? As Ogilvie and Richmond have pointed out, the carefully chosen position almost designed to invite attack, was not uncommon in British strategy.

In attempting to identify the site of the battle, geographical factors have to be considered, as also the nature of the country, not as it is today, but with mosses and forest much more extensive than now. Wherever the battlefield lay, must it not have been chosen by the Caledonians to offer them tactical advantages? A hill, not necessarily of great size, is to be sought; one near which the Romans may reasonably have been expected to pass. Rivers, peat mosses and mountains are amongst the natural features influencing an army's progress. The Forth and Teith, and their associated mosses together form the first natural obstacle to an army marching N from the Antonine Wall. Thereafter, neither the Tay nor the lesser rivers flowing out from the SE front of the Highlands are likely to provide clues to the site of the battlefield, for they are hardly major obstacles to the progress of an expeditionary force such as that under Agricola's command. It might be argued that Mons Graupius lay at some tactically advantageous point, not actually restricting the Roman advance, but one that it was militarily unwise

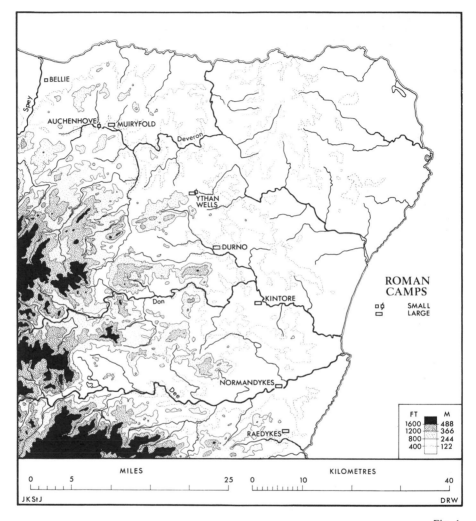

Fig. 1

to bypass, in that a hostile force was left in a position to cut lines of communication, and to oppose the army on its return. The hill mass known as the White and the Brown Caterthun, 7km NW of Brechin at the front of the Highlands, is such a point, and there are other possibilities.

Further N, there are at least two localities where geography imposes a restraint on an army's advance. The Highlands reach almost to the sea at Stonehaven, and if an army is to keep clear of the hills, it must pass within 2km of the coast. This circumstance attracted Crawford's attention, and he conjectured that Mons Graupius might have been at Raedykes. As to this, it may be observed that when the army had reached Raedykes, the constricted passage between the hills and the sea had been passed; moreover. that Raedykes, the smallest of the large camps N of Stonehaven, should be associated with the battle would seem curious. 75km to the NW, the neighbourhood of the Pass of Grange, the easiest route from Aberdeenshire to the coastal plain of Moray, has also been suggested as a possible site for the battle. However, the Pass is somewhat narrow, having regard to the deployment of the large forces involved, while by the time the army had reached the 109-acre camp at Muiryfold, the narrows between Little Balloch Hill and Sillyearn Wood had already been passed. The camp at Auchenhove, which can be accepted as Agricolan on account of its distinctive gate plan, lies to the W, at the far end of the Pass. If the Roman advance were halted at or before the Pass, access to the coastal plain extending W to Inverness, and including some of the most fertile land in Scotland, would be denied. Beyond that there was little land of value left to fight for.

North of Stonehaven the edge of the mountain mass turns northwest-wards, lying there within the basins of the three rivers, the Dee, the Don and the Deveron (Fig. 1). The straight margin of the Highlands, so marked further south, gives way to a much more dissected landscape, where granite intrusions form a number of conspicuous isolated hills, the Hill of Fare, Benaquhallie, Cairn William and Bennachie, rising in front of the main mountain mass. All the known camps N of Stonehaven lie within a corridor, where fairly easy terrain skirts the high ground to the W, the shortest route to the coast of Moray. The direction is at first northwards to a point about the confluence of the Don and the Urie, opposite the E end of Bennachie, and then northwestwards to the Pass of Grange. Bennachie overlooks Garioch, some of the best land in Aberdeenshire, and the presence in and around the mountain of at least six small forts, or defended 'settlements,' indicates a native population at a time not far removed from that of the Roman invasion. The view from the Mither Tap extends as far S as the Mounth, so that the approach of hostile forces could be observed from a distance. The situation is not unlike that at the White and Brown Caterthun already mentioned, but Bennachie is an isolated mountain with a far more distinctive profile, while 2km from its base lies the exceptionally large camp of Durno. The tactical significance of this camp is difficult to explain save in relation to Bennachie. The profile of the mountain makes it an easily recognised trysting place to which tribesmen could be summoned; the area affords an ample gathering ground for the large numbers involved, while the position, overlooking the most likely line of the Roman army's approach, poses such a threat to further advance as to invite attack.

As assault on a mountain occupied by thousands of tribesmen is a military operation with its own particular problems. Little can be gleaned from the generalised account of Tacitus. The Roman force included legionaries and auxiliary regiments, both of infantry and cavalry units. A total of 17,000 to 20,000 men has been conjectured:[16] the numbers that could be quartered in a camp of 144 acres might depend upon the size of the baggage train, and the space occupied by horses and stores. On the

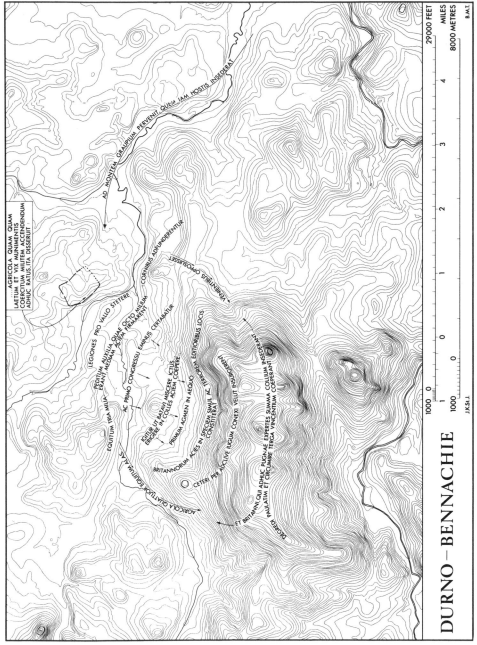

AGRICOLA QUAM QUAM
LAETUM ET VIX MUNIMENTIS
COERCITUM MILITEM ACCENDENDUM
ADHUC RATUS, ITA DISSERUIT

AD MONTEM GRAUPIUM PERVENIT QUEM IAM HOSTIS INSEDERAT

VENIENTIBUS OPPOSUISSET

CORNIBUS ADFUNDERENTUR

LEGIONES PRO VALLO STETERE

PEDITUM AUXILIA QUAE OCTO MILIUM
ERANT, MEDIAM ACIEM FIRMARENT

AC PRIMO CONGRESSU EMINUS CERTABATUR

IGITUR UT BATAVI MISCERE ICTUS,
ERIGERE IN COLLES ACIEM COEPERE

EQUITUM TRIA MILIA

PRIMUM AGMEN IN AEQUO

BRITANNORUM ACIES IN SPECIEM SIMUL AC TERROREM EDITIORIBUS LOCIS
CONSTITERAT

CETERI PER ACLIVE IUGUM CONEXI VELUT INSURGERENT

AGRICOLA QUATTUOR EQUITUM ALAS

ET BRITANNI, QUI ADHUC PUGNAE EXPERTES SUMMA COLLIUM INSEDERANT

DECORE PAULATIM ET CIRCUMIRE TERGA VINCENTIUM COEPERANT

DURNO – BENNACHIE

J.K.St.J.

29000 FEET

MILES

8000 METRES

B.M.I.

0   1   2   3   4

1000   0   1000

0   0

Fig. 3

Caledonian side, there is no means of checking Tacitus' figure of 30,000 armed men, which may be an exaggeration.

The land lying to the E of Bennachie, including the ridge upon which Chapel of Garioch stands, together with the valley to the south, would seem most suitable ground for military operations, particularly operations with cavalry. However, this would imply an attack on the narrow E end of the mountain. The deployment of troops in units of convenient strength would require adequate space, and there is room for a battle-line of more reasonable length on the ground SW of the Roman camp, in front of the N face of the mountain. This face has a concave slope, that is to say the higher ground is steep, but the spacing of the contours increases on the lower ground. Thus, concentrations of tribesmen moving down the slope might well appear to be massed 'tier upon tier' as Tacitus describes. The noisy manoeuvering of war-chariots formed the first phase of the battle, and such an operation is only possible with appropriate space. It has been suggested that an extent of 1·5 to 2km of ground at the foot of Bennachie – and by no means all of it is level – would be required for such manoeuvres.

When there are so many uncertainties any detailed discussion of the battle is wide open to criticism. Figure 3, which includes quotations from the *Agricola.* represents a possible reconstruction. The contours at intervals of 25ft. (7·6m) bring out the topography. The north slope of Bennachie, shaped into a great hollow, or 'amphitheatre,' opening towards the camp at Durno, is of not inappropriate extent for the engagement. The original account of the battle, including the preliminary speeches or exhortations, now accepted as rhetorical compositions of Tacitus, appear in chapters 29 to 37 of the *Agricola.* An analysis of the battle has recently been published[17] and need not be repeated here.

After the battle came the pursuit described by Tacitus in too general terms to be of help in identifying the terrain.[18] That the army would have remained at Durno for some days to allow time for disposal of its dead, for the clearing of the battlefield and the recovery of whatever equipment was worth salvage, is likely enough. Agricola then led his army, marching slowly, to the territory of the Boresti, a tribe nowhere else recorded. The two large camps to the NW of Durno, Ythan Wells at 11·7km distance, and Muiryfold 21·7km further on, may mark the progress of Agricola's main force at least to a point from which the sea will have been in sight.

The suggested equation of Bennachie with Mons Graupius rests largely on circumstantial evidence, which not everyone will accept.[19] There are two main heads of criticism, namely that the historical record of Agricola's campaigns is so imprecise as to be open to many interpretations, and that the evidence, necessarily incomplete, provided by the temporary camps, has been strained.[20] The battlefield may indeed have lain farther S, but the 30-acre camps at Ythan Wells and Auchenhove show that Agricola's operations extended almost to the Moray Firth. If a more distant site is in question, then temporary camps are to be sought in country where as yet there is no proof of the presence of the Roman army. The coastal plain between the Pass of Grange and Inverness, with extensive arable land, has been reconnoitered from the air for many years. The discovery of a camp gives a positive result: to prove a negative by this means is much more difficult. Certainly, Roman camps may lie unobserved, especially if their ditches are of dimensions so small that they seldom yield crop marks.

At Durno alone has a camp of exceptional size been recognised, representing a special concentration of military strength. Its position in relation to Bennachie suits the description of Agricola's famous battle. The axial dimensions are approximately on the ratio of 1:1.40;[21] while temporary camps of the late first century tend to be square in shape. Thus, Dunning and Abernethy have axial dimensions in the ratio of 1:1.05 and 1:1.09 respectively , the early camps at Raycross and Crackenthorpe on the route to Carlisle, and those at Newstead are nearly square, as are a number of camps with elaborate gates of 'Stracathro-type.' By contrast, the '63-acre' camps, assigned to the early third century have ratios that range from 1.51 to 1.64, with an average of 1:1.56.[22] The '130-acre' camps of similar date range from 1:1.13 to 1:1.48 with an average of 1:1.39. Of the six northernmòst large camps, Raedykes, with a ratio of 1:1.22, is unusually irregular in plan, because of the lie of the ground, while Normandykes, occupying a ridge-top, is long and narrow. The average of the axial dimensions of Kintore, Durno, Ythan Wells and Muiryfold is 1:1.38, implying a rectangular shape. Too much can be read into these statistics, for there are camps, indubitably early in date, that are markedly rectangular. Silloans, in Northumberland, which must surely be Agricolan, for it is earlier than Dere Street, has a ratio of 1:1.45, while for the nearby camp at Belshiel.[3] with internal claviculae – and thus presumably early – the corresponding figure is 1:1.53. Some of the 'Stracathro-type' camps, a group associated with Agricola's operations, show considerable departure from a square. The ratio for Castledykes, laid out on comparatively level ground is 1:1.22, while for Bochastle and Malling, two camps where the available space is constricted, the corresponding figures are 1:1.50 and 1:1.66. The camp at Stracathro occupying level ground, has a ratio of 1:1.18, while for the early camp at Ythan Wells, the ratio is 1:1.30.

Camps of large size, and those laid out on ground where the available space is constricted, may have their shape influenced by external factors, and with so small a sample only tentative conclusions can be drawn. The rectangular shape of Durno may have been a deliberate choice to ensure that the mountain was in full view of the camp: there could be no question of concealing preparations on the Roman side from watchers on the mountain, for the higher slopes command the whole area of the battlefield.

Whether or not the six northernmost camps may be regarded as the work of Agricola's army, the question arises as to how the troops encamped at Durno reached that locality; was it as a single force, or in separate contingents? The implication that many camps await discovery may well be true, but the country extending back to the Forth-Clyde isthmus, including the whole of Strathmore, has been extensively reconnoitered for the last thirty-five years. Camps are known, for example Belshiel in Northumberland, where for much of the perimeter the defences consisted of a rampart with no ditch. If such a site were levelled by ploughing, no trace would be

Fig. 4 (correct way)   Aerial photograph – J. K. St. Joseph

seen even from the air, but this explanation seems unlikely as at Durno a ditch was present save at the one corner where an outcrop of igneous rock made this impracticable.

The arguments supporting the identification of Bennachie with Mons Graupius rest rather upon other factors, such as the influence of geography on a major military operation like the progress of an expeditionary force far into NE Scotland. There is a limited number of places of considerable strength, where Caledonian tribemen could assemble so as to command or overlook the likely line of Roman advance, and invite attack. The evidence needed for positive identification must include a large Roman camp unquestionably associated with Agricola in a position not far from a suitable gathering-ground for the Caledonians, together with indications that a battle had actually taken place. As has been written elsewhere: 'Readers will form their own judgment on the identification of this elusive hill. A camp of unique size in significant juxtaposition to a highly distinctive mountain that it partly outflanks; ample space for the massing of large native forces; ground suited to the tactics of the battle; such details of the terrain as the concave hill-slopes and the mountain mass with its distinct peaks; interruption of the normal spacing of the large camps by the position of Durno; . . . . . these considerations taken individually, might be judged of little account, but the chances are overwhelmingly against there being in some other locality the significant association which is so evident at Durno-Bennachie.'[24]

FOOTNOTES

1. W. Camden, *Britannia,* ed. Gough (1806) iv, 47-49.
2. I. A. Richmond, *F.S.A.Scot.* lxiii (1939), 110-154.
3. O. G. S. Crawford, *Topography of Roman Scotland* (1949), 28-29; for subsequent excavations see W. A. Anderson, *Trans. Glasgow Arch. Soc.* xiv (1956), 35-63.
4. O. G. S. Crawford, *Antiquity* xiii (1939), 287-288, 291-292.
5. J. K. St. Joseph, *J.R.S.* lxiii (1973), 228-232.
6. Malling, Bochastle, Dalginross and Stracathro.
7. The areas of the large camps are given in imperial measure to facilitate comparison with previous papers on this subject.
8. *Agricola,* ch. 22.
9. J. K. St. Joseph, *Britannia* xi (1978), 278-279.
10. *J.R.S.* ixiii (1973), 231; *Britannia* ix (1978), 278-279.
11. *Agricola,* chs. 25,29.
12. *J.R.S.* lxiii (1973), 220-222.
13. The 33-acre camp at Ythan Wells occupies in part the same ground as the 109-acre camp there. Excavation at one of the points of intersection of the defences has shown that the 33-acre camp is the earlier of the two.
14. *De vita Agricolae,* ed. R. M. Ogilvie and I. A. Richmond (1967), 65.
15. *Topography of Roman Scotland* (1949), 131-132.
16. *Britannia* ix (1978), 283.
17. *Ibid.,* 283-286.
18. *Agricola,* chs. 37-38.
19. L. Keppie, *Scottish Archaeological Forum* xii (1980), 79-88.

20. See for example, G. Maxwell, *Ibid.,* 25-54.

21. Roman camps usually range in shape between a square and an oblong. The ratio of the axial dimensions is a convenient means of expressing the proportions which vary from 1:1 for a square, to as much as 1:2.1 for an exceptionally elongated camp like Kirkbuddo. The essential need was to secure an appropriate extent of reasonably level ground, having regard to the needs of defence. With large camps, uneven terrain often necessitated some departure from a regular shape.

22. Kirkbuddo (ratio of 1:2.14) has been omitted in calculating these figures because of its abnormal shape, probably dictated by the need to avoid boggy ground.

23. For Silloans and Belshiel, see I. A. Richmond, *The Romans in Redesdale,* in A history of Northumberland, xv (1940), 124 ff.

24. *Britannia* ix (1978), 286-287.

FIGURES

Fig. 1. Roman camps in north-east Scotland. (Bennachie is the mountain of which the summit, at 528m, lies 5·5km SW of Durno).

Fig. 2. The Roman camp at Durno (contours in feet).

Fig. 3. Map of Durno – Bennachie, with a tentative reconstruction of the tactics of the battle. (Contours at 25ft. intervals; the summit of Bennachie is at 1,733ft.).

Fig. 4. Durno – Bennachie, panorama looking SSW (p.89).
The Roman camp occupies the foreground: farms of Easterton (to left) and Westerton (right) lie within it. The small river Urie, largely hidden by trees, flows in a hollow beyond the camp. In the distance is the distinctive profile of Bennachie with its several summits, including the Mither Tap, the left-hand peak, crowned by a small hill-fort.

THE BATTLE O' BENNACHIE
(AD 83)

By Professor Duncan R. Mennie

Ae nicht atween the hay an' hairst –
The corn an' bere wiz stannin' braw –
A chiel cam ridin' frae Dunnottar
An' chappit at the yett o' Calgach's ha'.

'Rise up, rise up, Lord Calgach,' he said,
'Rise up an' lippen tae me.
The Romans sailt by Dunnottar the streen
An' the morn we'll their legions see.'

Their sailors hiz burnt auld Aiberbrothock,
The Angus lads tae the Mounth hiz taen;
Ah doot the lowe Ah saw i' the gloamin'
Wiz the lowe o' burnin' Aiberdeen.

The gweed Lord Calgach spak bit ae wird
As he hent his claymore doon frae the wa',
'They maks a desert an' ca's it peace;
Up lads an' saddle yer garrons sma'.

The fiery cross sped throu' the lan'
By Don an' Dee an' Deveron Fair,
An' seen wiz mustert on Bennachie
Thretty thoosan' men or mair.

The Romans marched frae Aiberdeen;
Ayont the Urie they bigget their dykes.
Syne oot i' the mornin' we saw them steer
As bees that bizzes frae herried bykes.

They sent the Dutchmen ower Urie Water
An' seen the spears wiz fleein' free
Frae hiz an' them. The canny Romans
Steed back an' lat the Dutchmen dee.

Noo up the hill they cam tae fecht us;
Fu' mony a straik wiz taen an' gien.
Oor claymores dang on shields an' helmets,
They pikit wi' sords as shairp's a preen.

Oor lads ran doon frae the Tap an' Shannoch
An' socht tae turn the Dutchmen's flanks,
Bit the Gaulish horse got roon ahin' them
An' their doonhill chairge, it brak oor ranks.

Lord Calgach lay deid aneth a breem-buss
His trusty claymore broken in twa;
The lads that wizna taen or killt
They fled tae the hielan's, hine awa'.

The Romans burnt oor corn an' steadin's;
The reek raise black frae Don tae Spey.
They got as far's the Laigh o' Moray
An' turnt at Forres; weel, that's the say.

Syne sooth they marched ower the Fords o' Frew
Sair trachelt wi' oor trock an' gear.
An' ne'er cam back. They'd hid their sairin',
Aneuch o' Caledonian weir.

BORN UNDER BENNACHIE

By May Thomson

The Battle of Harlaw, one of the three most important battles of Scottish
history, was fought in 1411 in the fields of Balhalgardy 'a lang Scots mile'
from Bennachie, between a great Highland host much superior in numbers
and the armoured chivalry of the North-East. It was a scene of such
courage as to leave an indelible mark on local memory for many centuries.

The last verse of the Harlaw ballad runs: –
> Gin onybody speir at ye
> For them that gaed awa'
> Ye may tell them plain and very plain
> They're sleepin' at Harlaw.

To defend their city, Sir Robert Davidson, the Provost of Aberdeen, sallied forth with his stoutest burgesses to join the fray. The Provost was killed, the only one of a long line to be killed in action. For nearly two hundred years, his memory has been kept green by the St. Andrew's Society of Aberdeen, as they meet annually on the night of the thirtieth of November. The chief toast, always the same is 'Sir Robert Davidson and the heroes of Harlaw.' The records show a long line of the cream of the guest speakers of 'Aiberdeen an' twal mile roon.' Incidentally two Bennachie men have given the toast more than once, Dr Alex. Keith three times and Dr Danny Gordon twice.

In this century we have had three Aberdeen Lord Provosts of distinction born under the shadow of Bennachie. The latest was Sir Thomas Mitchell, born at Daviot, the kenspeckle civic chief of the 1939-45 war, whose humour so warmed the heart of the present Queen Mother, that she made a special visit to his bedside a few days before he died. The earliest of the three was the fine bearded upstanding Provost Adam Maitland, who inaugurated the memorial at Harlaw in 1911, the five-hundredth anniversary of the battle, and presided at its opening in July 24th, 1914. He was born at Balhalgardy, where by tradition a Maitland was killed in the battle. Certainly written records show the fourteenth Robert Maitland in direct line farming to-day on the same farm, surely a unique record.

Comparisons, they say, are odious, but the third Provost of whom I write was, I feel, the greatest character of the three. He was born at the farm of Coldwells, Inverurie – Sir James Taggart, whose term of office included the 1914-18 war. He was a prince of story-tellers. I don't remember much about the 1914-18 war, but the Girls' High School was commandeered as a military hospital and temporary quarters for the pupils were found in houses along Albyn Terrace, where we were 'cribbed and cabinned' for five years. The figures of Provost Taggart and Lang Jimmy Smith, the minister of St. George's-in-the-West, now a military padre, were often to be seen in Albyn Terrace. Who could have been a better war-time Lord Provost than Sir James Taggart, with his fine carriage and ready wit, who never spared himself in public service. His tall slim figure in khaki uniform was everywhere.

Born at the farm of Coldwells of Inverurie, he became the owner of a granite works in Great Western Road. When war started, he became a grand recruiting officer, raising Taggart's Own Brigade of Artillery (City and County). He had his portrait painted twice, the first by public subscription for his own home in appreciation of the wonderful work he was doing, showing him in his uniform as Lord Lieutenant of the County of the City of Aberdeen. The second showed him in khaki, a striking likeness, painted for the Corporation, to be seen in the Aberdeen Art Gallery. After the war, his energies were directed to raising funds for the new Sick Children's Hospital. When he approached Lord Cowdray for a contribution, his Lordship demanded 'How much do you want?' to which Sir James replied, with a face as unemotional as the granite in which he traded 'How much have you got?!' He was knighted in 1918, and given the honour of LL.D. by Aberdeen University in 1919. He was the first president of the Aberdeen Rotary Club, as well as many other bodies.

A typical example of his humour occurred when he presented the Freedom of the City of Aberdeen to Earl Haig in 1919. Earlier in the day, the University had been honouring Lord Haig and Sir Roger Keyes, the hero of Zeebrugge and were carried shoulder-high down Broad Street by the students to the Town House. Incidentally Dr Danny Gordon was one of the four students who carried the Field-Marshal. After Haig had signed the Burgess Roll, Sir Roger Keyes made to do likewise, but Sir James stretched his arm across the Admiral's chest, barring the way, saying 'Na, na, nae you, we've got to draw the line somewye.'

The two great story-tellers of the twenties were Sir James and Lord Aberdeen (of We Twa fame), two public figures who were much in demand as public speakers. A competition for charity was arranged between them in front of a great audience. Sir James won.

In the Aberdeen Reference Library there are two booklets of humorous anecdotes by the contestants.

An example of Sir James' wit runs as follows-'Have you got *The Life of a Christian*?' asked a prospective customer of a bookseller's young assistant. 'The Life of a Christian' echoed the lad, 'I dinna hae the life o' a dog an' I'm leavin' on Saturday.'

A story from Lord Aberdeen's collection:

'I've seen better days' said a tramp to an Aberdonian who replied 'So have I, but I havna' time to discuss the weather the noo.'

When Sir James died in November 1929, the funeral procession was over half a mile in length, the largest ever seen in Aberdeen.

His old home, Ashley Lodge, is now a Church of Scotland Eventide Home. This would have pleased a man so kind and generous, who did not let his right hand know what his left hand gave.

WINTER FERLIE

By Dr Ken Morrice

Ae bonny day, Christmas nae lang bye,
blithely we stairted oot frae Esson's Craft
tae clim braw Bennachie, ablow blue
sky and gowden sun, sookin in the caller
air like wine. The wids were hapt
in snaw, trees feathered fite, their
airms ootraxed – a benediction o bricht angels.
Canty syne and weel-blessed, we pechd
oor wey up the steeny path at last
tae win the Mither Tap.

Weet-broued, gulpin braith,
we sat in sunlicht heich abune the lands
o Buchan – fairmyairds, wids, keeps,
and couthy toons – ootspread afore us,
rowin tae the sea.

But syne, growin caul
in the snell win, we rose stiff-jinted
tae styter ower Maiden's Causeway and find
oor path ere gloamin-faa, fan sudden-like
a bearded chiel appeared. A wee bairnie
happit in a shawl was craidelt in his airms;
and 'Cam awa, Mary,' he cries ower his shouther
at his young wife, reid-cheeked, labourin ahin.
'Grand day!' he smiles and salutes us, speirin,
'Is this the richt wey tae the Mither Tap?'
Bumbazed I stammer, 'Gin ye cairry stracht on . . .'

Sae in a dwam we watch the three o them.
And in the winter gloamin blinks oot
the star o Bethlehem, skinklin in the lift.

THE COLONY

By Flora Garry

Eence the crafts o' the Esson Men
Noo a broken wa';
Eence spaed an' scythe an' reekin' lum
Noo the green girss haps a'.

BENNACHIE

By John Garden

Statistics from *The Topographical Statistical and Historical Gazatteer of Scotland* –

1846 'Bennachie, a mountain in Aberdeenshire situated between Alford and Garioch and stated by Dr. Neill in his survey of Aberdeenshire 'To have an altitude of 1,440 feet.'
'The mass of mountain consists of reddish granite, traversed from North to South by great dykes of porphry.'
Over the years since then, statistics have varied and those arrived at now would seem to be final and accurate.
Other spellings were:
In 1355 – Benechkey, in 1359 – Benchye.
In 1897 the Mither Tap had grown to 1,698 feet.
Enough of statistics!

In the space of time since then, Bennachie, as it is now known the world over, has become a couthy place, far removed from the stark description of 1846.

This is highlighted as I read my copy of the book written by Mr James Allan on *Agriculture in Aberdeenshire in the Nineteenth Century*.

Slowly, to augment the small crofts clinging round the lower slopes, a group of hard working people started to laboriously cultivate for themselves a colony of smallholdings to provide a place to live and eke out a living for their families.

These hard working people became known as 'The Squatters.' Later on they earned a somewhat more acceptable title, 'The Settlers.'

Their stay on Bennachie lasted from around 1801 until the last of the Essons was buried on 31 May, 1939.

In the following I can write only of my own relations. There are many others and no doubt, at some future date, the story will be continued by others with knowledge of their own.

Where did the Settlers or their offspring go?

Curiously enough one answer is given in the *Scots Magazine* of January, 1958.

In this issue there was an article by R. M. McAndrew on 'The Colony on Bennachie.' Further on, in the same issue, an article by Margaret Aitken describing 'The Floating Shops of Kirkwall.'*

The above shops were owned by a Robert Garden who left Old Rayne to seek his fortune in Kirkwall, this in 1873! This could have been about the first of the Gardens to venture far afield.

My father was born at Croft Hill of Pitbee, Chapel of Garioch in 1882 and soon after my grandfather left Pitbee with the family to join his brother in Kirkwall. For many years he ferried goods across the stormy Pentland Firth from Scrabster for his brother's business.

Another son started a contractor's business near Turriff. From there his oldest son left for America around the turn of the century.

He worked his passage to Canada, conserving such monies he had saved, then worked his way to Calgary, where, with the money accrued, he bought some land which is now the centre of Calgary. Being a mason, he built houses thereon making the start of another successful enterprise.

Perhaps it was a good thing for some Settlers that their people were displaced and were forced to look further afield for work!

Another Garden became Mine Host of 'The Butcher's Arms' in Inverurie and from there, his family spread their wings and dispersed around the area.

It is pure coincidence that my mother's people, the Middletons, worked the farm at Dorlethen, close to the Settlers, but perhaps enjoying a little more security of tenure.

I can remember stories of the farm people who converged on Inverurie and who sooner or later became involved in arguments with The Butchers which often led to fisticuffs.

On one occasion a party from the foot of 'The Hill' arrived at the top of the road from the Old Railway Station when a party of Butchers accosted

*See *Days of Orkney Steam* by Alastair and Anne Cormack.

them, this just across from The Kintore Arms Hotel. A pendulum clock, bought in Aberdeen, was placed for safety behind the railings surrounding the house belonging to Mr Laing. When the fight started, packing protecting the mechanism became dislodged and the clock started to ring every few seconds. This interruption was sufficient to stop the fight for at least one night. I would like to add that this self same clock still ticks faithfully on my brother's sideboard after over eighty years! Time gentlemen!

One daughter left Dorlethen to work at Balhalgardy, this brings to mind James Allan's mention of a championship ploughing match held there at which nineteen thousand spectators paid for admission! Later, this same daughter worked in the Wool Mill at Burnhervie before going to a similar job in Innerleithen.

After leaving Bennachie, my maternal grandfather went to Haughton Farm where my mother used to ferry farmers and others across the Don. Mart day was sometimes difficult as some were unwilling or unable to board the boat without help.

My father went to Manar House to serve his apprenticeship as a gardener. Somewhere around he must have met the 'Lady of the Ferryboat.' They got married and in due course, I arrived on the scene.

During the Second World War the Gardens returned to Bennachie having bought Westerton Croft, a stone's throw from the original area occupied by the Settlers.

On one occasion my brother and I went to Westerton to discuss some necessary work with the foreman. We found him in rather an excited state having read in the newspaper that Chief Constable Strath of Banff had arrested a German spy who had been put ashore from a U-Boat. He was convinced another spy was hiding in Esson's Croft and had sent for the police and others. There were red faces all round when the said 'spy' turned out to be our cousin, on holiday at Chapel of Garioch, who loved to commune at Essons. Old family ties?

There are many pictures. An ancient, but valued one, a Middleton golden wedding on Bennachie where Middletons, Wights, Diacks and many others are present.

My uncle married one Mitchell Diack related to Hunter Diack who wrote the book *The Boy in the Village* and *The Village on the Don*.

A picture of the gamekeeper's cottage at Tillyfour where my wife was born. Pictures of a home from home at Westerton where we spent many happy hours and used as a base for the Riley Motor Club events. There was a competition for the fastest time up to Esson's Croft and back. Mad! Perhaps, but lots of fun for all.

Just recently I got a picture of Robert Garden's grandson who returned from New Zealand to learn to fly. After completing his lessons he bought a very second-hand Tiger Moth and flew it home. He did this journey with no sponsorship, no help and in spite of having a long delay in Greece through the lack of proper passports etc. He completed the trip in nineteen days. I met him last year at another cousin's who is now a vet in Methlick.

Finally, a picture of a house overlooking the Don at Paradise where my daughter and her husband have now chosen to stay.

Some time ago a friend and neighbour (Nida Rowe) who had been working on her ancestry discovered that she was directly related to not only the Essons, but also perhaps to the Gardens. Unfortunately this was never clarified as Nida has since died.

A recent true story of The Hill. A schoolboy friend of mine went to America some fifty years ago and when he died I was told quietly that his ashes had been taken home and scattered on Bennachie. Soon after, I was informed by an acquaintance that he had met this friend in Inverurie and spoken to him. He was quite insistent this was the case. Perhaps he had been seeking companionship and had strayed from The Hill for this purpose.

On another sad note. I had gone up country to buy a threshing mill for Westerton and on arriving home in the small hours of the morning my father gave precise instructions as to its installation. By morning he was dead. Needless to say, his last instructions were carried out to the letter.

Westerton was later sold, but we are told that a small piece of Bennachie still belongs to us and some old papers appear to confirm this. When cleared, what better place could there be for The Bailies to meet?

A house now built on a small piece of ground we sold bears the name 'Mither Garth.' Again? Where are they now?

There were at least two ministers, two schoolmasters, two doctors, many farmers, builders, that man from Kirkwall and last, but by no means least, an opera singer – Mary Garden.

The 'Hill Folks' and 'The Butchers' must have come to terms for at least two Gardens married Butchers. A host of Gardens now rest in Old Logie churchyard.

Finally, 'O gin I were where Gadie rins!' I have before me four versions of this famous song. How nice it would be were The Bailies to produce these four versions in some future publication.

An advertisement from the same book dated 1897: –

'Old malt whisky at 16/6 per gallon!'

A toast to The Bailies!

COPY OF A LETTER WRITTEN BY GEORGE ESSON TO ROBERT CORMACK IN 1938

Boghead of Tullos,
21st January, 1938.

Dear Robert,

I received your most kind and welcome letter some time ago and I intended to write to you sooner but have failed to get an opportunity to do so. I am still able to look after my croft and the various duties attached to it although I am not able now to go to work away from home as my feet

George Esson, 1937

Photo – Jeannie L. Cormack

and legs have failed me otherwise I am feeling in wonderful health. I am pleased to see by your letter that you have succeeded so well in the land of your adoption and that your family have all done so well. I was delighted to see your daughter up here to see me. It was very kind of her to come up to my Humble residence and my wife was alive then although an invalid in bed but she appreciated your daughter's visit to us very much and thought her a very nice kind lady. I am missing my dear wife very much. We had no family as we were well up in years before we married, she being a widow. I have her daughter here with me now but I am not sure how long she may be with me. I see you noticed the sale of the Fetternear Estates in the Aberdeen newspapers. They were sold by Auction in the Kintore Arms Hotel Inverurie, every place by itself. I intended to buy my place but my boundaries were not properly defined and they promised to me to reserve the sale of my place until this was done but in the interval the Farmer of West Fingask went and gave them a good offer for the Hill and my croft and they sold to him which I thought very mean. However I took my case to the Land Court and got my rent reduced and Fixety of tenure and Valuation for my Houses and for improving the land if leaving my place or in the event of my death and I have also the right to bequeath my tenant right so I have little to grumble about after all. The Tenant of Tullos,

Boghead of Tullos, 1937

Photo – Jeannie L. Cormack

McWilliam, bought his Farm for £435. It was cheap as there is a new steading there since you left this place. Bogmill, Capernook and Whitecross were not sold to tenants but were sold along with some more of the Farms to Mr Patterson of the Auction Mart, Turriff, and they are still in his hands. The House of Fetternear was Burned to the ground some years ago and the Laird was unable to repair it so it is a ruin. The House of Aquhorthies was sold to an Englishman named Mr Bagshaw. Crowmallie is a nice place. The house is built on the hill of Knockollochie and the Laird Sir Robert Smith, M.P. owns Knockollochie Farm, Pitbee, Backbrae, Hillhead and Craigmile. He is the Laird of Pittodrie's Uncle. I am pleased to know you have Dr Davidson's Earldom of the Garioch. I have a copy also. It is very interesting. Like you, I have a taste for History especially local and Antiquarian things. The old stone in the dyke below my place is still there; the Cup and Saucer as it was called. My Brother John is dead and his Collection of Antiquities was sold in Aberdeen about 20 years ago. The Gouk's Stone is still standing in its old place. The woods are all cut down all round Bennachie and the last bit is being cut down above old George Sim's place. There is to be a sawmill set down at the corner of the wood above Westertown. My Sister Jane and her Husband George Spalding are both dead a few years ago and two of their family. Sarah is living in a house at Burnhervie. She is now Mrs Mennie. Mary is dead. Also her husband, Wm. Milne, and Mr Connon. He did not live to be a very old man. He was living in South Australia. Annie Milne and her husband, John Sim, are still alive. I get a letter from them every New Year. Robert Milne is still in Aberdeen as far as I know but his wife is dead. The Hill of Bennachie was all burned round this side and the old house at the Linn is in ruins and all the trees round it cut down. A. Hay, Dorlethen, is dead a few years ago. There was a very mysterious occurrence about a child of his step-daughter. It was lost. It disappeared away from Dorlethen and its body was found on the Hill when they were cutting trees 7 years afterwards at the head of the Boddach road. It was just 22 months old and it could not manage to climb up there by itself, I don't think. There was a Public Enquiry in Aberdeen but nothing was decided about it as there was no evidence. I often think I should have stayed in America for I liked the Country but I was laid up with sciatica in my left leg and was unable to work. I was in Cleveland, Ohio. A very fine Country there about and I was doing well but I cannot regret that now. I have no doubt the Country is changed very much since that time. I think it would be better for Britain and America to come to a closer agreement about trade and other matters. It would do more to keep peace throughout the World than anything I know. We are living in constant dread of war breaking out in Europe again and the Government is making great Preparations for war. We are all to be served out with Gas Masks for fear of Invasion by Air and Gas Bombs and they are constructing Bomb Proof Shelters to hold all the population of the towns if invasion by Air does come which is causing a lot of work. There will be no peace until Germany gets back at least some of her Colonies and I am just afraid we may have to teach Italy a lesson very soon as she is getting rather impudent with us. As for Japan I think the United States and

it is no wonder my sight is getting weaker there is no one round here that was here when you went away bat John Walker Hill of Fetternear he is over 80 years of age and now I think I will need to draw to a close Give your Brother George my best wishes and your Daughter Jennie and wish them a happy New Year although it is some late and while expecting to hear from you again at your convenience and sending you my best wishes and a happy New Year and many returns of the Season

I remain

Yours Sincearly
George Eason

Britain will unite in settling her. She is I think going too far with her Invasion of China. It is just a pity we are so far separated for I would love a crack with you about many things but we can still drop a letter to each other now and again. I am not so good at writing now as my eyesight is failing me especially with lamp light. I am now 75 years of age and it is no wonder my sight is getting weaker. There is no one round here that was here when you went away but John Walker, Hill of Fetternear. He is over 80 years of age. And now I think I will need to draw to a close. Give your brother George my Best Wishes and your Daughter Jennie and wish them a Happy New Year although it is some late and while expecting to hear from you again at your convenience and sending you my best wishes and a happy New Year and many returns of the Season.

Yours sincerely,
George Esson.

THE CORMACK CONNECTION

By Helen P. Fraser

Although the Cormack Connection with Bennachie began nearly two hundred years ago, it was in 1977 that there began the Cormack Connection with the Bailies of Bennachie. In that year Miss Jeannie L. Cormack of Milwaukee, Wisconsin, paid one of her many visits to the Bennachie area. Before returning to her home, she left behind a wonderful collection of old photographs for the Bailies of Bennachie. These photographs had been 'taken' at the beginning of the century by her aunt Sarah Cormack. Since that time, Miss Jeannie has sent over many more of her aunt's photographs to the Bailies.

In correspondence with Miss Jeannie, it was clear to me that she knew Bennachie and its surroundings far better than many of us who live close by. Born in Iowa, Miss Cormack has crossed the Atlantic fourteen times, spending many weeks of each visit around Bennachie. Her memories of Bennachie go back to her first visit as a child, with a photograph by Aunt Sarah to prove it! During one visit, in July, 1937, she visited Mr and Mrs George Esson at Boghead of Tullos. Mrs Esson was confined to bed, but her husband, George, prepared tea for their guest. George Esson refers to this visit in his letter to Miss Cormack's father, Robert Cormack (see page 100).

Today there is a great interest, on both sides of the Atlantic, in researching into family history and Miss Cormack readily agreed to my request for details of her family and their connection with the parishes around Bennachie. So many people regret that earlier in life they did not ask enough questions of their parents and near relatives. Miss Cormack was fortunate in that she was able to supplement her own gleanings with the extensive notes left by her father, and it is mainly from these sources that the following account of the Cormack family is taken.

The earliest known ancestor was James Cormack, born at Monkshill, Fyvie, in 1754. James, along with his brother worked at Rothiebrisbane, but after a disagreement with the laird, they moved to Cross of Jackston. A search through the pages of the Spalding Club's publication entitled *List of Pollable Persons within the Shire of Aberdeen: 1696* failed to reveal any Cormacks in the parish of Fyvie, but there were quite a number of that name in the parish of Forgue. James married Barbara Ruddiman in 1779 and they set up their home at Mickle Rothey, and here they reared four children: Anne, James, Peter and Robert. It is the fortunes of the son James which are of interest in this family history and on reaching manhood we find him in Daviot where he worked as a millwright at Mounie. In 1807 he married Jean Tocher and they moved to Mill of Wartle. After giving birth to at least six children, Jean died and in 1822 James Cormack married again, his second wife was Sarah Ewing. They had a family of ten children, two of whom were born at Wartle. A very interesting reference is made to James Cormack's farming initiative in *A Century of Aberdeenshire Agriculture* by Isabella Bruce, published in 1908. Substantial sums of money were offered to farmers by the Garioch Farmer Club for the encouragement of land reclaiming, house building, cleanliness and neatness in house and garden, etc. In 1823, James Cormack, Mill of Warthill was awarded a premium 'for reclaiming 5 acres 13 poles by the spade; and the two following years he was obliged to plough the same by men, it being too soft for carrying cattle. It is now completely dry, and can be ploughed by cattle at all seasons.'

At the end of his lease James and Sarah moved to Mill of Durno where eight more children were born: Alexander, Isabella, Robert, Jane, Sarah, David, George, and Henry. In later life William, who was born before the move to Durno, recalled the celebrations in Durno and Whiteford to mark the wedding of Queen Victoria and Prince Albert. He remembered too, getting up at 3 o'clock to work in the Mill before setting off to school, up the Chapel Brae. One of his schoolmates was William Alexander of Johnny Gibb fame and the two boys frequently walked together part of the way. William Cormack became a minister and eventually settled in South Africa. One of his brothers, George Hall Cormack, born in 1837, trained to be a miller with his father. George was interested in the working of the mill machinery and he became apprenticed to George Annand, Millwright in Inverurie. He worked for a number of years in Inverurie and in 1867 married Mary Walker, daughter of Robert Walker, tenant farmer in Whitewell, Chapel of Garioch. George and Mary made their home at 68 High Street, Inverurie where, in due course, their three children were born: Robert, George and Sarah. After his father's death in 1866, his mother moved to Inverurie where she died in 1869 and the family ties with the Mill of Durno came to an end. Perhaps this fact influenced George Cormack when he made up his mind to go abroad. He had the urge to invent and expand and he may have come to realise that the prosperity of the small country mill was on the decline. The Inverurie Canal, followed by the advent to the Railway was beginning to have an adverse affect on the economy of many country pursuits, a way of life was coming to an end. In order to achieve his ambitions, George Cormack set off; firstly he went to Ontario, but two years later he settled in Rockford, Illinois, where he died in 1911. In one respect his dream came true and he prospered. He invented a number of machines for the process of rolling oats. He started up his own Mill and won a Gold Medal at the New Orleans Cotton Exposition for his 'Cormack's Nudavene Flakes,' where the first rolled oats on the market were placed before the public. Later his Company merged with 'American Cereal' to become the 'Quaker Oats Company.' He was appointed Mechanical Engineer in 1891, a position he held until his death.

Sadly, he was unable to persuade his wife Mary to join him in America. She stayed in Inverurie for a time but eventually returned with her children to her parents' home at Whitewell. Several times George Cormack returned to Scotland to see his family, always hoping that his wife would change her mind and return with him to America, but all to no avail. His many visits to Scotland were obviously enjoyed by his children – his daughter Sarah recalled his visit of 1909 when together they visited the graves of her great-grandparents in the Kirkyard at Auchterless.

One treasure which George Cormack was particularly pleased to have with him in America was the grandfather clock which had belonged to his

On Bennachie, 1909

Left to right – Mrs G. Cormack, Mrs R. Cormack, Bob Cormack, Mrs R. Cormack
Bill Cormack, Jeannie Cormack and Mrs G. H. Cormack

Photo – Sarah Cormack

Sarah Cormack at Whitewell, 1897

father. He had cherished memories of it in the home at Mill of Durno where it stood in the angle of the stairway. This far-travelled clock was made in 1812 by Alex. Sim, Aberdeen. It eventually became the property of Miss Cormack's father Robert, and it is now in the home of her brother Dr Robert G. H. Cormack, in Edmonton, Alberta.

Mary Walker's family had been in Whitewell for many years. At the beginning of the nineteenth century Alexander Walker moved from his native Tarland to the Garioch. For a time he worked with Dr Harvey, the laird of Braco, and at length he decided to settle near Bennachie. There were a number of crofts in the area and he was able to rent the holding at Whitewell, along with an adjoining stretch of rough ground, and here he made a home for his bride Elizabeth Hunter, and here they raised their family of six children. Robert the eldest was born in 1810. As the years went by, Alexander cleared a bit of his rough ground to add to his arable land and this task was continued in greater measure by his son Robert when in due course he took over the tenancy of Whitewell after Alexander's death in 1850. It was due to the labours of men like the Walkers, and James Cormack in Mill of Wartle, that many of the Aberdeenshire lairds of last century owed the increase in the arable acreage, and hence the increased value of their estates.

Robert Walker spent his early years working as a herd boy on neighbouring farms, and as he gained experience he was fee'd as a horseman. When the time came for him to take over the tenancy of Whitewell, he was already married; his marriage to Mary Reid took place at Kemnay in 1839. Elizabeth Hunter continued to live at Whitewell until her death in 1859. She was born in 1770 and remembered the late 'hairst' of 1782 when all the crops were ruined by snow and early frosts. There followed a time of famine and great hardship when many children and adults died of starvation. Her brother, Robert Hunter, was an innkeeper, probably nearby at Westerton of Braco, and it was said that he had more than a passing interest in the smuggling trade. She must have had many stirring tales to tell of smugglers and Excise men dodging each other on the slopes of Bennachie.

During Robert's tenancy, changes were taking place at Whitewell. Dilly's Dam was constructed, a new farmhouse was built in 1857 and alterations were made to the steading when a new barn was built in 1860. Robert Walker followed his father's example and continued to trench and drain the rough ground and he built the stone dykes round his newly reclaimed land. Whitewell was now a small farm of 50 acres. It is interesting to speculate at this stage why certain of the enclosures were given such names as 'Nearest Farquhar Park,' 'Upper George Park,' 'Lower George Park.' 'Little Brae Park,' 'Sawmill Park,' 'Back Whitewell Park' and 'Pump Park.' Robert and Mary Walker had three children: Robert, Mary and Margaret. All the children had to help with the farm work, harrowing and rolling with the horses. During busy times they had to take it in turn to stay off school. They helped to cart off the stones, whins and broom from the rough ground. Perhaps it was this experience that caused young Robert to think of another career when he became apprenticed to the joiner at Chapel of

Garioch. His sister Margaret died when she was quite young and Mary worked at home until her marriage to George Hall Cormack in 1867.

It was not all hard work at Whitewell. Robert Walker was musical; in his youth he played the violin and he had a good singing voice. He became interested in teaching psalmody and in this connection he would have met that great authority on psalmody, William Carnie of Aberdeen who, with John Philip, R.A., known as 'Spanish John,' was often a guest of the musical minister, the Rev. James Greig, at the Manse of Chapel of Garioch. A treasured possession of the Cormack family is a Psalm Book with the inscription, 'Presented to Mr Robert Walker by his pupils for his gratuitous services in teaching them Psalmody. Whitewell, 22nd May, 1858.'

The Walkers, although displeased that their daughter refused to join her husband in America, nevertheless welcomed the family to Whitewell where the three children, Robert, George and Sarah, spent a very happy childhood. In later years they never ceased to talk of the days they spent near Bennachie. They remembered their schooldays at Fetternear with their teachers: Miss Lizzie Scott, Mr Ramage and Mr Cruden. There were jaunts with their mother and grandmother, a visit to the New Market in Aberdeen where toys were bought for them, a trip by gig to visit Aunt Kirsty at Tough, via the ford on the Don at Pitfichie. There were also memories of the long walk with their mother, along the foot of the hill, past Pittodrie and Harthill Castle to the Kirkton of Oyne to visit Great-aunt Mary Sievwright. A welcome visitor to Whitewell, at least as far as the Cormack children were concerned, was that almost forgotten book-man, the 'Colporteur.' A tall man, John Reid carried his books and magazines in a leather case strapped to his shoulders. The opening of this treasure chest was eagerly awaited by the three young members of the family, while their elders were hard pressed to conceal their lack of interest when Mr Reid began to expound on his favourite topic. There were various other interests for the young folks to enjoy; home-made and homely family entertainments were a feature of life in the country districts.

The Walkers had very good neighbours at Tullos. It was in 1877 that Mr and Mrs James Milne took over the tenancy, moving with their large household from the farm of Yonderton in Monymusk. James Milne's mother, whose maiden name was Bell Beveridge, lived with the family as did Mrs Milne's parents, Mr and Mrs High. For a number of years the Milnes had quite a struggle to make a living; the land was poor and stoney and a lot of trenching, digging and blasting was done. At the end of a hard day's work in the fields, there was often an evening of games and dancing. Mrs Milne had a wonderful store of old ballads and there was always a request for her to sing Drumallachie. These happy evenings were shared with their neighbours at Whitewell.

Along with the last batch of photographs, Miss Cormack sent another treasured family possession to the Bailies of Bennachie. This is the Day Book of Whitewell, a fascinating daily record of the farm work, crops, livestock, implements used, with a record of all the purchases and sales effected for the farm. The first entry was made on 27th May, 1889, and the book ends with the entry for 25th January, 1893. As well as being a record of all the farming operations, there are numerous entries about helping neighbours at seed-time and harvest and of neighbous helping with seasonal work at Whitewell. The several families mentioned include Robertson, Sim, Soutar, Spalding, Hay, Reid, Milne, Clark, Sorrie, Harvie and Middleton. Other entries tell that peats were carted from Wartle where, in 1891, G. Fraser was Moss Grieve; brushwood was carted from Millstone Hill and coals were supplied by A. Lumsden. There are references to the various tradesmen and shopkeepers in the district – James Mackie was the blacksmith at Burnhervie and his counterparts at Balquhain and Chapel of Garioch were James Adams and B. Moir respectively. In Inverurie we find Wm. Rae and Son, Implement Makers, Wm Lauder, Builder, John Henderson, Saddler and J. Munro, Druggist. John Gordon was the General Merchant in Chapel of Garioch and J. McKnight is referred to as Newsagent, Pitcaple.

Although his name does not appear in the Day Book, John Esson was a near neighbour at Boghead of Tullos. He was obviously a man with wide interests and had earned for himself quite a reputation as the local antiquary. Certain it is that he had a large collection of flint arrows and stone axes. He also had in his possession an old sword with a solid silver hilt. He was interested in the origins of the numerous tumuli which he described as being near the farm of Auquhorsk: on opening some of them in 1880, he found decayed bones. At one time he owned an old church seat, dated 1629, taken from the Chapel of Garioch Church. It was thought, from the coat of arms carved on it, that it had belonged to the Abercromby family of Fetternear. John Esson was succeeded in Boghead of Tullos by his son George who, after a few years in America, returned to his native heath where he also gained for himself the reputation of a man of many talents and interests. The Bailies of Bennachie are very fortunate to have in their library, three books which belonged to John Esson in 1877 and which were presented to the library by Mr John Hird, Kemnay, who bought them at the Roup held at Boghead of Tullos after the death of George Esson in 1939.

Towards the close of last century, events were taking place which were to affect the lives of Robert, Sarah and George Cormack. Their grandfather, Robert Walker, died in his 82nd year, in 1891, and his wife Mary was in her 87th year when she died in 1895, both of them having lived through most of the nineteenth century. During that time they saw many changes on the face of the countryside around them, and they must have witnessed the sad occasion of the eviction in 1876 of some of the Bennachie 'Colonists' whose homes were but a short distance from Whitewell. Soon after the death of his grandfather, George decided to emigrate. Plans were set in motion and in 1893 he set sail for the United States to join his father. The lease of Whitewell was due to expire in 1898 and Robert and Sarah stayed on and helped to run the farm. The friendly association continued with their neighbours the Milnes who often had a houseful of young cousins to stay with them during the summer months, and it was soon evident that Robert was falling in love with one of the pretty young cousins, Miss

Jeannie Beveridge from Tough. It was a case of love at first sight for both of them. Robert's ties with Whitewell were severed when he set off to join his father in America where he readily obtained employment with the Quaker Oats Company. When Miss Beveridge arrived in America some months later, they were married in New York City before moving to the home which Robert had established in Cedar Rapids, Iowa. An extensive account of Mrs Robert Cormack's father and grandfather, both named William Beveridge, is to be found in *John Duncan, Weaver and Botanist* by William Jolly, published in 1883. Mrs Cormack's father was a noted wood-carver and his work can be seen in Balmoral Castle. He was a violinist who also made violins and it is known that Prince Albert bought one of them. The Beveridge family lived for many years in the hamlet of Craigh, Tough, near Alford, before moving to Aberdeen in 1873, when William Beveridge became curator of the Free Church College Museum.

Leaving Whitewell at last in 1898, Sarah and her mother moved to Kemnay where they lived for a number of years. Sarah was now more free to devote time to her interest in photography, an interest which she had pursued for a number of years at Whitewell. Her competence in this sphere soon became apparent and she travelled, mostly on her bicycle, all over the Garioch and further afield, with her camera. She was probably the first freelance lady photographer in Aberdeenshire. Not content with taking the photographs, Sarah also mastered the technique of developing them. The photographs which she took and developed at the beginning of the century, and which now belong to the Bailies of Bennachie, are the work of a skilled photographer and they form an unique record of places which in the intervening years have changed considerably. After her mother's death in 1911, she continued to make her home in Kemnay until, early in 1914, she met and married the Rev. Alexander Wilson and the final link in the connection with Bennachie was about to be broken. Mr and Mrs Wilson went to Canada, making their home in Hamilton, Ontario, where Mrs Wilson soon adapted herself to her new surroundings and joined in all the activity of the town. She did not abandon her photography, but she was particularly interested in music circles and was for many years a member of a choir. With her husband, she paid one last visit to 'dear aul' Bennachie in 1930, an account of which forms a chapter in this book. After a long, interesting life, enjoyed to the full, Sarah Cormack Wilson died aged 93, in 1963.

Mr and Mrs Robert Cormack brought their three children, Jeannie, Robert and William, on their first visit to Aberdeenshire in 1909, and that first sight of Bennachie made such an impression on young Jeannie that she has returned again and again. She has spent many hours driving along the roads around Bennachie, she has climbed Bennachie in all weathers and she too has a large collection of photographs to remind her of the homes of her ancestors who lived in the parishes around Bennachie. She remembers her parents' love of their homeland and she has a deep sense of knowing that she too belongs to Bennachie.

SELECTION OF ENTRIES
FROM THE WHITEWELL FARM DAY BOOK

1889

27th September – Cross-ploughing. Brookie cow served. Paid Acct. to A. Raeburn, blacksmith.

7th September – Went to Inverurie with 1 cart. Thatching hay. Cutting roads for reaper. Driving tares and green corn. Went to Chapel with gig. Bought from Aberdeen Commercial Co. 2 cwts oilcake @ 9/3 per cwt. Bought from Thomas Tait and Son, 1 Bol Meal @ 15/6, 1 sack Dust @ 1/8.

13th September – Dewy, misty day. Driving tares and turnips. Raking. Various. Went up the hill to see sproats. Making and adjusting pulleys to lift skylights.

28th October – Ploughing, finished stubble. Fauching. Ploughing to J. Robertson 1½ hours.

30th October – Ploughing to J. Robertson 4 hours. Went to Artannes for meal. Credit milling. Went to Whitehaugh for wood to make dam sluice 8/-. Took in sheaves.

30th December – Hard frost. Driving brush-wood. Went to Whitecross for water cart. Driving liquid manure on to new grass.

1890

16th January – Ploughing ley endrigs. Harrowing fauched land. Went to smiddy with horses, shoes re-toed.

8th March – Stormy. No horse work. Brookie dropped red calf.

22nd March – Went to Kintore with gig. Paid to Wm. Smith & Son, Nurseries, for fruit trees etc. 14/3.

14th April – Driving turnips. Driving nets to Pitcaple Station. Sowed Lower George Park with 3 qrs. 1 bush.

2nd May – Went to Wm. Ririe's for grubber. Harrowing and linking potato ground. Grubbering. Driving off weeds. Drilling potatoes.

7th May – Dragging. Went to Denhead for calf. Working in garden. Rolling tares. Paid to J. Raeburn £17/10/-.

10th June – Driving dung. Covering in dung. J. Robertson 3½ hours. Paid to J. Garden for breaking dung 10 hours, 1/-. To G. Sim breaking dung 17 hours, 2/6.

20th June – Went to Strathdon on bicycles for week's holiday.

1st July – Cutting hay. Washing carts etc.

22nd August – Putting up Sorrie's hay. Painting. Sledging and driving stones.

19th September – Wet. Various. Setting up stooks and making 'raips.'

6th October – Leading. Had Wm. Sorrie 3 hours. J. Robertson 4 hours.

7th November – Went to Aberdeen auction sales. Bought 3 Canadian bullocks @ £10/15/-. Paid for droving of same from Pocra Pier to Kittybrewster 1/-. Paid for carriage of cattle from Kittybrewster to Pitcaple 4/-. Travelling expenses 3/7.

20th December – Stormy. Took in part of stack, 2 loads. Household expenses 14/11.

1891

3rd January – Various. Pulling and driving 4 loads turnips. Trying to settle about the mill water with Mr Sorrie. Household expenses 8/8½.

21st March – Horses shod. Driving turnips 18 loads. George Sim 10 hours. Sold Canadian stot to J. Lyon, Aberdeen, for £18, to be kept for 10 days. Bought at Aberdeen 7th Nov. 1890. Price £10/15/-, leaving for nearly 5 months keep, £7/5/-.

2nd April – Driving 9½ loads liquid manure. Ploughing. Bought from Mrs Brown, Drumdurno, 2 pigs, 5 weeks old @ 10/-.

18th June – Hoeing turnips. Mrs Soutar 2½ hours.

28th June – Hoeing. J. Robertson 2 hours working amongst hay.

23rd October – Fauching. Ploughing. Spreading top dressing. Linking same. Paid to J. Sim for harvest work 15/-.

12th December – Went to Millstone Hill for 2 trails of wood. Cutting up do. for fuel.

29th, 30th, and 31st December – No Horse work.

1892

16th January – Been very stormy since last entry (2nd Jan.). Nothing can be done. Turnips very hard to get. Went to Inverurie for drum and materials to repair mill.

20th January – Putting in drum, James Rae and George working till 1 a.m. Tried the high speed drum at 1 a.m., working very well. Had another thrash before J.R. left.

16th February – Driving 1 load straw and 1 small load of bedding from G. Sim. Hummelling corn. Rather too much snow for ploughing.

18th February – Putting seed corn into loft. Hummelling corn for sale. Cutting up timber for fuel. Driving 8 small loads of dung, stiff work. Very stormy.

17th March – Dragging out trees in Aforsk wood. Mare ran off, came down and smashed herself dreadfully, especially her near fore knee. Afraid she will be no more use. Sent for V.S.

31st March – Driving top dressing. Went to Wm. McGregor's for horse which J. McG. bought on our account from Mr Strachan, Woodside. Paid J. McGregor for horse, £10.

25th April – Sowed part of Sawmill Park with 2 qr., fully. Harrowing. Working at Steam-mill at Mellonbrae.

7th May – Drag-harrowing. Went to sale at Drumdurno. George bought 2 old scythes, 1/3; 1 old bridle, 1/-; Lot books, 1d; Household things, 6d, total, 2/10 (14½p).

17th June – Driving brushwood from Millstone Hill. George and Sara left for Edinburgh. Sowed about 1½ acres turnips for the 2nd time.

24th June – Pulling turnips out amongst young corn. S. and G. home, enjoyed holidays.

1st July – George began making carts. Went to Pittodrie in the afternoon to a picnic.

2nd July – George and I went up to the Breenie Hill to see W. Jamieson.

6th July – Hoeing turnips. Went to St. Sairs Fair, drove to Oyne, then rode over.

21st July – Went to cattle show at Aberdeen. George hoeing turnips and working at steam-mill at Whitecross.

20th August – Went to Wartle Moss for 2 loads peats. Paid 10/- for 2 loads.

1st October – Very wet, nothing done except getting in tares and turnips. Threshing barley. George went to Aberdeen and bought a Camera.

7th October – Finished cutting to Wm. Sorrie. Came on wet as we finished. Making raips.

18th October – Making a lot of feeding troughs for cattle. Been very stormy all day. 3 weeks today since harvest began, and have still 1 day's cutting.

31st October – George and Sara started to lead at 2 a.m. Trucked 2 cattle for J. Lyon.

9th November – Leading. Took 'winter.' Driving rakings into barn. Drawing thatch.

31st December – No horse work. Snedding trees. George making new box to go into dam sluice, the old one having quite broken down this morning. Mill wheel also smashed.

1893

2nd January – Very frosty. George rose at 1 a.m. to get box for dam finished.

8th January – Mending dam. Got the loan of J. Hay's sleigh to go to Inverurie.

23rd January – Ploughing has been stopped for 1 month. Sent cow to be slaughtered, being we think affected by tuberculosis. Paid Income Tax on house property in Inverurie 10/-. Paid Fire Insurance for Farm Stock etc. 15/-. This has been an exceptionally fine day, quite a contrast to previous ones.

25th January – Ploughing. Driving turnips 8 loads, Swedes 4 loads. Bought from J. Gordon 1 brush for stable 1/3, ½ gal. oil 1/3. Bruised 4 bush.

GEORGE ESSON'S ROUP

By John Hird

One fine Saturday afternoon in the summer of 1940, my wife and I set off on our bikes to the roup at Geordie Esson's croft. We found Davie Burns and young Taylor all ready to start, most of the contents of the house being spread around on the grass. They included a dresser, girnal, odd dishes, pots and pans, a bed of sorts, spinning wheel, some gramophone records, a badger trap, harness for pony and cart, a hay rake, Flackster spade, peat-cutting spade and some books.

The spinning wheel managed to hold out until it was sold, but when set down rather heavily, it finished up as a heap of dust. I bought what books he had, later giving three of Scottish interest to the Bailies of Bennachie, who, I understand, had them re-bound. Nine volumes of Richard Harding Davies' works, all short stories and articles and in perfect condition, must have been valued very highly by Mr Esson for him to bring them back with him from America. Mr Tom Tait of the Port Elphinstone paper mill bought the Flackster and peat spades, and was waiting till the end of the sale to see if he could buy some stones he fancied. They were on top of the dyke beside the house. The only other people I remember who were there were Mr & Mrs Smith from Blairdaff Farm. Mrs Smith bought some bee skeps and gramophone records.

Now widowed and living in Kemnay, Mrs Smith (a Findlater) was born on the Hill of Bennachie, and one of 14 of a family, most of whom, she told me, were killed in World War I. Only her sister Bella and herself are alive today. When Bella married an Irishman named Malone, they settled in Ireland, calling their house 'Bennachie'; but the troubles there got too much for them and they emigrated to America, where Bella, aged 103, still lives.

LETTER FROM MRS SARAH CORMACK WILSON
to her brother, Robert W. Cormack in America
describing a holiday spent in Inverurie and around Bennachie area in 1930.

'We went by Hazelhead Park on the Skene road, Broadstraik Inn, and Skene, and Loch of Skene on the left. How I watched to get the peep of dear aul' Bennachie, saw it just after we went through Skene village. Wasn't it a dear familiar sight to me! It seemed in a way the Mecca of all my trip. Turned to the right at the Waterton of Echt, on through Kintore, reaching Inverurie at 1 p.m., where we had a very warm welcome from Betsy Drummond and the others. I think we all talked for hours without a pause.

After tea all of us drove up Blackhall Road, through the woods of Manar, Burnhervie, on past Mill of Braco – alas, no Lyons there now – past Bogmill and Cappernook to the 'Pole,' turned here, coming in 'by the fit o' Dorrie's Green.'

The whole countryside is changed, *all* the wood cut above Braeside and the Linn Burn at Pittodrie. Trees all cut above James Robertson's and not a vestage of his house or steading left, nor Jean Clark's nor Spalding's. Tullos and Whitewell look about the same. The little 'Commonty' near Tullos is the same, though the road to Sandy Porter's is hardly discernible. Tullos hedge just the same and the Brig also, though it does look very small.

The 'Muckle ditch' beside the 'Waird' has lost its depth being overgrown by weeds, and the roadie from the Brig to Jamie Sim's has almost disappeared. The 'new' road also looks small and narrow; all these I noticed that first afternoon. But more of this later on. I couldn't help thinking, 'She's nae oor Bennachie,' so changed is the general appearance of the locality, tho' aul' Bennachie's Tap changes not.

It does seem strange to me to be driving a motor car on these familiar roads where I have in years gone by, walked, driven a horse, and cycled. I know every turn, every rising ground, every down hill and even the stone dykes on the road side. The motor car goes so quickly that you can cover the miles in a few minutes from say Inverurie to Whitewell, you are there almost before you know.

One afternoon we all – meaning Betsy Drummond, her niece Bess (a daughter of Bob Drummond), Bess's husband George Smith and their little girl Elma, 2½, with of course 'we twa' – set out for Charlie Esson's and Bennachie. Parked the car beside three big 'busses' and set off, the path now very rough and stony. The view to the north was grand and clear, all cultivated. Saw to westward, Tap o' Noth, Buck o' Cabrach and Dunnideer, and to the north, Knock Hill. All around the bell heather was in full bloom and foxgloves in great abundance. All the scrubby trees are gone and looking from the Stey Knowe was like a strange country. All the woods between this and Pittodrie have been cut and the big old trees at the Linn of Falls are gone, and it looks dreadfully bare and desolate. Could see the little path to the Falls, but no Falls. From here, Stey Knowe, could have a view of Howe o' Braco where the trees blocked the view in our young days.

Not far from Hosie's Well is a sign board 'To the Mither Tap' which seems very odd to me. Hosie's Well is still there, still running its fine clear cool stream with soft green grass and spring moss all round. Left Bess and Elma and the food here. We went up slowly to the Tap. There was no sunshine, soft blue clouds with a high wind. Got up at last, but couldn't stand on the top, 'twas so windy. The Don valley looking towards Alford was lovely, while to the west, hills and more hills, and away to the south, the Deeside hills, and what we thought was Lochnagar.

The country eastward looked very beautiful – like crazy patchwork and we could see the Don winding down by Monymusk and Kemnay, while further away we got a peep of Loch of Skene, and the Hill of Fare, and to the east, the blue waters of the North Sea. Grand feeling to be once more on the Tap. Back to Hosie's Well and our tea and lunch in the shelter of a few old scrubby spruce trees, all that are now left. Then down much faster than we came up, into the car and we're soon in Inverurie.

Alex and I went to Whitewell one afternoon, and found both Mr and Mrs McGregor at home and very glad to see us. Talked for an hour or two, then had tea and then went all over the house. Upstairs into the bedroom where I slept as a girl with Mother, seemed small, same old grate. The 'girnal' closet and the other closet off my room just the same, with the corner of the door cut off to fit the sloping roof, where your old crib used to be. The very railings of the stair still the same. The main room the same with the same grate that we had. Your room later still with the fixed-in bed and the window in the gable. The kitchen floor has still the smooth blue Caithness pavement and the threshold stones at outside door, the same red Bennachie granite. Uncle Robert's room has a new grate.

Went all round the garden – not in so good order as of years ago. Many of the bushes too old now, especially the black currants. Still a seat on the east corner and some fine Canterbury Bells. All the gean trees at the front are still there, though they look hoary, limbs are moss covered. I think many of the branches have been broken off at the ends by rough pickers. The trees look stocky and are too thick in the centre. The dyke of the garden is broken down in some places, and the gates and paling are falling to pieces.

George's shoppie is now made into a wash house, and our seat with the ivy there, is now a wooden shed. Round the back all changed, duck and pig houses etc., all orra looking. Cornyard grown full of dockens, five feet high. The old mill wheel all broken, the 'owes' and spouting all in bits and only a trickle of water. Dam and lade all falling in, very little water, dirty and muddy. No water rushing over the spout at the dam. I can hear it now as I did 40 years ago, when I'd go out to listen for you or any of us who were late in coming home. The high speed drum and George's 'harp' are still in the barn and aye working, driven by a gasoline engine. The floor of the sheaf loft is rotten and is to be renewed soon. The stable and byres are the same, but all untidy looking. The old ash trees round the cornyard are aye to the fore, though considerably trimmed; only one has gone, one of the two *outside* near the hay ricks.

Alex and I went to Chapel Kirkyard. We visited the graves of our own family and those we used to know: Nicols, Hunters, Drummonds and Lyons. Grandfather, Grandmother, Mother, all sleep quietly in the shade of dear old Bennachie. Another cemetery has now been opened, about a year ago across the road from the north gate, or opposite the 'Merchan's steadin'.'

The 'Auld Kirk' has been all remodelled inside, with a built-in organ. I think the gentry's fine seats in the corners have all been done away with and the awful narrow pews have also gone. It looks the same outside.

We called on Mrs Porter, 75 years old, still hale and hearty. She asked much about you. Remembered you going past whistling when you worked the 'Smith's croft' long ago.

There are a few houses down towards the Manse but on the whole there is little change. The smiddy as such, is gone and a petrol pump stands there. The 'Lang Blair' road seems so small and narrow, wood has all been cut, except the big beeches along the side of the road. The 'green walk' still is green, bordered by raspberry bushes as of yore. 'The Cottage' Drumdurno looks the same as it did 40 years ago, and the walk from Drumdurno looks the same to the Kirk o' Chapel, tho' the gate at the Kirkyard is locked now.

We went through Inveramsay and Pitcaple many times. Inveramsay looks the same as when W. Jamieson was there. The old Inn at Pitcaple has not been rebuilt, seems to be only one or two new houses. Once we came up to the station and crossed the bridge to go up the brae. Halliday's house is still in the corner, past England, some new cottages there. Then the old school where we had the fine singing practices with old Halliday. The Free Kirk and Manse still stand among the fine old trees, tho' I think there has been some building behind the church. On up the brae, the school looks the same.

The brae is still as steep and much rougher than it used to be; past 'Hillie's' where Janet Middleton lived. I also visited in the 'Port' Davie

Halliday and his wife who was Alice Watt of Netherton, Balquhain. Davie has his father's fine gentle manner and pleasant smile.

Through Chapel and on to 'Dorrie's' road. The road looked so bad, more like a mountain torrent with the water gone, we were almost afraid to walk up. However we walked as far as the farm and walked to the Linn Falls. From the farm looking towards the Braeside crofts, it was a stange country. Felt as if I'd been planted down in an unknown Hielan' glen, that lovely winding road, bare and treeless, where the sweet smelling birches used to be, with fine fir and larch trees shutting in the road like an arch; blaeberry bushes almost all gone. But nature covers her bare spots fast, I never saw such rich heather than along the foot of the hill. Here I gathered some to take back with me.

Charlie Middleton's old croft with Mary's Schoolie, Mary Duncan's hoosie and 'Aul Roost's croft were like pelicans in the wilderness, only what looked like holly bushes at a bank of rocks, up above the Schoolie remains. Walked on, taking the path to the left towards the falls, which had been used as a trail road, and was rough. Came on the 'housie' with half the roof fallen in; the falls still falling, much as they used to look. But what a change! All around looks the picture of destruction and desolation, not a tree left, hardly a bush, even the pretty evergreen shrubs hacked down wantonly. Oh dear, no beauty now! I could have wept, and maybe I did and was almost sorry I saw it. However no change can take away my former remembrances of this lovely spot. Though lovely no longer, I can still see it as it was long ago.

Old Mrs Spalding lives in the hoosie at the end of Whitewell road. She was so pleased to see us, very stout, but real quick and nimble.

And now for another adventure, August 7th, Betsy Drummond and I made up our minds that we would go to the 'Tap' by the old road from the Whitewell side, 'just for the sake o' auld lang syne.' It had thundered and rained all morning but cleared up at 2.30 p.m. So we set out for Bennachie. Drove up to Geordie Sim's (now Booth's), lovely sunshine but the clouds gathered behind Millstone Hill and the Tap, as black as ink, on came the thunder and lightning and rain in torrents. We sat in the car at the back of Geordie Sim's cart-shed for 1½ hours. We ate our lunch then, and still determined to go up, set off carrying our walking sticks and holding up umbrellas, (we had the camera also) up the road that leads to the 'Braid Peel' by the Millstone Hill to the Heather Brig.

A little above Jean Clark's on the left, there is a fine young plantation of larch trees, that and a little scraggy wood near the back of Geordie Sim's house, are the *only* trees left. The old cart road is gone, even a horse couldn't walk now. Where the road turned sharp to the left at the end of the dyke, was like walking in a ditch of running water. The rain went off in a little and we saw the storm going to the north and east. We ploutered on, picking some nice heather as we went, to the 'Braid Peel,' mostly water now, little sand to be seen, our feet soaking wet at this early stage. On to the Heather Brig, the road almost grown over, hardly a foot-path. When we got here the sun came out, and the air was warm and so clean and fresh.

There were some dragon-flies darting around above the swampy 'Sproats' as of old, where we used to try and catch them. Then on up the path, now a mountain torrent, splashing and stumbling and stopping to rest a moment and look around. There was much more bell-heather here than when we were young, and it was lovely – could smell the honey. We struggled on and up, reaching the Tap at 6.30 p.m. The sun shone brightly and the Vale of the Garioch never looked more beautiful, so clear after the storm. Could see to the west, the Tap o' Noth, Buck o' Cabrach etc., also hills to the south.

The valley of the Don towards Alford, with the hills beyond, the river like a silver ribbon winding between oat and corn fields and the dark green fields of 'neeps,' was one of the most beautiful and peaceful scenes of our whole trip. Old Meldrum, Inverurie and Turriff were clearly to be seen. The thunderstorm lay all along the east and south-east, so didn't see the sea.

So much wood has been cut over the country that it took quite a while to locate what were once familiar places. Went on to the Bullet Crag and came down the face of the hill, past the little well, springing up as ever, no road but we waded on through the heather and water and went up past the old crofts; Jamie Gairn's and the Littlejohn's, grown over with broom twelve feet high. The holly and laurel bushes and the honeysuckle are still there, also gooseberry bushes and gean trees. Geordie Esson's croft and Geordie there as of old. We didn't pass there however, but found a good road to the 'ford' at Geordie Sim's.

Standing near Littlejohn's we looked around and felt like strangers in a strange land – almost. The old landmarks with which we were so familiar, had disappeared and it seemed as if we'd never seen the countryside before. The old woods cut down, young ones grown up, roads grown over. The 'Kewlie' woods – no more, and the road like a mere track, we could hardly bring ourselves to believe that it was the same place. Jean Clark's house, Spalding's, James Roberston's, as if they'd never been, not a mark nor a stone left. The land has gone to Westerton and Whitewell, and Janet Robson's and McConnachie's to Broadsea. Back to the car and to Inverurie, soaked to the knees but happy we had made the Tap again.

Footnote.

Sarah Cormack Wilson, with her husband, Rev. Alexander Wilson, took a trip from their home in Canada, to Great Britain, in 1930. They hired a car in Newcastle-upon-Tyne and drove north, to spend more than a month around Inverurie and Bennachie.

This remarkable lady died in 1963, aged 93 years, so at the time of her trip she must have been 60 years of age.

Editor.

THE RAID ON BENNACHIE
By Professor Ian Carter

On 5th March 1859 the legal division of Bennachie took place; eight landlords whose estates marched with the hill were apportioned parts of the hill land, and other individuals were granted limited peat-cutting rights. The legal process under which this divison took place allowed forty years for aggrieved parties to challenge the division. Forty years and one day later a Conservative newspaper noted that:

'Yesterday the title of certain individuals to the erstwhile commonty (or common lands) of Bennachie was fortified by 40 years' uninterrupted possession following on the division of the hill by the Supreme Court of Scotland. There is thus an end to all ideas of upsetting the judgement of the Court of Session; and the agitation for a reduction of the process of division – fitfully conducted by irresponsible parties – has come to an inglorious conclusion.'

Who were the parties? What was this agitation? The most significant attempt to challenge the division, given particular attention by the journalist just quoted, was the 'raid' on Bennachie on 23rd September 1889. This raid was organised from a most unlikely quarter; Aberdeen Trades Council, at that time a major centre of class-conscious socialist action. What was their interest in Bennachie?

To answer this question we have to consider what other groups lost when the lairds gained private possession of the hill. From a fine, and little-known, account of its days as a common we learn that:

'. . . anyone from far or near could come and take from it what they wanted, without money and without price, and many things it could produce. An extensive business was done by George Sim and William Mare in the supply of granite stones of all shapes and sizes. The granite was of the best quality, and was in demand for corner stones and lintels, or wherever strength and durability were required. There was a quarry on the east side of the hill from which stones used to be sent to England, and it got the name of the 'English Quarry.' A good deal of heather was taken every year from the hill for thatch, for which purpose it was very suitable, and lasted long, and it also supplied great quantities of peat and sods for the fire. So it may be said the hill kept the neighbourhood in comfort through the winter.'

This commentator, sympathetic to the use of the hill before 1859, was too tactful to mention that some of the comfort derived from Bennachie was internal. Others, taking the laird's part, were not; the common pastured large numbers of sheep, cattle and goats, and 'amateur sportsmen, who scorned the name of poacher, took care that (game) numbers should be kept steadily at vanishing point.'

All these uses had to end with the division. The lairds had three main purposes in pursuing an end to the commonty. The first, and now the most celebrated, was to control the Colony; the squatter settlement on the boundary between Oyne and Chapel of Garioch that was living proof that one could escape lairdly control and still farm on a small scale. The second purpose was to control access to the important, but rapidly diminishing, peat reserves on the ridge below Mither Tap. The third purpose was to cash in on the game potential of Bennachie. Thus the division of the hill was followed rapidly by its letting to shooting tenants. This meant not only that game watchers tried to prevent poaching, but that they tried to prevent local people from disturbing the birds by venturing on the hill to cut peat, quarry stone or pasture animals. From being an open resource for the neighbouring population Bennachie became a prominent symbol of the exercise of private property rights. Its symbolism was enhanced in 1878, when several squatters (rent-paying tenants since 1859) were evicted from the Colony. People who persisted in trying to exercise former customary rights, by cutting peat for instance, were served with legal interdicts prohibiting them from trespassing on private land. It must be said that this did not stop them all, though game watchers allegedly then resorted to more direct methods of persuasion by cutting drying peats to pieces and by beating up recalcitrant individuals.

This provides the background to the Trades Council's interest in Bennachie. At a meeting of the council's Executive Committee on 30th January 1889, the secretary reported:

'. . . having got a letter from a resident near Bennachie, in regard to the public right to that Commonty. After hearing the letter the Committee instructed the Secretary to communicate with the writer and inform him that they were of opinion that a test case should be made. That is to say an individual or individuals should go to the hill and take what they want, and let the lairds pursue.'

This decision was not endorsed unanimously by the full Trades Council; the Blacksmiths' Society objected that 'it would tend rather to discredit the Council than benefit the Community.' But the council ploughed ahead. Letters were exchanged with the Scottish Rights of Way and Recreative Society. Initial attempts were made to clarify the legal status of the 1859 division. Plans were mooted for a 'demonstration,' mass (and, illegal) march up Bennachie. The first date suggested for this march was 12th August – significant date – but eventually 23rd September was pre-ferred, since this was the Aberdeen holiday and working men from the city could join the throng.

The day dawned bright and showery. Special trains left the Joint Station for destinations all over the north east. The Trades Council having not been able to negotiate a special cheap price for the railway journey to Pitcaple, they took the regular 10.30 train. Once there, they were met by a disappointingly small group of local people: late September might have meant the autumn holiday in Aberdeen, but around Bennachie it meant the corn hairst, and everyone was at work in the fields. The only local group present in strength was the Kemnay granite quarriers, whose determination to join the raid had led to the Paradise quarry being closed for the day.

The raiders moved off, led by two pipers playing 'Whaur Gadie Rins.' They expected to be challenged by game keepers, and many carried stout walking sticks; purely for defence, of course. As they passed the entrance to Pittodrie House they saw that somebody had scratched the word 'interdict' in the drive's gravel. Eventually they reached the Mither Tap, unchallenged, and the four to five hundred raiders held a protest meeting. Speeches were made, and were heckled by a small section of the crowd. Two resolutions were proposed and passed. The first asserted:

That this meeting of the inhabitants in the District of Bennachie, and others interested in the preservation of Commonty rights, believing that the rights of the Public in the Hill of Bennachie have been wrongfully taken possession of by certain of the surrounding Proprietors hereby appoint a representative Committee with power to add to their number, and to take such steps they might deem necessary to establish the rights of the Public to the said commonty of Bennachie.'

The second motion advised voters to elect candidates to the county council that would look after their rights; the Trades Council was putting up socialist candidates in Aberdeen local elections by the 1880's, one of the first bodies in Britain so to do.

These resolutions passed, the raiders left the hill, and most returned to Aberdeen. The Trades Council did not rest content with the demonstration, however. A subscription list was opened to pay legal costs 'to test the Right to Bennachie.' The matter dragged on until June 1890, when the council received definitive legal opinion:

'. . . that Bennachie, even if it had at one time formed part of a Royal forest, was granted to the Earl of Mar, and possessed by him, and sub-feued by him to the predecessors of the proprietors amongst whom the common rights were afterwards divided. Had it been otherwise doubtless the advisers of the Crown would have interfered when the process of division took place to assert any right that existed beyond those of the proprietors who were parties to the action of division. Even had there been any rights not appropriated to private individuals, these would not have been left as a right to be exercised indiscriminately by members of the general public, but would have been taken charge of by the Commissioners of Her Majesty's Woods and Forests and Land Revenue, by whom such rights . . . are now exercised for the public interest.'

This opinion devastated the Trades Council's hopes for challenging the 1859 division. The action committee quietly dispersed, and the council turned its attention to other matters.

What are we to make of this agitation? The first thing to say is that it is odd that anybody should have bothered to challenge the legal status of the 1859 division, since the position was quite unequivocal. Long before, in 1794, James Anderson had written in his *General View of the Agriculture of the County of Aberdeen* that 'Of *commons,* in the strict sense of the word, I know of none in the county. Indeed, they are scarcely known in any part of Scotland . . . ; for however poor the soil may be, it always can be claimed by an appropriated owner: and though the line of march between different proprietors in extensive heaths, may not be very distinct, or strictly attended to, yet it is in general in the power of the proprietors themselves to settle that line of marches when they incline, without the interposition of Parliament.' That was still the position in 1859; the only reason why the division of Bennachie took such an unconscionably long time to accomplish was that the lairds concerned could not agree among themselves over who should get what: peat rights proved to be the most contentious point. The only ground for challenging the division would be for a laird to claim that his rights in the hill had not been acknowledged. Only one laird did so in the forty years allowed for objections: inevitably, it was the cantankerous Burnett of Kemnay who did so, but nobody took any notice of anything that he did or said on any subject.

An accurate understanding of the legal position underpins Conservative comments on the division, and on the Trades Council's raid. The Tory *Aberdeen Journal's* leader on the raid noted that 'seeing that they had no really agrarian grievance to ventilate they must needs formulate an imaginary one.' Another paper of like political persuasion extended the notion of private property in an interesting way, using it to criticise the Colony squatters:

> '. . . worst of all for the general welfare, certain individuals appropriated bits of the commonty – 'improved it, and even built houses, little enough but comfortable for the times. They appropriated for themselves what was locally regarded as the property of the public.'

This comment is two edged. On the one hand, it is clear that the colonists did believe that they had some kind of private ownership of their holdings: at the protest meeting in September 1889 an evicted squatter/tenant, Hugh Middleton, claimed that 'He reclaimed land, and he had built a house to himself, and so long as the mass of the people did not come and interfere with him he considered it was his own.' Against this, the Tory journalist quoted above notes the widespread public belief that the commonty was public property. It was this belief that Bennachie had been, and could once more be, a 'Free Forest' that led many people to ignore the simple legal position.

This was the view of the radical Liberals, and of those Trades Council members who were making the journey from radicalism to socialism. It is well summarised by the speech of the Trades Council's President, William Livingston, in the shadow of Mither Tap: after connecting the raid to the Covenanters' fight for religious freedom and the continuing struggle for political freedom he claimed that:

> 'They had persons around them who had suffered from the present state of things, and one old woman had told him that she had lived twenty years in bondage at the foot of the hill. Now, they knew that there was a free Crown forest, and they had taken legal advice on the matter, and had learned that, according to a law passed in 1769 or thereabouts, the landlords were empowered to enclose and divide the rest of the lands or commonties. Of course, they would see that this was a law made for the landlords, and one which must at once be abrogated. In the resolution which was to be submitted to them, it was stated that the commonty had been wrongfully taken from the people. They said that guardedly, but he could tell them that if that was a free crown forest they could redeem it with very little trouble or expense to the people.'

We have seen that legal opinion that the Crown had no rights on Bennachie dashed these hopes. But what of Livingston's ambition of abrogating the legislation that allowed Scottish Lairds to divide commons so easily? It was never undertaken, of course; but even floating the idea shows the basis for opposition to the 1859 division. Legal forms might have been observed, but the division was immoral. Quite how it was immoral depended on how far down the road from radicalism to socialism one had travelled. For those close to the radical land agitation which had narrowly failed to have the rights of small farmers and crofters protected in 1886 one looked backwards for moral justification, to some lost 'Merrie Scotland' before the naked pursuit of self-interest divided class from class; and set landlords dividing commons, and clearing small tenants from their land, in the interest of maximising the rent-roll. Those closer to socialism, by contrast, saw lairds' venality to lie not in the removal of individual rights from individual small farmers, but in the private appropriation of land which should have been held for the public good.

Thus the Trades Council's raid on Bennachie lays bare a tension that runs right through late nineteenth century agitation and discussion of 'the land question'; a tension between individual rights and communal rights. It lays bare a scond tension, too. This one is crucial for anybody seeking to understand the late nineteenth century Liberal Party. In 1886 the party had split on the rock of Gladstone's proposals for Irish Home Rule. The Gladstonian rump was the land radicals; one speaker at the meeting below Mither Tap proposed that the Irish rent strike tactic be applied to the lairds who now owned Bennachie. The other wing of the Liberal Party, the Liberal Unionists, opposed land radicalism. The large scale north-east land agitation between 1881 and 1886 had been orchestrated from the editor's chair of the *Aberdeen Free Press* by the Gladstonian William Alexander, the author of *Johnny Gibb of Gushetneuk*. When the party split he was forced out of that chair, and replaced by his Unionist brother, Henry Alexander. William was demoted to edit the *Aberdeen Evening Gazette*; thin gruel indeed after the *Free Press*, which was the most important Liberal paper north of the Forth. The Trades Council's raid shows us the result of this split, in the reporting of the events in the two papers. The *Free Press* gave a long account of the excursion to Bennachie, but written in a very hostile tone; more hostile, indeed, than that of the report in the Tory *Aberdeen Journal*. The *Free Press's* leader is even more striking, being written in a jovially insulting style:

'The leaders of that omniscient and energetic body the Aberdeen Trades Council, on the conclusion of their Bennachie enterprise on Monday, must have felt, it is feared, very much in the condition of the Three Jolly Huntsmen when, after all their hunting and hollaing, they found they had 'naught to bring away'.'

Compare that with the *Evening Gazette's* coverage. William Alexander had provided the Trades Council leaders with an accurate potted history of the process of dividing the hill. In his leader reflecting on the raid he recognised its tragi-comic elements, and went on to draw the moral.

'The holiday demonstration of Monday in defence of the public rights in Bennachie, carried out under the guidance of the Aberdeen Trades

Council, may be regarded either as a comparative failure, or as a considerable success, according to the view taken as to the fitting course of procedure, and the end to be ultimately aimed at. As an initial step towards restoration to the public of the four thousand and odd acres of commonty 'appropriated' by the eight neighbouring proprietors . . . (the lawyers and law courts aiding them) – some thirty years ago, the rather incompact gathering that assembled near the Mither Tap and passed a couple of resolutions, will not, we fear, count for a great deal. An accomplished writer on Scots law, the late Mr Cosmo Innes, in speaking of the many thousands of acres of commonty taken from the peasantry of Scotland in former days, lays the blame largely on the legal fraternity, who lent themselves to the service of grasping proprietors, while 'the poor had no lawyers.' Bennachie was practically a case in point.'

So it was. Resting their actions on the spurious assumption that 'land which belonged to everybody was of no use to anybody' the eight lairds took private control of what, immemorably, had been a valuable resource for people in the parishes surrounding Bennachie. The division of the hill, and later extrusion of squatters/tenants from the Colony, was resented by these people. As the final legal acts in the division were dragging their way through the Court of Session in Edinburgh somebody – quite who was never established – lit a heath fire near the Colony. It was dry spring weather, and the heather was like tinder. The fire grew rapidly; driven by the wind it raced up to the Mither Tap, and swept around the hill towards Pittodrie House and its woods. The fire was contained short of Pittodrie's policies, to less than universal rejoicing. The next market day in Inverurie saw a petition drawn up to abort the division of Bennachie: in vain, of course, since no popular petition could prevent the completion of the tidy division procedure devised by a landlord-dominated Scots parliament in 1695.

Division did not mean the end of resentment. Think of the name attached to the marker below Mither Tap where three laird's allocated lands met: the Thieves' Stone. Think of the Trades Council's raid. Read the continuing hatred of the lairds' appropriation of the hill that surfaces in Helen Beaton's book *At the Back of Bennachie,* published in 1923. It is all encapsulated in the last two lines of the anonymous elegy for the commonty:

> 'The lairds aroon' hae ta'en ye noo,
> Ye're nae oor Bennachie.'

William Alexander claimed in 1889 that if the division of the hill had been attempted in that year, rather than thirty years earlier, then it would not have succeeded. One doubts whether that is true. What cannot be doubted, however, is that the 1859 division made Bennachie the most celebrated lost commonty in the north east, and possibly the most celebrated in Scotland. It is the sense of loss, and resentment at private lairds profiting from communal loss, that underpins the reverence still felt by many north east country folk for the hill. Whenever I join the summer Sunday throng on the path from Pittodrie to the Mither Tap I do not look out for the women teetering upwards on ludicrously inappropriate high-heeled shoes. Nor do I look out for the children in track suits and trainers.

I search for the old men that one sees in flat caps, three-piece blue Sunday suits, and highly polished black boots. They are always to be found, and I have always felt that they regard the climb not as a pleasant afternoon jaunt but as a religious observance; keeping faith with those who held and then lost a vision of a different way of living in rural Aberdeenshire. It is these old men who understand the true social meaning of Bennachie.

THE COLONY

By James T. Kelman

There wis a time fan Bennachie,
An' ither sic-like hills,
Provided fowk wi' their grazin' free
An' water for their mulls.
As weel's a this, some quarried steen
Tae gi'e them hoose an' steadin',
An' cuist their peats i' the moss abeen,
An' aneth they cut nowt's beddin'.

In echteen-one there cam a man
Wi' eident han's an strang.
He biggit a hoose faur the Clachie ran,
An' thocht he'd deen nae wrang.
He wis the first tae gyang there
An' squat on Bennachie,
An' rive in grun' that hid lang lain bare,
Tae eke oot his meagre fee.

His dother mairriet a dyker chiel
Fa bore the name John Esson,
But 'twis aye the hill baith lo'ed sae weel
They hankert for a place on.
In God's gweed time they wan'ert back
Tae be wi' their aul' man,
An' John set tee wi' speed an' knack
Tae clear an' brak' in lan'.

A hoose he biggit wi' steen an' clay,
Weel thackit wi' divots and hedder,
An' afore verra lang he wis prood tae say
'We've gane up a fyou rungs o' the ledder!'
Syne ither faim'lies thocht that they
Wad stake their claims for grun',
An' seen were scrapin' a livin' fae
Crafts that were gey hard won.

There wis Littlejohn, the thacker man
An' Lindsay, the herrin' cadger,
Christies an' Findlaters – a' wi' lan',
An' the Beverleys tee, I waajer.
In the lang mirk nichts o' winter, I wat
Fan they'd little ither tae dee,
The men-fowk brcwed a starn o' maut
An' distilled some barley bree.

Nae customs duty did they pey,
Sae, nae doot they'd been vaunty
Fan sattl'd doon at the ein o' a day
For a news wi' freens fu' canty.
Some were a law untae themsel's
Wi' mair things gin the fusky,
An' Oyne an' Chapel fowk wid tell's
That tae own them wid be risky.

The Colony – as it wis ca'd,
Wis noo coveted b' the lairds,
Fa sa' hoo they could streetch their ward
B' mair gin a fyou squar' yairds.
The Coort o' Session they implored,
The Commonty tae divide,
An' in nae time ava the colonists heard
That b' leases they wid be tied.

A rent they'd tae pey tae Fetternear.
Nae langer were they squatters,
But 'tenants-at-will' an' livin' in fear,
An' some were peer, deen craiturs.
It fairly nettled 'em tae see
Their industry ignored,
For the mair they'd tyaved, the mair they'd tae gie
Tae an unscrupulous landlord.

Nae compensation did they get
For a' their brave endeavours.
Some were forced tae pack an' flit,
Nor gat they ony favours.
Three were evictit b' the Sherra
For haudin' back the rent;
An' seen their couthy biggins were a'
Riven doon wi' contempt.

In coorse o' time an' wi' some regret
The lave forhooie't the hill,
Barrin' John Esson, fa b' single let
Took ower a' the grun' 'imsel'.
Noo this John Esson was the second o' that name
Tae hae wrastl't wi' the breem an' hedder.
Syae 'is sin, George, took ower the aul' hame,
A dyker, like his fader.

An emigrant tae the States oor George hid been,
But his sojourn there wis short;
His health broke doon an' sae he wis keen
Tae be hame an' hae beasts tae sort.
For forty-echt 'ear he dyket a' roon,
An' high wis the standard he set:
A solitary chiel fa, since he'd been a loon,
Took tae workin' fae early tae late.

O did the craft tae him belang,
Or did he belang tae it?
Ae thing is certain – Far ivver ye gyang,
His marra ye'll nivver meet.
The breem took ower fan George passed awa'
An' the craft's noo plantit wi' trees.
A' that remains is but an anterin wa'
O' the hame that for lang wis his.

Nae gran' memorial will ye see
Tae oor doughty pioneers.
But is that true? – look ower the sea
Tae lands, far for mony 'ears,
The progeny o' the Colonists
Hae made their mark, I swear;
For ye'll find them in the honours lists –
A memorial indeed – that's clear.

THE GARIOCH MEDICAL ASSOCIATION

By Dr Douglas L. Stewart

Two years ago this Association was revived after being in abeyance since the '14-'18 War; it met sporadically in 1923 and 1924 and was finally disbanded in 1951. The Association had been founded in 1854 and I have had access to the Association's minutes from that date; I am sure you will be interested in some of its history and individuals. We have a photograph of the original letter requesting the attendance of prospective members. The provisional secretary, Dr Geo. Mackie, of Insch, was confirmed as

SIR,

A few Medical Gentlemen in the district of Garioch, thinking it very desirable that the Members of the Profession in that, and surrounding districts, should have occasional Meetings for the purpose of conversing on Professional Matters, and fostering friendly feeling, have formed themselves into a PROVISIONAL COMMITTEE for the attainment of this object. And believing that you would co-operate, I have been directed to request you to meet them at PITCAPLE INN, on TUESDAY, 11th April, at Noon, to assist in giving effect to their proposal.

I am,

SIR,

Your obedient Servant,

Geo. Mackie,

Provisional Secretary.

Insch, Old Rayne,

28th MARCH, 1854.

P.S.—You will be good enough to meet the other Members of Committee half an hour before noon.

secretary and remained so for thirty-two years, and sixteen members attended the first meeting. Dr Thomson, Inverury, was the first president and is referred to as the 'Father' of the society. In the minutes of the first meeting we read 'It was the unanimous opinion of the meeting that such an Association will do much to promote the Honor, the Usefulness and the Respectability of the profession in these districts by promoting friendly intercourse and free communication among the members and by establishing among them the harmony and good feeling which ought to characterise a liberal profession. The next meeting will be held at Cooper's Inn, Pitmachie, and the secretary was instructed to call it accordingly by advertisement in the Aberdeen Journal and Herald Newspapers.' (The spelling and capitals are as in the minutes).

Inverury became Inverurie in 1866, Old Rayne became Rain in 1890, then quickly became Old Rain and eventually Old Rayne again.

You will notice the postal address of Dr Mackie in the original letter was Insch, Old Rayne, the reason being that Old Rayne was on the turnpike road from Aberdeen to Huntly and mail was distributed from Old Rayne by packhorse or by postmen on foot to Insch, Oyne, Leslie, Clatt and Kennethmont.

What was going on elsewhere about this time? The Disruption had taken place in 1843; chloroform had been first used as an anaesthetic in 1847. There was in the Garioch a flourishing Farmers' Club which had started in 1808 and it is significant that I read that in 1858 among the committee of the Farmers' Club were Dr Mackie, Insch, and Dr Thomson, Inverury. Among the judges and prizewinners of that year were names like Sylvester Campbell, Kinellar, John Maitland, Ballhagardy, Peter Bruce, Myreton, and James Stephen, Conglass. Dr Thomson is reported to have been for many years one of the Club's most active members and became convener of the business committee.

The canal from Waterloo Quay to Port Elphinstone closed in 1853 after performing a very useful function to the Garioch, providing transport for coal, lime and guano, so essential for increasing the productivity of the land. The coaches that ran from Aberdeen to Huntly were still quite primitive and at one time known as 'The Scorgie'; this was a van for four passengers, doing the journey twice a week. Mr Scorgie was the driver and, if there were no passengers, he was inclined to go inside the van and allow the pony to carry on itself from Toll-bar to Toll-bar where it stopped for 'refreshment' for the driver and payment of the toll. Let's hope the poor pony got some refreshment too.

In 1852, Lady Elphinstone of Westhall had cut the first sod, near Oyne, to start officially the building of the railway – first of all from Inverurie to Huntly and then, with the closing of the canal, from Inverurie to Kittybrewster, the latter part making use of the track of the canal so that in September '54 the Great North of Scotland Railway opened to public traffic from Kittybrewster to Huntly.

In 1840 the Penny Post had been introduced, and Queen Victoria married Prince Albert. In 1854 the Crimean War began, in 1857 the Indian Mutiny. In 1865 Lister introduced 'Antiseptic' surgery and in the same year Tolls were abolished in Aberdeenshire. In 1872 School Boards were introduced and attendance at school became compulsory.

Item XI of the Constitution and Rules of the Association reads: 'That the object of the Association being to advance the scientific knowledge and practice of the profession in the district, Members are expected to volunteer contributions of the nature of cases, queries or essays of which they will require to give early intimation to the Secretary, and in no case less than fourteen days prior to the date of the meeting at which such business is to be brought forward.'

At the meeting in November '54, the secretary read a paper from Dr Keith, Aberdeen, on an operation of the excision of the knee joint performed by him in the Royal Infirmary on 17th May '54, which was heard with great interest. The meeting discussed the case and, considering the very unfavourable character of the subject operated upon, conveyed to Dr Keith their warmest thanks for the paper and their admiration of the treatment which had led to the successful issue. (The case was more fully reported by Dr Keith himself at a subsequent meeting and the patient had had severe tuberculosis of his knee joint with a large number of sinuses discharging copious pus. The femur was sawn through above the knee and the tibia below the knee and eventually the two bones joined together in firm union, allowing him to walk and eventually return to work).

Dr Abel, Inverury, read a paper in 1855 on Common Continued Fever, dividing it into two forms – Typhus and Typhoid and contrasting these. Also by Dr Abel in 1866, a paper on gout and rheumatism; discussion on the merits of Citrate of Potash, which had been found of great benefit. Little faith was expressed by Dr Abel in the curative powers of colchicine in rheumatism, but others differed, saying that larger doses would cut short the attack. Bleeding was advocated by some, but Dr Abel disagreed.

In 1855, Dr Keith remarked on the prevalence of influenza in Aberdeen and mentioned the suddenness of the attack, in some instances imitating an epileptic seizure. Dr Traill (of Monymusk) had seen numerous cases of it in his locality and stated that he had found leeches applied about and within the nose gave very great relief to the suffusion of eyes and pain in the frontal region so much complained of. To quote an erstwhile young colleague of ours, the mind boggles!

A meeting was arranged in 1856 for a small deputation from the Association to meet Lord Haddo, the local MP, to discuss with him the Medical Bill introduced by a Mr Cowper in Parliament. The meeting was unanimous that the Bill as a whole was suited to the wants of the profession, but they objected to the method of nominating the members of the Council. This Medical Bill established a council which would keep a register of all who were practising medicine, surgery and midwifery; a list was made of organisations which would nominate a representative to sit on the Council. Colleges were named which would in future educate and examine candidates who wished to become physicians, surgeons or obstetricians. A great deal of argument and petitioning went into the educational programmes and at one time it was decided that – no medical person would be a member of the Council organising all this – it was to this that Lord Haddo readily agreed to object.

In 1857, Dr Keith read a paper on the case of James Scott, aged 19, a draper's apprentice who called at the house of Dr Tom Keith, MD, MRCSE, Senior Surgeon at the Royal Infirmary, Aberdeen, and Lecturer in Clinical Surgery. (This is the Keith of Keith's Surgical Medal which is still being awarded to the best student in Surgery).

The case interests me so much that I give it in considerable detail, often in the words of Dr Keith who subsequently published a pamphlet with pictures of the patient before and after, a copy of which is illustrated here.

'James Scott complained of the constant weeping from a small wound in the bridge of his nose, between his eyebrows. His face was disfigured by a deep cicatrix (a healed scar) involving not only the soft palate but the nasal bones; the shrivelled remains of his left eyeball lay deep in the orbit. The face and forehead were dotted, under the skin, with grains of gunpowder. Inserting a silver probe at the slit, it came into instant contact with metal and the following particulars were stated in explanation.

'While shooting on the morning of 19th February 1857, on the seacliff near Aberdeen, his fowling piece burst; he stood stunned for a minute and then fell on the ground quite insensible, and so continued for half-an-hour. When consciousness returned, he found himself in a farm and within half-an-hour was seen by a surgeon. He had bled very freely all this time from a large deep wound in his face, between his eyebrows, extending from below the R eye across the bridge of the nose and into his L orbit, lacerating the lower eyelid and utterly destroying the L eyeball. The bones of the face proper seemed to have been so far separated from the frontal bone that the patient is positive the surgeon applied one hand under his chin, and the other on the crown of his head, and pressed them forcibly together.

'Be that as it may, the bleeding was staunched and the torn integuments(covers) brought together by stitches over a chasm said to have been large enough to let one see down into the top of his pharynx. No suspicion was awakened that any foreign body could be there lodged. The case progressed most favourably; the wound filled up by granulation and cicatrised except the little slit between his eyebrows. After confinement to bed for three weeks he began to get up; at the end of six weeks to go out of doors, and in the end of April he resumed his service at the desk.

'He had occasional headache, especially when he awoke in the morning, but he slept well at night and felt well through the day and never for a moment suspected the presence of any foreign body in his head. It was the constant weeping from the little slit that induced him to apply to Dr Keith to get rid of that annoyance – four months snd six days after the accident.

'On 25th June, having seated Scott firmly in a chair with his head steadied against the breast of the assistant, Dr Keith forcibly separated the nasal bones, so as to enable him to grasp the tip-end of the screw-plate of a fowling-piece breeching, and after splitting the nasal bones widely from each other, and fracturing the nasal process of the L maxillary bone, he was able by a strong twist and a steady downward

Before the Operation.

After the Operation.

pull (using both hands) to bring away the whole breech of a fowling-piece weighing two ounces and five drachms and measuring two and a half inches in length. The bleeding was profuse on the removal of the breeching.

'The bones so rudely separated were re-adjusted; and the skin, rather freely torn by the exit of such a bulky body, was neatly closed by stitching. At the end of a fortnight he was able to step about again, and before the end of six weeks he returned to his duties, the wound entirely healed. His face is marked by a deep indentation at the bridge of the nose; and the left nostril is so far closed, the olfactory nerve destroyed, that he is robbed of the sense of smell. The right nostril is however patent, and on that side the function of the nerve is entire. The shrivelled remains of the eyeball lie in the bottom of the orbit, retaining some prominence in the centre. This, with the eyelids very perfectly restored, give him a control over movements of an artificial eye, since then inserted into the left socket, so that it is now difficult to discover that anything very serious had ever befallen him.'

Any comment would be superfluous.

In 1859, the meeting considered the question of public vaccination against Smallpox and of certificates of the cause of death under the new Registration Act.

In 1860, only three members turned up at their winter meeting; the railway train arrangements were such as to prevent several members being present unless at the expense of much extra time and in the winter months the weather was so variable as to make long journeys across the country not very desirable, it was resolved to propose that in future the meetings of the Association be restricted to two – one of which to be devoted to medical papers and cases exclusively and the other to be devoted to the election of office-bearers, examination of the accounts and the Annual Dinner.

Dr George of Keith read a paper in 1861 on tobacco as a medical agent, giving notes of cases of Ileus, Neuralgia, small and incised wounds in which he had found it very efficiently curative and from his experience, urged its claims to more extensive trial. The members generally seemed to think it a most unmanageable remedy – its effects too seldom bearing a uniform ratio to the dose exhibited.

A Table of Fees was recommended in May '63 to the Association by their Committee as reasonable and leviable under an Act of Parliament.

Single or Express Visit	Within a mile of Practitioner's residence 2/6 to 5/-	
Single or Express Visit	At a greater distance, add extra 1/- per mile. Subsequent attendance – according to its length and the distance, and social position of patient.	
Night Visit	A double fee.	
Midwifery	Medium fee with extra fee in difficult cases. Attendance in Protracted Recovery at Visit Rate.	£1/1/-

These fees to be paid Half-yearly at Whitsunday and Martinmas.

The following to be paid when the Service is rendered.

Advice	At Practitioner's residence	2/6
Surgery	Extraction of teeth, vaccination and the minor operations of surgery:	
	At Practitioner's residence	2/6
	At patient's residence, charged as single visit.	

Other operations according to importance.

Certificates	Ordinary certificate	5/-
	Lunacy certificate	£1/1/-

Insurance Reports (chargeable to Company):

On Policies of £300	£1/1/-
On Policies under £300	10/6.

I must observe that these charges differ very little from Dr Mitchell's charges when I joined him in 1946, and the wage for a day's work by a casual agricultural worker at that time in 1863 was 1/-.

In 1899, Dr Watt of Turriff was accused by the other two doctors in Turriff of a breach of etiquette. The other two had appointments with the Turriff Parochial Board and Dr Watt had applied for an appointment although neither of these had resigned. He appeared before the Association and explained that some of his patients had told him to apply, so in all innocence he had done so, but he said he was 'prepared to cry 'Peccavi'.' Thereafter the discussion dropped!

Dr S. Davidson of Wartle, the last surviving member of the founders died in 1895 and a very splendid tribute to him was recorded in the Minutes. He had practised in Wartle for nearly sixty years and was described as 'a man of strong frame, marked personality, out-spoken, but kindly; he was a favourite with all his medical brethren, highly respected for his professional skill and sagacity and beloved for his genial and courteous manner, his kindly and steady interest in the Association's prosperity and that of its members.'

In the accounts of the Association, for the first time in 1902 we read of four chauffeurs having been given dinner at 1/6 each.

In 1903, the Jubilee Meeting was held as usual in the Kintore Arms Hotel, Inverurie, which up till 1898 had been known as Annand's Hotel, but about that date the hotel was taken over by Mr A. D. Hay.

On 26th September, under the chairmanship of Dr Patrick Mitchell, Old Rain, forty-three members and guests were present. We are not told what the menu was, but the bill was:

43 Dinners at 5/-	£10.15.0
32 Bottles clicquot Champagne, Vintage '95	£12. 0.0
2 Professional Waiters	£1. 0.0
43 Coffees	10.0
2 Bottles Fine Old Whisky	10.0
9/10 Bottle Very Old Brandy	6.0
1 Bottle Marsala	4.0
2 Bottles Fine Old Sherry	8.0
4 Syphon Sodas	2.0
Total	£25.15.0

There were fourteen members from Aberdeen, three from Inverurie, Two
from Huntly and two from Insch, one each from Old Rain, Forgue, Banff,
Alford, Tullynessle, Kemnay, Tarves, Dunecht and Kinnairdy; at that time,
though not present, there were, or had been, members in Oyne, Rhynie,
Ellon, New Deer, Foveran, Bucksburn, Kintore, Auchterless, Balnoon,
Aberchirder, Turriff, Keith, Echt, Cluny, Monymusk, Balfluig and Wartle;
doctors had been quite thick on the ground in these days. Among the
official guests were Sir Victor Worsley, a Consultant Surgeon at University
College Hospital, London, who was shooting tenant at Pitcaple Castle, and
various members had their own guests. The final sentence of the Minutes of
that Meeting reads: 'The after-dinner proceedings were of the most jovial
and hearty description and the afternoon appeared too short to complete
the toast list with the usual songs interspersed; altogether the Jubilee
Meeting will be a memorable day in the history of the Garioch and
Northern Medical Association.' I should think so too; I wonder if the
secretary wrote the Minutes before the dinner. I am surprised that any of
them remembered much about the Jubilee. They must have been made of
stern stuff; still, if champagne were 7/6 a bottle and whisky 5/-, one could
afford to go into training for such an event.

Mention of Dr Patrick Mitchell makes it interesting to me that my boss
and mentor in practice in Insch, Dr George Mitchell, became a member of
the Assocition in 1910, his father Dr Patrick Mitchell in 1887, and his
father, Dr Alex. Mitchell in 1858.

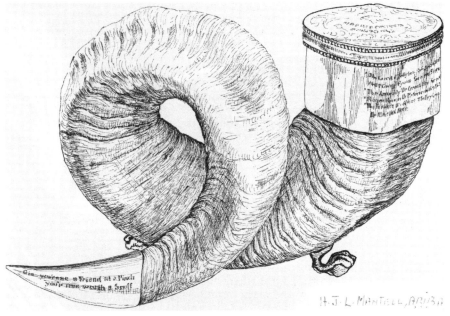

Ram's horn snuff mull

Our present treasurer may not derive any pleasure, but he may obtain some solace from knowing from the Minutes of 1905 that many members were heavily in arrears with their subscriptions, which were 5/- per year.

There is a minute in 1892 of the presentation of a snuff mull which seems to have been very important to the Association. 'It was presented by Professor Stephenson, Aberdeen, who, in presenting the silver-mounted ram's horn snuff mull to be placed on the table at the dinner of the Association with the view that the members may thereafter in passing it from hand to hand thereby express in the old Scottish style, the friendly feeling one to another which is the object of the Association to foster.' Snuff had meant more in these days than it does now, but the mull is such a splendid article, now in the safe keeping of the Aberdeen Medico-Chirurgical Society that I have had a drawing made of it by my son-in-law, Harry Mantell.

Meetings stopped in May '14 and the next was in 1922; eleven members are recorded as having lost their lives in the War. Two meetings were held in 1923 and two in 1924 and the final meeting, winding up the Association was held in July '51 when four members were present – Alexander Mitchell, Andrew Fowler, Gordon Bruce and Robert Richards. Many readers will remember these eminent medical men. 'In attendance' were Dr J. M. Gill, Inverurie, and Leslie Smith. The need for the Association had gone. The Medico-Chirurgical Society had taken its place and there were medico-political committees and the Local Medical Committee for the Counties of Aberdeen and Kincardine to whose Benevolent Fund the sum of £72.19.5 was handed over. I see the receipt was signed by Harry Ogston.

The Meetings of the Association seem to have been characterised by a multiplicity of toasts and the frequent singing of songs; members were identified with certain songs, similar to bothy ballads in a sort of medical way; in 1903 they published a booklet of their songs with the names of the doctors who sang them. Unfortunately, they did not publish the tunes and one cannot get the full value of the songs which embody the robust spirit and humour of the Garioch gatherings. Dr Mackie of Insch, for example, was linked in voice and personality with two songs, 'The Brave Old Oak' and 'The Ivy Green' and no meeting was complete without his singing them.

I will finish now with one of the songs, written in May 1910 by one W.S. The tune is obvious.

N'Rurie Where the Garioch Meets

O gin I were where the Garie meets
Where the Garie meets, where the Garie meets;
O gin I were the Garie meets
N'Rurie in rure.

In rure here, in urbe there
We're fain to meet, in mirth to share,
Mang a' our ploys nane can compare
Wi' meetings o' the Garie.
O gin I were . . . etc.

When fields in brere are bonnie green
An' when the corn's been a' led in,
We're trysted to foregather in
The fairy haughs of Garie.
So here we are where the Garie meets . . . etc.

We care na for the man o' ease
Wha stays at hame himself to please,
Grip ticht that hand that taks a sneeze
Frae the snuff-mull o' the Garie.
For here we are . . . etc.

When cronie lads agree to dine,
It's no the meat, it's no the wine,
It's just the tang o' auld lang syne
That draws us to the Garie.
So here we are . . . etc.

Then here's to Marischal and to King's
Round them, like ivy, mem'ry clings,
Fu' loud the Gaudeamus rings
At meetings o' the Garie.
Gaudeamus igitur, juvenes dum sumus,
Post jucundam juventutem, post molestam senectutem,
Nos habebit humus, nos habebit humus.

Frae daffin and fun, stay, ane an' a'
And doucely to the mind reca'
Ilk freen that's been, but noo's awa
Frae meetings o' the Garie.

(In silence drink)
To them that's awa'.

Tho' mute the voice, fond mem'ries hing
Round Garie sangs, each lilt will bring
Some auld freen' back, then let us sing
The auld sangs o' the Garie.
Then let us sing the Garie sangs
The Garie sangs, the Garie sangs;
Then let us sing the dear auld sangs
At meetings o' the Garie.

The photos by courtesy of the Library, King's College, Aberdeen,
and the drawing by H. J. L. Mantell, ARIBA.

THE COUNTRY MINISTER

By Dr D. G. Gordon

I think it was in *Punch*, the humorous London Magazine, that I first came
across the quotation –
> 'From quiet homes and first beginnings
> Out to the unconsidered ends
> There's nothing worth the wear of winning
> But laughter and the love of friends.'

Now that I am old and have more friends than money, real friends who not
only invite us to sit at their table to feed on the fat of the land, but come
for us and bring us safely home again. Over the years I could remember as
a country doctor among my friends many country ministers, some of them
Army Chaplains, most now sadly gathered to their fathers.

My first encounter with the cloth, was in the person of a young saint of a
minister, Arthur Shand, who came to the Rhynie Congregational Kirk in
the early years of King Edward the Seventh's reign. One summer afternoon
he arrived unexpectedly to visit us at our Tayloch home, when my
hospitable mother's supply of scones and bannocks had dwindled.
Dispatched to be out of the way, while my mother got the girdle on to the
peat fire, the kitchen deemie and I escorted the minister to the old garden
where the bees were kept. You can imagine what happened. Nellie's two-
year – old urchin charge managed to slip his hand out of hers and made
straight for the bee hive. Nellie screamed. I yelled. The minister rescued me,
removed a few stings from my face, and while Nellie up-ended me and took
down my pants, he picked one from my bottom. Naturally the story of how
he had run many yards with me from the pursuing bees, lost nothing in the
telling, and added to the congregation's delight in their grand young
minister. He was much loved, but there is an adage that the good die
young. A few years later, he developed acute appendicitis, turning into
peritonitis, known then as mortification of the bowels, which was fatal.
Although King Edward the Seventh had his appendix removed, operation in
the isolated country district was unknown at a time when travel and
communication were slow. After he had been ill for a day or two, his
fiancée in Aberdeen had been informed by letter and when she arrived at
Gartly station by train, the Rhynie carrier meeting the train asked if she
minded him taking a coffin on his little horse bus. Poignantly, it was only
when they got to Rhynie that she knew who the coffin was for.

Willie Barclay, the deaf Glasgow divinity professor who did so much to
cheer up the downcast in his television programmes, instanced Jimmy
Edwards as a maker of laughter, doing good like medicine in a Holiday
programme at Llandudno. But my boyhood memory of the country
ministers found little room for a joyful countenance. Coming home from
Kennethmont School where we were taught to touch our bonnets to the
laird and minister, we would meet the bachelor Rev. Dr Burnett, who got
his D.D. presumably for completing fifty years in one parish, salute him as

taught, and slink hurriedly past. There was no dearth of kirks or ministers then. The Disruption of 1843 was caused largely by the lairds' patronage of appointing the ministers from the relatives of themselves or their friends with a consequent deterioration of quality. The congregations wanted to choose their own minister. I imagine the lairds thought their right sacred, as they paid all the teinds or tithes which supported the Church of Scotland. Within a year or two there was a Free Kirk in almost every parish in Scotland, without a penny of teind to support them, an amazing sacrifice with the womenfolk doing without a new dress for years, and their Kirk collection plates brimming with silver. The Auld Kirk collection plates kept the brown hue of copper. I remember a leading elder of the Kennethmont Auld Kirk calling one Sunday morning at the back door of the local grocer, who was a staunch Free Kirker. His mission was to have a penny changed into two halfpennies, as he thought a penny too much for his collection. Naturally the grocer did not belittle this episode in telling of it to his customers for the next week. There were other denominations. The Congregationalists were active in Inverurie, Culsalmond, Insch, Duncanstone and Rhynie. Now all their Kirks are closed. Those of the lairds who were Episcopalians, known locally as the Piskies, not only paid their teinds, but built in Victorian times the beautiful chapels and manses still present to beautify our villages, but now sparsely attended, so that one minister or rector has to look after three or four of their congregations. Only slightly better is the Auld Kirk, the Church of Scotland, re-united with the Free Kirk in 1929, where now two of the parishes in our area have to be cared for by the one parson, or even three as in the case of Leslie, Premnay and Oyne, where five ministers preached every Sunday at the beginning of this century, when opposition between the different sects had a stimulating influence. Sometimes the Auld Kirk and Free Kirk ministers would cut one another dead in the street. An amusing instance of this was brought out by the Wartle doctor, Dr Sam Davidson, who practised there from 1835 to 1895, latterly with the help of his doctor son. His wife, who was an Episcopalian of county stock, had predeceased him and was buried at Folla Rule among her relations. When the old doctor was sinking, the family enquired where he would like to be buried. After a few minutes' thought, he gave a smile and replied 'Better bury me beside the wife, although when the last trump sounds and we all rise from our graves, it'll be an awful shock to the Episcopalians to find an Auld Kirker among them.'

One of the perks or perquisites which the ministers had was the glebe, often the best land in the parish, as was the case at Kennethmont where Dr Burnett had his own minister's man in pre-1914 days. I remember him well, a stocky chap, Willie Souter, with a small Highland cob and a cart scaled down for the size of the horse, a very neat job, in which he drove the peats from the manse peat bank, the only one remaining at that time in the Kirkhill Moss. Everybody else around had to dig turfs from the exhausted peat banks. He was also the beadle. Down at Blairdaff the minister was a very keen farmer and did all the work himself, and at funerals he wore a long black coat over his working clothes and great muddy tackety boots, as he appeared to be so anxious to get back to his farm work, that he had no time to change. There was an old saying that there was not one bad foot of land in Tarves and Tyrie parishes. So be it. Certainly the Tarves glebe was the richest of land and the Kirk Session in the 1950's got the local farmers to cultivate it without payment, and the kirk funds benefited substantially. I presume a rent was paid to the minister. I remember calling one day about 1965, I think, on the Chapel of Garioch minister, Dr Allan Main. He says 'Come and see this, doctor' and opened the door of the old stable, where I was shaken to find the two stalls in the stable brimful of barley. One of his farmer elders had lent him a tractor, and he had ploughed the glebe and sown and harvested the barley with a bare modicum of help. He is now a Divinity Professor at Aberdeen University.

Household expenses in the manses must have been helped by the produce of the glebe fields, and the walled gardens. Some ministers had private means like the Episcopal rector at St Mary's-on-the-Rock at Ellon, who at one time had eight of a domestic staff. At the opposite extreme was the Donside parson whose glebe was too poor to grow enough hay for his pony and he was grudging the expense of having to buy hay. About 1890 when the tandem bicycle became popular, he sold his pony and trap, and bought one of the new machines. His submissive wife, although inwardly boiling, pedalled away behind him on their parish visits. It was easy downhill, bearable on the level, but a hard grind uphill. Quite soon she discovered that she could rest her legs by taking her feet off the pedals, unbeknown to her husband, until one afternoon as the school was skalin', when the tandem came toiling up the school brae, one nickum shouted, 'Hey minister, the wife's nae cain.'

In the comings and goings of that peaceful age about a century ago, frequently the minister got stuck in his parish for many years, and tended to live a leisurely life. The old sermons were reputed to be kept in a barrel, and after a time could be resurrected and used again and sometimes again and again. One of my many cousins remembered hearing an old minister preaching in 1930, ending his sermon by assuring the congregation that they should all be proud and grateful that Mafeking had been relieved. Of course, interchange of pulpits saved a lot of brain work, no fresh sermon being required. Up in the Vale of Alford, there was a delightful short poem about the local parson who had taken his favourite sermon about the widow's cruse that never failed, all over the valley. Little scraps of it I remember.

> 'Up by Keig and Tullynessle,
> Twas aye the wifie and her vessel,
> Doon by Tough and up by Towie,
> Twas aye the wifie and her bowie,
> Through by Alford, up Strathdon
> Aye he drove the wifie on,
> Hame by Rhynie and Strathbogie,
> Cam the wifie and her cogie.'

Yes, there was leisure in the manse study. Some put it to good use. George Abel, who was born at Womblehill of Kintore, and who spent his days at the Free Kirk in Pitmedden of Udny, was a minor Doric Poet. His

'Wylins Fae my Wallet' being published in 1916. At another Free Kirk up at Lynturk by Muggarthaugh, Rev. James Bruce Duncan in the forty years in his charge up to his death in 1917, was the collaborator of the New Deer dominie Gavin Greig, in what is now recognised as the greatest collection of ballads in the world. Many volumes of prose, to-day rather dated, came from the pen of Dr James Stark, the Belmont Congregational parson in Aberdeen, who lived for a long period at 'The Braes of Bennachie' at the foot of My Lord's Throat, now the beautiful home of Tom Hutchison, the prominent Bailie who organised the Bennachie Ballad Competition in 1981.

Would you forgive me if I digress briefly to speak of Dr Stark's brother? Away back in King Edward's reign, this brother lived alone on a croft in Leslie and it was reported that his minister brother made him an allowance to stay on the croft, so small that it could provide him a living only as his weakness was a drooth which prevented him from passing the door of any hostelry. Now like some country folk, he was a grand rhymer. At Leith Hall in Kennethmont, lived the laird, the benevolent Charles Leith-Hay, whose estates spread down through Clatt, Leslie and Premnay, to parts of Insch. Dinners for the tenantry and presentation to the laird, when he brought home his lovely Irish bride, and other occasions were celebrated in rhyme by the crofter. Now Stark was a wit, a rhymer who could sum up in a few couplets the foibles of the local worthies. He was quite kind to my father, whose forebears had tenanted the farm of Tayloch for a couple of centuries and although not the largest farmer on the estate, he was a racy speaker, who had to make most of the speeches. Known as Big Bob Gordon or R.S. from his initials, he had three brothers farming closeby, all like himself over six feet in height. As a preacher he was greatly in demand by the ministers for a dozen miles around, Auld Kirk, Free Kirk and Congregational to give pulpit supply when they wanted a day off. He also ran a very popular non-denominational Sunday School. I remember him telling me he got no travelling expenses when preaching and the only reward he got was a cake baked by the Tullynessle minister's wife as he had an extra duty on that occasion as he had to dedicate the new extension to the kirkyard. On his demurring that he was unqualified, the minister replied that as an Alford District Councillor, he had been responsible for extending the kirkyard and he was just the man for the job.

The crofter's quatrain gives in a few words the 1908 picture:

> Then Big Bob o' the Tayloch clan,
> Stood up and waved his mighty haun,
> Richt gled am I so see this day
> God bless the bairnies, let us pray.

Mention of Tullynessle reminds me of the old story of the local minister who found by experience that if he visited early at the farms he was in time for the farm dinner at 11.30. One day the wife at Warrackstone at the top of the glen spies the minister away about a mile off toiling up the brae, and puts on a clean apron to greet him, thinking to herself this must be the third visit this summer. Seated at the table, he tries to count the great bevy of cats round the kitchen fire, saying 'Gracious, are all these cats yours?' 'Na, na,' she retorts, 'a' the hungry whaups in the countryside come here for their maet.'

Stern, unsmiling, even lugubrious were the faces in the pulpit in olden times. They have got more human as this century passes. We had a delightful young lad called Alistair Calder in the thirties at Ellon. He had trained at New College, Edinburgh, and used to tell of the shocking food. One day the soup was particularly bad. One of the wags among the students – and there were always plenty of them in my experience, especially in the divinity faculty-sent a sample of the soup to the city analyst. The report came back that they regretted their horse had diabetes.

He was very human. We took him shooting up to Broomfield. A hare got up. He emptied both barrels. I did the same. The hare kept running, but as it came past Davie Low the farmer, who was a top shot, it was too far out, and another two shots speeded it up the Hill of Ardgrain unharmed. At least not quite unharmed. It grew to a ripe old age at Broomfield, nicknamed Alistair, easily recognised from the missing tip of its left ear, the credit for which we gave to the minister.

We took our minister mackerel fishing at Collieston when the shoals came in July. We took him through the Larig Gru, the chauffeur I had inherited with the practice dropping us at Coylum Bridge, with instructions to pick us up at White Bridge on Deeside. When Borwick arrived at Linn of Dee, he mistook it for the White Bridge and stopped there and we had three extra weary miles to trudge. Alistair was exhausted and fell asleep in the car. He had been looking forward to seeing Balmoral, but he wakened up when we stopped at Tarland for a memorable feed of great quantities of beef and pickles. Yes, we made the townsman into a real country minister. When he trained a few years later in the Cairngorms as padre of the Glasgow Highlanders in the 52nd Mountain Division, he was ready for action in the Alps. The all-wise War Office sent them to the polders and mud flats of Walcheren instead. Asked what was his most exciting moment of his war, he said they were happily holed up one night out of the mud in a lovely barn among lovely straw. The guard woke them to say the Bosch was at the barn door. With their sten guns at the ready, the door was flung open and in marched a huge black and white cow, with gorged udder ready to be milked.

The finest country minister I ever knew was Jimmy Ross of Slains. He had been a trooper in the Scottish Horse in Mesopotamia in the First War. Born in Glenkindie, where his father was the local souter or cobbler, like his brother who became a doctor, he was the typical lad of pairts whose parents sacrificed their all to put him through college, the mother's laudable ambition that her son would 'wag his heid in a pulpit.' He had three charges in his life-time, Finzean, Slains and Glenbuchat. He was as much at home in the cottar hoose as the castle. Joseph Farquharson, the ageing artist painting the Finzean black-faced sheep in the snow-deep birch woods, found him a boon companion. He left Ross his dress kilt with green evening jacket. I used to borrow it before I could afford my own one. In his last charge at Glenbuchat he felt he was coming home to his own country and was welcomed by the men who were 'boys when he was a boy.' His chest had been giving him trouble in the cold clay of Slains and the North Sea gales howling ·in winter up the cliffs of Collieston and Cransdale. In 1946 after a ministry of twenty years in Slains, he returned to Strathdon, where he died at the Manse of Glenbuchat in 1950. He had come home. The simple granite stone in the kirkyard beside the ancient Glenbuchat Kirk tells of his three Aberdeenshire parishes.

Let me try to express the affection of the Slains folk for their minister. It was a small parish, of farm folk and fishers. Farming was at its most depressed, with oats at twelve shillings a quarter and the bankruptcies common. The farm workers in their cottar houses on £50 a year, with an earth closet at the foot of the garden, bare floors in the house apart from a scrap of linoleum or an old rug at the fireplace, slaved for ten hours a day with no half-day on Saturday. Six of the larger farms were occupied by a multiple absentee farmer, who used the farmhouses for his poor workers. The collection plate on Sundays suffered from the lack of six farming families. In Collieston the houses were occupied by the old fishers who had left in the 1890's to go to Torry for the trawling, and had returned to end their days in the old family homes, doing the line fishing and making the haddocks and whiting into the famous speldings. In the summer, holiday-makers were numerous, helping to fill the church on a Sunday. Lawrence of Arabia stayed in a fisher's cottage for six weeks in 1933. He described it as a hovel.

Slains was one of the last Aberdeenshire parishes to get a district nurse. There was therefore no district nurse at that time to look after a salmon fisher, whose long rubber boots leaked and the salt water continuously on the stockings produced dermatitis of the skin which became infected. It was one of the worst cases I ever saw. The whole of the legs up to the knees was one mass of suppuration, with dead infected skin scaling off to create massive ulceration.

For six months Jimmy Ross arrived every morning to dress the infected legs, until they gradually improved and finally healed. Presentations to ministers on their departure to another charge have always been commonplace. Something unique happened in 1934 when the Slains minister had completed seven years of service to the parish. The whole community, worried that jealous eyes from other parishes would be cast in their direction, combined in a spontaneous outburst of affection to make a grand presentation to Jimmy Ross to keep him with them. It was a great night, a packed house. Lord Caithness, Convener of the County presided. I remember it so well after half a century. I stuck in the middle of my speech.

Yes, he was a full man, a whole man, cheering the tinkers up on a wet day in their leaking tents, relieving the ploughman by holding the stilts of the plough for a round up and down the field, or taking his place as one of the best shots at the gun dog trials held by Lorna, Countess Howe, the great black labrador breeder, who came every autumn to Slains Lodge. Yes, he was a full man who followed His Master, who washed his disciples' feet.

Historically the position of the country minister has undergone enormous change. In the eighteenth century the minister and session were all powerful, punishing congregational lapses like non-attendance at the Kirk and sexual digressions with a heavy hand. Sitting in sackcloth on successive

Sabbaths did little to put any fervour into religious observance. The
nineteenth century, on the other hand, with the disruption of 1843 against
patronage, causing an amazing period of religious activity, was plagued by
the common defect of most virtues, in the shape of that outburst being
dissipated into too many sects. As we approach the end of the twentieth
century, when two terrible wars have impoverished and depopulated our
countryside, with empty kirks having their best congregations at weddings
and funerals, I feel the country ministers, now poor as church mice
compared with their predecessors, are honest men fighting religious apathy.
Let us give them our sympathy, and spare a double dose for their wives,
coping with the huge, cold Victorian manses without a Victorian domestic
staff.

They have humour. They need it. The other day a local minister told me
of a colleague and his wife calling in other days to visit a kindly hospitable
lady known as Clorty Kate. Fat and beaming and blowsy, she welcomed
them with 'Come awa in, sit down here in the kitchen and I'll get ye some
bacon and eggs.' When they had been served, the cat jumped on the
minister's lap and his wife exclaimed, 'Look John, the cat likes you,'
whereupon Kate, aiming a blow at the cat, cries 'Oh minister, I must've
gien ye the cat's plate.'

THE TAP O' BENNACHIE
By John Mearns

I find as I grow aulder
An' doon memory's lane I stap
That it's aye the happy memories
That come siftin' tae the tap.
An' the nicht, the 'Tap' I'm thinkin' o',
Wi' memories dear tae me,
Is the Aberdeenshire mountain
Ca'ed the Tap o' Bennachie.

It's mair than jist a mountain,
Atowerin' tae the sky,
It's the Guardian o' the Garioch,
An' that's the reason why
As a youngster, I wis longin'
For the day when I could see
The land o' my fore-fathers
Fae the tap o' Bennachie.

Then cam the day my wish cam true
When Dad said; 'Bairns, come here
Ye hinna hid a picnic not a holiday this year.
So the morn, if the weather's fine,
I'll tell ye what we'll dee,
We'll yoke the gig, an' picnic
On the Tap o' Bennachie.'

I hardly slept a wink that nicht,
Next mornin' it wis rain;
But, by the time the shalt wis yokit
The sun shone bright again.
So aff we set, five happier bairns
Ye couldna wish tae see,
A' itchin' tae set fit
Upon the Tap o' Bennachie.

At length we reached Pittodrie
Whaur the shalt wis loused an' fed,
Mum's picnic basket syne wis broached,
An' Grace was duly said.
Then, when hungry moos were satisfied
We a' set aff wi' glee
An' climbed the rocky roadie
Tae the Tap o' Bennachie.

We stood there in amazement,
As we viewed the country side,
Dad pointed oot the places
That he kent, baith far an' wide;
Tae the east we saw the ocean
An' ships upon the sea,
Lang syne they took their bearin's
Fae the Tap o' Bennachie.

When pointin' oot Harlaw,
He had a sorry tale tae tell,
How Highlanders and' Redcoats
Baith bravely focht an' fell;
The battle raged for near a week,
An' thousands had tae dee;
We could see the tower that marks the spot
Fae the Tap o' Bennachie.

Then a lovely picture faced us
That only Nature's hand can crane,
For the sun wis shinin' brightly
Ower the fields o' ripenin' grain.
'Twas the girnal o' the Garioch
Stretchin' far's the eye could see
We looked doon intae the hert o't
Fae the Tap o' Bennachie.

But we followed aye Dad's finger
Tae places that we knew,
Like Fyvie, roon by Turra
Wi' its famous Turra coo.
An' further roon by Huntly,
Where the Deveron flows sae free,
But we couldna see Drumdelgie
Fae the Tap o' Bennachie.

Baith Dunnideer an' Tap o'Noth
Were clearly tae be seen,
Aye, an' lots o' ither places
That lie scattered in atween.
Fae the Ury tae the Gadie
There wis sic a lot tae see,
We could hae bidden there for 'oors
Upon the Tap o' Bennachie.

But bide we could nae langer,
It wis time tae 'pack oor bag,'
Fan a muckle thunner clood
Cam glowerin' ower the Oxen Crag.
Wi' a lichtenin' flash for warnin'
There wis naething for't but flee,
For there's nae sic thing as shelter
On the Tap o' Bennachie.

So aff we set, the lot o' us
An' doon the hill we ran,
By luck we got some cover
When the heavy sho'er began.
But it pelted roon aboot us
Till t'was like the Linn o' Dee
That cam doon the rocky roadie
Fae the Tap o' Bennachie.

But the sun broke thro' the cloods again
As seen's the rain gaed aff.
We played tackie amang the heather
An' had mony a herty laugh.
Syne gaithered roon the basket
For some hame-made scones an' tea,
An' a slice o' clootie dumplin'
Like the Tap o' Bennachie.

But the shalt wis gettin' ristless,
So time for leavin' came,
By the time we'd crossed the Ury
We were thankfu' tae be hame.
We were tired an' fair forfochen
But as happy as could be
For we'd fair enjoyed oor picnic
Tae the Tap o' Bennachie.

Tho' half-wye thro' my seventies
I can see it a' again.
The shalt, the picnic basket,
The sunshine an' the rain.
It's a happy boyhood memory
That will live for aye wi' me
That day we went a picnic
Tae the Tap o' Bennachie.

BENNACHIE EXPEDITIONS

Compiled by Mike Davidson

'There is no mountain in Aberdeenshire – or indeed in the North of Scotland – better known, or more visited than Bennachie.'

These are the words you might expect to find in the introduction to a 1983 Guide to Bennachie, but they are in fact quoted from Alexander McConnochie's *Bennachie*, published in 1890.

Interest in the hill is obviously not new and I like to think that the first inhabitants of the area would have been infected with a desire to climb it, if only to escape for an hour or two from the pressures of life as Hunter-Gatherers.

In the year 84 A.D. the Caledonians were defeated at the Battle of Mons Graupius, by the Romans under the leadership of Agricola. Recent evidence from aerial photographs suggests that Bennachie may well be the site of the battle. In Tacitus' description of the battle no mention is made of a fortification on Mons Graupius and the fort on Bennachie may have been built following that defeat. The Maiden Causeway was probably built to facilitate the transport of materials during construction and afterwards as a quick route to the fort's safety.

This is largely speculation, but whatever the reason for the causeway's construction it provided an easy way to the top, and although the modern path follows a slightly different line, it remains the most popular route to the hill.

Before and during the time of the 'Colony,' tracks were built for the extraction of wood, peat and stone from the Royal or Free Forest of

Bennachie, by the local inhabitants. However, following the Division of the Commonty in 1859, this freedom of access was removed. Helen Beaton in her book, *At the Back o' Bennachie,* states that, 'Tourists who desired to ascend the hill were chased by keepers.' Thankfully, things have changed and any pedestrian is able to wander freely over the hill.

I doubt whether Bennachie has seen such a gathering on its slopes as on the day 30,000 Caledonians faced Agricola's army. However, in more recent times, there have been a number of well documented expeditions to the hill which are of some interest. The first record I can find of any excursionary interest in Bennachie is in an advertisement placed in the *Aberdeen Journal* on the 10th August 1808:

THE BENACHIE CLUB
Meets at the Mither-Tap, on Monday the 22nd inst.
Dinner at Pitmachie, at 4 o'clock.
James Philip, President.

Nothing is known about the Bennachie Club, except that some badges still exist and it was on these that the Bailies' badge was modelled.

If indeed access to the hill was restricted following the 'Division,' it was not long after that we find accounts of organised excursions by groups such as the Cairngorm Club and the Aberdeen Working Mens Natural History and Scientific Society. An article on the latter can be found elsewhere in this book.

In 1893 the Cairngorm Club's Autumn Excursion was to Bennachie. Good use was made in those pre-car days of the extensive rail network in the area, with convenient stations at Oyne, Pitcaple and Monymusk. In the account in the Club's Journal, the author tells us that, 'The original intention was to leave the train at Monymusk Station, drive through the grounds of Monymusk House to Paradise, and ford the Don.' This plan was thwarted by recent rains, making the ford impassable. The party alighted at Kemnay and, 'After nearly a two hours' drive, Dorlethen, a farm a mile S. by E. of Pittodrie House, was reached, and luncheon served. The ascent was thereafter commenced on foot, Mither Tap (1698) being first made for.'

After surveying the surrounding hills the party set off for Oxen Craig, the highest point.

'The distance between the peaks is barely 1¼ miles, and our bolder spirits attempted to cut right across the moor, but landed themselves in a peat bog, and only after a struggle overtook the others, who, plodding by the orthodox paths, had reached the Craig.'

The author then lists the hills which can be seen, including Garbit Tap, below which lived a local worthy, William Jamieson, 'the Heddie Craw o' Bennachie.' 'He was a social outcast, and, of more than local celebrity, acted the part of 'bogie man' to all the youngsters round about.'

'Bidding farewell to Oxen Craig, we descended the north slope to the scene of a 'waterspout' which, about two years ago, tore up a ravine for itself right down the side of the hill. It affords a capital opportunity of observing the extraordinary effects produced by water. It has rendered the peat road quite useless and beyond repair, and so made the direct route from Oyne station to the summit of the hill impassable in many places. The descent was made to the well-known 'Beeches,' whence we made our way to the Manse of Oyne, where, by the hospitality of Mrs Mearns, we were entertained to tea. It was a gay scene on the Manse lawn, although the members of the Club may have felt that their mud-stained mountaineering garb was barely in keeping with the appearance of the brilliant company that had met so kindly to make them welcome.'

The party left Oyne by train at 5.35 p.m. and arrived in Aberdeen shortly before 7 o'clock.

An interesting excursion to Bennachie is recorded in the diary of the late James Hampton Brown, Banker in Ellon.

'Sunday 5 Dec 1897 . . . On Saturday 13th Novr. Mr Fraser came out from Aberdeen he was anxious for a walk so about 4 o'clock in the afternoon we set out for Oldmeldrum which place after making two calls we reached at 9 o'cl. The night was fine and there was a good moon, we felt fresh, and it was predicted that there was to be a great display of shooting stars so at 10.45 p.m. we started for the summit of Benachie, the sky was clear save for a few fleecy clouds across the sky and we pushed on our journey, past Fingask, across the Urie beyond Pitcaple Station, through the hamlet of Pitcaple, and then underneath the line of Railway, past a farm which took us on to a hill road leading past Pitoddrie we past close past the House, till we got on the road to the top of the Hill, which after a time we left for a near cut and landed ourselves in a bog and there was nothing for it but to take right up the hill through the long heather till we reached the well near the summit where we sat down and took refreshment, and then make for the Mither Tap on which we found ourselves standing at 3 Oc. A.M. Not a shooting star did we see but in the solitude of the situation the stars above us shone in their places with a brilliancy which we never noticed before. We reached Oldmeldrum at 7 o'clock in the morning and went to bed and slept till between 12 and 1 o'clock.'

(Five years later, in 1902, Mr Brown, an enthusiastic mountaineer and member of the Cairngorm Club, was killed in an avalanche while descending the Wetterhorn in Switzerland).

The Cairngorm Club returned to Bennachie in September 1898, and this outing was described in the Journal by the Rev. Andrew Galloway of Oyne.

'The programme on that occasion was comprehensive, and did justice to the attractions of Bennachie: – Walk from Oyne Station; an inspection of the 'Waterspout,' Oxen Craig, Craig Shannoch, Mither Tap, Maiden Castle; dinner at the Home Farm of Pittodrie – thanks to facilities afforded by Mr Diack; and an inspection of the 'Maiden Stane O' Bennachie' en route to Pitcaple Station.'

Mr Galloway's article is well worth reading for his concise decription of the hill and its features of interest, including an account of the previously mentioned 'Waterspout.'

'In the early afternoon of 9th August 1891, a waterspout burst over the side of the hill a few hundred yards further up' (from Shannoch Well). 'For a time a great volume of water rushed down the peat road, washing out the gravel, and carrying immense quantities thereof and of stones down through the woods, and in the bed of the road to the levels below. Arrested at what is known as the Little Cut of '29, the waters, pent up to a great depth, at length burst, at right angles, through the east bank, tore down the hillside to the Gill Burn – the great torrent bearing with it trees and soil and boulders, and wearing out a wide gap in a rocky bed, in some places 40 feet wide and 30 feet deep. From markings on the trees at the side of the Gill Burn, the seething, roaring stream must have been eight to ten feet deep in some parts. The hopelessly ruined peat road, and the enormous quantity of sand, gravel, stones, and boulders lying everywhere in endless confusion, testify to the fearful force of the water, whose sound resembled rumbling thunder.'

Not only hill-walkers are attracted to the hill, but also occasionally climbers in the real sense of the word. In volume five of the Cairngorm Club Journal is found an account of two scrambles 'deserving of notice.'

'(I) the ascent by the long crack running up the central bastion to the top. This is difficult at the foot, and at the middle, where a traverse, not particularly easy, may be thought desirable owing to steep and slippery grass; (II) the ascent of the business side of the aiguille known as the Nether Maiden. Thence cross the path and gain the top by an interesting route up the N.E. end of the eastern division of the craig.'

New Years Day 1907 saw James G. Kyd and a friend ascending Bennachie from Oyne.

'We travelled from Aberdeen by the early morning train and managed to strap on our skis in Oyne station, and get through the village without any very great demonstration on the part of the inhabitants. The snow was in perfect condition until we got into the wood, but there it became somewhat heavy. We ascended Craig Shannoch, taking slightly longer than a fellow-clubman who was on foot, and struck over towards the Mither Tap.

'Once on the crest of the hill we flew downwards, soon reaching the woods of Pittodrie, then dodging in and out among the fir trees, kept on at an immense speed till we reached a farm about two miles from Pitcaple station. The good farmer was struck almost dumb at the speed with which we came down his sloping pasture; and on our enquiring how long we should take to reach Pitcaple we were informed that it took 'about half-an-oor tae walk, but ye'd gang in about twa meenuts on thae things!' However, he underestimated our time, as we found that the snow on the turnpike was not in very good condition, so our progress was slow. On reaching Pitcaple we kept on to Inveramsay, where we caught a suitable train home.'

On the 4th June 1904 . . . 'the Cairngorm Club, to the number of 30, bound on their climbing accoutrements and, instead of an 'alpenstock,' seized a cudgel and went forth to the Gariochland with the intent of again 'doing' Bennachie.

The author states that . . . 'the hill climber finds Bennachie a good beginning for the season's exploits, and might be taken as the first step of the training ground for the ascent of 3,000 feet which is the standard for membership of the Cairngorm Club.'

This recommendation is reinforced by a writer in 1903, who states that . . . 'Most of the members of the Club know Bennachie, or, if they don't, they ought to be heartily ashamed of themselves. In my opinion, no one should be admitted to membership who has not been on the top – in fact, on all the tops – of Bennachie.'

I might perhaps suggest, that this condition should apply to membership of the Bailies of Bennachie, but then, like the author of the last quotation, 'I admit I have a peculiar liking for Bennachie, that 'King of common hills.' '

THE LINTEL QUARRY

By Flora Garry

The Quarry roads nae langer there
Mason, House and Cairt are gaen;
But yonder the granite lintels lie
Fresh as if squared an' vrocht yestreen.

The Lintel Quarry on Bennachie.
Andrew Galloway Fordyce, Jnr., sitting on his father's lintel stones.

THE MYSTERY OF THE LINTEL QUARRY

By Andrew Galloway Fordyce, Jnr.

One evening last summer I made a flying visit to the new Donview Information Centre to see this latest added amenity to the great Bennachie Scheme. There, my wife and I met another couple who told us that they regularly climb the Hill with their dog. Conversation led to mention of the quarry. Our observant friend had felt that there was something strange about it? Why was it left in this state? He felt that for some unknown reason the quarry appeared to have been suddenly abandoned. He did not realise that by a strange coincidence he was speaking to the very person who could supply the answer, and whose father was most involved in the aftermath of this incident of just over 90 years and who personally was greatly affected.

My father was born and brought up on the edge of the heather and woodland, and to look south was upwards to Craigshannoch peak. My grandfather, his father, being a crofter was most versatile, and could turn his hand to almost anything. As a youngster my father helped with jobs on the croft, the corn mill astride the burn, bringing in wood, cutting peats on the hill top and sledding them down; and he knew Bennachie well. He started building contracting at the age of 21 and decided to quarry his stone from the Lower Oxencraig, 1,400 feet up. The old quarry and peat cutters road to the top was in disrepair. My grandfather offered to rebuild the road for £5; and he did it, single-handed. The quarry was worked successfully until a waterspout of great intensity struck the hillside near the quarry, washed the road away along with a mass of debris down to the lands below. It scooped out a long deep channel in the solid granite on the edge of the Hill and left a most remarkable geological phenomenon. It does seem strange that within a period of 60 years, a waterspout should strike exactly the same point on the Hill and coming from the same direction and with such intensity. Why did they so closely by-pass the Higher Oxencraig and hit the Lower Oxencraig? Could it be that the iron in the Hill conducted the elements in the oncoming storm cloud? Here is a problem for scientists to probe.

This then was the end of the quarry working, and my father's large, beautifully dressed stones were never recovered and have lain up there for over 90 years.

THE LIFE OF A BENNACHIE GAMEKEEPER

By William Wallace

Most people imagine that a gamekeeper has a gentleman's life, and that he just walks around, dressed in colourful tweeds, with a gun under his arm, a couple of dogs at his heel, and not a care of any kind. Indeed, friends of my own who are engaged in indoor occupations can think of no better way of spending their holidays than by coming to stay and join in our activities out of doors, but they, like most other onlookers, cannot know the other side of the picture. For the gamekeeper there are no such things as unions, no fixed hours with overtime rates and bonuses – he has a daylight till dark day, seven days a week, in all kinds of weather.

There are roughly three types of gamekeeping – purely grouse and stalking; purely low ground with no grouse or stalking; or mixed ground, that is, with grouse moor, low ground shooting, and often fishing as well. My present job comes into the latter category, so that there is very little time to 'let up' and holidays have to be taken when duties permit, not usually when it is most suitable. When I started work at the age of 14 in the Trossachs district of Perthshire, I had a wage of 15/- a week, and was given all the odd jobs to do – kennels, exercising dogs, and going round with the older keepers learning all the different duties of a gamekeeper. There it was grouse moor, killing vermin, and deer stalking, and I have many memories of days on the hills when darkness fell while one had still miles to go down over bogs and rocks, but we trusted to the sturdy hill pony finding its way with the stag tied to its back and we reached home safely.

On the high ground where grouse and deer are the chief targets, activities begin in earnest on 12th August with the opening of the grouse season, the earlier part of the year having being spent in keeping down vermin, and burning heather so that there may be plenty of young heather on which the grouse feed. The grouse season closes on 10th December, stalking goes on from September until the middle of October, and then activities ease off, usually by which time the winter storms have set in and put a stop to everything except trying to keep contact with the outside world.

For the purely low ground keeper, life follows a rather different pattern. There is no heather to burn, but there are large areas of woodland and agricultural land which must be kept clear of vermin, and on some of the very large estates the rearing of pheasants and partridges is carried out on an extensive scale. For the mixed ground keeper, his duties are many and varied. As you will understand, these depend on the season of the year. Grouse shooting begins on 12th August and ends on 10th December; partridge shooting begins on 1st September; and pheasant shooting on 1st October, both continuing till 1st February, so that the autumn is a very busy time. Fishing in the river Don begins on 11th February and goes on till 31st October. It is thus very difficult to take any one day and say that this is typical of my duties, but perhaps a general picture will do.

The day begins in the summer at about 6.30 a.m. when I feed my dogs and do out the kennels. In the winter this is usually about 7.30 a.m. After a short break for breakfast my assistant and I set out on our rounds in the Land Rover. There are vermin traps to look at, pheasant feeds to be made up, for after the reared birds are five to six weeks old they are put out into selected spots in the woods and are encouraged to stay around by having corn put down regularly. Then in these days of myxomatosis rabbits are becoming rather hard to come by, and as they are essential for dog food, one can spend a considerable time hunting for them.

During the shooting season, the men and beaters usually meet at 9 a.m. and drive in a few fields and strips of woodland ready for the shooting party at 9.30 a.m. The shoot goes on till the light fades, when the bag has to be counted over, records made out, and the game got ready for the market. If by any chance there is a roe deer in the bag, this must be skinned immediately and left to hang overnight before being cut up. By this time it may well be 6.30 p.m. when a hot meal and a good fire are very welcome sights. There is a feeling of excitement in the air when the morning of a shoot is bright and crisp with frost, but it is miserable going when the undergrowth is damp and clothes are soaked before one has been an hour in the field. There is nothing better than a fine August or September day on the moors. The guns usually walk in line for the first few days of shooting and later in the season they shoot from the butts when the grouse are driven to them by the beaters. The grouse moor under my control is the western slope of the Bennachie range, and on a clear day the view from the top over the surrounding countryside is wonderful.

Each spring I rear several hundred pheasants. A few pheasant hens and cocks are caught in February and penned near the kennels. A hen pheasant usually lays from 14 to 16 eggs in a season, and they can be relied on to begin around the 10th April. These eggs are put down in hatching boxes under broody hens which must be taken off and fed each morning for 24 days, as that is the time a pheasant chick takes to hatch. As they hatch the chicks are taken out to the rearing field and placed in coops along with the broody hen. They are fed 4 times a day, so there is a lot of walking involved, as coops are spaced 25 yards apart, and there may be 100 coops in the field. On some estates, where there is extensive rearing, a pheasant rearer is usually employed whose duties are solely the care of the young birds. They are in constant danger from stoats and weasels and hawks, but by using large netting-covered runs the tiny birds are kept safe from the marauders.

We do not rear many partridges, but they are a most interesting game bird, as they are counted as being the best parents to their young chicks. They lay their eggs around the end of April or the beginning of May, perhaps under a hedgerow, on the roadside, or any spot which appeals to them. Their first egg is usually laid bare in the nest, but after that the hen covers them with grass until she is about to turn broody. After 26 days they hatch, and if you are around when they are hatching, you will see that the cock partridge sits at the side of the hen, and takes the chicks from mother partridge when they are hatched. An old patridge may lay only 10 or 11 eggs, while a young bird will lay up to 20 eggs.

The grouse is a very hardy bird too, and starts nesting earlier, about the 10th to 20th April, and it is surprising how the young chicks stand up to the cold and wet to which they are subjected on the hills.

As to fishing, during the early part of the season the fishing beats are usually let to tenants, and apart from my possibly having to show the pools to the tenant who has not fished the water before, the river requires little attention. Later on, however, if there are any vacant beats, I have to fish these as time permits. An eye must however be kept on the river banks and pools after heavy spates as a tree trunk or heavy branch lodged in a good salmon pool can crate havoc with fishing lines later on!

One never knows too when a fox might be seen on the hill and then it is a case of all hands on deck as it were. A hurried phone call here and there and a party is got together to track the fox down. A call might come too from one of the local farmers whose sheep are being worried by stray dogs, not an enjoyable outing at any time.

One expedition which can be most enjoyable or miserable as the weather allows is duck shooting. If it is a dawn flight, this means we must be in position about half an hour before dawn. For the evening flight positions must be taken up just as dusk is falling. A dull night without a moon is perhaps the best time for this.

There is surely no job which does not have its compensations, and here there are the friendly greetings with one's neighbours, visits to help at adjoining shoots, reminiscences of 'that wonderful day a long time ago,' the post-mortem of a more recent shoot, and the stories of 'the ones that got away.

From all this it will be seen that there is variety in plenty in the duties of a gamekeeper. His knowledge of nature, weather observations and the stamina to be able to walk for miles and cope with all climatic conditions are all essentials to his work, but keepers who have spent all their lives in the profession – in many cases second and third generations – would not like to change with anyone, as it does not matter how old one is one is always learning something new about Nature and her many moods.

AIRCRAFT CRASHES ON BENNACHIE

By Adam C. Watson, Jnr.

The distinctive hill tops of Bennachie are often a valuable aid to pilots of light aircraft. Flying around the Grampians by visual navigation, they can easily recognise the unmistakable landmark of the Mither Tap, rising steeply out of the low-lying farm land of the Garioch. But in poor weather such a hill becomes dangerous. Bennachie's position and height have made it a hazard to aircraft flying round near the coast as a bad-weather alternative to crossing the Grampians directly.

Two Royal Air Force aircraft have crashed on Bennachie, with the loss of three aircrew. The first, a Westland Wallace biplane, crashed on the south side of Bennachie the very day war broke out, Sunday, 3rd September,

1939, with the loss of both crew members. A two-seat, general-purpose biplane, the Wallace entered RAF service in 1933. The radial piston engine gave a top speed of almost 160mph. When war was declared, the RAF had 83 Wallaces on strength. A few of these were converted for aerial target-towing and remained in service until 1943.

The aircraft in the Bennachie crash was a Wallace Mk. II target tug-plane, serial number K6028, one of a batch of 75 aircraft delivered between 1935 and 1936. To be easily seen from the ground, it had a bizarre colour scheme of yellow with black stripes, standard colours for aerial target-towing. At the time of the accident, K6028 was on charge to No. 9 Air Observers School (AOS) at RAF Penhros, North Wales, which formed in September 1939 to train observers in navigation, bomb aiming, photography and gunnery.

The accident record card for Wallace K6028 said that it was on a ferry flight from 1 AOS at RAF Wigtown, which had just been disbanded, to 9 AOS. For some reason, however, it actually flew from Wigtown heading for RAF Evanton, Easter Ross. It was on the Dyce-Evanton leg of its journey when it crashed, having presumably taken the lowland route rather than cross the higher Grampians in thick fog. Although the aircraft, flown

Some of the rescue party on their way down a forest road in Bennachie Forest, with the body of Pilot Officer J. B. Lightfoot. Fred Marr drives the tractor in deep snow with two members of the Gordon Highlanders search team and Tilliefoure gamekeeper George Clark behind. In the background the rocky peak of Bruntwood Tap.

by Pilot Officer E. H. Cummings, had taken the correct direction for Evanton, it was too low, some 30 feet below a summit on the south side of Bennachie. The Wallace hit the hill in very poor visibility and sadly P/O Cummings and his gunner were killed.

Mrs Charlotte Marr heard the plane loudly as it flew low over Blairdaff, near Kemnay, in thick fog at about 3 p.m. It took a long time to pass over and then the noise suddenly stopped. Local people wondered if the plane had crashed. Next morning, two Forestry Commission workers on their way to plant in the Bennachie Forest, spotted the yellow and black Wallace high on the hillside. They climbed the hill to find the surprisingly intact plane with both crew still strapped into their seats, apparently untouched. They must have died as a result of the aircraft's impact with the stony ground.

After they had reported the crash, scores of local people went up to see it. Many had seen aeroplanes fly over, but to see one on the ground would have been a novelty. Mrs Marr and a friend walked up the day after, carrying their newly-issued gas masks. By then the fog had lifted. They found the Kemnay policeman standing by the wreck, allowing nobody to come near the plane until the bodies had been removed by stretcher. As the Wallace was largely intact, it must have stalled flat onto the hill with a low

The body of Pilot Officer Lightfoot, wrapped in his parachute, is lifted o'ver a deer fence in upper Bennachie Forest, atop a piece of the Meteor aircraft wreckage. *Left to right:* Constable J. Fraser, Fred Marr, Constable A. Tough (barely visible behind fence), George Clark and Alan Rennie.

forward speed. The propeller had been knocked off and lay beside the engine, the fixed undercarriage had been crushed beneath the plane's fuselage, and the wings had cracked at the point where they joined the fuselage. Mrs Marr remembers that the tail of K6028 had broken off. The plane lay close to the summit of the hill, but its fuselage was flat on the hill and not buried in the peat.

Hence I believe that P/O Cummings had seen the hill looming in front of the Wallace a split second before the crash. He probably pulled the control column back sharply to climb whilst presumably also opening the throttle. The tail probably hit the hill before the rest of the aircraft, and thus broke off. Such rapid changes in power or attitude might have caused K6028 to stall, thus explaining why it flopped down onto the hill with its tail down and why it sustained moderate damage. Research has shown that aircrews are unlikely to survive tail-down crash landings, and nearly all of these occur in bad weather.

The RAF removed very few pieces of K6028 at the time, and did not clear the wreck afterwards. Once the RAF and the Kemnay policeman had left, local people removed many pieces. All that remains now is a small pile of twisted bits of metal, mostly wing spars and struts. At the site I have found an aerial target drogue canister, and flakes of yellow-painted fabric. Kinloss Mountain Rescue Team visited the wreck in 1965 and aptly described it as 'rusty old bedsteads!'

There is an interesting tale that finishes off this account of Wallace K6028's demise. Several years after the crash, somebody rolled K6028's Pegasus IV engine downhill, where it came to rest beside a forest road. It lay there for a few years before being pushed across the road and into a wood. Despite thirty years of Bennachie wind, rain and snow, the engine's condition had not deteriorated, and Mrs Marr told me that one could still operate it by hand. The Barr brothers from Muirton of Sauchen, while felling timber near by in the late 1960's came across K6028's engine. They removed it, planning to sell it when they sold their farm. Soon after, a group of RAF Officer Cadets, possibly from RAF Leuchars, Fife, arrived with a Land Rover at Mill of Tilliefoure, where Mrs Marr had moved when she married. The Cadets intended to remove the engine that day, for restoration at the RAF Museum at Hendon, London, because by then the Wallace type no longer existed. The late Fred Marr, Mrs Marr's husband, looked for the engine with the Cadets, but they could not find it. Having been told that the Barrs intended to sell the engine, they removed it from the Barr's farm for restoration.

Wallace K6028's engine may have been restored, but I have no knowledge of its whereabouts.

Another twelve years saw the second aircraft crash on Bennachie and a big jump in technology from piston to jet engine. A Gloster Meteor single-seat, turbo-jet powered fighter crashed on the west side of Bennachie on Tuesday, 12th February, 1952, with the loss of its pilot. The RAF's first jet fighter, the Meteor first flew in 1940 powered by Sir Frank Whittle's jet engine. It had an unorthodox design, with the two engines enclosed in separate wing nacelles.

The aircraft which crashed on Bennachie was the successful Meteor F Mk. 8, the RAF's main daytime interceptor jet from 1950-58. Armed with four Hispano cannon, it was the first RAF aircraft to have an injection seat fitted as standard. The Rolls-Royce Derwent jets gave a top speed of almost 600 mph. The Bennachie aircraft was Serial No. WA882 of No. 222 Squadron, RAF Leuchars. Formed in 1939, 222 Sqn. flew Meteor jets from 1950-57.

The 22-year-old pilot of the Meteor, Pilot Officer John Brian Lightfoot. belonged to Northallerton, North Yorkshire. At 09.58 a.m. he took off from Leuchars to carry out a low flying and cross-country exercise. Deep snow lay over north-east Scotland that day, with intermittent snow showers.

Mrs Marr, who lived then at Mill of Tilliefoure, at the bottom of Bennachie, told me that she heard the extremely loud roar of an aircraft flying very low over Millstone Hill and her own farm. Thinking something was wrong, she ran out in time to see the silver-painted Meteor flying west and very low over Glenton farm. Despite isolated snow showers, she could see the plane well. The Meteor then started a turn to the north, gradually losing height over the west edge of Bennachie. The plane banked steeply to the right as it turned, still descending. It continued to turn until it flew

This rare RAF photograph by Squadron Leader Peter Anson shows the accident-investigating party on Bennachie. Much of the snow had melted since the plane crashed. Mr Marr and his dog are second from left, John Smith third from right and Inspector Adams, extreme right. The others were airmen from RAF Turnhouse, including a doctor, and an Inverurie policeman.

in the opposite direction, east and towards the hill tops, and the
straightened out. Flying behind the plateau, the Meteor went out of Mrs
Marr's sight. Seconds later she heard a loud thud and a cloud of black
peat flew up from the hill top. Immediately after came a second, much
louder bang. A trail of thin smoke rose from the hill and spiralled up into
the sky.

Mrs Marr is sure that P/O Lightfoot must have seen the hill, yet at
10.20 a.m. the Meteor had ploughed a 14-foot-long rut into the peat on
the Bennachie plateau. The plane's inertia and the still-running Derwent jets
bounced the Meteor for about one-third of a mile. It then hit the
ground before exploding, scattering the wreckage over a half-mile square.
Sadly, P/O Lightfoot died in the accident.

Mrs Marr first thought of saving life, but she could not have climbed up
to Bennachie because of the deep snow. She ran down to House of
Tilliefoure, to the nearest telephone. A resident there phoned the Police at
Inverurie, and told them to come to the Mill, because Mrs Marr had noted
the exact direction where the cloud of peat had risen. The Police phoned
the RAF, who had received no radio messages from the Meteor and did
not know that it had crashed. The Police received many unreliable reports
of the Meteor's position, but Mrs Marr's observation was the correct one.

The Police organised a rescue party consisting of Fred Marr, Inspector John
Adams, Constables J. Fraser and A. Tough, Tilliefoure estate workers John
Smith, George Clark and Alan Rennie, and an *Evening Express* reporter.
They hurried up the hill at 1 p.m. in Mr Marr's tractor and trailer, through
knee-deep snow on the forest roads. An aircraft – possibly an Avro Anson
from No. 44 Maintenance Unit or 612 (County of Aberdeen) RAuxAF
Squadron, RAF Edzell, Angus – started circling low over the area. Mrs
Marr attracted its attention by waving a black jumper and making a 'V' in
the snow with clothes poles, pointing to the crash. The Anson spotted the
crash as it flew over Bennachie, and then waggled its wings as it flew over
the Mill. After Fred Marr's tractor became stuck on a corner in a blinding
storm, the party set off on foot. The *Evening Express* reporter had a
walkie-talkie, and told Police at the Mill, where other reporters had
gathered, that they had found the wreckage and the dead pilot.

A squad of Gordon Highlanders from Bridge of Don Barracks,
Aberdeen, arrived late in the day in a big lorry and field kitchen. They set
off to search for the plane, leaving one man behind as cook. Mrs Marr told
the soldiers to follow the tractor's tracks, but they separated and became
lost in the dense forest. Two of them followed the tracks and met the rescue
party on their way down. The party had put P/O Lightfoot's body into part
of his white parachute, and used a metal part of the fuselage as a sledge
which they trailed back to Fred Marr's tractor. They returned to the Mill by
4 p.m., to be fed with large piles of hot scones and bannocks which Mrs
Marr had baked specially for them! An ambulance waiting at the farm went
away with the pilot's remains. As darkness fell, the Gordon Highlanders
sent up flares from the Mill and the forest, to try to find each other. Later
that night, the local people saw a fireworks display as the flares whizzed out
of the forest all along the face of the hill above the Mill of Tilliefoure.

Eventually they all found each other and were safely off the hill by midnight!

Officers from 603 Sqn. travelled north from Turnhouse by car four days later, to investigate the accident. Also on 16th February, P/O Lightfoot was buried at Leuchars cemetery with full service honours. Squadron Leader Peter J. Anson, along with an RAF doctor, Inspector Adams, other policemen and airmen, spent a few hours investigating the crash. S/Ldr Anson told Mrs Marr that investigation was very difficult, because the Meteor had exploded into many pieces. However, he studied the wreckage and had found where the plane hit the ground a second time before exploding. S/Ldr Anson questioned Mrs Marr on what she had seen and heard, over tea at the Mill. Mrs Marr asked him if he had any idea why the accident happened; he replied that there would be an enquiry, but the cause would remain an unsolved mystery because the Meteor was built to climb in all conditions. Although Mrs Marr could see the Meteor, the RAF considered that P/O Lightfoot had been deceived by the poor definition of the deeply snow-blanketed contours and overcast weather. In the isolated

A photograph taken by Aircraftsman (AC) Bill Law of the RAF Edzell No. 44 Maintenance Unit team, at Mill of Tilliefoure. *Left to right:* Mr Marr, Mrs Marr, AC David Brown, AC 'Lofty' Kinnear, AC Watson and Corporal Thomson. The team's lorry is in the background.

showers, he may have suffered pilot disorientation and not realised the height or position of Bennachie.

A team of seven airmen, probably from No. 44 Maintenance Unit, arrived at Mill of Tilliefoure to bury the wreckage on 26th February, two weeks after the crash. The team, which stayed nine days, consisted of the cook, Corporal Thomson, who was in charge, and six Aircraftmen. No. 44 Maintenance Unit (MU) were based at RAF Edzell, Angus. In addition to maintenance, storage and repair of aircraft, they also salvaged or buried wrecked aircraft. The men were to have slept in their lorry, but the weather had deteriorated and become bitterly cold, and they ended up sleeping in a spare room in the house! The MU team walked up Bennachie each morning. Using axes, spades and hammers, they broke up and buried the Meteor wreckage, returning to the Mill just before dark. Many local people came up to retrieve parts of the Meteor for souvenirs or mechanical pieces. The MU team dug holes where they could in the hard, stony ground, and were amazed to see people uncovering pieces buried only minutes before, and then trail them off the hill!

The Marrs enjoyed the company of the RAF lads; after tea they would play monopoly and one evening they all climbed into the RAF lorry and went to the cinema in Inverurie! Mrs Marr went up to the crash just before the MU left. She took tea for the men, which they greatly appreciated because of the cold weather. Mrs Marr recalls the wreckage of the Meteor being very scattered, much of it covered in kerosene and oil. The MU obviously had an unenviable task. They told Mrs Marr that they had buried much of it, but large pieces lay scattered over the hill. About this time, the Marrs received a letter and photograph from S/Ldr Anson, thanking them for giving up so much of their time to help with the rescue operation.

Several years later, P/O Lightfoot's parents came up from North Yorkshire, to search for someone who knew about the crash, and they met the Marrs. In April, 1982, I finally located the crash site, after receiving information from Mrs Marr. The wreckage is scattered over almost a half-mile and pieces are now exposed, lying in the holes dug by the MU. The largest and most surprising find was an 8-foot long piece of the right wing. A large part of the wing and fuselage probably travelled much farther than any other parts, propelled by the engine, a typical feature of jet crashes. Thirty years of Bennachie weather had removed all traces of the painted serial number on the wing's underside. After 30 years, official information On WA882's demise became available in January, 1983, in accordance with the Public Records Act. The new information came just in time for it to be incorporated in this Chapter, which is therefore completely up to date.

Flying in bad weather imposes some odd mental and physical stresses. Pilots can suffer decompression sickness. Lack of oxygen and the imbalance of the inner ear can have startling results. Visual flying in fine, clear weather is standard practice. But in zero visibility, pilots have a psychological tendency to ignore or disbelieve flying instruments. Attempting to fly visually in bad visibility has often proved fatal, and I believe that bad weather was an important contributory factor in both accidents.

Note – The exact locations of the wrecks have not been divulged as I disapprove of wreckage being removed for souvenirs, so-called restoration of aircraft, or litter. I regard such wreckage as a memorial, sometimes the only memorial to the airmen who so often died.

Also, many people are interested in visiting such crash sites, and no doubt future generations will have the same interest, so the leaving of wreckage is an act of conservation.

I am indebted to Mrs Marr for giving up so much of her time to help my research. Mr Marr recorded details about the Meteor crash in his diary, and the Marrs kept a scrapbook of unique photographs and newspaper clippings. This chapter could not have been written but for Mrs Marr's help. Thanks are also due to the Air Historical Branch of the Ministry of Defence, and Keith Bryers.

I would be very interested to hear from anybody who knows further information about the Bennachie crashes, or any other in north-east Scotland.

BENNACHIE ABLAZE

By Algy Watson

One of my earliest recollections is of the thrill of a drive in a chauffeur-driven car, in the days when cars were much less common than at the present time. It occurred on the occasion of a very serious fire on Bennachie in 1933. The highly-polished limousine was driven by Mr William Sandison who was employed by Colonel George Milne of Logie House and he was taking hampers of food to the foot of the hill for the estate workers who were working exceedingly hard to control the serious outbreak of fire along the flanks of the hill. Bill Sandison asked my father to go along with him from Bogend (which at that time also belonged to Colonel Milne and where my father was grieve) to help to carry the hampers up the hill to the weary fire-fighters, and I was taken along as well.

There have been numerous fires on Bennachie since the time of the First World War, but three of these have been more extensive and serious than the others. These occurred in July 1933, February 1949, and April 1960.

July 1933

During much of June 1933 most of Britain sweltered in a scorching heatwave and this was probably partly responsible for the tinder-dry conditions which led to the fire which started to sweep across the hill on Saturday 1st July, and was finally declared under control on Wednesday 12th July, although the peat continued to smoulder for some time after that.

A fire carelessly left by campers is thought to have started the outbreak for near where it is believed to have originated were found traces of a camping party.

One of the first to discover the fire was Mr Alex Louden, head gamekeeper on the Logie Estate, which owned a considerable area of the north slopes of Bennachie. He immediately sent word to the Pittodrie Estate on whose land the fire appears to have started. Mr R. Laidlaw Smith, the proprietor of Pittodrie Estate rounded up all the men available and set off for the area where the fire was raging not far from the farm of Newmains, Oyne.

The flames swept with amazing speed over the shoulder on the east side of the hill, and a stifling cloud of smoke and scorching sheets of flame met the men. Operations to bring the fire under control were directed from two points. The Pittodrie party with Mr Smith and Mr James Clarkson worked from the Pittodrie side, while men on the Logie Estate worked from the Oyne side under the direction of Mr Louden.

One of the first tasks on which the men had to concentrate was the saving of a plantation of young trees extending to several hundred acres which had been built up during the years following the First World War. The belt was within 200 yards of where the fire started, but by working like Trojans amid the choking smoke and terrific heat from the flames the men ultimately succeeded in keeping the fire to the heather. Time and again it was believed that the fire had been brought under control but repeatedly the heather, bone-dry following the intense heat and drought of the previous weeks, blazed up again with a fury that almost defied all efforts to subdue it. When, in spite of the valiant work done by some fifty estate workers and a party of unemployed men from Inverurie and the vicinity, it was seen that they had not succeeded in getting the blaze under control, an urgent summons was sent to Castlehill Barracks in Aberdeen from where 30 Gordon Highlanders were sent out to give valuable assistance.

Moors on the estates of Pittodrie and Logie were the most seriously affected, although the Tillyfoure Estate was also involved to some extent.

Game and wild life generally went through a terrible experience. Countless hares could be seen running among the feet of the firefighters, frenziedly seeking safety, while overhead older grouse were flying wildly about, their screeches almost drowned by the roar of the fire. As the flames encircled them the younger grouse rose late into the air terrified, but their strength could hardly carry them and many fell exhausted into the flames.

Even after the heather had been thoroughly beaten with broom and branches of trees there was little certainty that the fire at any particular place had been extinguished and frequently the heather blazed up again after smouldering for a time. This was true during Saturday afternoon and again in the early hours of Sunday morning when certain areas burst into flames. Hardly had these outbreaks been brought under control, affording the firefighters little chance to snatch some rest and refreshment, than the worst outbreak of all occurred shortly before 10 o'clock on Sunday forenoon. It raged until nearly nine o'clock that night and even then was still smouldering in many places and throwing up clouds of smoke.

By two o'clock on Monday it was thought that all the efforts had succeeded in checking the flames after a fight in the most trying conditions. This was achieved partly by the hard work of the detachment of Gordon

Highlanders who helped to dig trenches in the peat to cut off the affected area. However, after most men had left the scene, leaving only a few on watch, the alarm was again raised at five o'clock in the morning for the fire had broken out anew and was once more out of control.

From all the estates in the district men were rushed to combat the fresh menace. Unemployed men came from Inverurie: Lord Forbes sent a group, and men from the estate of Major Leith of Petmathen assisted on the Oyne side. With picks, shovels and spades the fight was resumed with increased vigour and their efforts were again performed in trying circumstances – the heatwave continued throughout the area with the temperature Aberdeen 83°F; the grey curling smoke made their eyes smart and the flames eating up bone-dry heather swept dangerously among their feet.

The fire was at this time concentrated on the top of the hill in the peat moss and was smouldering to a depth of fully a foot. It was estimated that about four square miles of the hillsides and hilltop had been devastated.

By Tuesday 4th July the fire appeared to be completely under control although clouds of smoke were blown from the smouldering heather and peat moss by a freshening breeze. Thanks to the vigilance of the firefighters any fresh outbreak was contained and prevented from spreading to new areas and the fire was allowed to burn itself out. However on Wednesday afternoon a strong wind blew up and fanned the fire into a fresh fury. A very large plantation of young trees was almost devastated and fresh stretches of heather were swept by the flames, leaving a huge area of blackened land. For fully an hour and a half the farm of Newmains, Oyne, tenanted by Mr George Gardiner, was in danger of being destroyed for the wind had changed direction again, sending flames back towards the direction the fire had originally come from. They reached within 200 yards of the steading and there was a risk that sparks would set alight three ricks of hay that stood in the intervening field, from which in turn sparks could have been blown on to the steading. Around two hundred men drawn from all over the district, again including unemployed from Inverurie, Insch and Oyne fought the flames. In the early evening when the danger to Newmains threatened, an appeal was made for the assistance of the Aberdeen Fire Brigade, but as there was no adequate water supply available nothing could be done. Although the strong wind sent sheets of flame all along the Oyne side of the hill the farm was saved, but Nursery Cottage, occupied by Tibbie McIntosh, had a narrow escape, being separated on one side from the flames by a stream which flows into the Gill Burn.

During Thursday there was still considerable anxiety as time and time again the smouldering heather burst into flame. Only by maintaining the closest watch was the fire prevented from spreading rapidly and consuming additional areas. During this period of respite the men concentrated on the digging of trenches and the 'screeving' or surfacing of land some 150 yards distant, to restrict the spread of the fire – in particular to prevent movement in the direction of Pittodrie House, the Place of Tillyfoure or towards Lickleyhead. Again parties of unemployed from Aberdeen were used – 30 in the afternoon, 30 at midnight and another 30 early on Friday morning.

During the weekend, parties of workmen kept watch or dug more trenches to avert further danger. However they were hindered in their work by large crowds of sightseers who journeyed to Bennachie in cars and buses to view the scene of the great blaze – a scene of desolation, a huge area of charred and blackened stumps with here and there a skeleton tree replacing the normal luxuriant growth of heather and trees.

Heavy rainfall which occurred early on the Monday morning was indeed very welcome but in spite of this some peat continued to smoulder and was allowed to burn itself out. This smouldering kept going at least until the Wednesday, and although a watch had to be maintained all that day the fire was declared then to be definitely under control.

In the *Press and Journal* of Tuesday 11th July there appeared a public notice in the name of C. and P. Chalmers, acting for the proprietors' agents, stating that access to the Mither Tap would be permitted only by the path from Boghead. Camping and the lighting of fires were also prohibited.

February, 1949

The 1949 fire started near Castle Forbes a little before noon on February 22nd, when controlled burning of heather got out of hand. This undergrowth fire, fanned by gale force winds, advanced rapidly on a very wide front over the crags of Hermit Seat and the western slopes of Oxen Craig, eastwards to the Mither Tap.

Eighty soldiers from Bridge of Don Barracks at Aberdeen joined fire brigades from Inverurie and Insch, estate and farm workers, police and villagers in a desperate bid to halt the blaze. When darkness fell the flaming hillside could be seen 40 miles away like a torch. Late that night the fire was sweeping down the slopes, threatening woodland and crofts, so that many crofters and smallholders around the base of the hill spent a very anxious night.

Estates endangered included those of Castle Forbes, Logie, Druminnor, Pittodrie and Tillyfoure, and patrols of workers from these estates carried out a lonely vigil at strategic points on the hill in case of fresh outbreaks for two nights. The fire swept over 500 acres of unplantable land but fortunately no plantations were lost.

A second outbreak on Thursday afternoon fanned by a stiff westerly wind threatened to encroach on the farm of Mr R. Laidlaw Smith. Luckily the fire was kept under control and most damage was to gamebirds, gorse and heather, although a plantation of young trees was also badly affected. Patches of peat on the higher slopes continued to smoulder for some time.

April, 1960

I was able to record on colour transparencies scenes of the serious outbreak which started on 20th April, 1960. Controlled burning was being carried out on Forestry Commission Ground on the Premnay side of the hill but unfortunately got out of hand and the blaze quickly swept eastwards along the hillside reaching the Monymusk-Tillyfoure shoulder of the Mither Tap.

Forty soldiers from Gordon Barracks at Bridge of Don joined firemen from Alford, Insch and Kintore and forestry workers in an attempt to control this very fast moving fire. Fanned by a strong north-west wind it swept down into the forestry plantations at Braco and the adjoining Tillyfoure woods. One fireman is reported to have said that it roared just like a train coming down the hill, for flames were leaping 60 feet into the air.

The Forestry contingent of firefighters was reinforced by detachments from Forestry Commission stations as far afield as Huntly and Deeside, for there was a serious possibility that the fire would ruin 30 years of forestry work. The earliest trees destroyed had been planted that time ago and the most recent ones earlier during 1960.

On the forenoon of 21st April the Forestry Commission had to call in the Inverurie Fire Brigade when a strong wind caused smouldering heather to blaze up on the Mains of Afforsk-Chapel of Garioch sector of the hill. For several hours the firemen pumped water by relays for a mile from the Mains of Afforsk Dam, and the combined efforts of all the firefighters succeeded in getting the blaze under control. On this occasion some 584 acres of Forestry Commission plantations, involving at least 500,000 trees, and 400 acres of heather and scrub were laid to waste.

As I write this during the summer of 1982 radio and television are broadcasting appeals by the Forestry Commission to the public not to start fires in forested areas because of the extreme danger to plantations. The above examples of destruction by fire indicate that each and every one privileged to enter Forestry Commission and other forests must exercise great vigilance to prevent the repetition of such disasters. Picnic fires, lighted cigarettes and matches and, more recently, stubble burning, may all be responsible for starting disastrous fires. Even greater care is called for now that more of Bennachie is covered in valuable forests. I sincerely hope that no opportunity arises in the future for me or anyone else to write about fires on Bennachie.

On the dog's burial ground at Logie House near where Gaudie and Ury meet, one stone is inscribed:

'Ye cats rejoice. Terry lies buried low,
Foxes exult. Here lies your deadliest foe.'
From James Milne's Day-Book.

FAREWELL TO THE WIDS O' LOGIE
January, 1953
By James Anderson

All Januar of Fifty-Three
We aften heard the crash o' tree;
Then on the very hinmost day
Mither Nature stepped into the Play.

She took herself the leading role
And played the part wi' heart and soul;
For four and twenty hours did blow
The fiercest gale we ever saw.

The wind cam howling frae the west
A roarin', tearin', icy blast
The trees resist wi' might and main,
Bit a' their efforts were in vain.

Then, at last, wi' noise like thunder
Logie wids were torn asunder;
Where e'er I roam I'll always see
Those bonnie wids, in memory.

NATURALISTS ON BENNACHIE

By Stuart Hannabuss and Robert Bayliss

In their day naturalists like Philip Gosse and Frank Buckland were well known throughout Britain. Along with others like Hugh Miller, John Gould, and the Reverend J. G. Wood, they fed and stimulated the Victorian appetite for natural history through their many influential publications. It is easy to underestimate the vigour and enthusiasm of grass-roots activity, however, particularly that among working men and women. Many local societies were formed during the nineteenth century, and one of these was the Aberdeen Working Men's Natural History and Scientific Society.

The aim of this Society was to spread the knowledge of natural history and foster a love of the subject. It started up in October 1886 in a church hall in Nelson Street, and, under the lively presidency of amateur lepidopterist William Cowie, developed a programme of talks and lectures, exhibitions and excursions. The Society steadily grew so that by the late 1890's it needed better accommodation, and to its delight obtained the 'botanical class-room' at Marischal College of Professor James Trail, who had held the Chair of Botany at Aberdeen University since 1877. It took on a new lease of life and by 1911 had some 240 members.

From the Society's *Transactions*, which started in 1901, a clear idea of the membership is given. There was John Cobban, for example, a mason; Alexander Benzie, a farmboy, taxidermist and janitor of The Church of Scotland Training College; and James Smith who was successively farm worker, shoemaker, policeman and conservator in Marischal College's Anthropological Museum. The amateur status of members like this should not betray us into thinking that they were dilettanti. As was said: 'The true naturalist spirit striving after which can be relied upon, and which must ever be the bed-rock of all true research. If the foundation stone does not consist of facts, the edifice reared upon it must be flimsy indeed.' To this end the minute books record the plan to interpolate the names of important reference books (available in the Public Library) into accounts of the Society's activities 'so that intellectual strength may be acquired.' Such authorities as MacGillivray, Lankester, Darwin, and Wood were recommended. To this end, also, members meticulously documented and compared their findings, and men like George Sim earned substantial local reputations for their learning and publications. Many of those who addressed the Society at meetings were well-respected academics or well experienced naturalists. Two Professors at Aberdeen University, Trail and J. Arthur Thomson, were among the Honorary Presidents of the Society and were active participants in its various activities. Trail spoke at the Society's Union Street Exhibition of 1890 and closely identified with the majority of its members: 'he considered himself a working man as much as anyone in the Society, as he worked with his hands – he hoped with some success – as well as with his head.' Trail's influence was more local to the north-east than was Thomson's: Thomson was a great populariser of natural history, keen on the role of the field naturalist (see his *Natural History Sketches*), and interested in promoting nature study in schools. This last was also one of the aims of the Society itself, and members were very gratified that teachers brought so many children to their public exhibition of specimens in 1889.

Topics covered at meetings were astonishingly wide, reflecting the breadth of interest among the members. These included animal life along our sea coast, wild habits in domesticated animals, colour blindness, volcanoes, the *Scotia* Expedition, X-Rays, the origins of lakes, the use of the microscope, marine conchology of the Dee, and evolution among plants. There were 'hat' nights (when questions were put into a hat and drawn out and discussed) and lantern nights and exhibitions of things as diverse as African spears and geological fragments. This ambitious range of matters is symptomatic of the omnivorous approach to natural history and indeed to science as a whole during the period, cutting across more recent divisions of amateur and professional, observation and research. No wonder did the Majority Number of *Bon Accord*, called *Aberdeen Today* and published in 1907, say that the Society was 'full of buoyant and healthy activity, and is doing an admirable work amongst the class to which it appeals. This suggests the remark that among the working classes there is a decided increase of intellectual vigour and freshness of mind. One section of that class, unhappily, find their pleasures in alcohol, but the better type of working man studies natural history to good purpose, and the necessity for research in the fields is not only a potent safeguard against idle ways, but it is a source of real and elevating pleasure to men of observant disposition. Many of our working men are really authorities in certain departments of scientific study.'

And they were not unique, as studies like David Elliston Allen's *The Naturalist in Britain*, Lynn Barber's *The Heyday of Natural History*, and Peter Marren's *A Natural History of Aberdeen* suggest. In 1886, the year in which the Society was founded, there was a union of East of Scotland naturalists' societies, at which were represented ten societies including the Alford Field Club and Scientific Society, the Aberdeen Philosophical Society (which had been started in 1840 and had visited Bennachie in 1856), and the Aberdeen Natural History Society (the third such to be founded in Aberdeen, a group which had an active publications programme, and which became the Aberdeen Natural History and Antiquarian Society later in its life). The vicissitudes of these various groups are outside the remit of this discussion, except to say that the present Northern Naturalists' Club is an amalgam of the Natural History and Working Men's Societies and still meets regularly today.

Our main concern is to consider the excursions organised by the Aberdeen Working Men's Natural History and Scientific Society, in particular two excursions to Bennachie, one in 1905 and the other in 1909. Such excursions were (and still are with field clubs) integral to the life of the Society, and over the years they visited many places – Craibstone House at Bucksburn, Dunecht House, Edzell, Dunnottar Castle, the Loch of Skene, Cruden Bay and Slains Castle, and the Marine Laboratory and Fish Hatchery at Nigg. On one ill-fated day, the excursion was abandoned on account of the weather, and members sat in Aberdeen station and 'examined the contents of a member's vasculum, collected the previous day at Stoneywood.' These excursions were vigorously botanising in character, often accompanied by a guest expert, often punctuated by an 'excellent tea.' Sometimes more specialised 'sectional' expeditions took place, giving emphasis to botany or geology. These excursions were written up in the Society's *Transactions* and often information was provided for an entry in the *Aberdeen Daily Journal*. They were written up in the fullest way in the minute books.

Secretary John Davidson writes that, at the meeting held on the 12th September 1905, the membership was to be 'post carded' about the Bennachie excursion, and tea 'at the foot of the hill at 3 p.m.' should be organised. On the Aberdeen autumn holiday, 26th September, the excursion took place. There were many trips that day in the area by motor, charabanc and bicycle and the various railways (Great North of Scotland Railway, Caledonian Railway, North British Railway) were kept busy. The weather improved: 'Early in the morning there were heavy showers of rain, and dark clouds obscured the sky. As the morning advanced . . . conditions improved, and the overcast sky gradually gave way to brilliant sunshine. Although there was a sharp air, the weather was on the whole excellent, and the prospect for the day most hopeful.' This derives from the *Aberdeen Daily Journal* account of the day as a whole. As for the Society itself, the excursion was a great success, as John Davidson now records:

'The fourth and last excursion for this session was held yesterday (the September holiday), and turned out to be perhaps the most successful and pleasant outing held by our society. The destination was Bennachie and about 50 members and friends were conveyed by the G.N.S.R. in first class reserved carriages to Pitcaple by the 8.30 a.m. train – thence the party proceeded by the nearest road to the summit, turning up through below the railway a little way on the road to Oyne. By the roadside is a small quarry evidently for road metal and in it was seen a splendid specimen of a felsite dyke; many of the members took samples of the mica which was abundant here; the surrounding roads were of what is commonly called whinstone. The summit was reached after a slow but sure ascent by most of the party, although a few fell by the wayside, and those who reached the Mither Tap evidently enjoyed the outing as well as the rest on the top; there were few others on the hill but ourselves. Photos were taken of those who had been successful in reaching the top; and afterwards of those who had been successful in reaching the foot – at tea time, which I think everyone enjoyed. But for two slight drizzles of rain the weather was perfect although rather cold at the very top. The tea was served by Mr Kelty, Baker, Inverurie, at a small corner at the foot of the ascent and needless to say nearly all were present – 3 having gone round to some quarry near Oyne and lost their tea. The excursion was successful in another sense inasmuch as the party kept well together and did not break up into clans, everyone seemed to have pleasure in each other's company and the happy, social spirit which pervaded added a lot to the success of the outing. Up till now I have heard no complaints as I did last year [a trip to Haddo], and judging by that and the vote of thanks proposed to the Secretary by Mr Reay [Mr George Reay, President of the Society] I feel that the excursion was a thoroughly enjoyable outing. We returned again in first class carriages reserved from Pitcaple by 6.3 train. My own personal feeling is that instead of having 50 I fully expected 100, but we shall look for this at next Annual Holiday outing!'

Into the *Transactions* for the session 1904-5, only a shortened version of this went, although there was this addition: 'A little beyond [the road to the summit of the Ben], where the road passes to the west of the railway, is the Maiden Stone, a rude obelisk, with characteristic early sculptured figures on it. It measures in height about ten feet, nearly three feet in breadth, and a foot in thickness.' Also, they expatiated on the view obtained from the top:

'The summit was reached, after a slow but sure ascent, by most of the party, although a few fell by the wayside. But those who reached the 'Mither Tap' (1667 feet) evidently enjoyed the extensive view from the summit. To the west is seen the Deeside hills, with Morven and Loch-nagar forming the background. Northwards is the Tap o' Noth, Knock Hill, and the Bin at Cullen, on the Moray Firth coast. The whole of Buchan is to be seen, with the sea beyond, while at the foot is the little rivulet which gives its name to the well-known song and air, which is such a favourite marching tune of our Highland regiments. 'O gin I were where Gadie rins . . .'.'

There was a later excursion to Bennachie, on Monday 27th September 1910, another Aberdeen Autumn Holiday. Once again, the Society thoroughly enjoyed themselves, saw much of great interest, and had another tea. The Honorary Secretary at this time, Hugh Welsh, writes in the minutes:

'The fourth Excursion of the year took the form of a whole day outing to Bennachie, on the Aberdeen Autumn Holiday, 27th September.

'The party which numbered 36, left Aberdeen in reserved compartments in the 8.43 a.m. excursion train for Oyne, arriving there about 9.45 a.m. Leaving Oyne, the turnpike was taken on the left, and turning to the left after a distance of about ½ mile. The rough road leading past the farms of Ryhill and Hillfoot was now followed till it deteriorated into a track in the woods through which the Gillree Burn ran. The party now formed into single file and picked its way through the somewhat damp grass and bracken, till signs of the track of the famous cloudburst of about 23 years ago were struck. The bed of this huge ditch proved much drier than the banks, and afforded somewhat better walking. On nearing the upper reaches of the wood, the party broke up into sections, some going straight ahead, others cutting across in an easterly direction for the Gill Burn, where evidences of a more recent cloudburst are to be seen. The former sections continued up the Gillree burn until clear of the wood, and followed the rough cart track up to Little Oxen Craig where there are evidences of recent quarry working, several large blocks of roughly hewn granite lying about. One party climbed to the highest point of the Hill, Oxen Craig (1733 ft.), while the others, still following the track, crossed the commencement of the cloudburst, Moss Grieve, and made for the Mither Tap. The party which made for the Gill Burn, had by this time ascended Craig Shannoch (1600 ft.). On Moss Grieve, one sees the power a large volume of water has. Large areas of heather are torn away, leaving patches of blackened peat and whitened gravel. Across these peat areas, one can see the beaten paths of hares quite readily. On this part, one party was intercepted by what was probably a beater, who tried to turn them off, as there were sportsmen on the hill. Being on the footpath, however, and, moreover, the Hill being a Commonty, the party continued on its way, and were not further molested. The most imposing summit of the Hill, Mither Tap (1698) was in due course reached (at 1 p.m.) by almost all the party – others being seen on Oxen Craig and Garbit Tap, and Hosie's Well. On the summit of this majestic top, lunch was partaken of, and the atmosphere being fairly clear, an extensive view was obtained. Those inclined towards antiquarian subjects had ample opportunity of examining the remains of the Fort encircling the foot of the rock, upon which there have been numberless discussions. However, the origin and uses of this great mass of stones have not been arrived at satisfactorily. On the top of the Mither Tap is an inscription, and has puzzled not a few. This reads 'AD 1858 - B - P - LE' and indicates the point of junction of three lairds' lands, as marked by the Court of Session. The initials stand for Balquhain, Pitcaple, and Logie-Elphinstone. In descending the Hill, the Maiden Causeway – or as nearly as possible – was followed, and the old cart track through the woods on the west of Pittodrie, landing out at the farm of Boghead, at 3 p.m. Tea being at 4 o'clock several visited Castle Torries and a neighbouring harvest field, where photographs were secured. Tea was admirably served by Mr J. M. Kelty, from Inverurie, in a plantation of beeches near at hand, and was done justice to. W. Andrew Sim afterwards photographed the whole party. On the way to Pitcaple, the Maiden Stone was examined, a description of it being read by W. J. B. Thomson. W. J. Davidson here said that he would now take the opportunity of proposing a vote of thanks to the Secretary for his arrangements of this excursion. He was sure they had thoroughly enjoyed themselves and were all satisfied. The Secretary in reply, thanked those present for their appreciation of his efforts, and hoped that they had found nothing wrong in his arrangements. His one wish was that everything had passed off pleasantly.

'The way now lay through Chapel of Garioch and thence to Pitcaple station, with 3½ hours to wait for a train! Although it was now dusk, several small parties explored the neighbourhood. The others amused themselves with asking several boys questions on the district, and 'swapping' stories. The train duly arrived – 25 minutes late – and put an end to a most enjoyable wandering in the open air.

'The weather throughout was all that could be desired, although a trifle warm.

'One member of the party (Mrs Middleton of 60 Hutcheon Street – [*marginal note*] showed an excellent example to the younger members. This was a lady well advanced in years who went through the whole day's programme, and turned up at Pitcaple, bright and smiling. I am sure there are not many at her age who would have gone through the same.'

The excursion was reported both in the *Evening Express* for the 28th September and in the *Aberdeen Daily Journal* for the 29th. The *Transactions* reproduce a shortened version of the day, taking in the major points of detail and adding the fact that at lunch (from the summit, Mither Tap) 'the outlook was very pleasing' and that 'underneath lay the valley of the Don with its fields of ripening grain in all stages of harvest.' Some of those photographs taken by the party were of reapers at work. As for the weather that autumn holiday, the *Aberdeen Daily Journal* reports:

'. . . no sunshine . . . [but] pleasant enough, the sky being comparatively clear, and the atmosphere typical of the fall of the year, with a bracing touch of frost. The dullness in the early morning was not oppressive, and did not act as a deterrent upon the large numbers who had decided to spend the day in jaunts of various kinds, some proceeding long distances by train, others contenting themselves with shorter runs . . .'

These two excursions to Bennachie are imbued with the enthusiasm and optimism of the Society. They are in holiday mood and therefore the strict scientific tone of the meeting accommodates itself to lighter touches. Their interest in plants and geology, topography and archaeology, is only partly revealed from the explicit accounts, since there is ample evidence in the minute books and the *Transactions* as to the careful and thoughtful scientific approach that formed the context of field trips. Furthermore, in their interest for nature set within the landscape of the north-east, the members of the Society reveal other wholly admirable attitudes – the value of systematic collection and comparison, the need to be responsible and not indiscriminate in collecting, the openness of natural history to men and women of all classes and backgrounds, and the virtue of caring for the countryside and seashore, for plants and pathways and small animals, particularly with the increase of urbanisation. These themes emerge strongly from the activities and commitment of the members of the Society, and reinforce the view that, like the Bailies themselves, they are staging-posts in a tradition of stewardship over the natural history of North-East Scotland.

Note: We should like to thank Dr Mark Young of the Department of Zoology, University of Aberdeen, for allowing us access to the Minute Books of the Society.

THE FORESTER – MAN OF VISION

By Flora Garry

His saplins clead the bare knowe heid
Pine, spruce an' fir, the larick tree;
He plants and clears for comin' years
For lythe and wealth on Bennachie.

FORESTRY WORK ON BENNACHIE 40 YEARS AGO

By George A. Dey

True I had often gazed at the graceful profile of Bennachie from the road or railway en route to and from Elgin, or from Burnett's bus returning from holidays in the Buchan area.

The chance came of making closer acquaintance during a school Easter holiday of 1941.

This was not my first taste of Forestry having, the previous summer – that of the Battle of Britain – spent two sessions at a Grammar School Forestry Camp in Dalliefour Wood, near Ballater.

A friend and I had been keen to do 'our bit' and had been directed to Tilliefoure Forest, as it was then known, by Mr Newton, with whom we had had an interview in North Silver Street.

We cycled out via the tedious Tyrebagger, bicycles laden, and were inspired by the view to Mither Tap as we free-wheeled down to Blackburn.

We called at Kemnay to meet the Forester, Jimmy Allan (in temporary charge of Tilliefoure, Frank Anderson being seconded to Timber Control) who further directed us to Monymusk and beyond.

Bennachie was streaked with rotting snow and as we pedalled along, it gripped the attention, looming larger and larger in our landscape until we were swallowed up as the hills closed in on each side of the Don at Ramspot. We may not have realised it at the time but we were on ground where – back in the 11th century – Malcolm Canmore dealt effectively with a threat to his crown from the Moray men.

We were met by a young fellow keeping an eye out for us at Upper Woodend – now the site of the Donview Information Centre. He was one Ian Garioch, a student of Forestry from Edinburgh, awaiting Call-up.

We were put to work for the rest of the day on a new road being put in to a Forester's house. My first job, then, on Tilliefoure was to '. . . brak up big steens inta sma'er bitties' with a knapping hammer.

At Lousin' Time, Ian took us up the Oak Brae (the 'oaker') and thence downhill again to Lower Glenton farm, tenanted by Bill and Kate Fordyce and family of six. Thereby started an association with the Fordyces that was to last many years.

Lower Glenton – a small croft of perhaps 60 acres belonging to Castle Forbes estate – was set close to the Don in a natural enclosed bowl of land. It was contained by Bennachie to the north (particularly Oxen Craig, Hermit's Seat and Black Hill) Pitfichie and Cairn William hills to the south, the Oak Brae to the east and Lord's Throat to the west. To me it was a Shang ri La – in which I always found contentment.

In 1938 the Forestry Commission had acquired considerable areas of land from Mr Moncrieff Paterson of Tilliefoure, making a start to the land north of the Don at the north-west end, virtually on the lower slopes of Oxen Craig.

We had to wait a few days until the snow had thawed sufficiently to deem it safe for treeplanting. The first job of this nature was beating-up, the operation of replanting the occasional losses of previous seasons' planting. I can recall that in the company of a competent man to show me the ropes, I was introduced to one or two exotic species. There was the inevitable Sitka Spruce ('Serker sproosh' to the squad), Western Hemlock (Tsuga as it was then), Douglas Fir, and Abies Grandis (Grand Silver Fir), all along the Birks Burn behind Tilliebrack Farm. As a matter of interest I re-visited the Grand Fir stand in 1971 and was astonished to find some trees already approaching 60 feet high.

On my next morning the full squad set up the hill. We came to what sounded like a burn and I thought I would jump across on to a patch of woodrush. I went right through and landed up to my chest in a pool at the base of a small waterfall! I was hauled out gasping at the sheer surprise of it, water dripping from clothes and precious piece bag alike. Jimmy Duncan, the Ganger, looked at me without the slightest trace of emotion and said, 'Ye'll ging hame, an' change yer claethes. Syne came back an' fin' his lads up i' hill 'ere

This I did – gladly – and was back in a time that clearly impressed Jimmy! On my part I was impressed by Jimmy's humanity and decisiveness.

Planting was carried out with an ordinary garden spade, the edge of which we sharpened from time to time with a file. An L notch was cut – two incisions of the spade at right angles (hopefully avoiding stones), the turf prised up, the tree roots inserted and the turf firmed in again with the heel. This left the tree standing erect – the trees being carried in canvas planting bags in lots of 50 to 100 depending on size.

Jimmy Duncan used to come up behind us and tug the trees to see if they were firm. If not, he would shout 'Nae hud – nae hud ava',' haul them out and replant. Every now and then he would help out in a row and request a tree from the nearest planter with a simple ' – steck' (meaning stick, meaning tree). There can't have been many trees planted that Jimmy did not know was not firm!

Because planting was behind schedule we were invited to work overtime at the weekend – we still of course worked Saturday mornings in those days. Most of us jumped at the chance. We were planting Scots Pine and European Larch up as far as meet an existing wood of Scots Pine known as Blackwell. Being nimble on the hill, I kept going to the 'sheugh' for plants to keep everyone going. This enabled me to make a little for myself of the money I earned. As a youth of 16 I earned the handsome sum of 25/6 per week. As a concession, digs were knocked down to 23/-, thus giving me 2/6 pocket money. The overtime came as a bonus.

We were well catered for at the Glenton. Kate Fordyce gave us a shout about 6.30 a.m. and we descended to a plate of porridge and a bowl of milk poured the night before so that one's spoon broke through a delectable layer of thick cream. Generally we had an egg to follow, and all the while we put together our own pieces, from piles of loaf, egg, cheese, jam, cakes, etc., including the inevitable date scone as much part of the Aberdeenshire scene as a pair of 'nickey tams.'

I soon learned that bread was called 'loaf' and that bread – or 'breed' was the name reserved for oatcakes, a commodity baked to perfection by our landlady on a 'girdle' over an open hearth.

Then we set off on our bikes to our rendezvous at Parkstyle Farm where members of the squad were gathering in one of the stables. I delighted in hearing their gossip in the Doric – always ready to turn their conversation towards droll wit.

Finally, Jimmy would bring out his watch from his waistcoat pocket and say 'Weel, fowk, ah suppose we'll hae tae try't – .'

Ian Garioch and I climbed Mither Tap one weekend. We did it from the 'Heather Brig.' Ian did it in 14 minutes and I took a minute more.

Later I was to accompany him on a leisurely plod with Bill Fordyce's horse and cart to take his trunk to Monymusk Station. He was on his way to call-up.

Ian Garioch retired in 1981 as Chief Forester at Kilmichael Forest in Argyll.

I spent all summer of that year at Lower Glenton, joined by one or two school friends.

By this time we were on to the weeding and some fencing. Weeding was with a sickle – no herbicides in those days. It took time to become adapted but in the early stages it was a back-breaking business relieved by piece times and the 'crack.'

One job which came as a diversion was the checking of Pine Weevil traps. In this I assisted one of the squad, Dougal Mitchell, son of Drummond Mitchell, tenant of Parkstyle Farm and a senior member of the squad. Some felling of old trees along the Birks Burn meant that the insect was beginning to breed in the stumps, and threatening the young recently planted trees to whose bark it was extremely partial.

These were days long before insecticides, so the practice was to dig small shallow pits into which were inserted short lengths of fresh pine branches – about the thickness of one's wrist – and cover over with fresh pine foliage. On checking, the billets and foliage were inspected, and any beetles found were quickly popped into an empty but stoppered lemonade bottle.

That summer was a good one and as we worked on the higher slopes it was pleasant – despite the flies – to relax at piece time and gaze down at the arable lands on either bank of the Don valley.

The progress of each farm would be the main topic of conversation – most of the squad had agricultural backgrounds, with spells in the County Council's road squad or in Kemnay quarry when farm work was scarce. For them, Forestry could not have been more welcome.

'Ah see Cornabo reddin' roads wi' the scythe – he's surely makin' tracks tae start the haerst.' 'Aye – its real green stuffy.' 'Och – it'll ripen i' the stook.'

Then, about 4 p.m. the smoke from the farmhouse chimneys would intensify. 'That's the sipper rick risin', someone would say and one's digestive juices would begin to flow – .

Not content with a full working day, we helped out on the farm during evenings. In early summer, this meant the hay. Bill Fordyce had an old mower which he coaxed into slicing down the hay. This had to be gathered into sheafs, using 'tooshties a' hay' with which to bind them. This one did by taking a few strands of hay, parting them, twisting them deftly round the sheaf then simply pressing the twisted ends back in on each other so that the sheaf was bound firmly with the encircling band.

Then the stookin' commenced.

Two sheafs were picked up, one under each arm, and then put tops together, bottoms splayed out so that they stood in equilibrium. These were added to until two banks of four completed the stook.

The practice was known as 'gyting' and was followed by crofters who had their own mills, and wished to extract the seed for next year. It sounds easy, and one soon became adept, but was no fun – the hay was 'fool' and full of thistles!

All the while the 'skirly willies' (the oyster catchers) kept up a non-stop screachin' along the Don at the foot of the field.

But if there were no jobs to do in the evening I frequently headed up the burn which took me high into the old Scots Pine wood that still clothed the middle slopes below Hermit Seat. There I would look for signs of the roe and linger for the sunset eagerly seeking the distant silhouettes of Clachnaben, Lochnagar and even Ben Avon.

I returned at the turn of the year when we would assemble in mornings of deep darkness, twinkling stars and crackling frosts.

There was not much for it except cut and pile whins before burning them.

In April 1942 my diary records I spent another Easter holiday on Bennachie and I quote some extracts –

'6th. Beating up with Jimmy Duncan, Drummond Mitchell, Peter Rainnie, Willie Troup, Gilbert Adam and Viv Chambers' (the last two awaiting call-up). 'Later we joined the Lavenie squad at Heather Brig for a roe deer drive. We got one.' This last entry testifies to the fact that a second squad was recruited, based on the Lavenie/Blairdaff side of Bennachie and they had commenced similar afforestation work at Afforsk. They were under a ganger called Alex Reid. Other members of the early forties squad included old John Tevendale (from Paradise Lodge) and the humorous Willie Collie (from Fetternear). Both have long since passed on, as have Jimmy Duncan, Drummond Mitchell, Willie Troup and Gilbert Adam. Alec Reid died but four or five years ago.

'8th. Met at Parkstyle – waited Brown's lorries and loaded two loads of birch in the rain.' (If my memory serves me well, these loads went to the Turnery in King Street, Aberdeen, now the Bobbin Mill Inn).

'12th. Climbed Mither Tap with Viv and Bert. Good view.'

'13th to 17th. Beating up – mostly Sitka – gradually shifting east to Birks Croft.'

For the two months August and September of 1942 I was back on Bennachie prior to going to Aberdeen University.

For most of the time, the work was weeding – cutting bracken with a sickle to give the young trees more light and to ensure that during autumn and winter, a crushing weight of bracken would not smother them.

We were assisted by varying numbers of Landgirls who were hostelled in Abersnithack.

The weather was mixed and I can recall it as a bad season for hornets' nests. Every now and then screams would come from the girls and they would scatter from the focus point of a hornets' 'bike.' I remember Willie Troup – a nice old man from Monymusk – coming running to see 'fit we wis deein' tae the quines!'

One interesting diversion came on 13th August when I collected gean seed. It was quite legitimate to eat the flesh first from the fruit! Even amenity planting was practised in those days.

I see that 27th August was a very hot day and we completed Compartment 1 early in the afternoon. The next area meant a walk of a mile and Jimmy for once was at somewhat of a loss. So Bert Adam and I asked if we could break off early and so enjoy a 'dook' in the Don. 'Ah richt' said Jimmy. Then – remembering the Timber Control had a sawmill down by the Don, processing timber brought across from the Pitfichie side – added 'but dinna let the wid lads see ye!'

Early in September, Jimmy Duncan left the Commission. He did re-appear some years later as a Forest Worker. It would be nice to pay belated tribute to the contribution he made to the establishment of those early years of Tilliefoure Forest, on Bennachie. He was a ganger of the classic mould.

Bill Fordyce began his hairst about this time and dry evenings were taken up with stooking ('stook them tae the Netherton') and preparatory jobs like 'pinnin' steens' – marking large boulders with stakes so that the horse-drawn binder could avoid them.

By the third week of the month, he was 'leadin' – i.e. forking the sheafs on to a cart and from thence to a rick – although some went right into the barn to be threshed with his own mill. On one occasion young Charlie Fordyce – still on the back of the cart – was 'couped' into the barn, load and all!

I can recall relaxing thankfully against a stook as young Nan Fordyce helped us to tea and dumpling from the piece basket she had brought through the field.

The hum of the insects was incessant and as I raised my eyes I could see Mither Tap baking in the heat haze, a small white cloud floating above –.

To make full use of dry weather, we sometimes worked far into the night especially when the moon was full.

'Ye can aye dee wintin' sleep' said a neighbour over a cup of tea in Lower Glenton's kitchen 'if ye hud in the me't!'

Meanwhile out on the hill, the brackens gave way to the ditching. The progress of afforestation was slowly working towards the Heather Brig and took us under the outlying knoll called Bruntwood into whose slopes a Lysander crashed. Incidentally we found the remains of the engine among a strip of old pine high up near the plantation boundary fence.

Ditching involved slicing through the peat with large 'flachter' spades. These could be had with their cutting edges right or left, but one could cut down one side and then up the other. Turves were prised out between the two parallel cut lines with a crosscut spade, and pulled away to the approved planting distance with a hack or creeper – a wooden handled tool like a small fork with the prongs bent at right angles.

I was back in December at the planting and when this was rendered impossible by snow we cut trees – mostly birch – and burnt the branches. This task was accomplished by the fatiguing 2-man cross-cut saw and heavy axe. No power saws in those days!

I did not return until July 1943 and I worked on until my call-up papers came. It was the same old formula – cutting bracken for most of July. Landgirls were still helping out and their numbers varied from two to eleven. Two lady school teachers from Aberdeen – Muriel Buick and Mary Gibb – joined the squad as did an old school friend, John Ferries whose parents owned the 4 Mile Inn out the Echt road and who is now an eye specialist in Canada.

Towards the end of the month and into August, I was detailed off (as an experienced hand by then!) to join the road mending and ditching squad, Victor Johnson and Davie Donald. We were still in the Birks Burn area but by now in full view of Mither Tap – the sight of which put revived energy into tired muscles. The ditching operation also included the spreading of turves, through which it was intended to plant Sitka Spruce or a mixture of Sitka and Scots Pine. Davie Donald died a year or two back. He ended his working days at Kirkhill Forest. I'm not sure about Victor. If alive he must be close on 80. His main topics of conversation were of illness and death and the 'Loonie' – his only son.

I note that on August 5th Forester Allan came with the pay accompanied by District Officer Iain Gillespie. Little did I know it then, but years later – in the early 1960's – I was to become his next door neighbour in Argyll where we had adjoining districts and a shared office. Alas, Iain passed away in Lochgilphead in 1979.

The war for me came a little nearer and the sublimity of Lower Glenton was broken when three mysterious figures were spotted moving west along the banks of the Don. They turned out to be Italian prisoners-of-war who had escaped from their camp at Monymusk. It appears that pressure from midges made them change their plans. They were soon heading back in an army truck and we returned our scythes, pitchforks, etc., to the byre.

I was able to supplement my pay on one or two occasions by playing the saxophone in Jock Smith's Pitfichie dance band! This was generally on Friday nights and as well as Monymusk Hall, we went as far as Tilliefourie and even Midmar. We went by Bill Tytler's taxi.

Bill Tytler deserves mention. He owned a garage just where the road from Monymusk, having crossed the Don, forks three ways – for Kemnay, for Inverurie and for Don side, the Lord's Throat and Keig. He mended cars, bicycles, radios, etc., and there was little he could not put a hand to.

But to return to Jock Smith. He farmed at Pitfichie and led the band on trumpet and a curved soprano saxophone. The speciality was 'Oh Them Golden Slippers' which cropped up at a variety of dances including the Eightsome Reel.

I was lucky to be home by 3 a.m. from these sessions, just in time to snatch a little sleep before the call for breakfast.

Before finally departing for my call-up in early October, I had a last day on Bennachie, cycling out and back from Aberdeen with John Ferries. We did the circuit from Lower Glenton – Mither Tap, Oxen Craig and Watch Crag.

After four years in the RAF I came home to study Forestry in November 1947. I lost no time in taking up employment during the Winter, Easter and Summer vacations of 1948.

Much had happened in my absence. A hostel for forestry workers had been built at Woodend or Donview as it came to be called. As Mrs Fordyce had added a seventh member to their family, I stayed at the hostel later in the summer.

As a matter of interest, one of the hostel inmates in those days was Bert Aitken who returned as Chief Forester in 1971 to take over the amalgamated complex of Pitfichie, Corennie, Whitehaugh and Tilliefourie to be known as Bennachie Forest.

The University second term closed on 19th March, 1948.

I cycled out to Lower Glenton on the Saturday. At 9.30 p.m. I was called out by Frank Anderson (back as Forester-in-Charge after his Timber Control work). There was a fire on Pitfichie Hill and the Bennachie squad had to keep watch on a cottage above Paradise Wood felt to be threatened. Frank – a believer in the practice known as back burning – had us set fire to the heather around the cottage to leave a blackened area between it and the approaching fire. I finally got back at 8 a.m.

The fire was still smouldering on Pitfichie Hill on the 25th.

The following Sunday I was awakened at 4.45 a.m. to join a squad bound for the Hill of Fare where a fire had spread up from the Raemoir road and was threatening planations on Midmar. Our job was to patrol along the march dyke at the crest of the hill. My most vivid memory was of mist and a bitterly cold, raw breeze.

The fire had died down but there were one or two areas of smouldering peat and when we were relieved at noon on the Sunday we passed the

Pitfichie Fire Unit struggling to pump water uphill through a long stretch of hose. It transpired that water, sitting in a length of hose which dipped into a depression, had frozen . . .

(Incidentally Tilliefourie had its own fire scare on 22nd February 1949 when a blaze swept down from Oxen Craig and nearly entered the plantations in the Blackwell Wood area. A last minute change of wind direction saved the day. The glow in the sky could be seen from Aberdeen and, by coincidence, a fire broke out in Whitehaugh Forest only a few miles to the west. Ray Horne, the District Officer, was a busy man that night!).

Much of the work was by now on the slopes of the Millstone hill and it proved to be a very tough business planting trees among the boulders and tough heather and wet moss vegetation. If we managed 400 plants per day we did well.

A further acquisition of land in 1942 from Sir Arthur Grant of Monymusk brought an extension of the work in the Braehead area. Two smaller areas were added in 1945 at Longfold.

I vividly recall one incident from the summer of 1948 during weeding, in the vicinity of Tilliehashlich across the Don from Paradise. It took place on the 17th August, round about the time of the Lonach Gathering. The sky had grown ominously dark and the ganger said we should perhaps make for 'wir claethes.' We never made it. The heavens opened and I was soaked as effectively as if someone had thrown a bucket of water at me. With instructions to go home I mounted my bike and cycled towards Upper Woodend along a road which was already over a foot deep in water. I noted Ramstone was almost submerged and in fact the Don rose two feet in an hour. As I came abreast of the hostel/office complex I came to grief in what turned out to be submerged gravel only recently laid on the access road to the houses and washed down by the downpour.

Back at Lower Glenton I found Charlie Fordyce fighting with a terrified horse in an effort to prevent a hen-house from floating down the Don. To the accompaniment of flashes of lightning and cracks of thunder, frighteningly close, we succeeded in dragging the hut from the lapping waters on to drier ground.

After graduating in 1950, I was lucky enough to serve for a spell as assistant to Ray Horne, in whose District was Tilliefoure Forest. I was thus able to appreciate the Forest on a much more intimate and technical level which included surveying and planning. Several houses had been built at Donview and the hostel dismantled.

Although I went to pastures new after that for about 20 years (including service in Argyll and the South Wales coalfield) there was hardly a year of which I did not spend a day on Mither Tap during holidays up north. It was inevitable that the children would ultimately join me on such outings.

It is small wonder that when I returned to Aberdeen in 1970 to take over that District which included Bennachie that the seeds of opening up the Forest for recreation were already sown.

Large areas of new land had been acquired and planted on the northern slopes of Bennachie, some from Pittodrie Estate – overlooking Oyne, Insch and Auchleven.

It was extremely fascinating to return to those early areas of 1941-42-43 and 48 to see how well they had grown. The area was now well served by roads, and many of the plantations were in the 1st Thinning stage.

When Dr·Gordon wrote inquiring about car parking, I had already been at work planning and the whole Back o' Bennachie project at Puttingstones clicked into place.

Complementary with this I conceived the walk from Puttingstones to Oxen Craig quarry, the Millstone walk from Upper Woodend near Paradise, and a car park and walk to Mither Tap via Esson's croft from Woodend on the fringes of the Garioch. Many late evenings and weekends were gladly devoted to trail-blazing in these areas.

I think a tribute must be paid to Bennachie's Head Forester at the time, Jim Maxton, who took the whole matter to heart and very quickly put plan into practice. Nor should be overlooked the part played by Bill Clarkson of the Forestry Commission's Roads Branch.

Further ambitious schemes which were sketched out – the Information Centre at Upper Woodend – the hill walks linking Oxen Craig, Mither Tap, etc. – these fell to be completed by successor Foresters and District Officers.

Meantime, the Bailies had been formed and I for one felt gratified that my efforts to pay due respect to a fine hill were being put to good use.

ALEXANDER KEITH, M.A., LL.D.
1895-1978

By Dr D. G. Gordon

'Scatter my ashes on Bennachie; the rock from which I was hewn' – the last wish of A.K. as he was known to his many friends, among whom I am proud to be numbered. As I write it is the evening of Tuesday the 3rd August, 1982, as I sit in the sunporch of Coldwells of Inverurie, looking down on what our visitors call the bonniest view of Don. It has been another perfect day. The warm sun cleared away the morning mists, to continue the warmest summer in my memory since 1911, still reputed to be the finest summer of the century, when we went barefooted to Kennethmont School month after month. A feeling of nostalgia for the Mither Tap had come over me, similar to that feeling described by A.K. in the *Book of Bennachie*, and off I set after my mid-day broth and tatties, to find my legs not so swack as in other days, but my tongue as swack as ever in greeting my fellow climbers going up and down the Maiden Causeway. On the top it was balmy. I was all alone for nearly an hour. Commonly the snell wind makes five minutes enough. By our hopefully vandal-proof indicator, I looked west to Ben Avon and the great mountain vista at its heather purple best, and east to the great chequered tapestry of the fields golden unto harvest. There was no breath of wind. Coming down off the great Tor rampart on its southern edge, I picked a handful of the lip staining blaeberries to savour as I sat on a mossy bank in the warm sun, in memory the taste of boyhood. I returned home refreshed and contented.

I had been worrying about how I was to face the mammoth task of doing justice to the name of Dr Alexander Keith and the prolific literary output of a life-time. My worry was over. Let me write a simple personal memory. Let me leave a study in depth to great writers like Cuthbert Graham and Ian Bryce in that grand *Leopard Magazine* of Diane Morgan's; that vivid beacon of conservation in a dull materialistic age. I remember him well, when at the end of the 1939-45 war he became the farmer at Eggie of Balmedie, three hundred acres stretching down to the North Sea, when I became his Doctor, not that he needed much doctoring. We would browse in his great library as he showed me some of the unpublished poems of Charles Murray, his friend. Later when I was a medical referee in Aberdeen, you would find him at lunch time in the Club, the centre of a listening, laughing coterie. In my opinion he was the finest raconteur in Aberdeen. In his seventies, in ripe old age, he retired to Fetteresso Lodge in Stonehaven. A.K. a very knowledgeable gardener, took a special pride in showing his flowers and vegetables and shrubs, to be followed by refreshment in his ever-increasing library, where you could pick his brains, and for a reference he would go unerringly to the spot on his book-shelves for the required volume.

He had a presence. Square-built, deep-chested, he had good looks. He was always kind and courteous. He had both wit and humour. I remember many kindnesses. When I asked his permission to reprint his two articles *The Seven Taps of Bennachie* and *In Praise of Donside* in the 1976 *Book of Bennachie* he said 'You'll be needing a pound off me to join the Bailies.' 'No,' I replied, 'we'll be very proud to make you an honorary Bailie.'

'Keep your friendships in good repair' was the advice of the old sage Dr Samuel Johnson. A.K. had heeded this advice. He had so many friends, their number was legion. To mention but a few, he never forgot his old Dominie, Benjamin Skinner of Strichen, or the great researcher of *The Bards of Bon-Accord*, William Walker, of whom A.K. became literary executor in 1931, or the retired accountant, Eric Finlayson, a fellow bibliophile, whose congenial company supported him in later years.

Keith was born in Kintore on 18th August, 1895, under the shadow of Bennachie. His father, Alfred Keith was the local pharmacist, dying when A.K. was nine years old. His widowed mother, thrang with the business and a young family, was glad of the offer of her bachelor brother-in-law to take his young namesake to his farm of Burnshangle at the foot of Mormond, and put him to school at Strichen. A.K. writes somewhere that it was the best school in the County of Aberdeen. Certainly the Dominie, Benjamin Skinner, who had just arrived was able to teach six subjects at Higher level, a unique achievement. 'Uncle Alec' had been Headmaster at Methlick School from 1879-1902, when he started farming. A.K. was, therefore in a constant educational environment. It was not all education, however. A.K. had to be in bed at 9 o'clock as he had to be up early for his job of little bailie to clean out the byre and feed his cattle before hurrying to school at 8.30 for his Greek class. The years at school rolled on. One night in 1911, the year before his Highers, Uncle Alec had as his guest for the night, his fellow student, Gavin Greig, the Dominie at Whitehills of New Deer, the famous ballad collector, who had been the speaker that night at the Strichen Mutual Improvement Society. After supper, Gavin Greig was in full flow and a very sleepy A.K. did not get to bed until two in the morning, with the prospect of his job as bailie starting in three to four hours time. His chief memory afterwards was of Gavin Greig always letting his pipe go out, as the speaking interfered with his smoking and he smoked a whole box of matches trying to re-light his pipe. Writing years later, A.K. considered Gavin Greig the greatest of our ballad collectors, a distinction which the American ballad specialist, Professor Child gave to Peter Buchan of Peterhead a century earlier.

1912 saw Keith enter Aberdeen University to take an Honours degree in English in 1916, studying under the two professorial giants, Grierson and Jack, who built well on Skinner's groundwork, giving A.K's meticulous and immaculate English a style which graced everything he was to write. In 1917 he joined the *Aberdeen Journal* being passed unfit for military service, as he had a systolic murmur of his heart. By the 1939-45 war, medical knowledge had advanced to show that the murmur was of no real significance, as proved by his living 83 years. As a Platoon Commander in the Home Guard on manoeuvres up Caskieben in full kit, he was the first up. But over the years it was Bennachie which was his first love, his goal on many a Saturday, the journalists' day off. After hours on the hill he would take the road round by Burnhervie, to Coldwells, where a grand farmhouse tea would be waiting him, and a long news with his old Dominie. They had kept their friendship in good repair. Benjamin Skinner died in 1945.

It was a year or two later that I got to know him. I think he had a warmer feeling for me as the nephew of Benjamin Skinner. Our friendship ripened when I became a member of the Charles Murray Memorial Trust, of which he was the genial Chairman and we published in 1969 *The Last Poems of Charles Murray*. He presided over a goodly company of Hamewith devotees, the doyen being Dr Nan Shepherd, who wrote the wonderful appreciation of 'Hamewith.' Other personalities were Leslie Gavin, the Culter Oatmeal Miller, Archie Whiteley, the dominie of Monymusk and Kemnay and James Gordon the grand old man of Alford.

Memories of him are legion. He was especially at home among the bluff Buchan farmers who bred the Aberdeen-Angus beauties, and the shrewd business cronies of the Chamber of Commerce, of whom he was for long President, and who joined in a Town and Gown celebration when he got his LL.D. in 1967. He had a word for everybody, a tale to tell often against himself to cheer a weary day. As a guest speaker of renown he was in great demand. I remember him at the Aberdeen St. Andrew's Society Annual Dinner when he proposed the time-honoured toast of 'Sir Robert Davidson, Provost of Aberdeen, and the Heroes of Harlaw.' It must have been a record as it was the third time he had done it.

His literary output was phenomenal. In the Spring, 1979 number of the *Aberdeen University Review*, you can find the bibliography of the works of Dr Alexander Keith, compiled by Harold Watt of the Aberdeen University Press, a real labour of love. It extends to six pages. From 1917 to 1944, besides his long working days as a Journalistic Editor, masses of articles flowed from his pen, particularly under the heading of 'From a Scottish Study' when the A.K. Cognomen became so well known. In 1922 a selection of these was published under the title of *Mine Honourable Friends* – for me I think my favourite of his books. In 1925 appeared a mammoth collection of Gavin Greig's ballads, called *Last Leaves.* He was greatly helped by his friend William Walker but regretted that pressure of work prevented him finishing the work. The remaining mass of material has been deposited in the Aberdeen University Library. I can refer but briefly to his well documented volumes on the Glenlivet Distillery, the North of Scotland Bank, and the two volumes on the Aberdeen-Angus Society when he was Secretary. Perhaps in the period from 1955 to 1971, when he was unofficial editor of the Chamber of Commerce Journal, his articles on 'Eminent Aberdonians' show a mellowing maturity, a depth of vision, which must have involved a lot of burning the midnight oil at Eggie Farm. He was even able in 1963 to publish the history of the University Press, his own publishers.

In 1972, appeared his magnum opus *A Thousand Years of Aberdeen.* As he said when asked, it took him a long time in the making. He says that in his preface. He dedicates it to two wonderful librarians of the University of Aberdeen, Peter John Anderson and William Douglas Simpson. He tells of his pride in having been amongst their friends. What a mass of material must have been hammered on the anvil of his mind! It has already become the reference book of choice for students of the Granite City. Readable, informative and amusing, it tells the story of a city almost under the Arctic Circle, which bred far more of our Empire builders than any other city of a similar size.

Perhaps one of the most memorable and fascinating activities of A.K. was the secretaryship of the Sit Siccar Club, a genial gathering of the personal friends of Charles Murray, on his return from South Africa. As Secretary he never called a meeting nor kept a minute. He was by far the youngest, surely a remarkable tribute to his worth and reputation as a young author. Meeting as fancy dictated, the flow of conversation must have been a delight. Pause to consider the roll of the members – Dr David Rorie, the Cults Doctor, of Lum Hat fame, Fred Martin, the blind Buchan M.P., Lord Boyd Orr, John Buchan, the first Lord Tweedsmuir, Sir Ashley Mackintosh, the finest medical teacher I ever sat under, that great character William Tawse, the public contractor and engineer, Sir Patrick Duncan, and several more across the years. A.K. must have blossomed as a journalist and author in the wit and repartee of such a company. A similar Club called the 'Calm Soughers,' flourished under the leadership of Rorie and Mackintosh. Membership of the two must have overlapped. With Sir Walter Scott, of whose wisdom he writes in *Mine Honourable Friends*, he could say 'I dwell among my own people.' Yes among his own people he could count the intellectual cream of the Sit Siccars, the astute minds of the Chamber of Commerce and the patient weather-beaten wisdom of the Buchan man.

In the summer of 1978, I was asked in my capacity of medical referee under the Department of Health to go out to Stonehaven to examine A.K., as he was becoming forgetful and unable to look after himself. He greeted me warmly as an old friend and asked me to come and see his garden as I had done on previous friendly visits. As we wandered around among his flowers, he was very normal. His condition deteriorated, however, and he died on 5th October at the age of 83. Shortly before his death, Ian Bryce, hoping to write up A.K's life story for the *Leopard Magazine*, went out to Fetteresso Lodge in the company of Eric Finlayson. As Bryce acknowledges, 'without the recollections of Mr Eric Finlayson prompting so many of Dr Keith's reminiscent chuckles this profile would have been so much less.' This is a most worthy appreciation of the role played by his 'honourable friend' Eric in his latter days, a role to be continued at the cremation, when in the presence of a few chosen friends, he voiced our tribute in simple moving words. A few days later, he brought out A.K's ashes to Coldwells, long the home of his old dominie. It was a beautiful October day, as Algy Watson carried the casket up Bennachie, and I scattered the ashes of Alexander Keith on the Mither Tap, the rock from which he was hewn. Surely he could continue to say 'I dwell among my own people.'

GOWD AN' YALLA

By Rev. David Ogston

Faan my gowd an siller's deen
An I want an honest frien
Hine awa fae Don an Dee an Fae the Geerie
Gin ma hert be caul an teem
Gie me gowd an yalla breem
Fae the canny braes an breist o Bennachie.

Faan I traivel aa maleen
Hine awa fae Aiberdeen
An aa the hummle knowes an hills o Geerie
Faan I'm tint an trachled sairly
I am thinkin late an early
O the Mairches' rise an fa on Bennachie.

Faan I'm weary an despairin
Gin ye'd gie ma hert a fairin
Tae cairry wie's tae mind me on the Geerie
Syne I'd sattle for a steen
Fae the Mither Tap abeen,
Or a souch o caller win fae Bennachie.

Faan I'm deen an dowie weerin
Faan I raise the hinmaist feerin
Lat it be a mids atop the hert o Geerie
Gie me heather for a happin
An my yaird'll be the bracken
In the lythe aneth the hicht o Bennachie.

A ROCK OF OFFENCE: THE QUAKERS OF KINMUCK

By Rev. Dr C. J. R. Armstrong

Those interested in the highlights and the shadows of the historical record as it affects the district around Bennachie in the seventeenth century could do worse than immerse themselves in the contemporary journal of Alexander Jaffray of Kingswells. Jaffray, born in 1614, some time Provost of Aberdeen, Scottish Covenanting ambassador to Holland, brave soldier on the covenanting side in the thirties and forties, brings vividly to life both the physical turbulence of his age and its avid spiritual searching. The man who graphically describes how in Aberdeen in 1643 the then laird of Haddo, accompanied by the young laird of Drum, pistols in hand, chased him from room to room in his own house, plundered his possessions and finally imprisoned him; then his encounter with the young laird of Harthill who first shot at him at point blank range and then also imprisoned him in Pitcaple Castle, is the same who, a little later, writes in his journal:

'It is one thing to be *willing* to receive Christ, and to desire heartily that he *would come*; and another thing to know *that he is there already*. I know it is the judgment of many that Christ is in every one . . . but sure I am that every *believer* has Christ in him or else he is *none of his* . . . How sad, then, is it that He should be there and so little taken notice of as not to be known *how* he comes or *what* he says and does in the heart! 'Surely the Lord is in this place and I knew it not,' said Jacob; so, surely, may I say, Christ has long been in my heart sorely slighted and not observed. O for a heart to mourn for this!' (Spalding Club edition, page 144).

Jaffray, after his many adventures, including service at Dunbar and frequentation of the centres of political and military power in Scotland, became a 'convinced' follower of the Inner Light preached by George Fox and his followers and, in 1662, not long, therefore, after Fox's visit to Scotland in 1657, retired to his house at Ardtannies, hard by the present Port Elphinstone. It is from approximately this time that the burgeoning of the Quaker movement in the north east can be dated, cherished and stimulated at frequent intervals by 'travelling Friends' from the south, notably William Dewsbury and Patrick Livingstone.

It is tempting to relate the establishment at Kinmuck of a Quaker congregation or 'meeting' (as Friends themselves say) to Jaffray's presence in the neighbourhood, first at Ardtannies, then at Kingswells. John Barclay, editor of Jaffray's *Diary* and compiler of the account of Friends in the north of Scotland in the same volume, tries to do so by referring to an apparent title of ownership held by Jaffray in the parish of Keith-hall, where Kinmuck lies. If such a title existed, the least that can be said is that it was a subject of dispute between Jaffray and the local laird, Sir John Keith, and that in so far as Friends eventually *owned* property in Kinmuck they had it from the two other major landowners in the parish, the Forbeses of Craigievar and the Irvines of Drum.

Two views of the Quaker meeting-house at Kinmuck

It is not in fact necessary to postulate so early a connection between Kinmuck and one who was, after all, only a single if distinguished example among many in the area of the power of the preaching of God immanent in the heart of man. The Friends, being zealous and meticulous chroniclers of all that occurred to them and through them, have left several lists of names and places in the district connected with their early history. Many of the most notable 'conversions' from Presbyterianism occurred in the mid-sixties. By the early seventies the evidence of local concern at their separatist tendencies was echoing through presbyteries, episcopally presided synods (for we are in that hybrid phase of Scottish Church History when Bishops, too, had authority in the kirk) and in the Scottish Privy Council itself. The resulting edicts, remonstrances and savage persecution through imprisonment, fines, and confiscation, which reached a peak in the area in about 1677, can be followed in the pages of John Barclay's edition of Jaffray, Joseph Besse's *Collection of Sufferings* (1753, volume II) or George Burnet's *The Story of Quakerism in Scotland* (1952).

So far as Kinmuck is concerned the spiritual contagion seems to have spread (for religion after all is 'caught not taught') through the winning over in different contexts and on different occasions of a sufficient number of local inhabitants for them to form a 'meeting' of their own quite early on. From the seventies we learn of meetings of Friends at Ardiharrald (variously spelt – near Old Kendal?), Paties Mill, Tillykerrie (Tillakerrie), Aquhorthies (near Old Meldrum), Coliehill, Lethenty, as well as in Inverurie. The meeting, in other words, moved around. Some names of its hosts and main pillars can be discovered from our lists, e.g. Robert Burnet at Lethenty and John Glenny at Coliehill, both also prominent later in Quaker affairs and whose identity can be checked from the *List of Pollable Persons within the Shire of Aberdeenshire 1696* (Aberdeen 1844). These names appear with others on the first page of what almost immediately became the *Kinmuck* Minute Book, i.e. register of weddings, as members of the meeting 'at Lethenty' in 1679 who are willing to contribute money on a regular basis 'for the service of truth' twice yearly, viz. at 'Witsunday and Mertimes (so called)' i.e. at Whitsun and Martinmas (early November).

The evidence seems overwhelming that it was at this juncture that the Friends of the Inverurie district decided to base themselves firmly in Kinmuck and not only established their school there and met there regularly for worship, as they undoubtedly did, but also *built* for these purposes a meeting-house which was to be *both* school and meeting place and is identical with the Kinmuck meeting-house which happily survives to this day. The arguments for this contention, not yet disputed, have been set out elsewhere (see bibliography). Suffice it to say here that they depend mainly though not exclusively on cumulative evidence from, first, the deeds concerning the meeting-house and related properties as they survive to this day; second, the clear evidence in the official record of the contemporary authorities, both civil and ecclesiastical, that Quakers *circa* 1681 had dared to *build* themselves in Kinmuck a school and meeting-house (one building) which ought forthwith to be destroyed; third, the total silence about building activity in the only alternative period on offer to account for the present buildings, viz. 1709/1710, when we know that the present meeting-house site and grounds were bought from the then laird of Drum. Everything seems to indicate that it was the surviving building which a contemporary Quaker source proudly describes in the seventeenth century as 'a Stumbling Stone and Rock of Offence laid in Sion' (unpublished MS of Alexander Skene and others from the period).

In other words the available evidence strongly supports the conclusion that the numerous Friends of this district, having come through the fires of persecution and having decided in 1678 to set up a school in Kinmuck (as we know from the record that they did), thereupon not only bought the property then known as Allan's Croft (now Bankhead) in Kinmuck as a residence for their schoolmaster, John Robertson, and his family (wife, son and daughter in 1696), but also *leased* the plot of land immediately opposite from the laird of Drum, upon which to build their meeting-house and school. The collection of money and undertakings in 1679, which we have already seen, would have been to finance the whole enterprise.

Among the evidence the deeds for the purchase of Allan's Croft survive and are signed by the then laird of Craigievar, Sir John Forbes, 'Red' Sir John, whose fine portrait still adorns a bedroom of his castle. There is no recorded deed for the tenancy by John Robertson of the land on which his school lay but we do know from the 1696 *List of Pollable Persons* that he was a tenant of the Irvines of Drum for *some* property in Kinmuck (see pages 352f.). Furthermore, the surviving deeds for the purchase by Friends of the meeting-house site and surrounding ground in 1710 make it quite clear that the property is *already* occupied by John Robertson. It is a matter of some interest and no little irony that the laird of Drum who must have leased the land to the Quakers in 1680 or so was none other than the high-spirited and enraged young man who in earlier days had chased Alexander Jaffray through his house in Aberdeen. By 1680 the Alexander Irvine in question was every bit as *persona non grata* to the Presbyterians as were the Quakers, having reinforced whatever previous offence he may have given by becoming latterly a Roman Catholic. Quakers and Catholics did make common cause at this time although both parties cicumspectly denied any felonious intent.

The new meeting-house of 1681 was a solid piece of work as one can still appreciate today. It had two floors with a large fireplace at each end on the ground floor, and doors placed asymmetrically on each of the long sides. We can surmise that meetings were held in the ground floor room furthest from the road in front of the large open hearth and that the upstairs room or rooms were devoted to school purposes. No doubt dormers, of which traces remain, served to light this area. In a subsequent period both fireplaces disappeared, though the lums remained. That on the north (roadside) end gave place to a door; that on the south was filled up and panelled over to make a so-called 'ministers' gallery' in conformity with normal Quaker conventions. When my wife and I took over the building in ruinous condition in 1967 it gave us great pleasure to re-open this old hearth, as well as the two ancient ground-floor windows and the western doorway. All other internal features of the building, including the gallery,

The Loupin' Stane at Kinmuck

date from later periods. The gallery should no doubt be thought of as incorporating the north end of the original upper storey.

John Robertson, the first Quaker schoolmaster at Kinmuck, author of at least two published works, died full of years and honour at Kinmuck on the 21st October, 1714. His name, as that of George Gray, poor man and weaver, whose character and sanctity moved his brethren to publish a special testimonial to him on his death in 1690, should always be revered in connection with the heroic days in Kinmuck. Several testimonies exist as to the strength of its meeting, 'the largest in Scotland' in 1696, and it is evident that its school enjoyed a high reputation for several decades at least. It is conjectured that the school ceased to function before the end of the 18th century, possibly before 1781, and thenceforward the building served purely and simply as a meeting-house. The caretaker seems normally to have lived sometimes in the former schoolmaster's house when this became vacant, sometimes in the small cottage next the building itself and now called 'The Friends' Cottage.'

A high point in the meeting-house's later story can be said to have occurred when Elizabeth Fry visited the community in 1818. Her vivid description of her spiritual experience there can be read in the *Memoir of the Life of Elizabeth Fry* (volume 1, pp.326ff in the 1848 edition) published by her daughters, as well as in her manuscript notebooks. Her physical description of the place, of which there is, alas, all too little, supposes the existence *between* the present cottage and the meeting-house of the so-called 'Womens' Meeting-house.' This has disappeared all but its fireplace. Those interested can also read the still manuscript account of the same visit, with a good deal more local colour, written by Mrs Fry's brother, Joseph John Gurney, and which is also preserved at Friends' House, London. Background information concerning the area at this period can be gleaned from the 1792 *Statistical Account of Scotland* (volume 2) which tells us that, besides members of the established church, there resided in the united parishes of Keith-hall and Kinkell some '38 Quakers, 2 seceders, 2 Methodists and 10 Episcopalians.' (page 529).

Quakers ceased to use Kinmuck for regular meetings only in this century. The meeting-house and its attendant cottage were sold first in 1940, the old croft across the road some years later. The cemetery, with its characteristic notes of sobriety and uniformity, alone remains in Friends' custody, having been established from very early if not the earliest times (its present wall, despite the stone inscribed '1680,' probably dates from a re-building of 1846 when we have an account for the work). Both cottages, Allan's Croft and the caretaker's cottage, were re-built on their sites by Friends in 1832. The long line of stables attached to Friends' Cottage for the convenience of Friends coming to meeting has gradually been adapted for living space but the 'loupin' stane' or mounting block survives and is no doubt of great antiquity.

The meeting-house, too, still survives, a once proud sign of contradiction, a symbol of determination and unquenchable faith. Since 1967 it has been cherished slowly and carefully repaired and restored. It is now protected by a covenant with the National Trust for Scotland and the work continues.

There is no other Quaker meeting-house in Scotland of comparable antiquity ('The Pleasance' meeting-house in Edinburgh dates from 1790) so that it can claim a certain unique-status in the kingdom. But, apart from that, those who have knowledge of the record will esteem it for the human and divine values it embodies and reminds us of, values as undying as the glory of the sunset over Mither Tap as seen from nearby Cairnhill and, yes, perhaps even more glorious than that!

Bibliographical Note – Further detail concerning the early history of the Quakers and their buildings in Kinmuck can be found in my article 'The Kinmuck Meeting-House: a Seventeenth Century Scandal?' in the *Aberdeen University Review*, volume XLV, 4, No. 152, Autumn 1974, pages 369-379. George Burnet's *The Story of Quakerism in Scotland 1650-1850* (London 1952) is invaluable but somewhat confusing about the date and whereabouts of the Kinmuck school and meeting-house. Ian J. Simpson *Education in Aberdeenshire before 1872* (London 1947) is excellent on the history of the Quaker school in Kinmuck but does not state where exactly it was held. A chapter entitled 'The Peculiar Hand of Providence' is devoted by Mr A. Fenton Wyness to the Kinmuck Quakers in his book, *Spots from the Leopard* (Aberdeen 1971). Mr Wyness who held the Quakers and Kinmuck very dear, never disagreed with the version of the story given above although it differs in important respects from his own. He did not have access to the documents and background material used in its preparation and which need to be taken account of for an accurate history.

Reproduction of photographs by courtesy of Michael Beasely.

LOUISE DONALD
(M.A.Hons. 1923, LL.B. 1972)

By Flora Garry

In the summer of 1932 we had a holiday cottage at Newburgh on the Ythan. The morning after we arrived I learned that a Mr and Mrs Donald from Inverurie were staying nearby. Donald? That must be Louise. In our student days I knew her as Louise Turner. We often walked together to classes at King's. She had graduated with honours in 1923, gone to teach at Inverurie Academy and in 1927 married Robert Donald, Head of the English Department, where she was his assistant. Robert had held a commission in the Black Watch during the war and was nine years older than Louise. I never knew him. After graduation Louise and I had gone our separate ways; now was a chance to meet again. So I set off across the bents this bright blowy Sunday forenoon to look for her. There they were, down by the water's edge, Louise and two small boys, happy, sunburned and all three 'barfit.' To my regret they were going back to Inverurie the very next day. As it was near the bairns' dinner time I saw them to their door. The cottage was immaculate, everything ready, even a pretty Sunday pudding. How typical!

In March 1936 Robert Donald died very suddenly. Louise was left a widow at the age of thirty-four with three young boys and another baby on the way. What was she to do? She placed her husband's photograph by her bedside, where it remained for the rest of her life, and took thought for her children.

What were her resources? She had good friends but very little money. They say the back is made for the burden; in her case it was true. She had a granite streak in her make-up and physical and mental stamina with single-minded devotion to her family. After Elizabeth's birth she bought a flat in Aberdeen and resumed her teaching career, first at the Central School and then at the High School for Girls as it was then called. Finally she succeeded Dr Nan Shepherd as lecturer in English at Aberdeen Training College. She added to her income by broadcasting and journalism.

When she retired from the Training College Louise went to Rhodesia and in 1961 became an Assistant English Mistress at Arundel School for Girls in Salisbury. By January 1962 she was a Housemistress and in March 1964 was appointed Principal.

When she returned to Aberdeen in 1968 she decided that coffee mornings and the life of an O.A.P. were not for her. Her family – all of them graduates – had their own careers and were scattered. Louise wanted the discipline and stimulus of study once again. She found that in the Faculty of Law of her own University. Acquisition of new knowledge wasn't easy, her former power of recall was impaired – no wonder after the wear and tear of forty years! In 1972 she graduated LL.B. and promptly joined a firm of solicitors: as a side-line, she undertook the editing of the Roll of Graduates of the University of Aberdeen.

Louise was a skilled house-wife, a home lover: she ran her terraced house, close to the centre of the city, practically single-handed. To stay with her was a joy, you were cossetted all the time, your only worry that she was giving herself far too much trouble. Her twelve grandchildren were her favourite guests, her house was their second home.

I was never part of the main stream of her life. Our mutual interest in the dialect and poetry of the North-East brought us together: that, and our affection for one another as human beings: I envy those who knew her as teacher, administrator or lawyer. Therefore, all I can attempt is a vignette, blurred at the edges. (Could any one individual do justice to the gem of many facets that was Louise Donald?).

Ten years were to elapse between our first meeting that Sunday in Newburgh and our second in the Beechgrove studios of the B.B.C. during the war. She asked me home for supper and told me something of her problems. 'If I spend more than two pounds a week on food, I feel I'm overdoing it!' She spoke of her exacting daily routine as a teacher and admitted she became tired. 'But you get the strength somehow' she said, and, pointing to a picture of herself and the children, 'the lioness and her cubs.'

Her interests were not confined to personal matters. Once, while attending a course of lectures, she spent a night with us in Glasgow. I showed her some poetry I was struggling with. 'I like it' she said 'but I have reservations about that bit: try turning it round the other way.' She was right. On another occasion the two of us gave a Saturday Night Lecture in University College, Dundee. The subject was Modern Scots Poetry with readings: Louise was a skilled reader of verse.

Here, in Comrie village, we have a flourishing Poetry Group. Our leader and inspiration was John Graham, emeritus Professor of Systematic Theology in Aberdeen University and twice the city's Lord Provost. He knew Louise and suggested that we ask her to come to one of our meetings; we had a wonderful evening. 'Hamewith' and 'Aberdeen and Twal Mile Roun' were well to the fore. One of our members, Ninian Wright, once minister at Fyvie, asked Louise to wind up with 'There's Aye a Something'; she gave an inimitable rendering. Now, alas, neither Louise nor John will be with us again.

Only once did she and I have a day off together, a day that had nothing to do with poetry. We were both invited to the annual 'Women of Scotland' luncheon in Glasgow. Louise brought her car to Comrie and next morning off we set. Neither of us had a new outfit. But I gave her a pink velvet rose to tack on to her hat and I updated my hat by putting it on back to front. Louise wasn't a conventionally pretty woman, but her blue eyes, heart-warming smile and sense of humour were to make her one of the outstanding personalities at the lunch. Our road led past Glenartney, recalling old-time class rooms and 'The Stag at Eve,' over to Braco and the Roman Camp and on to Dunblane and Stirling. We were two old wifies in their seventies looking forward to a few hours on the ran-dan with as much zest as two student quines to their first 'Varsity Hop. With far more in fact since we were well aware that this day was a bonus, that we might not pass this way again. Next day Louise was up early and back to Aberdeen to tackle an afternoon's work at the Roll of Graduates.

How did she keep up this gruelling schedule? Partly because she was a born organiser, having learned early on to 'gar her heid save her feet.' She was never flustered or in a hurry, never a minute was wasted. 'When God made Time, He made plenty of it.' Not for Louise! 'Her candle goeth not out by night – she eateth not the bread of idleness.' Her letters usually ended: 'It's now past midnight.'

Of course, when she could fit them in, she took holidays, often with family or friends or at her cottage at Collieston. And one of her annual treats was the Bailies of Bennachie picnic rally. Inverurie and Donside had precious memories for her: she wore the Bailies' badge with pride. Some of us will remember that golden autumn afternoon when we listened with enchantment to her delightful voice sounding from the slopes of the hill as we gazed across the farmlands of Buchan to Bennygoak and beyond. We were so happy for her on that special occasion in 1979 when she was accompanied by all four of her family.

After holidays, back to work again, 'reculer pour mieux sauter,' cheerful and forward-looking, warming both hands before the fire of life. For Louise was no unworldly ascetic. A true Aberdonian, she was shrewd and practical, as all who served with her on University committees could testify.

She admired achievement and appreciated its rewards and didn't despise the little luxuries and graces. You had only to step inside her house to be aware of her delight in tasteful, harmonious colour and design, her liking for bonny things.

Although she knew her worth she was never completely satisfied with her own performance. Even about her admirable series of 'Profiles' in Aberdeen's *Leopard Magazine* she had doubts. She admitted to 'butterflies' before every public appearance. She was truly humble. The nearest she ever came to a confession of faith was in a casual remark, made half apologetically: 'When I am gone, I'd like it to be said of me "She hath done what she could".'

Our last meeting was in July 1980 at Cuthbert Graham's honorary graduation. Louise and I sat together in the gallery of the Mitchell Hall. What memories for both of us! She was convalescent after an operation, but made light of the long climb up the steep narrow stairs.

The last time I spoke to her was on the telephone. She wanted me to listen to her reading of two 'Hamewith' poems. She was due to record them later for a 'Scotsoun' cassette and would be glad to know if I thought well of her reading. I don't know if she ever heard that recording. She meant to be at Alford for the inauguration and launching of the cassette, but had the sad news that her grandson Malcolm had been killed in a climbing accident. She went straight to Ellon to try to comfort the other grandmother – 'in simple service simply given to her own kind in their common need.'

Her last letter was short, ending with the gallant understatement: 'They say further surgery is necessary. A nuisance!' The service in church that Christmas Eve was one of mingled grief and thanksgiving. She had enriched the lives of all of us. Then, convoyed by her friends, she took the Inverurie road, one of Bennachie's bairns going home.

OUT OF THE MOUTHS . . .

By Rev. Dr James S. Wood

The dissection of a rose does not enhance its fragrance, nor does the anatomisation of humour make it any more enjoyable. The rose for most of us is there for our delight and humour for the instantaneous pleasure it gives. Let's leave it at that. While humour varies from region to region I believe, though I may be prejudiced, that the north-east brand has a quality all of its own. There's nothing forced about it. It's a built-in attribute or as the natives themselves would say 'It's jist naitrel.' Occasionally it is used as a weapon, if one of the said natives thinks he's being 'taken the loan of.' As when an American standing on the top of Bennachie with a local lad said . . . 'I suppose on a clear day you can see the United States from here?' 'Na' was the reply 'bit on a clear nicht we can see a lot farther than that. We can see the meen!' No sting there but jist a quiet warning to the 'off-taker' to beware.

Some of the best stories I know relate to our bairns. Like the boy after a week at school, who was asked how he liked his teacher, replied 'She's that impident ye wid think it wis yer mither.' Obviously he resented a total stranger taking liberties with him that only his mother was entitled to take. (All these tales, by the way, originated in schools in the shadow of Bennachie or on the fringe of the shadow). Another laddie during his early days at school was asked how he liked it. 'Ach' he said, 'I wish I hidna jine't.' Had he been born before compulsory education he could have opted out!

Our north-east bairns, I have noticed, are very observant even at an early age, as the following true story illustrates. (*All* these stories are true, believe it or not!). It happened after the Christmas holidays when the teacher asked her infant class about the presents Santa had brought them. One child said a dolly, another a ball, another a barrow. Then very proudly, one wee lass said 'Please miss, we got a new baby.' Unaware of danger the teacher said 'It must be very nice to have a new baby.' The postscript was unexpected. When the class skailed the wee mite stayed behind. Having apparently detected a note of longing in the teacher's comment she said 'Wid ye like to have a baby Miss Smith?' What could she say but yes. 'Weel' said the compassionate child. 'I'll tell ye fit t' dee. Ging hame an' pit on a clean goonie an' gang t' yer bed an' sen' for my grannie.' Biology simplified! It is not related whether the teacher followed the instructions given.

There's a puritanical strain in some of our bairns. Once, going to a function in the country, I shared a taxi with a very prim retired teacher, then in her eighties. The memorable event she told me of took place in a school in the vale of Don. At the playtime interval one day a boy came to her with this report . . . 'Please miss, John Broon said a bad word.' 'Oh' she said 'And what was it?' 'I'm nae gaun t' tell you' was the reply. 'But you must tell me.' 'No' he insisted. 'But if ye ging ower a' the bad wirds ye ken, I'll tell ye fin ye come tilt.' Looking sideways at the demure old lady, I wondered just what was the extent of her vocabulary of bad words!

In the days of 'sklates,' before the arrival of exercise books or jotters, an old teacher friend of mine told how on their first day at school she had the bairnies write down the figure 1 (one) copying it from the blackboard. After a time a laddie came to her with his slate covered with '1's' saying 'Div ye wint me t' mak' ony mair girse?' He evidently took the figure 1 to be a blade of grass! That same teacher one warm day, noticed a boy sprawling across his desk and asked 'What's wrong with you Willie?' 'Nithing' he said. 'I'm jist tiret.' No finesse there, just a plain statement of fact.

A boy I knew, now a strapping six-footer and a vet, was always busy on his father's farm even before he went to school, 'hashin neeps,' 'hurlin' a barra' and so forth. His first day at school the teacher gave him a frame with beads to start him counting. After fiddling with it for a while he said, with a touch of scorn, to a surprised teacher 'This is nae wark for a man.' After the work he'd been accustomed to, this was child's play, and an insult to his manhood.

I myself have been cut down to size by a child's observation. One day I was up on a ladder painting the door of the Church hall with paint pot and brush wearing dungarees, my dog collar still showing. A lad on his way home from school stopped and looked quizzically at me and after a time said 'Hey, are e' a minister?' 'Yes, I'm a minister' I replied. 'Weel' he said 'fit wye are e' workin'?' I suppose he had the idea some people have that a minister is a man who does not soil his hands!

The inadequacy of my education was brought home to me once when I was helping with the hairst at Largie. I said to the young loon who was working alongside me 'You get a lovely view from here.' Looking up he said 'Aye, ye can see a fair daud on' the country.' Then he asked me 'Can ye mak' ban's?' 'I'm afraid I can't' I replied. 'I thocht ye gied t' the university' he said. 'Fit did they teach ye there?' Clearly the theological curriculum must be revised. As must be our concept of the hereafter for the laddie who was asked by his minister what his idea of heaven was promptly replied 'Cream on ma porridge an' swing on a gate a' day.'

To return to the classroom, teachers in the north-east tell me that from time to time, they have a lot to learn from their pupils. One boy, not the brightest of arithmeticians, was asked 'If five people came unexpectedly to your house for dinner and your mother had only four potatoes, how would she divide them?' The teacher was put firmly in his place by the answer 'She widna divide them. She wid chap them.'

And here's yet another example of the practicality and down to earthness so often found in our bairns. It was the drawing period in one of our country schools. All visible objects in the room had been used up so the dominie suggested the class might draw a turnip and sent a boy out to a nearby field for one saying 'Take a fair sized one Sandy, maybe about the size of your head.' After a bit Sandy returned with the desired vegetable and the teacher looking at it remarked 'That's almost exactly the size of your head, Sandy. How did you choose it so well?' 'I jist tried my bonnet on them' said the practical Alexander. One teacher I heard of, meaning to be funny, said to a boy who had just joined her class, 'I see you come from the Cabrach, Willie. Why were you born in such a wild out-of-the-way place?' 'Because I winted to be aside my mither' he said. What better reason!

Children I find, are amazed at the ignorance of grown-ups on matters important to them. When a lad from Tarves was in London on holiday with his mother an English lady asked him where he came from. 'Tarves,' he replied. 'Tarves? Where's Tarves?' she queried. 'Guidsake, div ye nae ken faur TARVES is!' The colossal ignorance of these Sassenachs, not to know where the very centre of the universe was located!

A highland minister having preached for an hour paused and then said 'There is a lot more I could say if it would only occur.' I could give many more examples of north-east humour without waiting for them to occur but then I would risk the charge of having entered my anecdotage. However, I'll risk one other true tale. A friend of mine was standing at his garden gate when a lad of six or so on his way to school with his bag on his back, stopped and asked him what he did. 'Oh' said my friend 'I'm retired.' 'What does it mean to be retired?' was the next question. 'It just means you don't have to work any more.' 'Wish I was retired' said his interlocutor, as he continued his unwilling journey to school. So, at this point I too will retire, firm in my conviction that the humour of the north-east, conscious or unconscious, has a quality, and an appeal all of its own.

GLITTERING STONE CIRCLES

By Aubrey Burl

In the shadow of the Bennachies, at the far corner of Scotland, the Grampian mountains are approached by low and peaceful hills whose sides are neatly partitioned into fields by hedges and lines of trees. It is a quiet region but it is dominated by the harsh ridge that rises to the peak of Mither Tap, the legendary body of a goddess whose granite breast overshadows the countryside around here. This is the homeland of Scotland's famous recumbent stone circles. The ruins of over eighty still survive and at least another forty were destroyed in the nineteenth century.

In 1773, while they were in Aberdeenshire on their journey through Scotland, Dr Samuel Johnson and his friend, James Boswell, visited the house of Mr Fraser of Strichen who, wrote Johnson, 'shewed us in his grounds some stones yet standing of a druidical circle, and what I began to think more worthy of notice, some forest trees of full growth.' For once Johnson's scholarly curiosity had failed him. What he found so lacking in interest was, in fact, the wreckage of a stone circle, already 4,000 years old, one of a group of ancient rings in which rituals involving fire, death and astronomy had been performed.

That these were places of heathen sacrifice had long been suspected. The ring at Innesmill was called the 'Devil's Stanes,' and Chapel o' Sink was believed to be an unfinished church that the Devil had dragged halfway down into the earth one night. But to understand what these old and abandoned places really meant to their builders we must understand something about the strange design of these rings.

Although the ruins of more than a thousand prehistoric stone circles exist in the British Isles these magnificent Scottish sites possess a unique feature. In the south-west quarter of their circumference they have a huge block, the recumbent, lying prostrate between the two tallest pillars of the circle. From this pair of flankers the other stones descend in height. There is only one other region of similar circles, a small group in southern Ireland 400 miles from the Scottish rings and no one knows whether there is any connection between them.

The origins of the Scottish circles are just as uncertain. They may have developed from two separate traditions, the Clava Cairns around Inverness and the carved stones at the entrances of Irish passage-graves such as Newgrange. Yet although their ancestry is unclear what these rings do provide through their mysterious architecture and the objects left inside them is an insight into the thinking of prehistoric people whose beliefs were far more subtle than was once believed.

Even the people themselves are little more than shadows. Not one homestead of theirs is known in Aberdeenshire and the only burials found are cremations in coarse urns hidden under large, overgrown cairns. But from the circles have come stone ploughshares, flint arrowheads, heavy stone axes, tools of local flint and stone, and it is possible for us to imagine peasant families working the rich soils, felling trees, grazing lean cattle in the clearings. These were short-lived people, living in sturdy timber cabins, skilled in husbandry, self-sufficient but superstitious. To safeguard themselves against the perils of nature and to honour their ancestors they erected sacred enclosures for their rituals. Today the people are gone and only their lifeless circles of stone survive.

A hundred years ago the rings were dismissed as 'rude stone monuments' but they are not that. The position of the recumbent stone, the measuring and laying-out of the ring, even the deliberately counted number of stones all demonstrate the preconceived plans of the builders who must have spent months on the construction of a megalithic instrument whose components were vital to the community. Even the choice of situation was important as the circle at Dyce shows.

Here the tapering flankers and recumbent jut from a terrace high above Aberdeen airport. This elevated position is typical of the discrimination shown when a location was searched for. Virtually every one of the rings was placed on a hill-shoulder or at the end of a ridge where the recumbent could rest ponderously above a valley or an expanse of lower ground.

If several sites were available then the one nearest a source of stones was chosen. Sometimes, though, good situations were hard to find. Occasionally steepish hillsides had to be accepted and then the site was levelled. At Druidsfield, a circle put up many centuries before the Iron Age druids, men and women cut a shelf into the slope. At Loanhead of Daviot, only six miles NE of Mither Tap, other people laid down stones and rubble to make a level platform. At Berrybrae, a ring excavated by the writer between 1975 and 1978, we found that a thick layer of clay had been heaped up to make a flat arena on which the circle would stand. Such discoveries reveal what efforts the builders would make to ensure a perfect setting for their ring.

Then the recumbent was dragged to the site, its position already decided by astronomical observation. It is noticeable that the source of these great stones was frequently different from that of the other pillars. The recumbent had to be a massive block and even though slender boulders and erratics might lie in the circle's vicinity it cannot have been often that the people found a suitably gigantic block nearby. At Easter Aquorthies the circle-stones weigh on average about 1½ tons and are of a local porphyry but the 12-ton recumbent is red granite from some distance away. The sillimanite monster at Old Keig, weighing some 50 tons, may have been backbreakingly hauled several miles from the river valley.

Other features are just as distinctive. Surveys have shown that the 'circles' were indeed circular and carefully laid out. The length of the 'yardstick' used in measuring the radius may well have been based on personal body-fathoms from fingertip to fingertip of outstretched arms, differing slightly from circle to circle but measuring about 2ft 8ins.

The fact that the circle-stones rise in height towards the recumbent was noticed long ago but what is not so apparent is that the workers counted the stones they put up. The number varied from 8 to 16 but two numbers were preferred. Of 31 well-preseved rings no fewer than 22 consisted of 10 or 11 standing stones. This preference was not decided by the length of the circumference. The Hill of Fiddes with a perimeter of 144ft had 11 stones but so did Sunhoney with a circumference 260ft long. Garrol Wood with a circumference of 186ft and Old Rayne, 283ft, both had 10 stones, a number preferred in the earliest rings where the stones were erected in five opposing pairs. In later sites an eleventh stone was introduced, perhaps to mark the place from which an observer looked across the ring towards the recumbent. Whatever the reason, such numerical preferences show that these societies were capable of counting.

Inside these elegant circles it is quite usual to find a ring-cairn, a low dome of stones with an open centre. Well-preserved examples can still be seen at Whitehill Wood and at Auchquhorthies in Kincardine. In the central spaces pits were dug to receive burnt human bone, sometimes in crude pots fashioned in the centuries around 2200BC.

In 1693 James Garden of Aberdeen University wrote to John Aubrey, the first British archaeologist and author of *Brief Lives,* telling him that 'many years since, they did see ashes of some burnt matter digged out of the bottom of a little circle, set about with stones standing close together, in the center of one of those monuments . . . near the church of Keig,' a record of one of the earliest and probably one of the worst excavations of the cremations inside a recumbent stone circle. Nearly 200 years later, in some enthusiastic but rather haphazard investigations, the Victorian antiquarian, Charles Elphinstone Dalrymple, unearthed cremations in several more rings. Since then still more have been discovered at Loanhead of Daviot, Old Keig and Berrybrae.

Scatters of white quartz have also been found, usually close to the recumbent. At Berrybrae fragments were thick there. At Strichen pieces were exposed brightly when the turf was removed. Quartz and white pebbles have often been found with burials in prehistoric Britain and the conjunction of bone and quartz in the recumbent stone circles suggests that the rings had been erected for rituals symbolically concerned with death.

Cupmarks were carved upon some stones. These depressions, rarely wider than a drinking cup and half as deep, were made by grinding with a hard pebble. Perhaps one ring in ten was cupmarked but it was only the recumbent, its flankers or the stones alongside them that were decorated. Even there the markings were few. Normally there were only two or three cupmarks although some rings such as Sunhoney, ten miles south-east of Mither Tap, or Balquhain have many more, and the amazing recumbent at Rothiemay near Huntly has over a hundred cupmarks on its inner face.

Cupmarks tantalise the imagination. It seems impossible ever to decide their meaning. Being often on the side of stones they could not have been receptacles for sacrificial blood. Nor were they primitive plans of village huts or tallies for herds. In 1920 Major Tilney thought that Sunhoney's cupmarks were arranged in the pattern of *Ursa Major,* the Great Bear, but constellations are not represented elsewhere and the major's interpretation must be considered more ingenious than perceptive.

Cupmarks, quartz, numbers of stones, graded heights, levelled recumbents and burnt bone, these by themselves do little to explain what the circles were. Standing or fallen, flecked with glitters of summer light or romantic in the dusty greenness of a forest the stones exist in a stillness as empty of life as a Siberian snow-plain. Yet, bit by bit, slowly, we are realising what mysteries they conceal.

Until recently the only clues to their age were the objects found in them, ugly urns, an archer's stone wristguard, Bronze Age articles made between 2500 and 1700BC. Confirmation came from Berrybrae. This ring had been vandalised by prehistoric enemies from whose depredations we got charcoal for two Carbon-14 dates of 1500±80BC and 1360±90BC. Because such 'dates' from radiocarbon give results which are too young they have to be adjusted. It seems that Berrybrae's damage occurred around 1750BC. This small, elliptical ring in the farthest corner of Aberdeenshire was possibly built around 1900BC. Early circles such as Loanhead of Daviot may already have been hundreds of years old.

With no huts or settlements found in the entire region almost nothing is known about the builders. Yet the rings stand within two or three miles of each other, far too close to have been tribal centres, and each was probably put up in the homeland of a single family who farmed a territory of four to six square miles, land enough to support 10 to 20 people who grazed cattle and grew crops on the hillsides overlooking the coastal woodlands. In his letter to John Aubrey, James Garden added that local inhabitants believed that at the ring of Aquahorthies pagan priests 'had caused earth to be brought from other adjacent places . . . which is given for the reason why this parcel of land, though surrounded with heath and moss on all sides, is better and more fertile than other places thereabouts.' Nowadays we know from modern soil-maps that the rings stand alongside but rarely on large patches of rich, well-drained soil, a revelation of the expertise of those early farmers.

Lacking trace of domestic rubbish the circles were not for occupation. Nor were they workshops for potters or metalsmiths. Without substantial banks they were unsuitable for defence or cattle pens. James Fergusson in 1872 wrote that they were 'the graves of chiefs, or sometimes, it may be, family sepulchres,' but the cremations are too few for the rings to be burial-grounds. No more than one or two people's bones rested in most circles. Had any ring been used as a cemetery for only a hundred years a family of twenty would have suffered some eighty deaths in that time. Nor are men, women and children equally represented. At Berrybrae only the partial cremations of two children were discovered. At Loanhead of Daviot over five pounds in weight of bones were found, mostly of adults but with fifty or more smashed fragments of children's skulls amongst them.

That the rings were shrines rather than graveyards is made even more probable because of the strict conditions imposed upon their design. The position of the recumbent was of great importance. These heavy and awkward stones were without exception placed only between the SSE and SW of the circumference. As long ago as 1520 Hector Boece, Principal of the newly-founded Aberdeen University, knew this and in his *History of Scotland* described how 'huge stones were erected in a ring, and the biggest of them was stretched out on the south side to serve for an altar whereon were burnt the victims in sacrifice to the gods.' How Boece learned of the hidden cremations is a mystery unless folk memories of pyres and burnt bones had endured for 4,000 years. It is even more surprising that although he correctly noted the southerly position of the recumbents no good explanation for this was forthcoming for more than 400 years. There was no common lie of the land to account for it, it was not the direction from which pioneering ancestors had come, there was no prevailing wind or sacred mountain towards which all the circles faced. The answer almost certainly had to be astronomical and several astronomers have looked for the answer.

In 1909 Sir Norman Lockyer, Director of the Solar Physics Observatory, examined 29 recumbent stone circles. Rather strangely, he assumed that the sightline in them was from the recumbent to the other side of the ring rather than the reverse. He concluded that 15 rings pointed towards the risings of the stars Capella and Arcturus, 3 to midsummer sunrise, 2 to May Day sunrise, 5 were 'special cases' facing north or west, and 4 were simply non-astronomical. An archaeologist, Alexander Keiller of the famous Dundee marmalade family, was forthrightly scornful of these and other 'verbose fatuities' uttered by 'irresponsible cranks and monomaniacal theorists.'

Sixty years after Lockyer, Professor Alexander Thom of Oxford University investigated 30 circles and, to him, only 4 seemed to be of astronomical significance. Oddly, in his sites not one of the nine suggested alignments passed over the recumbent stone. Instead, they were directed towards inconspicuous outlaying stones or to other rings. Like Lockyer's they too were composed of a variety of heavenly targets, sunrise at midsummer, midwinter, May, October and November, sunset in November and the northerly setting of the moon. This lack of uniformity suggested a casualness that was belied by the symmetry and elegance of the circles.

As with other discoveries the solution was teasingly simple. Fifty rings are still in good enough condition for the compass-bearing of the recumbent stone to be established. Every one fell between 155° (SSE) and 235° (SW). Forty-two were between 155° and 204°, well south of the sun's midwinter risings and settings, seven were between 229° and 235° and only a very questionable alignment of 221° from the ravaged ring at Stonehead was anywhere near midwinter sunset. It was likely, therefore, that the rings had been orientated on some target not when it was rising or setting but when it was up in the sky. It was the full moon.

Unlike the sun the moon's circle is complex. Every midwinter the sun rises at the SE and sets at the SW. The moon is different. In the latitude of Aberdeen its southerly risings shift over a period of nine years from SSE to ESE. At its most southerly it will rise around 154° and set at 206° although a hilly skyline might reduce this arc to as little as 160°-200°. Then over the following years it will gradually rise and set farther from the south until it is coming up at 127° and setting at 233°. Having reached these limits it will then slowly return to its most southerly extremes of 154° and 206°, the complete cycle taking 18.6 years.

Because 42 recumbent stones lie between 154° and 204° it seems likely that the rings were aligned on the moon when it was in the sky between these southerly limits. Seven other circles with recumbents between 229° and 235° may have been built by people looking towards the moon at its setting at its other extreme.

From this it might be thought that any family intending to build a recumbent stone circle might have to wait up to nine years for the full moon to reach its desired position in the night sky but this was probably not so. Families already settled in the area would have known when the right time was approaching and there is quite positive evidence that several groups must have joined in the work when a stone circle was being constructed. The sheer weight of the recumbent proves this.

If those recumbent stones that have flat upper surfaces are inspected it will be seen that often their tops are perfectly horizontal. Their undersides are slightly peaked or else one end tapers so that once the stone was in position it could be tilted up and down, balanced on the pointed bottom. Perhaps putting a water-filled trough as a kind of improvised spirit-level on its top the people manoeuvred the recumbent until they saw it was horizontal. Then they jammed bulky stones underneath it, packing them so tightly that often the block has not shifted since that time. Such chockstones can be seen at the circle in Midmar churchyard where it is obvious that the recumbent was levered up and down on its thicker eastern end until the builders were satisfied that its top was level.

If, however, each ring was the shrine of a single family then so few men and women could never have budged a recumbent weighing ten tons or more. Whether it had to be moved two miles or two yards such a mass needed at least 20 and probably 50 adults to drag it. Draught oxen are unlikely and the easiest explanation for this puzzle is that neighbouring families joined in the task, an indication of peaceful co-existence, sadly different from the disruptions of hostile newcomers in later years.

Such co-operation also explains why similar orientations are found amongst the stone circles, each small district around the Bennachies having its own preference. Near Old Deer most of the rings face roughly to the south. The circles close to Inverurie are aligned towards the SSW but, not far away, by Echt, SW was the desired direction. Quite unusually, the late recumbent stone circles south of the Dee were oriented towards the SSE.

Such local preferences presumably originated in the orientation of the earliest circle in a district. Its builders could, quite casually, have aligned their recumbent stone upon the southern full moon as it rose, or when it was high in the night sky, even when it was setting. Whatever its orientation this would become the norm for later circles whose workers would have been aware, by long tradition, of when the moon was approaching the 'right' position. They would know from experience when the moon was once again reaching its southern limits or even when the moon, in the intervening years of its cycle, happened to be close to the desired position. A sightline for the second circle could then be set up, repeating within a few degrees the alignment of the older ring. The people, seemingly, were not much concerned with precision. It was the moon that mattered, not its exact situation in the heavens.

Certainly there was nothing well-defined about these sightlines. Looking across the 66ft diameter of the average circle towards a recumbent 15ft long there would have been an arc of some 14° between the flankers, far too wide for astronomical research but ideal for people engaged in ceremonies that were long drawn out and performed only when the moon was visible. At Sunhoney it would have taken the moon more than an hour to pass between the flanking pillars, its light shining past the recumbent on to the centre of the ring-cairn where in 1868 Dalrymple found fire-marked stones and burnt human bones.

Fire, death and the moon are the vital elements of these circles. At their centres the earth is often reddened where pyres blazed before the scorched bones were picked out, the ashes raked away and the ring-cairn built. Every thing and every action was a symbol. Sometimes things were smashed and 'killed' to accompany the dead. Near the middle of Loanhead of Daviot one lump of charcoal, one potsherd and one splinter of bone were buried inside a curve of stones that resembled the new moon's crescent.

So spectacular would the moon have been, framed between the silhouetted flankers, that this, surely, was the effect desired by the builders. In most rings, moreover, there would have been an even more dramatic occurrence when the moon was at its most southerly. Then the full moon would have risen barely a degree above the skyline. It would have seemed to

Loanhead of Daviot, Aberdeenshire.
Recumbent Stone Circle.

drift along the very top of the recumbent. One wonders what symbolism there was in the cupmarks there or in the moonlit quartz that gleamed whitely against the darkness of the ground around it.

What the moon meant to those distant people we may never know. Quite clearly it was essential to them just as the sun was to other communities. Miles to the south, near Stonehenge, a little girl was killed, her skull split completely in two. Her body was buried inside the rings of posts at Woodhenge, placed so that she was in line with the midsummer sunrise. Similarly, in recumbent stone circles, children may have died so that their spirits might merge with the potent moon. There is a scrap of supporting evidence. Boece, the mediaeval scholar, not only mentioned cremations in his *History* but added that rituals inside the rings demanded a monthly offering and 'that is why the new moon was hailed with certain words of prayer.'

One wonders whether Boece was repeating folk-stories that had preserved memories of human sacrifice at the time of the new moon, rites that were committed 200 generations before his time. This seems incredible and yet, having encountered other signs of the symbolic thinking of these early people, it is possible that they constructed likenesses of the new moon inside their rings. A crescent of small stones was found inside Loanhead of Daviot. There are comparable but grass-grown settings at Loudon Wood and at Whitehill Wood, a ring now blurred with mildew, moss and the green corruption of antiquity.

Our excavation at Berrybrae uncovered a crescentic platform, littered with quartz, along the inner face of the recumbent. Another excavation at the smashed site of Strichen revealed a crescent of heavy stones lavishly strewn with lumps of wax-white quartz. Such horned and white-lain settings may, like the cupmarks, have been images of the moon just as the graded heights of the circle-stones may have symbolised its rising and descending journey through the sky.

Much remains unknown about these decayed rings. We no longer think of them as crude enclosures but neither are they delicate observatories. They are pagan places, places of country folk who acted out their rituals of life and death inside these rings of stone. From circle after circle one sees the dark and everlasting body of the Bennachies and Mither Tap looming over the countryside, lilting in bars of sunlight or blurred by the gloom of heavy, sinking clouds. Beneath these ancient hills the stones survive, deserted 3,000 years ago as rain swept across the dying of the Bronze Age.

William Wordsworth in *The Prelude* wrote of 'small circles glittering idly in the moon.' Moonlight still shines on Loanhead of Daviot, Old Keig, Cothiemuir Wood and scores of other rings. One day – or night – we may understand why.

————

CIRCLES WORTH VISITING
In State Care
EASTER AQUORTHIES. NJ 732208. 2¾ miles W of Inverurie. Splendid recumbent and well-graded circle-stones.

LOANHEAD OF DAVIOT. NJ 747288. 5 miles NNW of Inverurie. Ring-cairn, cupmarks on stone east of east flanker.

TOMNAVERIE. NJ 486034. ¾ mile SE of Tarland. On edge of quarry with dramatic views.

Privately Owned.

COTHIEMUIR WOOD. NJ 617198. 3½ miles NE of Alford. In forest, 200 yards from road. Stones graded in height, well-shaped flankers. On Forbes Estate.

MIDMAR KIRK. NJ 699064. 2½ miles W of Echt. In churchyard. Chockstones under recumbent.

SUNHONEY. NJ 716056. 1½ miles W of Echt. Ask permission at farm. Cupmarked recumbent, graded heights, traces of surrounding bank.

THERE'S BENNACHIE

By Sheena M. Kelman

There's Bennachie we say
And we know what we mean.
A landmark, a focal point
you offer the reassurance of familiarity
to those who set their stooks
or draw the furrow straight
with an eye on Bennachie.

And those who pitted the stubby legs of infancy
against your sides can find you yet;
distilled images
woven with childhood's vigour
into our own mythology.

Yes, there's Bennachie.
We know where we are.
And with a foot on such firm ground
we dare to mock at our own uncertainty
for even when we peer beyond gnarled heather roots
chasing elusive history. We know
we've made a mountain out of you, Bennachie.

Seeking our own identity?

SCHOOL DAYS ON BENNACHIE

By John Philip

My first encounter with Bennachie was when I was a schoolboy at Gordon's. I think it was early in the summer of '24 that probably the first major school excursion to the hill took place. The instigator was one of the worthies on the staff – 'Boothie,' the geography master, whose teaching was always far removed from academic study. He planned to take all volunteers by special train to Oyne, climb the Mither Tap, descend to Monymusk, and pick up the train, by now in position there on the Kintore-Alford branch line.

The morning in Aberdeen was dull but dry and so it continued until the lower slopes of the hill. From there on it was very different. We climbed through dense woolly mist with no idea of what lay ahead.

In addition to a number of members of staff, the expedition was led by Dr Douglas Simpson – 'Fossil,' who in previous summers had made one of his earliest archaeological digs with the aid of his own Grammar School Troop of Scouts on the fort on the summit. He was to tell us of his discoveries when we arrived there, which we finally did. After his talk we ate our sandwiches while already conjuring up the delights of the feast of pies and peas we had been promised at the baker's at Monymusk, and had already been paid for, being part of the total outlay for the day of two shillings.

Now another important character in the tale looms up. This was no other than Mr Williams, the chemistry master, whose nick-name 'Pea Soup' well fitted our circumstances. With nil visibility the question was how to proceed. We gathered from various mumblings that we were not to go directly downhill but were to veer along the ridge before making the descent. 'Fossil' Simpson and 'Pea Soup' Williams were to lead; Fossil because it was reckoned he knew the hill like the palm of his hand, while Pea Soup had the only compass in the company – one very small circular model attached to his dangling watch-chain.

So off we set and then it seemed very little time before we were going downhill. As we descended the fog thinned and suddenly we were in full sunlight, but deep dismay! We had descended the wrong side of the hill! Bennachie stood between us and the pie and peas – not forgetting the tea and the train!

Poor Boothie! He was the one who had taken our money. The fog still lay thickly on the upper slopes, so it was decided that another attempt at crossing was out of the question. What to do? Members of staff were sent off along to Chapel of Garioch to phone the railway authorities and see what could be done, and being those days, it was possible to have the train re-routed back to Oyne without major delay.

The winner that day was the shop-keeper at the Chapel of Garioch – he was besieged! Poor Boothie was well out of pocket placating the pupils that he had so successfully persuaded to take part in what he proclaimed would be, and in truth turned out to be – a Day to Remember.

That was my experience as a pupil. Later I was to carry the responsibility that Boothie had that foggy day. In 1950 I became an assistant at Tertowie Residential School, and for a number of years on every third Thursday of the teaching year it was my responsibility to take a party of Aberdeen City School pupils to the top. And that was regardless of the weather – at least that was how it turned out, for the bus was ordered at the beginning of the session, and the pupils were primed for the occasion from the day of their arrival. It was not just a trip to the hill, it was a tour of the Garioch. The headmaster at the time, George Dickie, was himself a Garioch loon, and before we made for the hill we visited such places as the Quakers' Cemetery at Kinmuck, the Bass, the Maiden Stone, and after the climb had a conducted tour of the Pittodrie Home Farm, then internationally famous for the world record-priced Shorthorn bulls – Pittodrie Upright and Uprise.

But it was the hill climb that seized their imagination, and no more so than when the elements were wild. I can see them still, one living line, each wrist securely grasped by his neighbour as the wind swept them across the Devil's Causeway and staggered them with the force of its impact. Or in the spring when the burn was still filled with snow, racing down its course against all advice, and then all of a sudden disappearing right up to the armpits. That was a lesson they would not forget! Or on a day when the heat was such that you could hardly touch the bare rock faces to keep going regardless of the temperature and then bewail not having drunk at the well because of the determination to be up there looking down on class-mates still making the climb.

At this period I reckon there were hundreds of Aberdeen children making the climb, when many an adult in the Garioch had never set foot on it. Yes, I am all in favour of encouraging the school on to the hill, for I know indeed how much and in so many ways Bennachie has to offer.

THE MONYMUSK STONE
By Dr Jon Whiteley

One hundred and fifty years ago, the best known antiquity in Monymusk – the Donside parish rich in associations with the past – was the Monymusk Stone. Not a familiar name today, but in those days it was a conspicuous monument. The laird, Sir Archibald Grant, moved it in the late eighteenth century from a field by the Don about a mile downstream from the village and set it upright by the side of the recently completed Kemnay-Monymusk road near the farm of Nether Mains. Given a coat of whitewash with its decorations picked out in black paint to render them visible and more lively according to Alexander Duff, the minister of the time, it presented an object for exercising the talents of the antiquaries. The symbolism of the cross raised no particular problems but the accompanying step shape with the knob-like ends and the triple discs below have exercised the ingenuity and scholarship of antiquaries ever since. The oddest explanation was offered in 1805 by the schoolmaster of Kemnay, Charles Dawson, who thought the marks were hieroglyphics and translated them as:

'Here lies John Aikenwall beneath this lang stane
At the fight of Platecock, his life from him was taen.'

Now that the morphology of Pictish 'symbol' stones is fairly well
established, we know that the Monymusk Stone was carved about 800AD in
the tradition of the earlier pagan 'symbol' stones of Pictland which are
abundant in the North-East. It belongs with the Maiden Stone and one or
two others – at Migvie, Formaston and Dyce – among the earliest Christian
monuments in the area. Indeed, the Monymusk Stone could well be the
earliest tangible relic of Christianity in Aberdeenshire, for, as
Dr W. D. Simpson pointed out some years ago, the style of the design,
outlined on an undressed boulder, belongs to a native tradition which
presumably antedates the relief carving on the Maiden Stone and elsewhere.

Enthusiasts for the art of Northern Pictland will always prefer the refined
assurance of the native incisions to local attempts at relief carving imitated
from the art of the West and South. Picts in the Grampian peninsula had
an art of their own which was, as the carver of the Maiden Stone found
when he tried to translate his native outlines into rounded forms, ill-adapted
to the bas-relief. The carver of the Monymusk Stone made no such
concessions, skilfully matching his surface pattern to the angles and texture
of his material – a seven foot slab of dark grey granite, hard as iron, and
scored by the ice which left it in the valley thousands of years before. He
placed the cross right of centre to incorporate a vertical striated ridge which
gives the shaft the barest hint of three dimensions; this incipient relief and
the typically Irish knot-work on the arms and the three-ply interweaving on
the shaft – awkwardly dropping a thread towards the base, perhaps an error
or revision – in medias res – draw attention to the fact that the cross was a
recent import into the thriving two-dimensional art of the Northern Picts.

The design of the cross and two 'symbols' is large and bold, outlined
with ruler and compass and then pocked and chiselled from the metallic
surface. The final cutting of the design, however, is broad and shallow,
making an indistinct effect, best viewed in a raking light. The hard granite
is, perhaps, to blame but I wonder, unnerving though the idea may be,
whether the design, like the inscriptions on the contemporary and similar
runic stones of Scandinavia, was not intended to be filled with colour?

Two or three ideas seem worth considering among the suggested
meanings. In 1956, John Stuart, secretary of the Spalding Club, saw a
likeness between the circles and an ancient brooch-like object in Trinity
College, Dublin. The Rev. William Macpherson, author of the modestly-
titled *Materials for a History of the Church and Priory of Monymusk* was
reminded of a hinged box by the step-shaped design. There is a consistency
about the minor details of the best and earliest of the so-called symbol
stones which tends to confirm that the artist had an object in his mind. The
three lines, for instance, joining the outer rings to the central disc, look like
no mere pattern-making, but probably correspond to an aspect of this
original. The step-like design could represent a wooden box with sliding lid.
Carved boxes of this general type are not unknown in the Celtic world – but
the extreme rarity of surviving wooden or metal objects from Pictland
makes identification hazardous. Dr Simpson once suggested that the main

element might represent a processional cross. His attractive idea, if true, strengthens the likelihood that the Pictish artists thought in terms of familiar objects rather than abstract symbols. The type of equal-armed and shafted cross recurs on a later slab at Dyce along with the brooch-like object and again on a badly-cut stone in Wick which features our 'box' on the reverse side. Presumably these items had a commonplace significance taken in isolation or together but we shall probably never know what this is.

At the turn of the present century Sir Arthur Henry Grant, Bart., one of the great improving lairds of Aberdeenshire, moved the stone a second time to a new billiard room in the House of Monymusk where it was fitted for its protection into a specially-built cupboard. It had survived twelve hundred years of exposure to the weather extremely well but the move came too late to save it from the agent of the Ordnance Survey who defaced it with the familiar broad arrow as it stood by the roadside. In moving to the safekeeping of the House, however, the Monymusk Stone, once a familiar landmark on the road to Alford, disappeared from public memory. How many sharp-eyed visitors to the ancient parish church have puzzled over the decorated stone included, at the suggestion of Dr Simpson, in the design of the east window of the chancel?

Now, however, moved for the third time in its history, on the 4th May, 1979, it is safe, visible and very-aptly housed in the vaulted-entrance to the church, built eight hundred years ago for use by the Culdees, a Celtic brotherhood associated with Monymusk. If they did not themselves set up the stone by the riverside some four hundred years earlier, they would at least have been familiar with the use of the stone and the meaning of its emblems.

The writer gratefully acknowledges the help of Lady Tweedsmuir and Dr Revel Coles, Oxford, in preparing this article.

THE MAIDEN STEEN

By James D. Glennie

Th' sojer'd seen a thoosan' sichts
Bit this faer bleirt his een,
Aul Bennachie in the caul caul licht
O' a big roon hervest meen.

He steed at th' fit an' gaukit up
An' a' wis calm an' still,
Fin a silken shrood fell ower th' meen
An' happit oot th' hill.

Fin mist gid bye he saa a sicht
Nae mortal e'e hid seen,
For th' Deil wis there wi' horn't heid
Droolin' ower a heath'n steen.

Neist he saa a thackit hoose
An' a lass her bannocks bakin',
A lichtsim' cheil wis at th' door
An' baith th' twa wir claikin'.

Th' cheil he said, 'Afore yir throwe
A road a'll big o' steen
Tae tak ye easy tae th' Tap
An' we'll mairry fin a'm deen.'

Sh' toss't her heid an' gid a lauch
Her cheeks wir growe'n rosie,
'A' richt ma lad ging big yir road
An' a'll tak ye tae ma bosie.'

Wi' gloatin' smirk th' cheil ran oot
An' left th' bonny Janet,
Wi' forket flash an' muckle soon
He big't a road o' granit'.

Th' Deil wint back tae claim his bride
In monstrous shape he wis noo,
Th' lassie kennen she'd bin trick't
Ran skirlin' ower the' girss o.

Th' Deil leuch an' skirl't abeen
'Nae mortal man wull wed ye,
Satan's wife ye said ye'd be
An' Satan he wull hae ye.'

He noo rax't oot a horny han'
An' touch't her on th' shooder,
Th' quine lat oot a piteous soon
Bit th' Deil he leuch th' looder.

Th' sojer saa in th' licht o' the' meen
A rikkin' steen upstannin',
He look't at th' steen an' winner't sair
O' th' Deil an' his hellish waddin'.

Th' sojer'd seen a thoosan' sichts
Bit this faer bleirt his een,
A Maiden Steen in th' caul caul licht
O' a big roon hervest meen,
A Maiden Steen in th' caul caul licht
O' a big roon hervest meen.

BENNACHIE LOVE STORY

By Gillian M. L. Davidson

For all that we, as hard-working and diligent Bailies, care for and look after our hill, we know in truth there is a much older and more potent power guarding Bennachie – the aged giant known as 'Jock O' Bennachie.'

Jock, who may in actual fact merit the title of 'the original Bailie,' guarded his hill against all-comers, frequently by the expedient of hurling huge boulders at them. He was, nevertheless, of an essentially gentle and peaceful nature, and looked often for a wife to share his lonely existence. Legend has it that he was finally captivated by the beauties of a certain Lady Annc, a love which was to prove his undoing, for according to the ballad 'The Key o' Bennachie' quoted in A. I. McConnochie's *Bennachie*, she was instrumental in enchanting him and placing him, under lock and key, somewhere inside the hill he loved. In there he is trapped, until one day

'An' ae sin wi' ae e'e,'
'Tis sagely said, 'sall, some day, 'fin'
The Key o' Bennachie.'

In a second ballad quoted by Mr McConnochie, entitled 'The Rival Giants,' the Lady Anne shunned Jock o' Bennachie in favour of his great rival Jock o' Noth. Jock o' Bennachie, in his jealousy, hurled a stone from Bennachie to Tap o' Noth, and killed the two lovers. So, whichever version of the tale you prefer, whether you believe Jock lies enchanted and trapped below the hill, or whether he has disappeared, mourning his lady love, do not think that the spirit of Jock has vanished totally from this mortal world. On those misty days on the hill, when you are alone, and every sound rising from the whiteness which surrounds you takes on an unknown quality, go and stand on Craig Shannoch, close to Jock's bed, 'Little John's Length,' and listen. Is that the wind whistling round the stones, or is it the call of a lost spirit, crying in despair for a love no longer held in this world? . . .

> 'Swirling mist was the hill's cloak that forenoon,
> And Craig Shannoch in damp whiteness was won,
> When a heart-felt sigh whistled suddenly by
> 'Lady Anne, O Lady Anne, have you come?'
>
> It held the despair of a drowning man,
> When the last straw clutched has finally gone –
> As it screamed to the sky its age-old cry
> 'Lady Anne, O Lady Anne, have you come?'
>
> Ice cold breath of that voice blew by the stones,
> Freezing, chilling me right through to the bone,
> And the ghosts I heard could not be dispersed –
> 'Lady Anne, O Lady Anne, have you come?'
>
> Does the wind play strange tricks on a listener's ears?
> Or the cry of a ghost ring out through the years?
> And does Jock still await, entwined by his fate,
> 'Lady Anne, O Lady Anne, when will you come?'.'

FIGHTING LESLIES: FROM BENNACHIE TO RUSSIA

By Dr Paul Dukes, University of Aberdeen

Some years back, I was lucky enough to live at the back of Bennachie in the parish of Leslie, and as a professional historian, naturally enough I became interested in its past, of which I was continually reminded every day by looking out from a house built around 1794 on to a castle begun in 1661. These edifices as well as much else about the parish of Leslie have been evocatively described in the *Book of Bennachie* by William Leslie Gavin, and I would not want to repeat anything already said by him, although I do think that the story of the origin of the family that bears his middle name is worth telling in somewhat more detail, especially since it leads on to the main part of what I have to say, which concerns the manner in which members of the family learned the trade of arms on and around the slopes of Bennachie, and then went off in the period just before Leslie Castle was built to ply it on the battlefields of Europe. As a specialist in Russian history, I was astonished to discover that fighting Leslies were to be found in the first half of the seventeenth century in many parts of Eastern Europe, including Muscovy, as Russia was usually known at that turbulent time.

Who were the Leslies, and why were so many of them available as mercenaries in Eastern Europe in the early modern period? Appropriately enough, as the family's historian, Colonel K. H. Leslie tells us, the founder was probably Hungarian, Bartholomew or Bartolf, arriving in Scotland in

1067 as part of the retinue of Margaret, the sister of Edgar, Anglo-Saxon claimant to the throne just usurped by William of Normandy. Fleeing from the Conquest, Edgar intended to take his family back to Hungary, where several of them, including his mother and his sister Margaret, had been born. However, the refugees were blown off their course to the continent by bad weather and were forced to seek shelter in the Firth of Forth. At St. Margaret's Hope, Queensferry, as it became known in commemoration of the event, they were well received by the King of Scotland, Malcolm Canmore, who took a fancy to Margaret and soon married her. Bartholomew also appealed to Malcolm Canmore as a trusty retainer, and the King made him governor of Edinburgh Castle, dubbed him knight and granted him lands in several parts of Scotland, including what was to become Aberdeenshire. According to family legend, the King said that the knight could have all the lands for a mile around any point where he found it necessary to rest and feed his horse while on a journey to the north. On his return to court, in order to identify the place where it had stopped near Bennachie, the knight said:

> 'Between a lesse ley and a mair,
> My horse it tyrd and stoppit there.'

An apt title coming to him as well as an equal gift for metrical rhyming speech, the King answered:

> 'Lord Lesley shalt thou be,
> And thy heirs after thee.'

Whatever the basis for the legend, it is undoubtedly the case that Bartholomew did obtain a grant in land at Leslie, even if the name itself came about in some other manner and the man himself, as some accounts have it, was of Flemish rather than Hungarian origin.

While another branch of the family established itself in Fife, some of Bartholomew's successors remained at Leslie, Aberdeenshire, to become one of the first families of the county that formed the largest part of the north-east of Scotland, cut off from the rest of the kingdom in early times by distance and difficult terrain. At the beginning of the sixteenth century, John Major wrote of a more formidable barrier than Bennachie, namely the Mounth, as the 'Alps of Scotland . . . impassable by horsemen.' Remoteness necessarily made the local inhabitants self-reliant against the vagaries of their climate and the continued incursions of unruly highlanders. 'Wild Scots' normally at war rather than peace as Major described them. Discord could be domestic, too, as was indicated about a century later when the Synod of Aberdeen in its complaint to James VI and I early in 1606 talked of the miserable confusion of the region and gave as specific causes:

> 'In commonweill, FIRST, Monye deadlie feudis arysin amangst Forbesis and Irwingis, Leslyes and Leythis, quhilk are licklie be thair pairties to draw on the haill country to bloodie factionis. SECONDLIE, That every man that plesis wearis gunis, pistolis, rydis with jacks, spearis, knopsknais, without controlment.'

The complaint of the Synod notwithstanding, the confusion and factions continued. An apt example comes from the Register of the Privy Council of Scotland for 1634, when a complaint was made by Adam Abercrombie of

Old Rayne that, in contravention of the laws forbidding the wearing of hagbuts (or muskets) and pistols, John Leith of Harthill, with a great number of 'sorners and broken men' (accomplices and outlaws) came 'under cloud and silence of night' in the month of March to the dwelling house of one Henry Clerk, tenant to the complainant. The sequel is best described in the legal record's own inimitable language. The marauders:

'. . . brasht the doores thairof, tooke one of the said Adams men, callit Thomas Clerk, and band him hand and foote, held another of his servants, callit John Mitchell, till they searched the said Henrie his hous, resolving if they had gottin him to have slaine him, and missing him they tooke a broust of new beir, drank out a part thairof and spilt the rest upon the floore, brake up his kists and beeff fatts, cutted his seekes with swordes and durkes, spulzied and away tooke his haill salt beiff, muttoun and other victuall being within the hous, with his bed cloathes and what ellis they could find in the hous. And thereafter the same night they came to the dwelling hous of George Mathesone, another of the compleaners servants, strake up his doores, searched the poore man throw the haill hous with candle light, and missing him they threatened to hold his wifes soles to the fire whill she sold tell both where her husband and his moneyes wer; and they took with thame suche small geir as they fand in the hous. And upon the 17 day of the said moneth of Marche they came of new to the said Henrie Clerks hous, patt violent hands on his person, tooke him captive, being his Majesteis free subject, band his hands and caried him as a prisouner with thame to the dwelling hous of Johne Alexander in the hill brae on the north side of Bennachie where he lay two nights in the yrnes, and caried him over the hill to the dwelling hous of Thomas Gordoun in the Glentoun upon the south side of the said hill, quhair they laye him three nights in the yrnes. And the said Johne gave command to his Hieland men to sticke the said Henrie how soone they perceaved anie man to come to releeve him; and before he lett the poore man goe he tooke him deepelie sworne that he sould never strike pleuche nor harrow in the lands of Aldrayne, and he forced the said Henrie to give him ane hundred merkes. And when his poore wife had sauld her best plenishing to gett this hundreth merkes and she having offered the same to him for her husbands releefe, he refuised the same till Johne Leith of Newlands his wife became cautioner for the other dollar. Lykeas the said Johne Leith of Harthill be himselfe and his commissioners threatned the whole tennants of Aldrayne nather to strike pleuche nor harrow upon the saids lands, otherwayes he vowed to God to hang thame everie man over thair awne balkes. Upon occassioun whereof the haill labourers and occupyers of the lands of Aldrayne left the ground, so as there wes not a reiking hous within aucht plewes of the saids lands, aucht crofts and a myle of ground, except onelie Johne Ker, who maried one Leith to his wife.'

Although John Leith and his henchmen attempted by threats to stop their deeds from coming to light, enough witnesses stepped forward for the said John Leith to be confined in the tolbooth in Edinburgh from which he was released on probation a year or so later.

Among the witnesses against Leith of Harthill had been two members of the rival Leslie family, including one Alexander, who was probably the bearer of that name to be involved more actively in another fracas recorded by the Privy Council that took place in Edinburgh Canongate in 1635 as a sequel to the burning of the tower of the House of Frendraught in 1630. It was probably in retaliation for the attribution of the fire to their family by the Crichtons of Frendraught that Alexander and other Leslies fell upon David Seton, servant to the Laird of Frendraught, 'and toukit him, and thairafter drew thair suords and whingers, and cruellie persewed him of his lyffe, strake out a nomber of straiks at him and hes wounded himn to the effusion of his blood.' Citizens of Edinburgh intervened to save the life of David Seton, for the attempt on which Alexander Leslie was placed in the very tolbooth from which Leith of Harthill had just been released.

Among the several other Leslies bearing the name Alexander we will take one descended from the Balquhain branch of the family as an exemplar of the manner in which the fighting qualities learned on the slopes of Bennachie were exhibited on the battlefields of Europe. This particular Alexander Leslie spent some time in both the Polish and Swedish armies before entering the Russian service in 1630. It was probably in 1618 that he had his first close contact with Russians when taken prisoner along with other Polish soldiers during the siege of the fortress of Smolensk, In spite of this setback, the Poles duly took their siege to a successful conclusion, and then held on to what became an important part of the defence of their extended eastern frontier, while the Russians under the first member of the Romanov dynasty, Michael, planned to recapture it. Alexander Leslie became an important part of these plans; having helped the Poles to besiege Smolensk, he was now to be involved in a Russian siege of the same fortress.

For this purpose, he was actually sent to Moscow by King Gustavus of Sweden, who was hoping for the support of Muscovite Russia against the Poles and their allies in the great struggle that became known as the Thirty Years War. Having willingly exchanged one patron for another in 1630, Leslie set off for Western Europe at the beginning of 1631 on a mission to secure more men and materials for his new Romanov master. Among those giving a favourable response to Michael's appeal was his brother monarch, Charles I of England and Scotland, who sent out warrants for the levy of mercenaries in both his kingdoms. One of these is to be found in the same records of the Privy Council that tell us about the more informal hostilities of a domestic nature occurring at about the same time. In March 1633, Charles I ordered his officials north of the border to assist 'Sir Alexander Leslie, knight, generall colonell of the forrane forces of the Emporour of Russia' in his attempt to complete his mercenary force by raising one more company for the purpose. Leslie himself was actually back in Russia by this time, participating in the siege of Smolensk along with brother Scots, some English and other mercenaries, whose number was probably augmented as 1633 progressed and then well into 1634.

However, those British soldiers who are known to have arrived in the northern port of Archangel in July 1634 were too late to have any effect on the outcome of the siege, for the Russian commander had been forced to conclude an armistice with the Poles at the very beginning of that year. And among the circumstances that had brought about this disappointing conclusion was a feud between Alexander Leslie and an English officer Thomas Sanderson, in which not only the tensions between the two nations were in evidence but also the quick temper and combative tendencies developed over years of squabbling on and around Bennachie. We are fortunate to have at our disposal both sides of the argument, although it is difficult to know which is more accurate. To take them in turn, Sanderson's widow and brothers submitted to the 'High Court of War' in Moscow a declaration and accusation against Alexander Leslie for murder on 2 December 1633. Here are the two opening points:

'1. Collonell Lesseley on the 28th of November last did earnestly invite Collonell Sanderson to dinner, where hee was merrie and well entertained untille eveninge and then parted ffriendes;

2. Collonell Lesselley next day beeinge the 29th November called Collonell Sanderson hundsfutt, spatt in his face and violently laid hold on Collonell Sanderson's sworde and drewe it halfe out; all this was done publiquelie . . .'

Then, according to the Sandersons, although the Russian commander commanded Leslie to keep the peace, on 2 December the Scotsmen took offence for some unknown reason, followed the Englishman who was out on a reconnaissance sortie and, as the last section of point 7 puts it:

'. . . suddenly rides up to them, and without a worde speakinge, shootes Colonell Sanderson into the head soo neere that hee fired his haire and hatt brims, so as he fell starke dead from his horse, not haveinge time to speake a worde or to call to God for mercie with sighs and groanes . . .'

Although we do not have the records of any trial that may have taken place in Moscow as a response to this complaint, we do know that Leslie was allowed to leave the country soon after the failure to take Smolensk, and that possibly the intercession of merchant friends in the Muscovy Company was necessary for him to do so. In England, on 23 September 1634, Leslie was granted a pardon in a warrant under the Privy Seal, with the explanation that Leslie:

'. . . having long endured intemperance of language frequently and in intolerable manner hurled against him both in camp and in arms in the presence of the troops, being overcome by the atrocious nature of his contumacies, killed a certain Sanderson an Englishman by nation and when living a subject of ours and a colonel in the same unit.'

English, Scottish, German and other witnesses supported Leslie's explanation, according to the warrant, and he was admitted to an audience with the 'Emperor' Michael to kiss his hands before departure. Back in Muscovite service three years or so later, Leslie performed his duties in an exemplary fashion, helping Michael's son Alexis finally to take Smolensk, and then becoming governor of that fortress city. He was there to welcome later Scottish mercenaries such as Paul Menzies from Aberdeen and Patrick Gordon from near Ellon and lived to an advanced age. He became an

Orthodox Christian, and his family were russified, some of his descendants still surviving near Smolensk today.

Many other stories could be told of the fighting Leslies, including at least one other Alexander from the Fife branch, more famous as the first Earl of Leven, who returned from the Thirty Years War to play an outstanding part in the Scottish and English Civil Wars. And much still remains to be discovered in the archives of Moscow and elsewhere, including Prague, where there are many documents known to be in existence concerning the career of Walter Leslie, who was made Count of the Holy Roman Empire. Meanwhile, inspiration for this work will no doubt continue to come from return visits to Bennachie, from the slopes of which one can clearly see the restored Harthill and at least the location of the ruins of Leslie and Balquhain castles. And who knows? Buried under the heather may well be some of the 'gunis, pistolis, . . . jacks, spears, knopsknais' with which the fighting Leslies along with other feuding families used to ride 'without controlment.'

Footnote – The ruined Castle of Balquhain was the home of the ancient family of Leslie, the first Baron of that name being created in 1340 and the 29th Baron died in 1948. He was succeeded by his son, Alistair P. C. Leslie, 30th Baron of Balquhain, who resides at Rotorua, New Zealand. His daughter can succeed to the title as First Baroness of Balquhain.

It is interesting to note that the ancient Castle of Leslie is in the process of being restored.

The Editor.

FETTERNEAR: FIFTY YEARS ON

By James Duffus

In *The Book of Bennachie,* Alan Mackie related on page 114, how the Fetternear Estate was sold off. The prices quoted looked to be in the region of ten years rental. What an opportunity to get a home for £250 to £500 – if you were the sitting tenant of course! One wonders if it had been just as difficult to scrape that kind of money together, as it is today at present day values. One thing for sure a mortgage would be unheard of and the banker would have little sympathy.

In the recession of the 'Thirties,' land was cheap, plentiful, and few wanted it. But the Sale of Fetternear Estate meant most of the tenants became owner-occupiers, and many of the same families are still in their 'Placie,' or a younger generation has taken over, which has stabilised the population to some degree in this area, unlike some areas where large tracts of land have scarcely a house or a croft to be seen. Values of these properties will now have increased one hundred fold and more.

The focal point of Fetternear Estate, namely the Home Farm, and the former laundry to the Old Fortress, converted to a very substantial dwelling-house, were purchased by three ladies, who having seen and shared in the beauty of the Estate, with all its trees and policies, with the Don flowing along its boundary, felt it was the ideal place in which to settle down. In 1942 they acquired the farm of Netherton, which had always been part of the Laird's farm. The year 1943 saw Ardiebrown added on. After almost fifty years, two of the ladies, namely Miss E. M. E. Berry and Miss P. M. Chetwynd, still live on and farm this attractive little estate. The third partner, Miss Violet Arbuthnott-Leslie died some thirty years ago.

With the ending of hostilities in 1945, life in the country-side began to return to a more normal pattern; and with the easing of some restrictions, people had more freedom to plan and enjoy the social side of life. Fetternear was no different from other districts, but the only drawback was that the local school was the only building where such functions could be held. Much as the use of schools was appreciated, most of them were limited in capacity and usually lacking in other facilities. So it was on 24th October, 1946, a preliminary meeting was held in Fetternear House, to discuss the possibility of building a hall for the community of Fetternear. From this point on, a Committee was formed and efforts to raise the necessary funds were begun. Dances, Whist Drives, Garden Fetes, Treasure Hunts, and all sorts of functions were arranged until 1950, when well over £1,000 had been raised. But the project had to be abandoned then, as the Government stopped all grants and cash aids for such projects.

By 1957, however, the grants were again made available. There was a resurgence of enthusiasm, and it was decided to again proceed with the efforts. A new secretary had to be found at this stage, and that is where I personally became involved, and to date, I still am Hall Secretary. But with the rekindling of interest, after three more years of money-raising functions, Fetternear Hall finally became a reality, being officially opened by Major David Gordon (the late Lord Aberdeen), in August, 1960. Again this was made possible through the generosity of the Fetternear House ladies who gifted the excellent site on which it now stands. It provides the ideal centre for rural community activities a district like Fetternear needs. The regular users are the W.R.I., Youth Club, O.A.P.'s, the Children's Committee, the Bowling Club and other outside organisations who wish to come and make use of the Hall, which is a monument to those who worked so hard and gave so much to get it, and one hopes will be an asset to those who follow on. Unlike so many rural areas, Fetternear is far from being depopulated, in fact, the opposite, houses are being modernised and new houses are springing up, with young families moving in; surely this must be right for the future.

Maybe the wayward actions of the old Laird of Fetternear, causing the Estate to be broken up and sold, have turned out to be the best for this area after all. We wonder what the next fifty years will bring?

GRANNY TOLD ME

By Kay Needham-Hurst

Her nickname among the family was 'Jobbie,' for she always had 'just one more jobbie to finish' before she would sit down and rest; but while she worked she talked and I loved to listen.

She was Margaret, born 1845, the eldest daughter of Alexander Adam and Rebecca Bruce of Cairnfold, in the Parish of Lochiel-Cushnie. I don't know how long the family had been in Cairnfold.

The earliest item she recalled for me was of seeing *her* Granny put to sleep in the box bed in the kitchen and of how she could be heard saying aloud her prayers with many directions to the Lord as to how He should deal with her and her family.

She went to school near the Mill of Craigievar, around 1850, and when she was no more than six or seven, some boys were fighting in the playground and she was accidentally knocked over. A sharp stone penetrated her face over the cheek bone and for the rest of her life she had a small hollow there. She was always very conscious of this – though no-one else was – and would sit with her left elbow on the arm of her chair, so that her first finger would comfortably fit the hollow and thus hide it.

Many times Granny told me how she was up in the woods above Cairnfold doing a little courting one summer evening, when she saw a wild cat. They were rare even in her day.

How vividly she would describe to me how a woman in one of the farms started to hiccough and nothing would make her stop. At length in despair, she was put to lie in a cart lined thickly with straw – she was too weak to sit up – and as she was driven through the village all the women came to their doors to listen to the poor soul hiccoughing her way to the hospital in Aberdeen and her death. This must have before 1859 when the railway came.

'Once when I was a young girl' said Granny 'I was visiting the Andersons at Wellhouse. I was left alone in the drawing room and was nursing the baby. Under a cushion I found a copy of Jane Eyre and I was soon away into it, when Mr Anderson came into the room and snatched the book away. Later he wrote an editorial in the *Aberdeen Free Press* on the dangers of allowing young girls to read such wicked books..'

Now this could not have been when the book was first published as that was in 1847 and Granny was then only two years old. It must have been a later edition. In 1857 there was an expunged edition. Granny would have been twelve and quite old enough to mind the baby – she had already 'minded' five babies in her own home.

Meanwhile there was Grandpa, William Reid, in Greystone. He went to the school on Gallow Hill, taking his peat for the fire and studying under the firm guidance of Mr Hugh McConnach.

Grandpa had his stories as well, starting with the finding of an unidentified object in 1862, when he was twelve years old. He was leading the horses at the plough and turned up a curiously shaped 'thing.' He kept it all his life and towards the end he tied a luggage label to it with the description 'stone age salt cellar.' The mental picture of a caveman 'passing the salt please' makes one smile. I showed it to the Department of Physical Planning, Grampian Regional Council with the following result:

'An oval waisted stone object now broken in two and held together by an old 'A' string of a violin. Overall dimensions 60m x 48m x 41m with an oval depression at the top; in the base a roughly pecked depression. Possibly an ink-well with traces of a metal lid or an unguent jar or a small mortar. Probably made within the last three hundred years.'

At fourteen he left the Alford school and spent a year with his uncle, William Minto, Minister and Dominie of Clatt, staying there during the week and coming back over the steep pass between Bennachie and Coreen Hills, and over the stone Bridge of Alford built by his maternal grandfather, William Minto of Annfield, in 1811. Then he was ready to join his father on the farm.

When he was about sixteen he was driving a cartful of lime down the Brae of Ardballoch, when the horse shied and bolted. The lime rose like smoke around him, burning all exposed skin and seriously affecting his eyes. He recovered the sight in the right eye, but the left eye was almost useless. Few people realised this however, and he was an excellent shot.

In 1868 Granny married this red haired, hot blooded, quick tempered eighteen-year-old man – and she was five years his senior! From then she never celebrated her birthday. It was not until I read her death certificate that I found she was born on February 17th.

My Mother, the first child, was born in May 1869. Three weeks later Grandpa went down to Mr McConnach to register the birth. 'What are you calling the bairn?' he asked. 'Oh, Maggie Jeannie I suppose.' 'You'll do no such thing' replied McConnach. 'It will be Margaret Jane' and thus it was – though all her life she was just Maggie.

The young couple started life in Carnaveron and soon the young father was carrying his daughter wrapped in his plaid, down the three mile walk to Greystone. Horrors! In the distance he saw the Laird coming up the hill in his carriage. The disgrace! For a man to be seen carrying a baby! He dropped the well-wrapped bundle over the dyke and strode on, acknowledged the greeting of the Laird and stepped out firmly until he was sure that all was safe and only then turned back for his child.

One day, when Maggie, the baby, was about a year old, she was in her high chair having tea with her mother in the front room at Carnaveron, when shouts and screams were heard coming from the kitchen. Granny ran down the passage way and found all the back part of the house on fire. The maid had been scrubbing the floor of her bedroom, leading off the kitchen, and being extra thorough, had gone under her bed with a lighted candle. The bed caught fire and soon everything was ablaze. Fortunately the men working in the nearby fields saw the smoke and came running. A human chain was formed to the pump and buckets went up and down until it was out. Only then did Granny remember her baby; she opened the door to the passage way and there was little Maggie. She had, for the very first time, climbed out of her high chair by herself and made her escape. The door shut behind her and the two cats in the front room were suffocated.

In 1870 Jane Minto died. She was the wife of James Reid and Grandpa's Mother. Granny and Grandpa moved into Greystone to keep him company and for Granny to act as housekeeper. Granny was already pregnant again and on January 1st 1871 the first boy was born, and called William. It was a night of terrible snow and wind and it seems that right up until he was seven or eight, visitors could be entertained by getting young William to tell how he and his father had such a struggle to get the pony and trap over the hill to fetch the midwife on the night he was born.

There was a fine peacock at Greystone, but one day in the driveway it attacked young Willie, just able to toddle, knocked him to the ground and stood on him, pecking into the back of his head (there was a hole there for the rest of his life). Maggie's screams brought men with pitchforks from the byre, and that afternoon Maggie, my Mother, was driving beside her Grandfather James, perched high in the dog cart and she remembered as if it were etched into her mind, looking into the ditch as they turned from the driveway into the road to Alford – and saw the many coloured head of the peacock. She was three years old.

My Mother declared that she could read the Bible by the time she was four. I always doubted this, but I have since heard of other such children.

1872 was a particularly severe winter, and Granny said it was the piping and moleing of the fields that finally brought Grandpa to the decision that he must go south to find a better life in London, but I suspect it was also the clash of Reid tempers. Two of them on one farm would be a constant storm. Added to this, I suppose he saw his elder brother James at Greystone, Tullynessle, as the one who would take over the family farm on the death of his father. How could he foresee that his brother would die next year?

Grandpa went on ahead and obtained work in Smithfield Meat Market. This would have been easy through his father's reputation as a breeder and exhibitor of Aberdeen Angus cattle.

Soon he had taken a house at 98 Johns Street, Bransbury, within walking distance of the Market. Granny followed by steamer with the two children and the luggage. This was the easier way to travel before the Forth Bridge was opened in 1890 and obviated the need for changing trains.

Poor Granny – she said she began to cry as she looked out from the window of the cab on the shabby, dirty, crowded streets they traversed – the only city she knew was the sparkling granite of Aberdeen; but she dried her eyes when she saw the little garden of her new home was full of flowers.

Three more children were born here, and Grandfather James Reid came down for the Smithfield Show each year. After he left there were always five gold sovereigns on the mantel piece.

I must return to Alford.

James Reid by himself at Greystone was lonely and took to driving the short road down to the Haughton Arms and in 1873 he married the landlady, Margaret Stewart. Granny and Grandpa must have returned for the wedding taking Maggie with them; for my Mother could remember standing on the steps and crying with rage at 'this woman who was taking away her Grandpa' as the pair departed. Soon there were two sons, James and then George, so that Grandpa had step-brothers younger than his two eldest children.

Mrs Stewart (she never seems to have been called Mrs Reid) died in 1890 and James was alone again. He moved into Waterside Cottage, and my Mother remembers on a visit finding a riding habit in the attic, that had belonged to her Aunty Jeannie (Grandpa's sister) and wearing it with delight as she rode the pony along Donside. Perhaps it was on the same visit, when she was seventeen, that one of the highlights of her life occurred. She was invited to a ball at Craigievar Castle. More than sixty years later I took her back and her Marie Tempest eyes sparkled as she described how she was dressed. A bodice of terra-cotta satin with a skirt of cream lace – and she danced with the Laird, Sir William Forbes! To him I suppose it was just one of his 'duty dances' with the daughters of the local farmers, but to Maggie Reid it was a fairy tale that remained vivid until the end of her life.

In the meantime Granny's sister Elizabeth, born 1851 had married Mr Law of Dorsell as his second wife. He was said to have married first for money and second for work, and certainly Aunt Lizzie brought up his two children John and Belle as though they were her own and worked in the house and farmstead all the hours available.

When the Forth Bridge was opened and the train journey to Aberdeen was rather less arduous, it became the regular custom for the whole London Reid family to return to Alford every summer to stay at Dorsell. At first they went in the early coaches which were divided into separate compartments *without* corridors. Imagine the rush at the few stations where the train stopped – and the queues – especially with young children. They took with them two deck chairs of the old type which were opened in the space between the seats. Two people lay head to tail on either seat and any really small children went on the luggage rack. They were able to hire pillows and rugs at King's Cross Station but a huge hamper of food had to be packed. Hot drinks could be bought at stations, and the cups and saucers left under the seat to be handed in at the next stop, for there would have been no time to drink the scalding tea. Some of the stress was reduced with the introduction of corridors; but it was still a long night especially if one failed to get a corner seat.

They left King's Cross at 7 p.m. and reached Aberdeen at 7 a.m. next morning, always to be met by one or more of the Alford folk who had flitted from the village to town life. There were huge breakfasts and a tidy up; then they went to the quayside market to buy fish straight from the boats, and so on to the train for the short ride to Alford.

Maggie Reid took her fiancé John Stone, to meet her grandfather in 1895 shortly before he died, only to be told 'Are you really going to marry that foreigner? I had hoped you would marry a minister or a doctor, not just a business man.'

By then James Reid had built a fine reputation as an Aberdeen Angus man. I quote from the history of the *Aberdeen Angus* published in 1910.

'Mr James Reid, Greystone, who was one of the largest and most successful exhibitors of British cattle at the English Christmas shows, had a very good herd of pure bred cattle. Polled stock had been at Greystone for a long time, a few animals of Mr Reid's herd having been entered in No. 1 of the Herd Book, but it was later that particular attention was given to registration. For upwards of forty years the late Mr Reid was an extensive exhibitor and it was estimated that during that time some 1,400 prizes had been won.'

The first official list of judges drawn up by the Aberdeen-Angus Society contains twelve names and one was James Reid. This was in 1884. He was judging at the Smithfield Show as early as 1883 and was on the first board of Judges of the Aberdeen Angus cattle.

On his leaving the farm in 1894, the herd numbering 34, was disposed of; the average price being £26.11.5d.

After his death a granite pillar was placed in the graveyard of the Auld Kirk stating:

Erected to the Memory of

JAMES REID

Farmer at Greystone Alford.

By his numerous friends in the North of Scotland, as a mark
of respect on account of his distinguished merits as a
prominent agriculturist, and of his many kind and ready
services amongst his neighbours and acquaintances.

Born January 4th 1825. Died 16th November 1895.

Yes, Grandpa told me many a tale of his Father James and often a little girl in London laughed at that well-known story of William McCombie of Tillyfour and his parade of A.A. cattle before Queen Victoria . . . and she cried as, in imagination, she stood beside her Great Grandfather watching his face tortured and reddened by the flames of the great pyre of his cattle when foot and mouth disease first smote his herd, though he was completely in favour of the new law.

By 1900 the grandchildren were joining the throng. Dorsell must have been packed to the roof, and usually one or more of the Alford folk would go back to London with them. My Mother remembers overhearing two cousins discussing their forthcoming visit. 'Do you think you will like staying at Uncle William's in London? They *kiss* their parents before they go to bed you know.'

At the peak of the annual visit to Scotland it must have been of some interest to the Alford congregation to see the London Reids pour into the front row of the gallery in the Auld Kirk with James Reid. When they settled down for the long sermon there was a handing out of pandrops for the children and ladies and of snuff for the men. James would sit in the middle and turn to pass his snuff-box among the men in the row behind as well (I have it still).

Five years ago I sat in that pew myself; alone! With thirty ghosts for company.

Sometimes Granny would tell with a smile how one year she proudly wore a new bonnet on the first Sunday, bought at Peter Robinson's in

Oxford Street; it was said to be the latest style from Paris. Imagine her feelings when on Monday she saw exactly the same model in the window of the general store in Main Street at Alford. 'Most provoking' or 'Very vexatious' would have been her comment.

How Granny loved those yearly holidays in her beloved Alford. She said that one of the greatest pleasures was to lie in bed in the hot August mornings and to hear the men trouping in for their breakfast, silent but in proper order. First horseman, second horseman, first cattleman, second cattleman and the orra boy.

Late in her life – and without preamble – she began to tell of a young woman living in a croft well up the side of Bennachie. One day she was hanging out the washing, when suddenly she missed her young child, barely able to walk. After a frightened search she called her husband who was with the gamekeeper. 'We'll search Bennachie' said the keeper and whispered 'best bring a small box.' Some hours later they were back – and the box was filled with small bones – eagles! Was this a folk memory that rose in Granny's old mind or was there truth in the tale? She told it as though she had been there.

One year Granny said the family decided to climb Bennachie. There was a great borrowing of pony traps from neighbours and a packing of whole hampers of oat cakes and baps and scones and butter and ham and jam. There was buttermilk for the children, and a bottle of whisky for the men. The women relied on tea.

They left Dorsell early and were over the 'Minto Bridge' by 10 o'clock. Then to the right through the Lord's Throat, past the one-time crofters settlement and so round to the back of Bennachie and the Maiden Stone. There the ponies were taken from the shafts and hobbled, a fire was lit for the kettle and half the picnic was eaten. Then began the climb, straight up the steep dry course of the burn to reach a small cairn. Here Granny and her sister turned back but the others pushed on through the heather and bog.

There were no carefully tended pathways then. Most of them reached the final great crags of the Mither Tap, but the ladies had to be pushed against the wind. Finally they peered over the rocks to view the whole of the Vale of Alford with the silver Don snaking through it.

The wind was too cold for delay and tired or not they had to start down again. How thankful their legs were to reach the picnic site and the fire and the teapot! Was there a faint odour of whisky about the teacups? Then came the slow drive back with everyone too sleepy for much talking, but it was a day to remember. Few in Alford had made the climb.

It was 1908 before I joined the annual pilgrimage – and it was the last one. Suddenly it seemed the London family split up and went their different ways. Then came the Great War and it was 1919 before Granny and Grandpa went back to Scotland taking me with them. We still travelled third class and most uncomfortably, and stayed in Aberdeen. I was taken by train to Alford for the day. Grandpa hired a car and a driver and we whisked around all the farms and the churchyards that were but names to me and which meant so much to them. By that time not a Reid nor an

Adam nor a Minto was left in Alford and even Mr Law and Auntie Lizzie
had moved to a farm near Stonehaven.

I was only twelve but even I could sense something of the powerful
mixture of joy and grief that was passing through their minds. I knew it.
Granny didn't have to tell me.

MEMORIES

By John Hird

Monymusk, 1904-1910

The Monymusk I remember was a typical rural village. In the Square were
all the day-to-day facilities required. The shoemaker's residence was next to
that of the builder-joiner, then the library, the sawmill, and, across the
road, the farmhouse of 'Gloies,' with a house between it and the police
station. Then into the Square, the general merchant's and sub-post office
on the corner, where it still functions today. On the same side was the old
inn – a dwelling house then, but now the Grant Arms Hotel. There were no
licensed premises in the village. Postman McGillivray, who lived on this
side of the Square, had a wide country area to cover on his round.

Miss Dunbar, a schoolteacher, lived on the other corner, next to the
baker's shop, Mr Kinghorn the baker having his house at the other side of
the shop. The builder's shop and Mr Gray the blacksmith's premises were
just beyond the row of houses on the roadside. Mrs Barron lived on the
corner next to the Church opening, the old school being at the rear of that
row of houses. It is now the attractive village hall, used for all sorts of
village activities. The old church has been renovated, but, in my humble
opinion, it has lost its old world character, the loft along one side having
been removed or shut off. No longer would it be possible to see the elder
with the long-handled collecting box working the loft.

The minister in my day was the Rev. William McPherson, author of the
History of the Church and Priory, who christened me and who now lies at
rest in the old churchyard, where William Watson, the author of *Glimpses
o' Auld Lang Syne* is also buried. From the churchyard there is still the
opening through to the manse, whence the minister used to appear wearing
his robes on a Sunday.

Continuing along the Square, the only tenant I can remember carried on
a tailoring business in the end house. John Strachan, the shoemaker,
conducted a very successful business, the building which housed his shop
having a house at each end, one of them being my birthplace. Buchan the
builder, whose father built the Locomotive Works, the 'Colony' houses and
most of the houses in Harlaw Road, Inverurie, had a thriving business.
Mr Mathieson, who farmed 'Gloies,' was in partnership with Mr John Main
in the local sawmill business. He also partnered Robbie Davidson, whose
yard and sawmill in Inverurie stood on the site of Inverurie's first railway
station between (Old) Station Road and Wardes Road.

Josie Badenoch lived in the combined house and library, his wife being in charge of the library. He was foreman at the sawmill next door, and, a very good amateur gardener. He always topped the list of prizewinners at the village Flower and Vegetable Show. The Jamieson family lived next door to the police station. Hendry Petrie, the grocer and sub-postmaster, later served in World War I, but never settled down after it, emigrating with his wife, daughter and son to Australia, where I met them in my wanderings. His daughter, Hilda, visited me some three years ago here in Kemnay, at which time her mother, just on the borders of 100, was still alive in Melbourne.

The Tough family (Scots pronunciation) lived in the old inn, and there was also a family of Macdonalds living in the village, because I remember Lennie. I think they lived above the Toughs in the old inn. I must not forget Grigor, the miller, who had a daughter whose name I cannot recall. His mill and dam were up the back dykes, and you had to pass the McLean family cottage on the way up there.

There were some three of four stands or water pumps in the Square, supplying water for the surrounding houses. The nearest doctor was Dr Hendry at Kemnay, who used to arrive with his pony and gig when requested. If, however, he was approached by someone else in the village to look in and see another patient 'noo that ye're here,' as likely as not the response would be that a request should be made at his surgery in Kemnay. The new school, just out of the village on the road to Paradise and opposite the Deer Park, had just been completed in 1907. Mr Simpson was the schoolmaster, and stayed in Beech Lodge, now the residence of Mr Whiteley. The Territorials' camp was held in the Deer Park every year, when the Terriers from surrounding towns slept under canvas. It was a free holiday for them, and an inducement to join the Terriers.

John Strachan the shoemaker, in whose workshop my father was employed, had two or three 'souters' working permanently. But when hard pressed to keep up with his orders, he got Forbes Donald, a rare character who was employed by Johnie Grassie, the shoemaker at Sclattie, to come across to help out. Forbes was a bachelor and always in great demand with his fiddle, and was a familiar figure cycling round the countryside with his fiddle case strapped to his back.

Working boots were then made by hand, and of horse hide because it does not absorb water. (Hill shepherd's shoes are still made of horse hide). When the price went up to 12/6 a pair from 10/- because of the increasng price of leather, it was hard times indeed for the farm servants, who had very poor wages. Mrs Edwards, the banker's wife at Kemnay, later told me that when the price went up to 12/6 she felt ashamed when putting out her father's accounts, he being a shoemaker in Lumsden. Shoemakers' wages were around 21/- a week, and father told me that a newspaper at the end of the week was all the luxury they could afford. When a kirk elder bought a new pair of Sunday boots, the shoemaker had to put some French chalk between the inner and the outer sole to make them squeak, thus to warn members of the congregation that the elder was approaching with the ladle or plate.

Early Memories of Inverurie

I remember my first day, in 1910, at the 'little schoolie' at the back of the Square in Inverurie. On entering the playground, I was greeted by two black holes like huge gaping eyes in one half of the building which had been gutted by fire. Another early memory was assembling in the Square to march to the field just beyond the South Lodge at Keithall, where the King George V Coronation Picnic was held; scrambling for new 1911 pennies; running races; and coming home with a Coronation mug.

The Feeing Markets were held in the Square, and were great days for children to look forward to. Stalls everywhere, selling lemonade, ginger beer, and all kinds of candy and boiled sweets (you could buy a halfpenny worth at that time). There were paper balls almost as big as tennis balls, with strands of elastic attached to them, the purpose being to flick them in people's faces! Shooting galleries abounded, with ping pong balls balancing on jets of water to shoot at, etc., etc. The usual few young farm servants who had drunk too much were escorted to the Police Station between two bobbies, to be released later that night less a 5/- or 10/- fine.

The only circus to be allowed in the Square was Biddle's. I can remember a man pulling a lump of candy from a hook on the side door of the tent, later to be broken up into small pieces and sold for twopence a bag at the performance. Shepherds moving their flocks around their various pastures used to rest them in the Square, camping overnight if necessary. When the Town Council threatened to enclose the Square, the shepherds came with their flocks and rested all day as a gesture of defiance, but it was only a matter of time before the Council had its way. Only the horse trough, fountain and weighing machine were left outside the railings.

Horse markets, menageries, Bostock and Wombwell's Circus and Sanger's Circus were always held in the Market Green in North Street, well clear of the Inverurie Cricket Club's pavilion and pitch at the top half of the ground (the Alsops and Prossers were then in their prime). At that time, the Inverurie Pleasure Park lay off Souterford Road, behind the Gasworks. Equipped with permanent swings and football pitches, one could say it was Inverurie's first golf course, the holes being situated in the perimeter of the park. I remember being paid sixpence for carrying the players' clubs.

My First Visit to the Hill of Bennachie

My first visit to the hill of Bennachie was in the early summer of 1914. The Rev. Mr Sellars, minister of the steepled Wesleyan Kirk in High Street, Inverurie, was a very energetic man and a popular figure in the town. We used to sing in his choir – probably at the instigation of Alice McGregor, daughter of Councillor 'Stoney' McGregor.

Mr Sellars was over six feet tall, and used to take us out on long walks to the top of the Crichie and Selby hills, and to the memorial erected but a few years earlier to commemorate the Battle of Harlaw. But he surpassed himself when he decided on Bennachie as our objective. Meeting at his lodgings at 'Stonehouse' early one morning, we walked all the way to the hill and climbed it. I remember nothing of the actual climb, but he must have seen how very tired we were, for he shepherded us down to Pitcaple railway station and paid our railway fares to Inverurie. There must have been half a dozen boys on that outing. Mr Sellars went off to the 1914-18 War later on, and I cannot remember if he ever came back to his ministry in Inverurie.

During the summer holidays in 1914, World War I broke out, and I remember being wakened through the night by a bugler going along the streets calling out the men. Next day, the Terriers were all gone in special trains, headed by Captain Smith of Pittodrie, their Commander, who, along with so many others, never returned.

When Sunnie Nicol's traction engine trundled up Church Terrace (where we lived) in 1919 to thresh the ricks on Mrs Fraser's croft, I carried round the 'caff' bed to empty and refill it with fresh-smelling chaff. Her croft was where part of George Square is now, the boundaries being Wyness, the butcher's field at the back of his shop on one side, the road leading to the Manse from High Street on the other, and the Manse Roadie at the top.

MONYMUSK LIBRARY

By The Editor

Nowadays when public libraries are a common-place and in country districts library vans trundling along country roads are a part of everyday life, it might be of interest to know of the origins and struggle for existence of our small village library in Monymusk which was in its own way quite unique.

The history of the library begins in a room at the farm of Bluefold, where a young headmaster, named James Kerr, held an adventure school. The year is 1834. These adventure schools were to be found all over Aberdeenshire, but alas! the level of teaching was often very poor indeed. But James Kerr was a notable exception. A similar exception was James Beattie, a cobbler who had an adventure school at Auchterless for over sixty years. He received no fee but in 1836, he was presented with 'a most handsome silver snuff-box for his exertions.' Among the books he used were story-books: 'for,' he used to say, 'Ye ken, bairns maun like their books.' 'If ye dinna think o' the meaning,' he reminded his pupils over and over again, 'hoo can ye be richt?' It is reported that the financial return from teaching in these adventure schools was so poor, several schoolmasters supplemented their meagre income by keeping illicit stills!

If one cares to look, one can still see the traces of the stones of Bluefold Cottage and traces of its garden where neglected gooseberry bushes still grow among the weeds. There is a tradition that some of the stones of this cottage were used for the battlemented top of the tower of the twelfth century Norman Parish Church of Monymusk when its spire became dangerous and had to be replaced. Anyway James Kerr, obviously hungry for books to read in the dark months of winter, and lacking the means to buy them, decided to form a library for the farmers and their servants in the Parish round about. The farmer lent him a room and forty-eight members enrolled. One can imagine the scene. The small, farm room, lit by a fir-root pushed into one of the links of the swey, perhaps a rush-lamp or two. Not much wonder that one of the first imperative needs of the library-to-be was a supply of candles in addition to books so in the cash books we read such entries as: 'To Candles – 2½d.'

As well as James Kerr, the teacher, there were farmers from all the farms in the district, with old names that go back in history – such names as William Emslie, farmer at Gauldnock, Robert Taylor, farmer of Balvack, Charles Wilson of Meadowbrae, Robert Thomson of Glenton – with farm servants, labourers, two wrights, two gardeners from Cluny Castle, the local blacksmith, the general merchant, the toll-keeper, and Alex. Watt of Pitfichie who deserves a special mention as he was a pensioner from the Battle of Waterloo. Two enterprising women, probably housekeepers to local farmers, joined the library. One, Anne Fullerton, passes into oblivion after joining, but the second – Elspeth Robertson, Nethermains Farm – comes into prominence several times by having to pay a 2d fine for neglecting to take back her book in time. Some of the names mentioned are very interesting such as that of Peter Anderson, a journeyman-carpenter in the village, who was the brother of the famous Rev. Duncan Anderson, for a short time schoolmaster of Monymusk and then a minister in Canada, where he became a friend of the Marquis and Marchioness of Aberdeen at that time Governor-General of Canada. Rev. Duncan Anderson published several books and poems about Monymusk. Taken in all, this was a very representative group of the people who lived in the parish at that time.

We know so much about this from four manuscript books still in existence. These books are made of once-white paper now yellowed and ragged at the edges with covers of brown wrapping paper bound togther with a string. Holding a page up to the light one can read the watermark – 'Annandale & Son, 1833.' The writing in fadeless ink, is in beautiful copperplate, obviously that of James Kerr, the head of the adventure school. The first book is the *Monymusk Reading Society's Minute Book, 1834.* It gives all the Rules and Regulations. It begins by saying, 'The Advantages of Reading Societies and the Propriety of establishing one in Monymusk having been laid before a number of individuals by James Kerr and a Meeting of those favourable to the establishing of such a Society having been called by him, a good many came forward and the following Rules and Regulations were adopted.' The most interesting of these rules was Rule 11, namely that 'The Library shall consist of Religious Books and books connected therewith, such as Church History – with select volumes on other subjects such as Voyages, Travels, and Missionary Journeys.' Rule 11 further added: '*No Romances, no books of a Socinian or Deistical tendency and no books of whatever description which lead to the Subversion of True Religion shall have a place in the Library.*'

One cannot but applaud those farmers and servants of a bye-gone age. Members had to pay 2/6 Entry Money and 1/- annually. Others paid 2d per Lunar Month. Some with true Aberdonian instincts, instead of paying the initial 2/6 fee, brought a book instead and paid 1/6; but this was put a stop to after a while as possibly the books did not come up to the standards required. If members kept a book longer than three weeks they were fined

1d for each night overdue. Great care had to be taken to preserve the books from injury. Again fines were imposed for damaged books. In passing, it is revealing to note that the Schoolmaster was excused payment of an Annual Subscription in view of his being the Clerk and Librarian – this being his only remuneration for his services.

The Library was started by the Clerk inviting a well-known Aberdeen bookseller, George King, to send out, via the local horse carrier, a selection of books on approval. To pay for the books selected, a sum of £5 was borrowed from the local general merchant, one of their members, at 4 per cent interest. At the end of the first year the loan with its interest was duly repaid and the Library Committee promptly borrowed another £5 on similar terms to add further books to the Library.

The Entry Book gives the names of the subscribers, with their signatures, and the fees paid. The Cash Book gives such details as: 'To Books – £4.19.7d,' 'To Paper – 10d,' 'To Candles – 4d,' 'To Flour for making Paste – 1d,' 'To Pasteboard for Binding Books – 1d,' 'To Cloth for Book Backs – 8d' – evidently a lot of book-binding was required.

The Fourth and most interesting book is the *Catalogue of Books – 1835.* Here we have such books as Booth's *Reign of Grace, Essay on the Kingdom of Christ, Divine Sovereignty, Dodd on Death, The Economy of Human Life,* with *Lives of British Admirals,* and MacKenzie's *Man of Feeling,* and books of Travel to cheer the members up after perusing such books as *The Afflicted Man's Companion,* and *Anecdotes of Christian Conduct.* Later on the novels of Sir Walter Scott were permitted; and then with the stories of Annie S. Swan came the turn of the tide – novels, detective and Wild West stories duly found their way on the book-shelves and the older books were weeded out.

This small library flourished at Bluefold till it was removed to the Toll-house at the head of the brae which leads to Monymusk Village. The new librarian was a Nellie Duncan who lived with her father, the toll-keeper. When a girl herding cows, it is recorded that she used to memorise scraps of an old translation of Virgil's *Aeneid.* Her annual salary consisted of enough yards of cloth and braid, bought at the local shop, to make a dress for herself. But, in addition, she had always the books to read. In particular she loved books on Theology. Two famous divines of Monymusk at this time were members of the Library: Dr MacPherson, the author of *The Monymusk Church and Priory,* and Dr William Walker, the Episcopal clergyman, the author of *The Life of Dean Skinner* of Tullochgoram fame, and *The Ewie wi' the Crooked Horn,* which inspired Burns to write *The Elegy on Auld Mailie.* Dr MacPherson and Dr Walker selected suitable books for the Library including *The Life of David Hume, the Philosopher.* Nellie refused to put this book on her library shelves and she would have warmly applauded the Aberdeen fish-wife who refused to help Dr Hume when he was stuck fast in the mud in Old Aberdeen until he recited to her the Lord's Prayer.

When Sir Francis Grant succeeded to the estate in 1887, he built a new house and Library for Nellie, using the stones of a disused local distillery for this purpose. To mark the opening of this new Library, a ball was held and Sir Francis himself led off the Grand March and Reel with old Nellie as his partner.

To supplement the funds of the Library lectures were given by prominent personalities. Their titles and the income from these public lectures make interesting reading. A lecture on the Highlands brought in the sum of £1.8.6½d; 'On China' – 5.11d; 'Chicago' – 17/10d; 'Music' – 14/5d; 'A Tour Round the World' – £1.4.6d; 'Life in the Arctic Regions' – £1.0.4d; 'The Sudan' – £1.5.0d; 'Atmospheric Dust' – 8/-; 'Dickens' – 8/5d; 'Handel' – 16/7d; 'Longfellow' – 16/0½d; 'Beethoven' – 15/6d; 'Rome' – 8/3d; 'Pompeii' – 9/5d; 'Lucerne' – 17/1½d; 'Paris' – 13/3d; 'Johnny Gibb of Gushetneuk' – £1.15.7d; 'Livingstone' – 7/9d; 'Aviation' – 11/6d; 'Life Among My Ain Folk' – £1.17.6d; 'Robert Burns' – £1.17.4d; 'Tuberculosis' – 5/8d; 'Bannockburn' – 15/7d. But surely the most popular of them all was 'The Relief of Mafeking' which brought in the princely sum of £3.11.6d!

In 1896 it is recorded that the first cinematograph entertainment ever given in the North took place in Monymusk in aid of the funds of the Library. Alas! neither the titles of the films nor the total proceeds from this epic event are recorded!

Regrettably the old Monymusk Library no longer exists. Its function has been taken over by the Grampian Region Library Service which serves the community as a worthy successor to those who did so well in the past for their own generation.

THE FAIRY CIRCLE
IN PARADISE, MONYMUSK

By Alexander Gordon

Do you love to roam through the forest glade,
    Where the sunbeams faintly creep,
Where the fir and the plane throw a gloomy shade,
    And the dew charged branches weep?
Then come; I will show you a lovely spot,
    Enamell'd with shrubs and flowers,
Where no sound is heard save the cushat's note,
    And enraptured we gaze till we've almost forgot,
We are banished from Eden's bowers.

Yet here is a place which knows no spring,
    Here no flowers or grass will grow,
And a circle of beech trees their shadows fling,
    O'er their name-carved trunks below,
'Twas here that at even – the aged tell –
    A woodman wearied and worn,
Sat down to rest and in slumber fell,
    Till awoke by the tinkling sound of a bell,
And the blast of a tiny horn.

In the green hillside was an opening made,
    And forth came a fairy train –
On the withered leaves fell their pattering tread,
    With a rustling sound like rain,
And he saw from the throng the Queen advance,
    And spellbound brook and rill –
When the fairies joined in their moonlight dance
    All nature was hushed in a silent trance,
And the rushing Don stood still.

O'er the low red fire that lonesome night,
    His wife his absence mourn'd –
She look'd from the door in the grey daylight
    But the woodman ne'er returned.
They search'd the hill and hollow; and came to the place
    Where they saw that the woodman had been –
A wild look of terror o'erspread every face,
    While his wife sank down with a cry of distress –
For last night was the Hallowmass E'en.

They waited till that day year came round,
    When the moon rose o'er the hill,
And here by the side of this circle they found
    The woodman sitting still.
He turned and a look of surprise he cast
    On his wife and his altered child –
He wondered the daylight had faded so fast;
    But when he told that a twelvemonth round had passed,
He never again once smiled.

Now here you may wander at eve undismayed,
    For afar to some highland vale,
They've raised their green banners and trembling fled,
    From the sound of the Sabbath bell,
No unholy sound will meet your ear,
    No unhallowed form your eye,
But the murmuring rush of the river near,
    Or the dusky form of the startled deer,
As he glides like a shadow by.

                                Monymusk, February, 1847.

THE FAIRY CIRCLE IN PARADISE, MONYMUSK

By Alexander Gordon

The Editor is grateful to Mr T. G. Smith, Boysmeade, Newbury, Berkshire, who submitted this poem, along with a biographical note of the poet, Alexander Gordon, who was his Great Grandfather.

'Alexander Gordon was born in Aberdeen on September, 1808, and at the age of nine entered Gordon's Hospital (College) as a pupil. He remained in the school until the age of 15 when he left to become an apprentice blacksmith with the firm of Duffus and Co. At the age of 18, he joined the 78th Highlanders and served at Fort George but his service was interspersed with periods of illness at Chatham Hospital and, eventually, he was discharged from the army at the age of 20. The next documented record we have of him is his enlistment and service in the British Auxiliary Force which fought in Spain from 1835 until 1838. In a brief biography of him in the *Bards of Bon-Accord,* it states that in 1838 he entered the service of a Mr Shepherd, who was then planting the Hill of Kinellar. It seems that for the next 20 years he was employed in forestry having moved to Monymusk some time around 1840. In 1848 he married Annie Watt, daughter of Peter Watt, farmer of Brownieshill Farm, Monymusk. About 1851 he took up the tenancy of the croft of Laggan, Cluny, and lived there until he moved to Inverurie in 1860 where he had a small shoemaker's shop at 71 High Street, and he died there in 1873. During his years in Monymusk and in Inverurie he wrote a great number of poems. Many of his works are signed, 'The Planter,' presumably a reference to his occupation in the Monymusk area.'

THE LAYING OF THE RAILWAY TRACK
AT TILLYFOURIE IN 1858

The following notes have fallen into the Editor's hands and he feels that they will be of interest to many of the readers.

It is evident from these Minutes of the Police Committee, dated 14th September 1858, that Industrial Action in Labour Disputes is no new thing!

The members of the Council of the Bailies of Bennachie are grateful to Inspector John Duff for his research and to the Grampian Police for their help.

The whole of the Alford Valley Railway from Kintore to Alford was opened in 1859 and closed to all passenger traffic in 1950.

Alford Valley Railway.
The Chief Constable's Remarks on the Strike of Labourers,
7th and 9th August, 1858, and
Pay of Labourers, 10th and 11th August, 1858.

No notice of this strike and pay of labourers was sent to the Chief Constable until he received a telegraph message on Monday, 9th inst., at 9 p.m., from Messrs. Dean & Son, Contractors, to send 10 or 12 constables to Tillyfourie next day, as they were 'Compelled to pay their men'; and at 10 p.m. on the same evening, a special messenger arrived, with a letter from the same parties, requesting 12 or 13 constables and that they were quite agreeable to pay off expenses that might be incurred.

The Chief Constable immediately made arrangements and gave orders to Inspector Smith to arrange for 1 Sergeant and 3 Constables to proceed from Aberdeen by first morning train for Tillyfourie. Communications were sent to other Constables, so that by 1 p.m. of the 10th inst., there were at Tillyfourie, 1 Inspector, 1 Sergeant and 13 Constables, present at the pay.

Inspector Smith reports that a series of squabbling and disputes continued all through the pay, between Messrs. Dean and their labourers, but that on the whole the pay went off as quietly as could have been expected. The pay continued till 9 p.m., of the 10th; again commenced at noon of the 11th and finished at 3 p.m. of that day. The Inspector, Sergeant and Constables who were sent from Aberdeen, returned at 9 p.m. of the 11th and reported themselves at Headquarters, leaving several of the Constables on duty at the Inns during the night of the 11th, in consequence of the continued drinkings and fightings of the labourers.

In order that the Chief Constable should be enabled to arrive at the origin of the strike, he proceeded, with Superintendent Cran, to Tillyfourie, and when within about three to four miles of that place, began to meet the labourers, some of them very much the worse from drink, others cut and their faces clotted with blood. There were a number of them at 'Lawsons,' a Grocer and Spirit Dealer, near Tillycairn Castle, of which shop the Chief Constable has given special orders to be looked after.

On arriving at Tillyfourie, the Chief Constable met Mr N. Dean, one of the partners of the firm, who, on being questioned, stated that the strike commenced on Saturday, at noon, yet the month was not up till 6 p.m. that day; that they, the Contractors, required some days to make up their books, and had fixed Thursday, the 12th, as the pay day. On Monday, the 9th, the majority of the labourers were inclined to proceed with their work, but those who were about to leave (having previously engaged themselves for harvest in the Lothians) being joined by others, stoned the well-disposed off the works. The Contractors said they had made all haste with the books and had settled with the labourers correctly, with a few exceptions.

Mr Dean further stated that several of their Gangers and Foremen had been drunk since Saturday and were then drunk in bed, and that in consequence of this, several squads of the labourers had been kept from commencing their work on Wednesday morning and that they (the Gangers) were the best of their hands, still they had no control over them. Mr Deans also stated that the labourers received no pay for the day they attended to get their wages.

The Chief Constable then recommended to Mr Dean the Course that should be taken, to obviate a like occurrence, viz. that there should be only from two to three hundred labourers paid at one time; that the books should be made up correctly, so as to give no cause for squabbling; then that number could be settled within an afternoon and thus avoid confusion. Mr Dean said they would adopt this course.

The Chief Constable questioned several of the labourers. Some stated that they had been cheated of their time, and had been so on previous pay days; that the foremen made them believe they would get a higher rate of wages, but when the pay time came the sum was reduced from what they were lead to expect and a high rate charged for lodgings in the bothy. The Chief Constable proceeded to Whiteley Inn and there he beheld a fearful scene of.debauchery; some drinking, some dancing, and others fighting. The Chief observed that during the short time he was there, two of the labourers fought and drank with each other three times, and then appeared satisfied. The railway constables were at the inn for the purpose of observing that the labourers did not interfere with strangers and others passing; but took no part with the squabbles that the workmen had amongst themselves.

The Chief Constable questioned Mrs Paterson at Whiteley Inn (her son being absent) but elicited nothing of much importance, with the exception that when the Chief told her that by continuing to give drink to those intoxicated, she was committing a breach of the Licence Certificate. In reply she said if they (the labourers) did not get what drink they asked for, they would take possession of the house or pull it down about their ears.

The Chief Constable then proceeded to Monymusk, but found there had only been a few of the labourers drinking there, and that all had passed off comparatively quietly.

EDUCATION AROUND THE FOOT OF BENNACHIE
A HUNDRED YEARS AGO
Information from Log Books and School Board
Minute Books (1873-1900)
By Miss Mary Simpson

In spring of 1873, according to the Education Act 1872, School Boards were elected in every parish. Very frequently the local laird was appointed Chairman. The keeping of the Minutes and the detail recorded therein depended very much on the Clerk to the Board.

A bank account was opened and a code of rules and bye-laws set up. One of the first things each School Board had to do was to take a census of all children in the parish aged 5-13, and then assess the adequacy of the existing school buildings. Remember, before this time education was available, but not compulsory.

e.g. **Keig**   Census of children 5-13
Male   85   Female 78   Total 163
Not attending School   45
Adventure School Male   5
                  Female 9   14
Premnay   Educational Census
331   children in Parish under 13
199 = 101 Boys   98 Girls aged 5-13
 90 = 49 Boys   41 Girls are at school in this parish
 58 = 30 Boys   28 Girls attending school in other parishes
 51 = 22 Boys   29 Girls are not attending school
∴132 must have been under 5 years of age.

Oyne   Census of children 5-13
428 under 15 years
250 aged 5-13
174 receiving instruction at school
 76 not at present attending school
111 attend the Parish School
 19 attend Old Rain (Female School)
  9 attend Chapel of Garioch
  8 attend Braeside of Pittodrie (Female)
  7 attend Insch
  3 attend Premnay
  3 attend Keig
 14 attend Lord Cullen's School

Oyne School Board Minutes gives the following details from 1871 census:

Population of Parish	1050
Number of Families	190
Area in Imperial acres	10151

The Parish School, recently enlarged and repaired contains an area of 918 square feet, is capable of affording accommodation for 114 children, allowing 8 sq. ft. for each child, and according to cubic measurement, allowing 80 cu. ft. for each child there is accommodation for 129.6 children.

The School Board fixed the School Fees, dates of Quarter Days by which they had to be paid, appointed teachers and paid their salaries, arranged for the cleaning of schools and improvements, extensions or building of new schools, supplies including text books and equipment and fixed holidays.

After the census most School Boards decided that improvements in the school buildings required to be made.

e.g. **Keig** –

It was agreed that with the view of keeping the boys and girls schools separate, plans and estimates for a Female School and residence be prepared. Quote – 'The extent of ground in connection with the new residence for the teacher of the Female School was a right-angled parallelogram, 121 ft. along the public road by 120 ft. back, being ⅓ of an acre.' (Isn't that a rectangle?). In 1881 these schools were amalgamated.

Premnay –

Following the census, the unanimous conclusion of the School Board was that new school buildings in a central part of the parish be required.

These were the offers accepted:

Mason Work	Wm. Beattie, Marnoch	£599. 0.0
Carpenter	George Isaac, Rettie	£410. 0.0
Slater	Andrew Rhind, Inverurie	£ 79. 5.0
Plumber	A. Robertson, Aberdeen	£ 60. 0.0
Plasterer	John Logie, Huntly	£ 58. 0.0
Bells	James Laing & Co.	£ 4.13.0
		£1210.18.0

By the time it was completed and walls, desks, fittings, architects fees etc. were paid the total cost was £1,573.16.11d. The opening took place on Monday, 28th October 1878.

Oyne –

In December 1873 Sketch of site and plans were forwarded to Scotch Education Department, London, for approval and to ascertain the amount of the grant. No detail is given of the building planned, but in November 1874 an estimate from George Isaac, Builder, Gadydale, Premnay, to execute the whole mason, carpenter, slater, plumber and plaster works for £100 was accepted.

Kemnay –

A new building adjacent but distinct from the other to be a Girls and Infants School.

Estimates accepted:

Mr Fyfe as mason	£268. 0.0
Mr Middleton as carpenter	£165. 0.0
Mr Rhind as slater and plumber	£ 64.12.9
Chisholm & Son plasterer	£ 20.17.0
	£518. 9.9

An entry February 1878 stated that the schools were now entered as one school.

Fees charged in 1873 –
1. Elementary Branches, viz. Reading, Writing and Arithmetic with English, Grammar and Geography, per quarter of 12 weeks:

Pupils preparing for or under Standard	I	2/-
Pupils preparing for or under Standard	II	2/6
	III	3/-
	IV	3/6
	V and VI	4/-

2. Higher Branches, viz. Mathematics, Latin, Greek, etc.:

One higher branch with or without elementary branches	5/-
Two higher branches with or without elementary branches	6/-
Three or more	7/-

Pupils to supply their own ink, pens and pencils.

Fees to be paid in advance on third Monday of each quarter.

In Oyne an extra 6d in each of first two quarters to pay for fuel.

The Board fixed the Holidays. One week at Christmas (usually Old Christmas) or New Year. The Fast and Thanksgiving Days in the Parish at Communion Seasons, including Harvest Thanksgiving. The annual excursion holiday, and three other days throughout the year at the discretion of the teacher, with six weeks vacation in the autumn. (In addition there were one or two days after annual inspection).

Quarter Days (Oyne 1874) –

First from 14th Oct. to 9th Dec.	8 weeks
(Fees for this period to be ⅔ rate for quarter)	
Second from 10th Dec. to 10th March	12 weeks
Third from 11th March to 2nd June	12 weeks
Fourth from 3rd June to 2nd Sept.	12 weeks
Teaching weeks	44

These last paragraphs are taken from Oyne School Board Minute Book which gives most exact detail, but approximately the same fees and other arrangements are quoted in Leslie, Keig, Premnay and mentioned in others.

Quote from Attendance Officer Pemnay: 'I find it is hard for a common labourer to keep more than two children at school at one time, and the common practice is to fee out the eldest in summer as soon as they are able to do anything, returning to school again in winter.'

Oyne School Board agreed to accept the Dick Bequest Scale of fees with the modification that where there are four in a family at school, the youngest should be exempted from payment of fees. Unfortunately in order to qualify for Dick Bequest this was not allowed.

At Keig fees had been slightly higher before 1873. In September 1874 the School Board, taking into consideration the difficulty felt by many parents in paying school fees, deem it necessary to fix a reduced scale, viz. the lowest suggested by Dick Bequest.

Fees were discontinued in 1889.

The Dick and Milne Bequests were of great benefit (a) in raising the standard of living of the parish schoolmasters in Aberdeenshire (b) in raising
the standard of education (c) in extending opportunities for the same in Aberdeenshire.

The Dick Bequest.

Mr Dick, a West Indies merchant who died in 1828, left most of his fortune to encourage active schoolmasters in the counties of Aberdeen, Banff and Moray, and gradually to elevate the literary character of the parochial schoolmasters and schools. It was decided that a schoolmaster benefiting by the Bequest must pass an examination (Dick Bequest Examination) and must submit to a periodic inspection of his school. The total income of a schoolmaster qualifying for Dick Bequest had to be at least £80. In addition, he had a house and garden and was usually session clerk, for which he was paid a fee.

The Trustees of the Dick Bequest saw to it that some provision was made for aged and infirm masters, so that they might be induced to retire.

Dr Kerr, who was Chief Inspector of Schools in North of Scotland, wrote of the Dick Bequest: 'It has done more for the promotion of advanced education than any fund with which I am acquainted.'

The Milne Bequest.

The primary aim of this Bequest was to give the children of the poor the opportunity of education.

Dr John Milne, who was President of the Medical Board on the Bombay establishment, as an experiment offered £20 a year to certain schools in lieu of fees of poor pupils. The Parish of Skene was chosen for the start of the experiment. By 1871, 89 schoolmasters selected to benefit from this scheme. They benefited, but far more did the poor of the parish benefit, for in return for £20 a year, a schoolmaster was bound to instruct daily in religion and in usual branches, 25 pupils selected by Kirk Session.

Schoolmasters' Salaries.
Keig 1874. Headmaster's salary to be £50 from Rates + £30 Government Grant + School Fees. Added to this would be Dick Bequest and Milne Bequest. Assistant to be paid £40 + her School Fees.

Oyne 1873. Schoolmaster's Salary as when School Board was set up —
From Heritors £50. Present Government Grant £18. Allowance from Milne Bequest £20, from Dick Bequest £32. Average of School Fees over 5 years £40.15.10 yearly, and Dwelling House and Garden £13.0.8.

29th November 1873, Miss Robb accepted post of Assistant with salary £50 to be paid quarterly — six weeks notice either way.

At Premnay in 1875 new female Assistant and a female Teacher to teach children of Rothney Village in old Free Church School, Insch, were each to be paid £65.

Premnay. Advertisement for new Headmaster offered a salary of £70 stg. per annum + ⅓ of government grant earned in school along with a house and garden, 3 months notice either way. (This was usual notice). Addition of Dick and Milne Bequests if entitled to them).

These examples show how important the fees and the grants were a century ago. Unless a requisite percentage attendance was made, pupils could not be presented for annual inspection and amount of grant received depended on their ability to satisfy H.M. Inspectors, in basic subjects and specific subjects in which they were presented.

Here are some examples of Grant Results —
Leslie, 1883.

Claim on average attendance —			
1 General @ 4/-	64		
2 Music @ 1/-	64	64 × 6/-	£19. 4.0
3 Ordinary Discipline 1/-	64		
Infants 4-7: Presented 11 @ 8/-			£ 4. 8.0
Examination in standards			
Presented	46		
Passed in Reading	41		
Passed in Writing	33		
Passed in Arithmetic	36		
	110		
Passed in Art. 19B3	6		
	104 @ 3/-		£15.12.0

Grammar/Intelligence	57 @ 2/-	
Geography/History	57 @ 2/-	£11. 8.0
Specific Subjects – Latin	4 @ 4/-	£ 0.16.0
		£51. 8.0

Oyne, 1875

Claim on average attendance –

(1) General @ 4/-	90		
(2) Music @ 1/ –	90	90 × 6/-	£27. 0.0
(3) Discipline @ 1/-	90		
Infants 4-7 Qualified for presentation 2			
Presented 1 @ 8/ –			£ 0. 8.0
Examination in standards –			
Qualified for examination 89			
Presented	73		
Passed in Reading	73		
Passed in Writing	73		
Passed in Arithmetic	61		
	207 @ 3/ –		£31. 1.0
Grammar & Intelligence	86 × 2/-		
Geography & History	86 × 2/-		£17. 4.0
	Total claimed		£75.13.0
	Reduction		£ 8. 3.0
	Received		£67.10.0

By 1891 Grant Earnings had increased as follows at Oyne –

(1) Fixed Grant	100 × 10/-	
(2) Singing 6d or 1/-	100 × 1/-	
	100 × 12/6	£62.10.0
(3) Order & Discipline 1/- or 1/6	100 × 1/6	
Needlework 1/- on average		
attendance, girls only	54 × 1/-	£ 2.14.0
In and under Standard III		
1/-, 2/-, 3/- or 4/-	62 × 2/ –	£ 6. 4.0
Above Standard III		
1/6, 2/6, 3/-	38 × 2/6	£ 4.15.0
Class subjects –		
(1) English	88 × 2/-	£ 8.16.0
(2) Geography	88 × 2/-	£ 8.16.0
(3) Special Subjects		£ 4.12.0
		£98. 7.0

Intensive preparation was given before the Inspector's visit, which was always intimated in advance towards end of school year, which was often February 28th.

The day, sometimes two days, following annual inspection, were granted as holidays, needed I'm sure by pupils and teachers alike.

In schools like Chapel of Garioch, Leslie, Premnay and Keig, inspection in February/March when roads were so often impassable and weather conditions prevented full attendance, seems rather surprising.

Special, or specific subjects as they were usually termed, varied greatly from school to school, year to year and interests and qualifications of head teacher.

Monymusk – 1877 refers to Latin, French, Domestic Economy, Literature and Animal Physiology. **Oyne** 1876 – Literature and Latin are mentioned. **Keig** 1864 – Five boys named commenced Latin Rudiments. 1868 mention of four boys taking Greek. **Leslie** 1876 – Latin, Elementary and Advanced, Greek and Mathematics successfully taught. **Premnay** 1891 – French, Latin, Maths and Domestic Economy – other references to Mathematics, Latin, Greek and Euclid.

In addition to annual Government Inspection, there were inspections by Dick Bequest and Milne Bequest inspectors. In August/September every year, immediately prior to the Harvest vacation, an examination in Religious Knowledge was given by a local minister, representatives of school board being present. Prizes were often presented on this occasion, very often these were donated and presented by local laird.

We tend to think that there were few holidays but it is surprising how many there were. Six weeks Harvest vacation seems to have been statutory, New Year's Day and Old Christmas (January 6th, known as Aul Eel). The number of days given then varied from year to year and parish to parish. In Monymusk in 1884 Christmas holidays were given on December 19th for a week and a day. Entry January 1st – attendance poor (24 in all). 1885 December 24th to January 5th Christmas holidays. Keig Female School in 1869 gave holidays Christmas 25th December to 3rd January inclusive – Kemnay 1874 Christmas Holy Days commenced January 4th for one week.

Oyne 1874 – dismissed for New Year holidays December 31st to January 11th 1875.

Communion Fast Days (twice yearly) usually Thursday before and Thanksgiving Monday following. In some parishes these were given for Parish Church only, in others for both Parish and Free Churches. The Harvest Thanksgiving service was a special week-day one, usually on a Wednesday. If harvests were late it was very often in first week of December. In Keig 1903, October 30th was to have been observed as a Fast Day and school closed but owing to lateness of harvest it had been agreed to have no day service in Established Church and it was resolved to keep school open, since the day was not to be generally observed. Occasional holidays – some quotes – **Monymusk** – February 29th 1876, half holiday being Bannock night. February 17th 1883 – scholars were let loose at 2 p.m. in compliance with their petition that they might be allowed the afternoon to make their bannock.

December 2nd 1886 – Holiday and Treat from Sir Francis Grant on occasion of his marriage.

Chapel of Garioch. November 19th 1879 – Holiday – Majority of Mr H. W. Knight Erskine of Pittodrie.

July 28th 1882 – To-day 61 of the older scholars had a trip by rail to Elgin with their teachers. A most lovely day as to weather and recreation.

In 1876 on August 19th Oyne had a holiday for a Parish Railway Excursion.

'The Age of the Train' had arrived.

Leslie 1878 – March 8th Wednesday last a holiday for Annual Sourée to parents and children. August 16th – Half-day Annual Flower Show at Alford. This was a usual holiday also at Keig.

August 4th 1882 – Attendance very good considering the annual holiday time when many families go to the seaside for a week. (How many I wonder could do this?).

St. Sairs Market was usually observed as a holiday at Insch, Premnay and Leslie. In same way Lawrence Fair, Old Rayne on third Wednesday of August was taken as a holiday there and at Oyne.

In 1891-92 etc. A menagerie at **Insch**. Premnay records – A large proportion of scholars asking at the instance of their parents to be allowed off for the afternoon. Oyne and Leslie also attended.

Kemnay. August 13th 1876 – had a Berry Treat at the Manse. **Keig** – a treat by Lord Forbes.

Sir Arthur Grant's Delab. On August 8th 1892 – had a half-holiday owing to a treat given at Tilliefoure. 20th June 1897 – Two holidays owing to celebration of Queen's Diamond Jubilee.

1891 – Opening Tea on Monday 12th January to children of both parishes, i.e. Monymusk and Oyne. (This school opened on 13th January 1891 and replaced Lord Cullen's School.

Keig 1877 – records many pupils absent on account of a picnic given to the Sabbath School pupils at Benachie (apparently not a holiday).

Kemnay 1867/77 – The School Board agreed to the recommendation (of Head Teacher) that the Christmas holidays should be taken after H.M. Inspection, so April 14th 1877 – Holiday not taken at Christmas taken this week.

One comment typical of others – General neglect of lessons, consequent on approach of close of session and over-frequency of occasional holidays.

Schools were closed for other reasons besides holidays. Weather conditions could be very stormy, then as now, in some of the parishes round the foot o' Bennachie.

All the log books contain frequent references to the weather. Here are some examples – **Monymusk** 1878 December 13th-20th, 27th, school closed for three weeks. 1881 – Repeated closures half days and days from mid-January to end of February and for week March 7th-11th.

1883 March 28th – Roads all but impassable for last 14 days. Attendance almost nil.

Chapel of Garioch – 1876 March 21st. Snowstorm. Access to school impossible except for a few close to school. School inspection to have been to-day, deferred.

December 22nd – Severe frost, heavy fall of snow.

1877 January 12th/19th – Roads blocked.

1878 March 22nd – Stormy weather for 10 days. 29th-30th – Roads blocked.

April 1st/2nd – Roads were blocked. This continued until April 12th.

1878/79 December 13th – Great snowstorm.

20th/27th – During these weeks school did not meet as roads blocked.
O/P Oyne, Monymusk.

1879 January 10th – Many still unable to come to school. Comment: 'This storm has been more injurious to school than an epidemic.'

January 17th – Fever now prevalent in addition to stormy weather and blocked roads.

April 4th – Owing to snow being off the fields which have been covered for 16 weeks, farm work being actively pushed forward; some pupils are occasionally absent.

Inspector's Report 1879.

In common with most schools of the county this one has suffered much hindrance to progress from the severity of the weather. Mr Selbie (Headmaster) has thought it wise to offer no scholars for examination in specific subjects.

1879, December 29th – Last evening, Sunday 28th, a most fearful hurricane of wind, amid most brilliant moonlight, blew for hours from 6 p.m. Damage very great. Many scholars are absent assisting to put houses etc. to rights. There has not been such a hurricane since 3rd October 1860.

Oyne School Board Minute Book has an entry 1880 13th February. Mr Milne, Slater, Inverurie, employed to repair the damage to roofs of school and schoolhouse, occasioned by terrific gale of wind 28th December last. That was night of Tay Bridge disaster.

Oyne 1878, December 13th, 20th, 27th – Heavy snowstorm.

27th Monday, 23rd – Snow was so deep and untrodden, female teachers unable to be present.

1880, October 22nd – Severe snowstorm – (This appears to have been a stormy winter through to March).

January 14th – Frost of extraordinary intensity 'From benumbed state of the fingers scholars unable to handle pens or pencils.'

February 12th – Scholars utterly incapable of working owing to intensity of frost – excessive cold.

March 4th – Another wild severe snowstorm burst over the parish with unexampled fury.

Keig. 10th February 1881 – More drift to-day – no scholars.

The winters from 1878 to 1882 seem to have been very severe around Bennachie and of course there were no mechanical devices available for snow-clearing.

Another major cause of absences and closures were the epidemics of infectious diseases, e.g. –

Leslie 1878, October 21st – Re-opened after harvest holidays. This was delayed two weeks on account of fever. This outbreak continued until school was shut from December 7th to January 27th 1879.

1882, March – Influenza.
       April/May – Whooping cough.
       May 19th – Chickenpox.
       May 26th – Mumps.
1893, February 2nd – A very unsatisfactory year has ended – one epidemic after another the whole year.

Chapel of Garioch.
1888, January 13th – 3 cases of typhoid fever (seems to have been confined to these).
1890, March 13th – School closed until Monday 24th but measles still spreading so did not re-open until April 1st.
1894, August 7th – Diphtheria – school closed. After 10 weeks, school re-opened on October 16th. (This was 4 weeks + 6 weeks harvest holidays).
1898, May – Epidemic of measles, school closed.
1901, January 25th – Measles – closed until February 28th.

Keig. 1865, October 14th – a week later in opening because of fever in neighbourhood.
October 20th – Few have come up this week because of fear of fever.

Kemnay, 1878, June 21st – Fever. July 9th – Holidays given out on doctor's advice.
September 3rd – School commenced after eight weeks. Fever still lingering.
October 4th – A boy died of fever.
December – Fever spreading.
January 10th – Fever still spreading.
       This epidemic began in June and went on to following January.

Monymusk, 1884, May 22nd – Reduced attendance. Probably by fear of an infectious disease being abroad.
June 13th – School closed by order of the School Board, to be opened on Wednesday 18th. A measure of caution against possible spread of diphtheria. Three of a family have died. Remainder of the family isolated from village.
No further mention of the disease.
       Influenza, bad throats and colds were frequently reported in log books.
       Schools were very often overcrowded, hygiene unheard of and sanitation leaving a great deal to be desired. Most of the people were poor and therefore often undernourished. Today's cures and preventative medicines were unknown and furthermore all doctors' visits and medicine had to be paid for. Therefore we can easily understand how, a century ago, illness and infectious diseases in particular were dreaded.
       Attendance was much affected by the seasonal work on farm and croft.
       Children helped at home and older ones were fee'd out to help with loading, seed-sowing, potato planting, turnip hoeing, peat-cutting, haymaking, harvesting and lifting of potatoes.
       The return to school after Harvest Holidays began with younger children mainly and the others gradually appearing. In a bad or late year, the

records show that it was often end of November or beginning of December before all had re-enrolled.

Finally, some random quotes and references.

Kemnay – Mr Wm. Rogers, Kemnay, elected as Singing Master – 2 hours per week.

Chapel of Garioch – Mr Wm. Nicol, Kintore, Certificated teacher of music began to-day to teach music in this school from 3-4 p.m. on Wednesdays – Visiting teachers of music.

Frequently in Inspectors' Reports – 'A ball frame would be a great help in Infant classes.' Also 'The use of fingers and strokes must be discontinued.'

Keig Female School 1867 – As a substitute for Ball Frame, have procured a number of marbles with which to illustrate the arithmetical lessons given to classes 2,3,4.

A hundred years on, what a change in our Primary classrooms.

Quotes – 'The dull routine of the week's work once more accomplished.'

'New books, considerable animation.'

'New books, alacrity and zeal.'

'No pupil teacher to 'grind up,' so teachers' duties would be reduced and therefore would not merit increase in salary as requested.'

'One family fitfully present because of Homesickness.'

'In July 1874 Great heat and consequent torpor.' Similar remarks in various log books.

'Timely arrival of new tags.'

'The ventilation is imperfect.'

'Extreme frost making it a great hardship to sit in seats distant from fire. Relaxed organisation to permit visits thereto.'

'Half an hour of candle or lamplight would help materially on nights like last.'

After prolonged storm – 'Many very much rusted.'

'General neglect of lessons, consequent on approach of close of session and the over-frequency of occasional holidays.'

Today we hear much of community schools, but these old buildings of a hundred years ago served this purpose. There were few public halls and School Boards had requests for use of schools for all kinds of social and adult educational uses.

There are few references to individual pupils, but one is a letter dated 16th October 1882 from John Benton, former pupil of Keig School, who became Mayor of Rochester, sent after re-visiting Keig. In it he says, 'My memory looks back with pleasure to those days when I received the education which has helped me all through life and without which I never could have occupied the honourable position I have during the past year.' He enclosed a draft for 50 guineas to be invested and the interest applied annually in providing books for distribution as prizes – the School Board to use their discretion in manner best calculated to promote the work of Education in school of Keig.

Let us hope that many of those, who have received their early education in the schools at the foot of Bennachie, as elsewhere, will look back with appreciation, as he did.

For reference to the Dick and Milne Bequests, see Dr Ian J. Simpson's excellent book entitled *Education in Aberdeenshire before 1872*. I feel sure Bennachie was much loved by Dr Simpson whose father was the highly respected headmaster of Monymusk for many years.

The Editor.

The former Brae's o' Bennachie School, in Mannville, Alberta, Canada. It is now a Community Hall. Mrs Hubbard, the writer of the article 'Memories of Brae's o' Bennachie,' is standing at the door.

MEMORIES OF BRAES O' BENNACHIE

By Mrs Annie Hubbard, Mannville, Alberta, Canada

The name Braes o' Bennachie is one of beauty and renown. I was born in Bennachie in a stone house up the road known as the Lodge. My father, Alex Allanach and wife Helen, had a family of five born in this home. One girl died at an early age. My father was a crofter. I can remember him snaring rabbits.

I spent two years at Bennachie play school. My teacher's name was Frances Burnett. I corresponded with Frances until her death. She was a kind and loving person. She had a wee dog called Barney. I remember one day she was visiting mother and wee Barney jumped up and tore my pinafore. Frances was really upset about it all. The first Christmas I can remember was at Bennachie. When Santa Claus came Dr Stark said he had to come down the stairway as the chimney was too small. My gift from Santa was a little white muff of rabbit hide and lined with satin. I ran home to show my folks and then up the road to show Grandpa and Grandma who lived at the Glenton. The valley and the heather hills were beautiful. My Grandma and I used to pick the heather. One day we walked to the Mither Tap.

My brother and I used to sit by the Birks Burn and shake jumbojine in a bottle and suck the froth. What fun! On up the road from our house there was a beautiful rowan tree behind the stone dyke. An enjoyable walk was up the Lord's Throat. My brother went to Keig School. Then there was the Tinky's well and ladle by the road where anyone could drink.

In 1910 my youngest brother was born. He was to be called Alexander Charles. The cook at Bennachie, Mrs Reid, baked the baptismal cake and put 'Donald' on it. Anyway, he was baptized by the first name but got Donald all his life. When he became a man he changed his name to Donald Alexander. My father was out on his bicycle one night and fell off and was rendered unconscious. A Jimmy Cruickshank picked him up and took him in to a neighbour's. A few years after we came to Canada, father found out Jimmy was just a few miles away. In Bennachie Dr and Mrs Stark's work in God's service lives on. I have his book on *Bennachie*. The last New Year we were in Scotland my dad and mother took me out for Hogmanay. I can remember a wee bit of coal, and we were never empty handed. We stood outside a neighbour's window with friends and sang:
> 'Rise up, guid wife and shack yer feathers
> Dinna think that we are beggars.
> We're only bairnies come to play,
> Rise up and gie's oor hogmanay.'

In the spring of 1910 my dad decided to come to Canada. We had a sale and prepared for a long tiresome journey with five children and one only three months old. I remember my grandfather giving me a bag of rock candy for the journey. It was a sad farewell of tears. We spent two nights in Aberdeen with an uncle. Then on to our boat, the *Brittania*. Everyone was seasick but we finally arrived in Montreal. The train trip across Canada was long and tiresome. We arrived in Mannville on June 1st. A livery gig took us out to our friends who lived 12 miles out. Our bachelor friend had just a wee, two-room shack. Good Scotsmen can always persevere and my parents surely did just that.

Dad took a homestead and built a fairly-good home. The first thing he thought of was a school for the children. Five men got together and the Government granted them permission to build a school. This was built of brick. A name had to be chosen and three names were sent in to the head office. My dad's choice was the name given, *Braes o' Bennachie*. It is built between hills with the river running by. Just a beautiful valley! In the year 1914 my dad bought a farm just across from the school. We could all run home for lunch then instead of walking 3½ miles.

The school is just used for entertainment now but there is still a strong community. We had a reunion on our 50th anniversary and many pupils came back. Last year we celebrated Alberta's 75th birthday and we had a two-days' celebration. My brother and I and our first teacher were the only ones there who had started the first day at school. We have had relations from Scotland and they said a school could never have been named better as the setting is so much like Bennachie in Scotland.

We are getting on in years now. My hubby, Archie, and I retired from the farm in 1967.

These are my memories of good old Braes o' Bennachie and I hope you enjoy them. The name will live on in Alberta as well as in Scotland.

Footnote – The Braes o' Bennachie School, Mannville, Alberta, Canada, celebrated its 50th Anniversary a few years ago when staff and pupils met to honour their old school which has now been turned into their local Community Centre.

On the occasion of the 50th Anniversary, the little 'red brick school' was exquisitely decorated with signs reading 'Braes o' Bennachie School, Golden Anniversary, 1912 to 1962,' with the number '50' in gold, with thistles painted around the lettering, to remind the company of their Scottish connection with their own Bennachie.

Gold and white gladioli, marigolds and white daisies graced the dining tables, the dinner consisting of cabbage rolls, ham turkey, with all the trimmings, served by the ladies at midnight.

The Editor.

FAREWELL TO THE BRAES
By John C. Fiddes

Farewell the Braes, the Bonnie Braes,
The Braes o' Benachie!
I'm on my way, a gey sad day
Nae mair for ye I'll dee.

Y're braw but big, wi' extra rig,
Wi' muckle steen and tree;
Gey hard to dig, aye picking twig
At the Braes o' Benachie.

The burnie's sweet they ca' the Birk
As it runs blythly on;
But like mysel gey near its end
For soon 'twill reach the Don.

Tae work beside ye is a treat
Just to lis'n tae y'r rill
Wi' beauty all around tae see
Of bird and tree and hill.

Y'vc worked me hard, I lo'ed ye weel
'Tis sure all will agree;
So fare ye well, my Bonnie Hame,
The Braes o' Benachie.

Composed by Mr John C. Fiddes on the occasion of his leaving 'The Braes'
to reside in Huntly.

SOME MEMORIES OF THE BACK O' BENNACHIE

By Mrs Jean Thow

Looking back, most of us see the sunny days, and beside the Gadie it
seemed to be sunny all summer. Having to leave Premnay when I was
eleven years old, to live in Paisley, I missed my friends and the Back o'
Bennachie very much, often dissolving into tears when I heard 'Whaur
Gadie Rins' played on the wireless.

School at Premnay for me was walking past the shoemaker's, my
relatives. Rachel Brewster's dressmaker's shop, next to the soutar's where
we as children called to look at her pattern books, and pick up the pins
which she had dropped on the floor. Hay's, Grocer and General Merchant
was on the opposite side from Rachel's shop, past Thornbank on your left
up to the Pint where the hotel was on your left. Tough, the tailor, was on
the right opposite the hotel and next door but one was Aggie Brewster who
had the Post Office in her living room and kept her money in a purse with
the stamps. They installed a phone in Aggie's room which she hated using.
Across from Aggie's in the square was Dawson, the General Store, and
Mennie, the baker on the opposite corner where the smell of bread was so
inviting. The vanmen were usually loading the two horse vans and the
motor van when we passed on our way to school in the morning. On the

right past Mennie's was Robertson the vricht where the boys and girls called, to see the men piling up the 'spells' on the floor while using a plane on the wood. Down the Premnay road to the Hallie beside Aggie's was Archie Smith, the Garage, who had a car for hire. Then farther down were Willie and Alexander Ironside – they had a garage as well and had an Essex two-passenger car for hire and were the first car hirers in the village. During the summer holidays we used to buy one pennyworth of broken biscuits from Hay's and with Boston Cream had a picnic by the Gadie or some other nice spot.

The headmaster was Mr Cruickshanks and the Primary teacher was Miss Tough, followed by Miss Stronach – or Polly Sids – her father being the miller in the village. Mr Cruickshanks used his tawse or strap with great gusto. We used to cover our hands with rosset from the soutar's shop; this helped to deaden the pain of the tawse. The school was divided into two rooms by a partition and had around sixty pupils. The pupils came from as far as Brindy, Brackla (up the Keig road), the Widdy at the 'Isles' on the Insch road and Grassick's farm on the Leslie road, and from the Mill o' Barns on the Oyne road, nearly to Daies. Robby McDonald from Newton on the Oyne road was one of the loons who pinned a bell on the dominie's jacket as the old man was nearly deaf by the time he retired. Our new headmaster was Mr Robert Roberts, nicknamed 'Double Robbie,' and he had a more modern approach to teaching, starting a football team for the boys and netball for the girls with nets outside in the playground. You went on to Insch at 11-plus or stayed at Premnay until 14, then left school.

The wool mill was still to the fore when I lived in the village. It was at the Gadie Brig where there was a lade, and further up the Gadie was the Grain Mill where Mr Stronach was the miller. Mr Ledingham was the blacksmith and I was used to the noise of horses walking down by the back of Jubilee Cottage – where I lived – on their way to be shod, and I heard the clang of the anvil as the shoes were made. This was a favourite place to visit, and the boys often went to the garages to chat with the Ironsides and with Archie Smith.

On Friday nights in the wintertime, my cousins and I used to hide in the rolls of leather – they stood about 3ft high – to listen to the men who came in for a 'news' at the soutar's where they discussed every subject, and sometimes the discussion got very heated. This was their way of relaxing after a very hard week's work. I hardly ever remember seeing a farmer wearing a good suit in my young days – they seldom had a day off when they could dress-up. Some of the men smoked Bogie Roll and the shop was thick with smoke by the time Aunt Maggie knocked through the wall from the house to try and get them to go to their homes.

On Saturdays sometimes my cousins and I took the meat up to Brackla, looking forward to the newly-baked scones which Elsie made and gave us, hot off the girdle spread with syrup or jam. They were very big and delicious. The floor at the Brackla was stone and scrubbed and so were most of the other things in the kitchen. The Brackla was built by the Dauns themselves in the days when men built their own houses. As well as the butcher's van, a fish-van came to the village from Whitehills.

The winters were normally hard with drifting snow, often after a white Christmas. There was a Christmas tree in the Hallie where every child got a present, usually someone special presented them, very often from Lickleyhead Castle. I remember one Christmas getting in my stocking a pair of shoes with straps and buttons, and in a box! It was my very first pair of factory-made shoes as ours were usually hand-made in the soutar's. We all walked to Waulkmill Manse one Christmas to Mr Hart's, to a party for Barbara Hart, his daughter. We walked hand in hand as the roads were like ice with the moon shining on the snow and I had to hold on to the rest of the children very tightly as I remember I wore my new shoes. I also remember singing the solo part at the Christmas service that year. It was the hymn 'In the field with their flocks abiding.' Unless the weather was very bad, we went to church every Sunday morning. The Sunday School was before the forenoon service and I remember having to learn the Catechism. In the afternoon we went for a walk and in the evening we read by the light of a paraffin lamp. In those days we were not allowed to sew or knit on Sunday.

The school had a picnic in the summer when we marched from the playground with a piper leading us down the village to the field at Lickleyhead Castle where we had games and races. Each child got a bag of buns from Mennie's and tea poured from big jugs. Some years later, we went by charabang to Cullen for a day's outing with a picnic on the beach.

In the summer and autumn we spent hours beside the Gadie at the Widdy at the Gadie Brig where we played 'housies,' guddled trout and made dams with stones and earth. We also 'beat' for grouse in August, being paid two shillings per day. There were always guests invited to the shooting at Lickleyhead. Across Bennachie there was a line of butts for the guns, while we walked, beating with sticks to raise the birds.

I came back every year to stay with my aunt in the summer, until I was about 15 years old. The first bus to run from Aberdeen to Rhynie started to operate in 1927, daily except Sunday. The first operator was called Benton and he was followed by Scott. From Aberdeen, where I caught the bus at Blackfriars' Street, I used to hope that coming over Tyrebagger Hill it would be clear enough to see the Mither Tap when I would feel that I was nearly home again.

Each year we spent a whole day on Bennachie, starting at the Roadie beside the site of the former Poorhouse. We walked across the hill to the Mither Tap and back the same way, having our picnic before we reached the Mither Tap. We used to recruit one or two friends for this outing but we dared not attempt Bennachie until Aunt Maggie said that we should not encounter mist. I can still hear her opening the curtains in the morning and asking,'Well, are ye for the hill the day?'. We were up like a shot, collecting everybody and on our way! The view from the Mither Tap was glorious and as usual, we had the hill to ourselves. In those days Premnay people went up the hill, but it was an occasion, perhaps once a year, not organised like the walks today on the hill. We came back the same way in the evening, running down the hill and barking our shins but we were so tired we did not feel it. We would hear Nicol the gamie's dogs barking – he kept them beside the house – we were terrified of them.

We also climbed The Satter to pick blaeberries and cranberries for Aunt Maggie to bake a pie which she did to perfection. One of the days during my holiday we cycled round Bennachie via Keig, Monymusk, Chapel of Garioch and Oyne, usually stopping at the Kirkyard then up past Premnay Kirk and the Quarrie, then free-wheel past Newton to the Hallie. We had a few stops on our run to have a rest and to admire the scenery.

One year when I was about 13 or 14, the Flower Show was held at Insch and there was a competition for a Children's Poem about the district. Entry was for local children and as I was no longer resident, my cousin entered it. He and I composed the poem and we got 1st Prize, much to our delight. Here is the poem.

MY AIN GADIE

There's a burn that I love dearly,
It runs through my native shire;
The most beautiful in Scotland,
It ripples like a lyre.

They named this burn, Gadie,
A name that's suited well.
It sounds more sweet and homely
Than many a glen or dell.

It runs from Clatt to Logie,
Past the foot o' Bennachie.
But where ever I may wander,
By Gadie may I dee.

First Prize, Insch Flower Show.

THE RHYNIE BREED

By Dr D. G. Gordon

Ten doctors in one year – that was the fate of Rhynie in the vacancy of 1966-67. It is a long story. Rhynie does not belie its name of the Muir of Rhynie, for lying at the top of the Strath of Bogie, its one broad, bleak main street runs north to meet the full blast of the winter winds. Its one redeeming feature is the lovely green square to the south-west with kirk and steeple in the midst.

Lulath, the son of McBeth was killed here in battle by MacDuff in 1025. That is incidental. What Rhynie is proud of is the Roll of Honour of its famous sons in the local school, the largest roll of any village of its size in Aberdeenshire. In the 1840's, the Rev. Robert Harvey Smith started the Mutual Improvement Society movement which spread all over the country.

His ancestor and the common ancestor of many on the list, parsons and pedagogues and doctors, was Peter Smith who was out in the forty-five and was killed at Culloden. After the battle when his widow went to look for him, all she found was the battered hilt of his sword, which is now in the Culloden National Trust museum.

The School Roll of Honour is amazing. It cites the four McDonell brothers, reputed to have been brought up in a but-and-ben called Poorin on the Tap O'Noth where the heather joins the farm lands. George became a K.C. of Lincoln's Inn, John of the Inner Temple became Sir John and a third was editor of the *Daily Telegraph*. My mother once told me that the Poorin children got a handful of oatmeal in their jacket pocket with them to school for their dinner.

In the 1860-1900 University of Aberdeen Roll of Graduates, there are eight medical graduates with the surname of Cran, six of them sprung from the Cran family of Rhynie. The line of greatest local fame was that of Dr Alexander Cran of Tarland who graduated in 1824, and his two sons, Robert 1876 of Ballater and George 1875 who practised in Banchory for more than fifty years, keeping up for that period a running battle of wit and invective with his colleague Dr McHardy.

The Peter Smith of Culloden line survived in direct descent for five generations, the last being Dr Peter Smith who graduated in 1860 and practised in Australia. He had three wives but died childless. His sisters, however, made up for it, and Troup, Skinner and Nicoll nephews were medical graduates of Aberdeen. Three Nicoll doctor brothers came out of the Congregational Manse, one going to Queensland, one to New Zealand, and the youngest, Dr Patrick Smith Nicoll, to London. Incidentally their nephew, Captain Archibald Smith, Captain of the S.S. *Otaki* in the 1914-18 war, attempted to ram the German raider *Moewe*, went down with his ship, and got a posthumous V.C. to add honour to his old school, Robert Gordon's College and give rise to the long list of Otaki scholars of that school.

So much for this line, this breed of Rhynie men. What of the men who practised here? Dr Alexander Mitchell of the old Rhynie family, born in 1843, was in Rhynie for twenty years and died at the age of 41. He was succeeded by a Lonmay man, Dr Peter Galloway, who must have found the going hard and stayed only five years, going south to England's green and pleasant land. One would not blame him, for Rhynie is by far the stormiest practice in winter in Aberdeenshire. Dr John Ross of Fraserburgh, who was locum at Rhynie from 1939 to 1945 when Dr McKenzie was on war service, tells that in the six winters he spent there, the road from Rhynie to Gartly was blocked with snow five out of the six, for periods of from two to six weeks when no traffic got through. When Galloway left, he was succeeded by Dr Thomas Grant, who graduated in 1889 at the age of 21. He was a fellow student of Dr Patrick Nicoll who graduated a year or two earlier. Born in Tomintoul, an even stormier practice than Rhynie, he was just the man for the place. Tall, handsome, weather-beaten, a big man, he needed a great mount of seventeen hands. The good folk of Clatt and Kildrummy and the Cabrach would wake up to hear his horse clip-clopping through the night, and wonder whether it was a young wife giving birth, or an old wife wearing away. The furthest west point of the practice, more than a dozen miles from Rhynie at the foot of the great seven miles stretch of mountain and moor, separating the Cabrach from Glenlivet was the Aldivalloch and the three Daughs. The middle Daugh is known as Reekimlane, so named as the only farm to be occupied in the terrible winter last century when early frosts ruined the late corn, and as there was food for neither man nor beast, the Cabrach folk took refuge in Dufftown for the winter. Last to leave was the Reekimlane family. As they came down to the ford which was frozen over, they saw below and half-frozen in the ice about twenty salmon. It was a good omen. They hacked one out with an axe, retraced their steps to home. The peat fire was soon going. With salmon from their natural deep-freeze, an odd grouse or red deer, their chimney lum reeked on till spring, the only reeking lum for miles.

This ford figured in an episode when Grant rode off on a call to Reekimlane at midnight, the roads hard frozen, and a full moon on the white landscape. It was after three in the morning when he got to the ford, which was lightly frozen. The full moon shining on the ice frightened the horse, which refused to cross. Grant had to dismount, back his horse into the water and wade across himself. On the return journey the ice had refrozen and off he had to get and repeat the process. By the time he got back to Rhynie, his trousers, leggings and boots were frozen solid and he had no feeling in his feet. He got undressed, swallowed a large whisky, and tired out, got into his cold bed – he was a bachelor – and slept for two hours. When he woke up, his feet were still numb. As he said later, he was worried, but he got on with the day's work and gradually the warmth came back, whether due to his Tomintoul blood, the whisky, or both.

As I said earlier, Grant and Nicoll had been students together. Nicoll settled at Stratford, then the eastern outskirt of London. He had a very fine practice, driving out in his coach and pair to attend many of the Essex County families. He had rooms in Wimpole Street. He was the general practitioner physician at Stratford Hospital and when he was able, through one of his titled lady patients to get Queen Mary to give her name to it, Stratford Hospital became Queen Mary's Hospital for the East End. Nicoll lived to become senior physician with Harley Street men his juniors. Every autumn he came back on holiday to his native Rhynie, staying at the Gordon Arms, and his student friendship with Grant ripened over the years. Often Dr Grant's gig would pick him up of a morning and the two bachelors would go the country roads, the London physician's job being to hold the reins at farms and croft and castle, when Grant stopped to pay his visits. Nicoll must have compared his own pleasant way of life with his friend's in these wild northern uplands of the Grampians. He made up his mind to build a small cottage hospital for his native Rhynie, with a maternity bed or two to ease Grant's burden.

The day of the gig passed, the war came and Dr Grant got his Tin Lizzie, but still Nicoll's joy was to join in the doctor's rounds. In the autumn of 1926, Dr Nicoll on holiday died suddenly on the steps of the

Invercauld Arms at Braemar. Shortly after Dr Grant had a stroke and although paralysed, he was driven round the countryside for his visits for a further year, but in 1927 he called it a day, and Dr James McKenzie, born in the moors of Dinnet came to Rhynie.

Dr Nicoll's will left a few thousand pounds to build the little hospital. It was opened in 1931. As Rhynie was part of the great Dukedom of Gordon the Duchess was asked to open it, while the money was enough to build the hospital, there was no endowment and Dr Nicoll's relatives, including his old partner and cousin, Dr George Troup stepped into the breach generously. In spite of this, funds at the start were pitifully meagre. The Rhynie folks buckled to with fêtes and concerts and other money spinners. Gradually over the years the financial position eased a little. When my father, who was chairman, got a gift or a legacy for sums of fifty or a hundred pounds, it delighted him. In fact he was more pleased than if the money had come to himself. The hospital with its six beds was a godsend to Rhynie. As McKenzie and Ross said, they would not have enjoyed practising without it. Gordon Bruce came out and did the operations. Accidents, medical emergencies, maternity cases – all were catered for.

All went well until 1957, when Dr James McKenzie after thirty years at Rhynie, had to retire due to ill-health. He was the kindest of doctors and received his proper mead of affection from his people. He did not have the same physical exposure as Grant. The horse had passed, but often he had to go to Reekimlane and Aldivalloch and the upper Cabrach farms and when the direct road of a dozen miles was snowbound, he had to make the journey of over thirty miles north to Huntly up Deveronside and across the moors.

He was succeeded by Dr Farrell, who gave yeoman service for nearly ten years before leaving the uplands, to practise in the more genial climate of lower Spey. 1966-1967 was the year of the ten doctors, locums in the vacancy. The Health Services Executive Council built a grand house for the doctor with modern surgery. Dr George Sorrie was appointed and with his lady doctor wife made a first rate partnership. When Dr Sorrie was appointed to succeed Paddy Rice in Aberdeen, I was bemoaning Rhynie's loss to a consultant. His reply shook me. He said it was 'time we brought Sorrie in out of the cold.' Who is going to stay out in the cold? A lad from Tomintoul and a lad from Dinnet stuck it between them for sixty-seven years.

In 1948 the Nicoll Hospital and its by then considerable endowment was handed over by the trustees to the North-Eastern Regional Hospital Board. In 1957 the Board decided to close the hospital. Several reasons were given. It was too small. Costs were too high. Staffing would be difficult. The matron, dedicated if ever anyone was, on call the twenty-four hours, was due to retire. New nursing regulations were in force; all to the good I feel, because I consider that the medical profession in the first half of the century must have some sense of guilt in not doing more for the nursing profession.

The Aberdeen and Kincardine Health Services Council and the Local Medical Committee sent a deputation of protest to the Regional Hospital

Board. Their spokesman likened the hospital to a regimental aid post or a field dressing station. He went on to say that as a trustee handing over the hospital and its hard-won endowment to the Board, he felt like little Red Riding Hood dealing with a kindly grandmother. Today as he comes trembling and pleading before you, it is as if he says 'What great teeth you have, grandmother' and your reply in effect is 'The better to eat you with.'

The hospital was closed.

The rural scene changes, the stock of the Smiths and the Crans remains. Fewer in number, they are still there in these Grampian foothills. The sickness of cities is bringing a trickle return to the countryside. It will take time to make a flood. Against the miracle of modern medicine must be set so many evils of this quick changing age. Bigness is all. The clever men in the mushroom industrial companies take over the family firms to strip their assets. The little firms with their own way of life decay as they are engulfed to make ever bigger units. The high flatted towers keep so many feet away from mother earth. As a peasant of the Smith breed over many generations since Culloden, I think the feel of the soil is the true touchstone of conscience.

REMINISCENCES OF BENACHIE

By an American Exile

Away ye naked prairies, ye forests dark and drear,
Ye sluggish streams and marshes, that spread so widely here;
Ye little hills and valleys, ye lakes that stud the plain,
Ye have beauties for the natives of this wide and rich domain,
And for the Yankee traveller who never saw before
The scenery of any land beyond his native shore;
But with all your boasted grandeur ye have little charms for me,
For I was born in Albin, at the foot of Benachie.

That bold and rocky mountain soon caught my infant eye;
I scanned its azure mantle, its crags so wild and high,
And every day till manhood it loomed before my gaze,
A monster wall of nature to hide the distant maze,
And so oft my idle fancy, when I was all alone,
Would shape it 'n its animals with blood and flesh and bone,
The mammoth and the mastodon that long have ceased to be
Of which I often heard and read in sight of Benachie.

And when by years of training, my limbs were waxing strong,
I mounted to the summit among the labouring throng;
And merrily till evening we trundled out the peat,
Laughing, talking, singing, sweating with the heat.
For the goodly mountain yielded fuel for the fire —
Stone to build the dwelling-house, the barn and the byre,
Heather for the roofing and all were gotten free
For no oppressive landlord could swallow Benachie.

And in the balmy summer when the heather was in bloom
Giving out its odours, its rich and sweet perfume –
When bees were ever busy providing winter food,
Buzzing, humming, gathering honey sweet and good,
I often scaled the mountain alone to labour there,
And like the bees around me for the winter to prepare.
And till my work was ended I was busy as a bee,
That I might have a leisure hour to spend on Benachie.

And everything seemed beautiful in my happy mood:
Beautiful the mountains and beautiful the wood,
Beautiful the valley, and beautiful the stream,
Beautiful the white clouds, fading like a dream,
Beautiful the mansion, and beautiful the cot,
Beautiful the corn-fields, and every grassy plot,
Beautiful the landscape as far as I could see,
Beautiful the heights and depths, and slopes of Benachie.

I've listened to the music of the plover and curlew,
That often in their rambles across my pathway flew,
The cackling of the muir fowl, the bleating of the sheep,
The frisking of the lambkins upon the heathy steep,
The bubbling of the fountains, the rushing of the streams,
The sparkling of the quartz in the sun's refulgent beams.
Those sights and sounds of nature, with my nature did agree
And oft till late I lingered 'mid the scenes of Benachie.

I've traced the mountain torrents in their deep and dark ravines
That flooded by the summer rain afforded stirring scenes;
I've watched them in their windings, their pauses, and their swells,
Their curves and foaming cataracts, their pools and rocky wells,
Their gambols and caprices as they sought to reach the plain,
To join the peaceful river that would bear them to the main,
And teach them to be gentle ere they mingled with the sea,
Far distant from their sources – the springs of Benachie.

I've often viewed with rapture when the morning mists were gone,
The fairy Vale of Alford stretching far beyond the Don;
With many a princely residence of beauty and of pride,
Mid forests, groves, and hedges, and fields so green and wide.
Backed by the lofty mountains of Leochel and Cromar,
While far beyond their summits rose Byron's Lochnagar,
In all its sombre glory beyond the rapid Dee,
Far higher, steeper, grander, than my own loved Benachie.

But often in the morning when the mountain top was clear,
A heavy mist enveloped the plains and valleys near;
And I have bathed in sunshine and in the balmy breeze,
When all the world below me seemed buried by the seas,
And on the level surface stretching far away –
Were foaming waves and breakers, all motionless and grey –
It seemed the human family were all engulfed but me,
And I was left a hermit on the top of Benachie.

But oftener still the mountain was shrouded in the gloom,
And drizzling fog and vapour soaked the heather bloom;
And then the scene was dreary, and bleak and dark and chill
For nought to me was visible but objects on the hill –
Stone and rock and heather, and moss and clay and sand;
A waste and cheerless wilderness, confined on every hand;
For corn-field, and garden, cottage, grove and tree,
Were hidden from my vision by the mists of Benachie.

And in the stormy weather, the mountain clad in snow,
Gazed like a giant spectre upon the vale below,
Looking wild and angry, and lonely in its pride,
Abandoned to the elements that warred on every side;
Forsaken by the workmen, and those who fondly roam
In quest of health and pleasure, far away from home;
For birds, and beasts, and bees, and men, were glad to flee
For shelter from the tempests and blasts of Benachie.

But even then the mountain was useful in its way,
For when the sun was shining it told the hour of day;
When the clock and watch were absent or resting from their toil,
Or in the hands of workmen, and under brush and oil –
The granite crags were pointers, that pointed ever true,
And told us when 'twas meal time, and time to yoke the 'plough,'
And ever in the morning we fondly rose to see
The prospects of the weather from the looks of Benachie.

O Benachie! thy beauties still linger in my eye,
I see the blooming heather and thy rocks that pierce the sky;
But a long and weary distance of many thousand miles,
Divides me from thy glories, thy frowns and welcome smiles;
And I would leave the prairie, the forest and the stream,
To gaze upon thy features that haunt me like a dream;
And though youth and early manhood are now denied me,
I still would range with rapture on the heights of Benachie.

This poem was sent to the Editor by Mrs Annie Hubbard, Alberta, Canada.
She received it from her cousin in the United States of America but regrets
she does not know the name of the author.

AN OOTSTAN'IN DAY FOR THE
BENNACHIE BAILIES

Press and Journal Monday, 19th July, 1982

The volunteers who look after the interests of Aberdeenshire's favourite hill, Bennachie, heard they were to be presented with a conservation award in London.

So the Bailies of Bennachie, as the volunteers are known, nominated Inverurie exile Mr James Milne, now living in London, to receive the award on their behalf.

Mr Milne, now in his 70's, has stayed in the capital for more than 30 years, but maintains strong connections with the Garioch.

One of his many hobbies is writing Doric-style prose. The Bailies' award and its presentation were natural subjects for the Milne pen.

Sir – Ye reportit that the Bailies o' Bennachie hid gotten a special mention certificate fae the Keep Britain Tidy Group on the occasion o' the group's second annual awards ceremony te commemorate the Queen Mother's 80th birthday, she bein' patron o' the group.

There canna be ony doot aboot the wye the group got te hear o' the Bailies. They hiv a directir in Aul Reekie, an' een o' thon craws that fowk coont mileages bi, maan hae flutter't doon 'is lum some nicht, stracht fae the Mither Tap, an' tell't 'im fut a gweed job the Bailies hiv deen on the hill sin their birth jist nine 'ear ago.

The inspired genius – or geniuses – fa conceived the idea o formin' this body o conservationists an' kirstnt it wi' sic an apt name, maan be richt prood the day.

Then there's thon doctir chiel Danny Gordin o Ca'wulls. He wis at the birth, an' fut better Howdie cwid a buddy wint?

Fae the ootset there's been a wise cooncil an' hardwirkin' office-bearers at han't te mak siccar that the lusty infint wis weel brocht up.

An' there's the common or gairden Bailies o' baith sexes fa hiv chaavt awa' on the hill an' hinna grum'lt (weel, nae muckle) at gettin' sair backs an' han's cut an' claartit wi' dirt fae the rubbish orra fowk hiv dumpit on wir hill. Is't ony winner that the craw couldna hud its whisht ony langer?

Bit you, sir, as weel as Radio Aberdeen an' Grampian Tillyveeshzin maan hae coppit the ee or lug o' the Aul Reekie directir chiel at least some o' the mony times ye've gi'en the Bailies' activities gweed publeecity.

Ye war deein't lang afore the feathert cratur made its lang journey te hae a wird wi' the directir, bit it wis that wird that clinchtit.

There wis nae prooder Bailie than maesel on the day o' the ceremony, for, bein' Lundin-based, I shared wi' ma dother (ma wife bein' laid low wi' a lumbackit back) the great honour an' preevlige o' representin' the Bailies at the awards ceremony in the Guildha'.

Fin I read the list o' companics, local authorities, banks, organisations, the media an' individuals that earned awards for ootstan'in effort in promotin' environmental improvement, particularly throwe litter abatement, ma kist swall't wi' pride till I wis some feart ma sark buttons wid flee aff. For then, an' only then, did the fu measure o the Bailies' achievement strik me . . .

Oot o' a total o' 94 awards, jist three gid te Scotlan'. It wis an odd, bit happy, coincidence that, wi' hunners o' fowk there, we happen't te sit doon neist te the representatives o' a distric cooncil up Largs wye.

We hid a crack wi' them, an' we a' agreed that tho' Scotlan' wis oot o the Warl Cup an' wisna ower weel representit in the awards list, the Keep Britain Tidy Group couldna hae deen better than ging there for the premier award.

That trophy, a crystal triangular prism acht inch heich bi twa inch wide, wis the wark o' Caithness Gless Ltd., jintly won bi the Girl Guides Association an' the Scouts Association.

Aifter Michael Heseltine hid presentit the awards, tea wis ser't in the crypt, o' a' places! It wis bit dimly lichtit, bit if I hadna kent far ma moo is at my age, I wid lookit roon for a niche te crawl intil.

There wis nae sign o' the craw, bit I'll sweir that fin his time comes, he'd raither rist his weary wings somewye nae ower far up wir ain bonnie hill.

I widna winner gin he wis on anither eeran, tellin' fowk o' the glory te be gotten throwe membership o' the Bailies o' Bennachie.

James Milne, 12 Sportsbank Street, Catford, London, SE6 2EX.

By courtesy of the *Press and Journal*

THE RUINS AND VANISHED FOLK OF FOUDLAND

By Rev. Dr J. S. Wood

My leave was well timed for a ski adventure. I came home to find the entire landscape deep in snow, waiting for winged feet.

So I lost no time on 'waxing up' and getting ready to realise a dream which carried me through the grey wet November days.

In bright forenoon sunshine I set out across the fields to Foudland, a hill of curved white loveliness – a hill with no dominating peak but a gently rounded, wind-blown summit.

A Scottish Gazetteer published in 1845 pays but scant tribute to this hill, saying it rises only 300 feet above sea level. Its actual height is 1529 feet.

My path lay over the meadowlands, along the hare's way, over burn and dyke, by croft and farm, skirting dark little firwoods, skimming down steep ploughed fields and along bare beech hedges.

Baps and a Tumbler of Milk

Near a picturesque little farm I stopped a baker's van and purchased a few baps. The farmer's wife came out with a tumblerful of milk. At least she called it milk. But if yon was milk I'd like to taste her cream. It was grand.

So on and away again through the clachan of Boddam where the children ran out to see the 'mannie wi' the lang skates.' Then over a road where men were 'casting' the snow, cutting it out in blocks of the purest marble.

Though I did not cross the Jordan I passed not far from Jericho with its old distillery, to which the 'caerts have lang syne stoppit ca'in the barley.'

The last habitation past, I took to the hill and was soon threading my way between clumps of breem and heather knowes. The snow streamed in little frozen banners from any heather that was left uncovered.

I startled a brown hare and a covey of muircock as I climbed.

Every now and then I would pass an old slate quarry with its cairn and rubble. Some contained miniature frozen lakes. Some were deep and grotto-like with fantastic ice formations on their rugged sides. Geologists say that a vein of slate beginning at Foudland, runs right across Scotland to the south-west, coming out somewhere about Ardnamurchan Point.

On Summit in Virgin Snow

By 2.30 I judged myself to be on the summit and I stopped to enjoy the beauty of the quiet world around me. To me nothing is lovelier than virgin snow in winter sunshine, many-faceted snow, kaleidoscopic in its everchanging beauty.

Bennachie, whose peaks I had ski-visited the year before, slept peacefully beneath her white winter blanket. Ben Rinnes in the far western distance was a shining pyramid of light. To the north the rounded Knock threw back the sunshine like a great mirror.

Somewhere to the north-west I saw a field of orange light, a phenomenon I witnessed last year from the Mither Tap.

Directly beneath me at the back of the hill lay Scotland's stormiest glen, a wild and storied place and a centre of the Disruption in the north-east. In the Muckle Storm of 1838, the old stage coach was storm-stayed in the glen for six weeks, every effort to clear the road being fruitless as snow fell continuously.

At Bainshole, not far away, it is said that more than one foul deed was committed in bygone days. Who knows but some Roman reconnaissance patrol surveyed the country from on which I stood! There was a Roman camp near Glenmellan.

Below me to the south lay the crofts and farms of Cairnieston and Largie and Lenchie. Here and there, nearer the hill, stood the snow-dusted ruins of cottages long since forsaken, where bairns had played and wives had baked and men had laughed and sung.

These whitened tumbled ruins set me thinking of the vanished community, the folk who worked in the slate quarries and fought for a living against the ever-encroaching heather and breem.

What did they do, I wondered, on the long winter nights on that wind-swept hillside? What were their pastimes? What were their names? Where had they gone and what memories had they left?

I determined to learn something about these unrecorded people.

In the late afternoon I navigated my way through the network of quarries on the western ridge and slipped away into the deep white hollow below.

There, in ski-parlance, I 'wrote my signature' on the hillside in winding telemarks, unpunctuated by a single full-stop!

Something of the Old Folk

Crossing over to the Red Hill, I 'slalomed' down between the breem-bushes, coming out at Brankstone Croft. And there I learned something of the hill-folk from one who had lived on the hill since 1859.

As she said, I 'hadna fessen eneuch o' the day wi' me' to hear a long story. But I sat and listened till the shadows lengthened, and in that croft kitchen, in the lowe o' the fire, the vanished folk came back again. And as the voice went on I shared with them their joys and sorrows, played their games, endured their hardships.

A simple life it was and a hard. But happy too. The speaker had played as a quine in the quarries and minded fine on the men working there. At that time there were, she said, 'dizzens o' crafts aboot the hill.' A 'man fae Balgaveney' and her father had trenched the croft out of the heather and built the house.

In the 'bonnie days,' she said, the hill was a great picnicking place for the bairnies and a favourite spot in blaeberry time. The women folk made extra money by knitting for the woollen mills in Huntly. For themselves they did their own spinning.

My informant told me of an old woman who was quite illiterate but had a flair for history, and 'mony a nicht,' said she, 'I had to gang ower by an' read Mary Queen o' Scots till 'er till I was seek o' the sicht o' the name.'

Something of a pastime was the nightly Bible reading. 'Ivery nicht my father read a chapter as we a' sat roon the fireside.' Then each was asked how much he remembered.

On one memorable occasion a brother said, 'I mind what you read aboot backbiters.' 'Oh,' said the father, 'an div ye ken what backbiters is?' 'Fine that,' says the son, 'golachs!' A picturesque exegesis.

That brother was afterwards in the siege of Mafeking and in his last letter home said he would never forget how, before leaving for Africa, he had climbed the Hill o' Foudland and thought that 'a' the warld was lyin' at his feet.'

There was the reading of the weekly paper, too, by rushwick or fircandle. And on special days, special diversions like rubbing sowens at Auld Eel on the doors o' 'fowk ye didna like' or 'pu'in' casticks at Hallowe'en.'

I could have listened long enough, but the day was wearing on and night ski-ing without a light is not much fun. So I set off at last reluctantly for home, arriving when it was quite dark.

Conditions in the Quarries

It was shortly afterwards that I visited, again at the darkening, the man whose father had worked in the quarries. From him I learned something of the conditions under which the menfolk worked.

The Laird of Logie was the contractor and the men were paid by him. There were those who were actually in the quarries. And there were the 'ri-vers' who considered themselves craftsmen, not mere 'barra' men.' They split and roughly dressed the big blue slabs.

They had little dugouts where they took shelter and ate their meals, bread and cheese and 'tatties rossen aneth the peat ess.'

The biggest quarry was the Gutter Quarry on the Bainshole side, where a number of men worked. A man named Bissett lived in the cottage highest on the hill near his quarry.

The whole world knows, of course, that Foudland 'sclates' were carted to Balmoral for the roofing of the Castle. But they roofed and floored many a house and kirk in the district, too. I have Foudland 'flags' on my own kitchen floor.

An old residenter who visited the quarries some sixty-five years ago said he saw only two men working there. And 'ye daurdna say' to them that the industry was dying out. They were very sensitive on that point.

Cottages are now deserted

I believe a survey of the hill was made during the last war with a view to re-opening the quarries. But the haphazard system employed by the old quarriers had rendered the project impracticable on the ground of expense.

The folk who worked on the hill in those days had names like Mackie and Bissett and Coutts and Davidson and Meldrum. A few of their descendants are still in the district. But many are in the far places of the earth.

To-day the breem is creeping down the hillside, outflanking the deserted cottages and taking back the little fields these hard-working folk fought to make fruitful.

Some there be that have no memorial, but not so the vanished hill folk of Foudland. Their quarries are silent and filled with snow. Their homes are in ruins.

But the slates they hewed from the hill-face went to the building of better homes for other men, for common folks, aye, and for kings.

All the hills of Foudland have . . . 'a gently rounded, wind-blown summit.'

By courtesy of Press and Journal

POSTSCRIPT TO CREATION

By Rev. Dr James S. Wood

The first sax documentit days were past.
The great Creator's wark was deen at last.
It's sair wark makin' a'thing oot o' nocht –
'I'll tak' it easy for a day,' He thocht.
Then ere the saxt day's licht began to fade,
He lookit doon on a' that He had made,
An' 'saw that it was good.' Noo surely that is
Fat ony man can read in Genesis.

But here's a secret, niver oot til noo!
The seventh day cam', an' lookin' ower the view
'I'm nae quite satisfied wi' a' I've deen,'
The Maker mused. 'No, something quite supreme
I maun create – aa little Paradise below,
An' nae far fae't, a heavenly hill,' and lo!
They're there for a' mankind to see
The earthly Paradise – an' Bennachie!

By courtesy of *Press and Journal*

PERSONALIA

James Allan, a farm worker in the Garioch, had the story of his youth on various farms given a final polish by his son-in-law, Dr A. A. Cormack.

Rev. Dr C. J. R. Armstrong, M.A., Ph.D., formerly Lecturer in the University of Aberdeen, 1968-74, resided at Friends' Cottage, Kinmuck. He is at present Director of Academic Studies and Tutor at Westcott House, Theological College, Cambridge.

Robert Bayliss is Senior Lecturer in the School of Social Studies at Robert Gordon's Institute of Technology, Aberdeen. He includes Victorian Science and Social History among his many interests.

Aubrey Burl is a world-wide authority on Stone Monuments whose books such as *Stone Circles of the British Isles* and *Prehistoric Avebury* are among the most important studies of our pre-historic stone monuments. He carried out a short time ago a very successful lecture tour in the United States of America.

Professor Ian Carter, formerly a member of the Staff of the Institute for the Study of Sparsely Populated Areas at Aberdeen University, now resides in Auckland, New Zealand, where he is Professor in the Department of Sociology in the University of Auckland. While in Aberdeen he published many notable books relating to the social history of the North-East

Michael Davidson, B.Sc.(Hons.) is Assistant Biologist to the North East River Purification Board. His great love for Bennachie is evident in the keen interest he takes in anything pertaining to the Hill.

Gillian Davidson is an Honours Graduate of St. Andrew's University. She is Personnel Officer with the Telecommunications Board. She is a keen bird-watcher and shares with her husband, Michael, the enjoyment of outdoor activities.

George A. Dey, B.Sc.(Forestry) has been instrumental in the making of the Back o' Bennachie beauty spot. His imaginative planning and meticulous care made smooth the co-operation between the Forestry Commission and the Garioch District Council. The Bailies as a mark of their appreciation presented him with one of the first copies of *The Book of Bennachie*.

James Duffus, Manager of the Fetternear Estate Farms, takes an active interest in the affairs of the communities in the Chapel of Garioch and Fetternear. He is well-known in farming circles, which is not surprising since he is descended from a hardy race of men and women who farmed in the Chapel of Garioch for more than two hundred years.

Dr Paul Dukes, a Specialist in Russian History at Aberdeen University, has made a detailed research into the careers of the Leslies of the 17th Century, with special reference to the manner in which they and other families used the slopes of Bennachie as a battlefield for their feuds.

Marc Ellington is a member of the Historic Buildings Council for Scotland and a member of the National Executive of the Historic Houses Association. His own restoration of Towie Barclay Castle along with the invaluable help of his wife, Karen, has been a very notable achievement.

Andrew G. Fordyce was born at Nursery Cottage at the foot of Craigshannoch. This most successful Kent business man has shown many kindnesses to the Bailies since the start of the Bennachie project. His forbears worked the Lintel Quarry on Oxencraig.

Mrs Helen P. Fraser. was sometime Chairman of the Keep Aberdeenshire Tidy Campaign. She has been a tireless worker on the Bailies Council since its inception. For the past five years as Clerk to the Bailies her Minutes of the Meetings have been a model to all. As one of the most enthusiastic bibliophiles in the Garioch, she has charge of the Bailies' Library.

John Garden. Both his grandfathers were colonists by the Clachie Burn, breaking in their tiny fields from the heather moor. With such blood in his veins, he was naturally a very fine Inverurie Nurseryman on the fertile Ury banks.

Flora Garry. Described by Dr Cuthbert Graham as the finest living lyric poet of the North-East in *The Book of Bennachie,* she puts the Bailies deeper in her debt by her moving article on her life-long friend, Louise Donald. Her Doric quatrains in the Forestry Information Centre at Donview on the edge of the River Don, on the road to the Lords Throat illustrating the murals are real gems.

Dr Daniel G. Gordon, Founder member of the Bailies Association, and its first Senior Bailie, was recently created a Life Member of the Council as a token of appreciation and thanks for all he has done for the Association. His beautifully-written booklet, *Welcome to Bennachie* was a best-seller. Before retiring to Coldwells, Inverurie, he was the well-loved physician at Ellon. He is Chairman of the Dr Charles Murray Memorial Trust and an enthusiastic member of the Dr David Rorie Committee.

Miss Joanna Gordon is the daughter of the distinguished North-East historian, the late Cosmo Gordon of Insch. A graduate of Cambridge University, she taught in Ghana where she was involved in the re-habilitation of the tribes on the Volta River before the Volta Dam was made. She is also a very talented artist and has illustrated books on flowers and botanical studies. For several years she was the very enthusiastic secretary of the House of Gordon Council. A friend of Professor St. Joseph, she now searches for relics of the Battle of Mons Graupius on the northern slopes of Craigshannoch.

Dr Cuthbert Graham, LL.D. No LL.D. has been better deserved, In his *North-East Muse* corner in the Saturday *Press & Journal,* he has done a noble job in encouraging the writing of Doric Verse. He published in volume form a selection of the best on an edition of 3,000, sold in a few weeks. The Bailies are grateful for his help at all times.

Stuart Hannabuss lectures in Librarianship, Literature and Management at Robert Gordon's Institute of Technology, and sees Bennachie in all its moods from his house in Kemnay.

John Hird spent a number of years in Australia when he was a young man. His interests are wide and varied. He played golf for many years and he was also a keen fisher. It would be true to say that he now angles for information of local interest.

Dr Robert House. This Sassenach doctor from Tewkesbury who since serving in the 12th Casualty Clearing Station with our first Senior Bailie, Dr Danny Gordon, has been his close friend. He has come under the spell of the Mither Tap, and climbed it often. The vandalism of the Indicator on the top of Bennachie moved him to make a generous contribution towards its repair.

Mrs Annie Hubbard, who resides in Mannville, Alberta, Canada, writes fondly of her early days near the *Braes o' Bennachie.* We rejoice with her that the name *Braes o' Bennachie* will long live on in Alberta.

Mrs Kay Needham-Hurst, L.R.A.M.(Eloc.), L.G.S.M.(Eloc.), was an Examiner in Elocution in London Academy of Music and Dramatic Art for 30 years. Better known in her professional career as Kathleen Stone, her work as a Lecturer and Adjudicator took her all over the British Isles, and in 1970 she spent five months in Southern Africa.

Professor J. K. S. St. Joseph, C.B.E., M.A., Litt.D., F.B.A., is Emeritus Professor of Aerial Photographic Studies in the University of Cambridge. The Bailies are deeply grateful that such an international expert in aerial archaeology as Dr J. K. S. St. Joseph should have placed at their disposal his account of the most exciting and recent discovery that the Battle of Mons Graupius was fought at Durno, under the shadow of Bennachie.

Michael G. Kidd, M.A. In addition to his facility in writing verse, he has spent many hours in delving into history of Jericho Distillery and the Callander family who made the famous brand.

David C. Leslie, Baron of Leslie, Dip.Arch.Abdn., A.R.I.B.A., A.R.I.A.S., F.S.A.Scot., born and lived in Aberdeen all his life, attended Aberdeen Grammar School and the Scott Sutherland School of Architecture, Aberdeen. He is at present an architect with the Aberdeen District Council. He is married and has a family of two daughters.

James R. Mackay, B.Sc., M.I.Biol. Head of the Biology Department of Inverurie Academy and former Senior Bailie. The Bailies owe a tremendous debt to Mr Mackay for the many projects he has carried out on the slopes of Bennachie and for his tireless enthusiasm. He is probably now the most knowledgeable expert on its fauna and flora, its stones and its topography. Meticulous in his every action, his work on the *Maiden Causeway* has already produced results. His 'Guide' is now in universal use.

David Merrie is a chartered mechanical Engineer who has lived at Oyne within sight of Craigshannoch for six years. He has had a life-long interest in Natural History, particularly of the mountain and moorland environment, and is a member of various Ornithological Societies. In his garden at Oyne, he has counted over sixty-five species of birds.

The late **James Milne.** We deeply regret the sudden death of Mr Milne in London. The son of James Milne, tinsmith, Inverurie, who published *Twixt Ury and the Don* and *The Gangrel Flute,* Mr Milne was first a Banker and then took an Engineering Degree at Aberdeen University before moving to London. The members of the Association of the Bailies of Bennachie are very conscious of the great debt of gratitude they owe to him.

John Philip. Now retired on the Hill of Kintore, the well-known Dominie Philip of Tertowie, bred from Buchan farming stock, was ideally suited to give a taste of country life to the short courses for city children sent out from Aberdeen to be under his care.

Prasong Sananikone went to Inverurie Academy in 1962 as a teenager from Laos. Later he graduated from Aberdeen University with the Degree of B.Sc. in Agriculture. He returned to his native Laos in 1969 where he supervised agricultural and educational projects. When his country's political masters changed in 1975 he was imprisoned. Later he was released and 'invited' to resume the work he had previously been doing. Conditions became progressively more impossible so that at the second attempt he, his wife and family escaped across the Mekong River into Thailand. In the spring of 1981, as political refugees, they arrived in Scotland. Now, he and his family live in Aberdeen.

Miss Mary Simpson, for long headmistress at Oyne School, is now retired in Kintore. With the help of her scholars, her Campaign against the Bennachie litter has been the most effective and continuous of our time.

Mrs Erica Smith of Pittodrie, a lover of garden and trees, has recently since the death of her brother, Mr Alexander Patrick Moore, spent many hours preserving the great garden of Newton. The care of the fabric of Harthill Castle by her father-in-law, Captain George Smith, a Company Commander in the Gordons, killed in action in 1915, facilitated the reconstruction seventy years later.

Dr Douglas L. Stewart, for many years the well-respected and popular doctor of Insch, is now enjoying retirement. He is keenly interested in the history of the area and is a recognised authority in this sphere. One of his many interests is that of Scottish Provincial Silver, with special reference to that of Aberdeen and Banff.

Joe Sutherland, an enthusiastic archaeologist, has written numerous articles across the years on our castles. He is ranked amongst the first three experts on Heraldry in the North-East.

Miss May Thomson. Formerly Librarian at Aberdeen City Reference Library, Miss Thomson is an expert in the history of social customs. She is a welcome guest speaker at W.R.I., and Woman's Guild Meetings all over the North-East and her recitations in the Doric of the poems of Charles Murray and Dr David Rorie are a sheer delight.

Mrs Jean Thow lives in Prestwick, but visits her native Premnay as often as possible. She likes to wander around the old familiar places with her camera.

William Wallace was Head Gamekeeper at Castle Fraser, 1954-71. He now resides near Beauly in Inverness-shire. His article on the *The Life of a Bennachie Gamekeeper* was to have been a talk in the 'sixties to the pupils of Inverurie Academy but unfortunately it had to be cancelled.

Adam C. Watson, Jnr., until recently a pupil at Banchory Academy, is waiting to commence his University studies at Aberdeen. He has a real gift for research and his article on *Air Crashes on Bennachie* will create much interest. Like his father, Dr Adam Watson, the author of the Book entitled *The Cairngorms,* Adam is keenly interested in history.

Algy Watson, M.A., B.A., Born at the Back o' Bennachie, he has just been deservedly chosen as the Senior Bailie. A skilled photographer, perhaps his most dramatic effort was the yellow broom in the *The Book of Bennachie* jacket. His illustrated lectures on *Bennachie* have been much appreciated for many years.

Dr Jon J. L. Whiteley, M.A., D.Phil.(Oxon), F.S.A.Scot. Born in Monymusk, Jon lived his early years within sight of Bennachie. He won international fame as a child film star and was awarded an Oscar by Holywood. He is now Assistant Keeper in the Department of Western Art in the Ashmolean Museum, Oxford and is also a guest lecturer and writer.

Colin Wood. His ambition for many years to restore a castle has now been fully realised. The *irremedial ruin,* according to the words of the late Dr Douglas Simpson, is now a sheer joy and delight. He has been most generous with his time in showing visitors round his lovely castle.

Rev. Dr James S. Wood, D.D. His lasting love affair with Bennachie since he skied on its slopes in training as a Chaplain in the 52nd Mountain Division in war-time, has made him one of the most generous friends of the Bailies. In addition to the many books he has contributed to our library, his work in prose and verse has enhanced both our books.

BIBLIOGRAPHY

1. *Bennachie* by Alexander Inkson McConnachie, 1890.
2. *Twixt Ury and the Don and Round About* by James Milne, 1947.
3. *The Province of Mar* by Dr Douglas Simpson, 1943.
4. *The Earldom of Mar* by Dr Douglas Simpson, 1949.
5. *Inverurie and the Earldom of the Garioch* by Rev. John Davidson, 1878.
6. *Aberdeenshire Castles* – James Giles, R.S.A., with *Memoir of Giles* by Dr William Kelly, edited by Dr Douglas Simpson, 1936.
7. *Place Names of Aberdeenshire* by Dr William M. Alexander, Third Spalding Club, 1952.

8. *The House of Forbes,* edited by Alistair and Henrietta Taylor, Third Spalding Club, 1937.

9. *The Leiths of Harthill* by Francis Bucklay, 1937.

10. *Rhymes and Recollections of a Handloom Weaver* by William Thom, 1844.

11. *Bog Myrtle and Peat Rick* by Pittendreigh McGillivray.

12. *At the Back o' Bennachie* by Helen Beaton, 1915.

13. *Glimpses o' Auld Lang Syne* by William Watson, 1905, Aberdeen University Press.

14. *A New History of Aberdeenshire* by Alexander Smith (two volumes), 1885.

15. *Hamewith and Other Poems* by Charles Murray.

16. *The County of Aberdeen* – Third Statistical Account, 1960.

17. *Dunnideer and its Three Fortresses* by G. M. Fraser, 1927.

18. *Donside* by Alexander Inkson McConnachie, 1901.

19. *Second Book of Legends* by Fenton Wyness, 1943.

20. *A Century of Aberdeenshire Agriculture* by Isabella M. Bruce, 1908.

21. *Education in Aberdeenshire before 1972* by Ian T. Simpson, M.A., ED.B., PH.D., 1947.

22. *A School History of Aberdeenshire* by Jim Buchan, M.A., ED.B., 1961.

23. *The Inscriptions of Pictland* by Francis C. Diack, 1944, Third Spalding Club.

24. *Murmurings Frae Ury* by T. L. Morrison, 1921.

25. *Johnie Gibb of Gushetneuk* by William Alexander, 1880.

26. *Let's Look Round the Garioch* by Fenton Wyness.

27. *From the Tone to the Don* by Alfred James Monday.

28. *The Cairngorms* by Sir Henry Alexander.

29. *Songs of the North-East* edited by Dr Alexander Keith.

30. *Last Leaves of Aberdeen Ballads* Gavin Greig, edited by Dr Alexander Keith.

31. *The Book of Buchan,* edited by Dr J. F. Tocher.

32. *The Heather Bells o' Bennachie* by Alexander Beattie Campbell.

33. *The Statistical Account of Scotland* – Aberdeenshire, 1843.

34. *Balquhain Castle* by Dr Douglas Simpson – Aberdeen University Review, 1936.

35. *The Castellated Architecture of Aberdeenshire* by Sir Andrew Leith-Hay, 1870.

36. *Braes o' Bennachie* by Dr James Stark.

37. *A Benzies Quest* by Frank Benzies, M.B.E., 1972.

38. *Materials for a History of the Church and Priory of Monymusk* by Rev. Dr William M. MacPherson.

39. *The Cairngorms* by Dr Adam Watson.

40. *The Mountain of Light* by Dr Catherine Gavin, 1944.

This list is by no means complete, but it contains the bulk of what has been written about Bennachie and round about. In many other local publications, casual reference to Bennachie will be found.

The following titles may be of additional interest: –

The Gavin Greig Collection of Folk Songs of the North-East – a series of 600 articles contributed to the *Buchan Observer,* 1907 to 1911. The original manuscripts are in King's College Library, Aberdeen. These were edited and a selection was published with notes by Dr Alexander Keith.

Old and New Bridges over the River Don at Inverurie (Tawse & Allan).

Historic Earls and Earldoms of Scotland – John Mackintosh.

A Thousand Years of Aberdeen – Dr Alexander Keith.

Aberdeen and Deeside, – Cuthbert Graham, 1972.

The North-East Lowlands of Scotland – John R. Allan.

William Thom, the Inverurie Poet: A New Look – Robert Bruce.

The North-East of Scotland, prepared for the visit of the British Association to Aberdeen in 1963.

From a Scottish Study: weekly articles in *Aberdeen Press & Journal* by Alexander Keith while Assistant Editor.

Lord Cullen by Rev. Dr James Stark, 1912.

Met by the Way by Rev. Dr James Stark, 1915.

Rev. John Skinner of Linshart by Rev. Dr William Walker, 1883.

The White Rose of Drumminor by Lilianne Grant Rich.

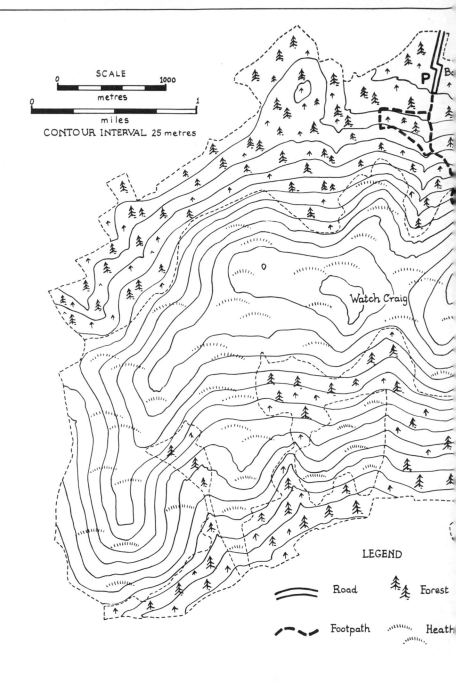

SCALE

0   1000

metres

0   1

miles

CONTOUR INTERVAL 25 metres

Watch Craig

P

B...

LEGEND

Road   Forest

Footpath   Heath

FOOTPATHS on BENNACHIE